ABOUT THIS BOOK

Y OUR PERSONAL GUIDE in the Western techniques of personal transformation and spiritual evolution is here. Discover the innermost secrets
of the most successful and popular system of ceremonial magic in the
world. *Circles of Power* opens up exciting new territory for students of the
Western Tradition. A definitive, contemporary guidebook to the Cabalistic magic of the Golden Dawn, *Circles of Power* takes you step by step
through the basic building blocks of ritual to powerful, advanced techniques of energy work and personal transformation.

More than just a "cookbook" of magical practice, *Circles of Power*
reveals the core principles underlying each ritual. Clear, straightforward
explanations and easy-to-follow guidelines illuminate the practical hows
and whys of Western ritual magic.

John Michael Greer explains the inner workings of Western ceremonial magic in a practical and down-to-earth manner. *Circles of Power* is
essential reading for anyone seeking to learn the authentic techniques of
real magic.

"Where the beginning student is usually given no more than the
Lesser Pentagram Ritual of the Golden Dawn in the average introduc-
tory text, *Circles of Power* takes the novice through such esoteric subjects
as Evocation, invisibility rituals, and the celebration of the Equinox.
Circles of Power provides a wonderful, ordered analysis of ritual work
and offers new insights for even the more advanced ritual practitioner.
If any writer is capable of reducing the most complex of all Golden
Dawn magical correspondences for the beginner, my guess would be
John Michael Greer."

David Allen Hulse
Author of *The Key of It All, Vols. I & II*

ABOUT THE AUTHOR

John Michael Greer first encountered the Western esoteric tradition in 1975 and has been actively involved in it as student, practitioner, and teacher ever since. The author of *Paths of Wisdom: The Magical Cabala in the Western Tradition* and a number of articles on magical subjects, he also co-edits (with Al Billings) *Caduceus: The Hermetic Quarterly*, a journal combining practical and scholarly approaches to the esoteric arts. *Caduceus* has a page on the World Wide Web at http://www.memoria.com/caduceus. Unlike at least one other Cabalistic author, he occasionally attends writers' workshops, owns a cat, and has practiced several martial arts. He lives in Seattle.

TO WRITE TO THE AUTHOR

If you wish to contact the author or would like more information about this book, please write to him in care of Llewellyn Worldwide, and we will forward your request. Both the author and publisher appreciate hearing from you and learning of your enjoyment of this book and how it has helped you. Llewellyn Worldwide cannot guarantee that every letter written to the author can be answered, but all will be forwarded. Please write to:

Llewellyn Worldwide
P. O. Box 64383, Dept. K313–1
St. Paul, MN 55164-0383, U.S.A.

Please enclose a self-addressed, stamped envelope for reply, or $1.00 to cover costs.
If outside the U.S.A., enclose international postal reply coupon.

Llewellyn's World of Magic and Religion Series

Circles of Power

Ritual Magic in the Western Tradition

John Michael Greer

1997
Llewellyn Publications
St. Paul, Minnesota 55164-0383, U.S.A.

FIRST EDITION
First Printing, 1997

Cover photo ©1995 Digital Stock Corporation
Cover design by Tom Grewe
Interior illustrations by Anne Marie Garrison and Tom Grewe
Book design by Darwin Holmstrom
Editing and layout by Deb Gruebele
Project management by Ken Schubert

Library of Congress Cataloging-in-Publication Data
Greer, John Michael.
    Circles of power : ritual magic in the western tradtion / John
Michael Greer. -- 1st ed.
        p. cm.
    Includes bibliographical references and index.
    ISBN 1-56718-313-1 (pbk.)
    1. Hermetic Order of the Golden Dawn. 2. Magic. I. Title.
    BF1623.R7G74   1997
    135' .4--dc21   97-10760
                                                               CIP

Llewellyn Publications
A Division of Llewellyn Worldwide, Ltd.
St. Paul, Minnesota 55164-0383, U.S.A.

Llewellyn's World of Magic and Religion Series

At the core of every religion, at the foundation of every culture, there is MAGIC.

Magic sees the world as alive, as the home that humanity shares with beings and powers both visible and invisible, with whom and which we can interface to either our advantage or disadvantage—depending on our awareness and intention.

Religious worship and communion is one kind of magic, and just as there are many religions in the world, so are there many magical systems.

Religion and magic are ways of seeing and relating to the creative powers, the living energies, the all-pervading spirit, the underlying intelligence that is the universe within which we and all else exist.

Neither religion nor magic conflicts with science. All share the same goals and the same limitations: always seeking truth, forever haunted by human limitations in perceiving that truth. Magic is "technology" based on experience and extrasensory insight, providing its practitioners with methods of greater influence and control over the world of the invisible before it impinges on the world of the visible.

The study of world magic not only enhances your understanding of the world in which you live, and hence your ability to live better, but brings you into touch with the inner essence of your long evolutionary heritage and most particularly—as in the case of the magical system identified most closely with your genetic inheritance—with the archetypal images and forces most alive in your whole consciousness.

DEDICATION

To my teachers and my students.

TABLE OF
CONTENTS

Table of Rituals and Ceremonies viii
Table of Illustrations x
Foreword xiii

PART I: PRINCIPLES OF RITUAL MAGIC
Chapter 1: The Nature of Ritual Magic 3
Chapter 2: The Magical Macrocosm 19
Chapter 3: The Magical Microcosm 43
Chapter 4: The Tools of Ritual Magic 63
Chapter 5: The Practice of Ritual Magic 111

PART II: PRACTICE OF RITUAL MAGIC
Chapter 6: Invoking and Banishing 137
Chapter 7: The Middle Pillar Exercises 157
Chapter 8: Opening and Closing 171
Chapter 9: Working Tools 193
Chapter 10: Talismans 219
Chapter 11: Evocation 239
Chapter 12: Invisibility and Transformation 265
Chapter 13: Spiritual Development 287
Chapter 14: The Formula of the Equinox 309
Appendix: Cabalistic Symbolism 339
Bibiography 355
Index 359

TABLE OF RITUALS
AND CEREMONIES

Cabalistic Cross 139
Cleansing Ritual for Preparing Talismans 223
Descending Light, Ceremony of the (Equinox formula) 325
Elemental Working Tools, Ceremony for Consecration of 198
Equinox, Ceremony of the (for solitary working) 316
Evocation Ceremony for Knowledge 251
Evocation Ceremony for Practical Magic 255
Exorcism, Ceremony of 262
First Degree Ritual of Opening and Closing: Basic Form 172
First Degree Ritual of Opening and Closing: Expanded Form 176
Hexagram, Greater Ritual of the 149
Hexagram, Lesser Ritual of the 146
Hexangle, Ritual of the 152
Holy Water, Consecration Ritual for 130
Invisibility, Ceremony of 269
Invocation of the Higher Self, Ceremony of 300
Invocation of the Name, Ceremony of 290
Lamen, Ceremony for Consecration of the 202
Lotus Wand, Ceremony for Consecration of the 211
Magical Eucharist 181
Magical Mirror, Ceremony for Consecration of the 214
Magical Sword, Ceremony for Consecration of the 207
Middle Pillar Exercise, Greater 168

Middle Pillar Exercise, Lesser. 162

Pentagram, Greater Ritual of the 143

Pentagram, Lesser Ritual of the 141

Revolutions of the Breath 167

Rising on the Planes, Ceremony of 295

Rose Cross, Ritual of the. 153

Scrying Mirror, Ritual for Consecration of the
  (Equinox formula) 322

Second Degree Ritual of Opening and Closing. 183

Talismans, Ceremony for Consecration of (Basic). 227

Talismans, Ceremony for Consecration of (Elemental). 229

Talismans, Ceremony for Consecration of (Telesmatic) 231

Talismans, Ceremony for Deconsecration of 236

Third Degree Ritual of Opening and Closing 187

Transformation into Animal Form, Ceremony for 281

Vibration of Adonai ha-Aretz, Ceremony of 292

Vibratory Formula of the Middle Pillar 166

TABLE OF ILLUSTRATIONS

Diagram 1: Levels of Being 10
Diagram 2: The Spheres 27
Diagram 3: The Planets 29
Diagram 4: The Elements 30
Diagram 5: Proportions of the Middle Pillar .49
Diagram 6: Closed and Open Positions 67
Diagram 7: The Sword Hand 68
Diagram 8: The Sign of Silence and the Sign of the Enterer 70
Diagram 9: The Signs of Fire, Water, Air, and Earth 72
Diagram 10: The Rending of the Veil and the Closing of the Veil . . .74
Diagram 11: The Signs of Isis, Apophis, and Osiris 76
Diagram 12: The Heptagram of Colors 87
Diagram 13: The Greek, Latin, and Rose Crosses 92
Diagram 14: Attributions of the Pentagram .93
Diagram 15: Attributions of the Invoking Pentagrams 94
Diagram 16: Attributions of the Banishing Pentagrams 95
Diagram 17: Attributions of the Hexagram .96
Diagram 18: Attributions of the Invoking Hexagrams 97
Diagram 19: Attributions of the Banishing Hexagrams 98
Diagram 20: The Elemental Forms of the Hexagram 99
Diagram 21: Attributions of the Pseudohexagram 100
Diagram 22: Attributions of the Invoking Pseudohexagrams 101
Diagram 23: Attributions of the Banishing Pseudohexagrams 102
Diagram 24: Magic Squares of the Planets 104
Diagram 25: Magic Squares of the Planets 105

Diagram 26: Tracing the Sigil of Zazel 106
Diagram 27: The Seal and Sigils of Saturn .106
Diagram 28: The Seal and Sigils of Jupiter .106
Diagram 29: The Seal and Sigils of Mars 107
Diagram 30: The Seal and Sigils of the Sun 107
Diagram 31: The Seal and Sigils of Venus .107
Diagram 32: The Seal and Sigils of Mercury 108
Diagram 33: The Seal and Sigils of the Moon 108
Diagram 34: The Horoscope as a Map of Ritual Space 126
Diagram 35: The Altar with Furnishings 129
Diagram 36: The Tau Robe 131
Diagram 37: The Invoking and Banishing Pentagrams 141
Diagram 38: The Hexagrams of Fire, Earth, Air, and Water 147
Diagram 39: The Invoking and Banishing Hexangles 152
Diagram 40: The Rose Cross 154
Diagram 41: The Rose Cross Ritual 155
Diagram 42: The Centers of the Middle Pillar 161
Diagram 43: The Elemental Working Tools 198
Diagram 44: The Lamen 202
Diagram 45: The Magical Sword 206
Diagram 46: The Lotus Wand 210
Diagram 47: Two Sample Talismans 226
Diagram 48: A Circle for Evocation 248
Diagram 49: The Equal-Armed Cross 293
Diagram 50: The Earth and the Sun 312
Diagram 51: The Triangle 350
Diagram 52: The Square 350
Diagram 53: The Pentagon and Pentagram 351
Diagram 54: The Hexagon and Hexagram 351
Diagram 55: The Hexangle or Pseudohexagram 351
Diagram 56: The Heptagon and Heptagrams 352
Diagram 57: The Octagon and Octagrams .353
Diagram 58: The Enneagon and Enneagrams 353
Diagram 59: The Decagon and Decagrams .353

FOREWORD

RITUAL MAGIC IN THE GOLDEN DAWN TRADITION

THIS BOOK, LIKE THE TRADITION ON WHICH IT'S BASED, had unlikely origins. It began as part of a chapter in my previous book *Paths of Wisdom: the Magical Cabala in the Western Tradition*. After covering the theory and symbolism of the magical Cabala, the essentials of practice, and some of the basic ritual work of the tradition, I hoped to summarize the more advanced methods of Cabalistic ritual magic in a few pages before going on to the chapter on meditation. Those few pages ballooned into a chapter and a half before I realized that my plans were going to have to change. The material that needed to be covered outstripped the space I had available in *Paths of Wisdom*, and in time it became obvious that it would need a book of its own.

Circles of Power: Ritual Magic in the Western Tradition is that book. It's intended as a practical guide to the system of Cabalistic ritual magic developed by the Hermetic Order of the Golden Dawn in the late nineteenth century. That system is the most complete and fully developed of the living traditions of Western magic, and forms the foundation for much of the current occult revival throughout the Western world.

The Golden Dawn itself was the product of an earlier revival of magical traditions. Founded in 1888 by William Wynn Westcott and Samuel Mathers, both of them Freemasons and practicing magicians with some claims to scholarship, it attracted a circle of men and women who saw magic as a way toward spiritual as well as practical ends. In pursuit of these ends, they drew together magical teachings from a dizzying array of sources and assembled them into a coherent and effective system of mystical and magical philosophy, theory, and practice, which deserves to rank among the world's major spiritual traditions.

Problems in its organizational structure caused the collapse of the Order itself in 1900, but many Golden Dawn members went on to found other magical orders along the same lines, using much of the same system. These successor orders—the Stella Matutina, the Fraternity of the Inner Light, and many others—produced many of the most important magicians of this century and gave the Golden Dawn system wider exposure. The process culminated in 1938–41 when Israel Regardie, an ex-member of the Stella Matutina, published an extensive collection of rituals and papers in four volumes as *The Golden Dawn*. Since then, basic elements of the system such as the Lesser Ritual of the Pentagram have become all but universal in modern magical circles.

Too often, though, Golden Dawn techniques have been simply copied blindly, without any attempt to put them in the context of a coherent system or to work out their potentials and their applications to practical and spiritual goals. The more advanced levels of the Order's magical work have received very little attention in recent years, and many of the possibilities for expansion built into the system—possibilities that seem never to have been developed within the Golden Dawn or its successor orders—have been left equally neglected. This has been especially true of the ritual methods developed by the Order. This is unfortunate, because the higher reaches of Golden Dawn ritual magic involve some of the most fascinating and powerful aspects of the whole system.

In the chapters that follow, then, I've tried to present as complete a view of the Golden Dawn's Cabalistic ritual work as possible, from the basic elements of ritual practice up through advanced ceremonial methods. In the process, I've included a number of practices and applications of my own, and made some corrections to the tradition's methods where this seemed appropriate. The whole point of tradition, after all, is that it grows and develops over time, drawing on the contributions of many hands and minds.

How to Use This Book

Circles of Power is designed as a complete introduction to the Cabalistic ritual magic of the Golden Dawn tradition and can be used on its own by the complete beginner. It does not, though, contain the complete Golden Dawn system of mysticism and magic. That would require a library, not a single book! Some of the subjects left out should be obvious enough—I have not, for example, covered Golden Dawn methods of divination, or of lodge work. Two exclusions deserve some comment.

The first of these is that I haven't covered the theory and philosophy of the magical Cabala in this book. The Cabala is the foundation of the entire Golden Dawn system, the framework that links together every other aspect of the Order's work, and it has a similar role in the work of most of the Golden Dawn's successor groups. It's possible to practice Golden Dawn ritual magic with only a small amount of Cabalistic background, though, and since that background can be picked up from a number of widely available sources—including, of course, my book, *Paths of Wisdom*—I've limited the amount of theory covered in this book to that actually needed to understand what's going on in the context of magical ritual.

The second exclusion is a little more problematic. The Golden Dawn drew on two main sources for its system of ritual magic. The first was the Cabala, as developed and expanded by Renaissance magicians such as Pico de Mirandola and Cornelius Agrippa. The second was the Enochian system devised by, or revealed to, the great Elizabethan occultist John Dee. These two sources share similar roots and similar approaches, but they are not the same. Each has its own structure and symbolism, its own language and applications, and putting both into a single book would have required either far too many deletions or far too many pages. Furthermore, on a more personal level, my main focus in the Golden Dawn tradition is the magical Cabala and its applications, and my work with the Enochian system hasn't been extensive enough to make me sure of my ability to teach it.

As a result, I've left the Enochian system entirely out of this book and revised certain ritual techniques so that they use a wholly Cabalistic symbolism. There are, again, a number of good books on Enochian magic available at present, and those who are interested in that system can find what they seek there.

In learning the material in this book, it's a good idea to take the chapters in order, and to be sure you have a clear grasp of the material in one chapter before going on to the next. The basic ideas presented in Part I provide the framework for the fundamental techniques covered in the first three chapters of Part II, and these in turn form the basic building blocks for the ritual applications given in the rest of Part II. The methods covered in each chapter draw on those covered in earlier chapters, and a step-by-step approach will make sure that you know how to do what's needed at each point.

It's also worth noting that ritual magic is an art, and an art that has to be learned. Without regular practice of the basic techniques, none of the rituals presented here will have any significant effect. The daily practice of the Lesser Middle Pillar exercise, which is given in Chapter 7, is a vital part of magical training. So, in a broader sense, is the regular performance of magical rituals themselves. Just as a musician doesn't learn how to play without practicing and playing, a magician doesn't learn how to work magic without practicing and performing rituals. As with anything else, what you get out of magic is precisely measured by what you put into it.

A Note on Sources and Spellings

The major sources for the material covered in this book are the surviving documents of the Hermetic Order of the Golden Dawn, especially those collected by Israel Regardie in *The Golden Dawn*. Several other sources deserve mention, though, and there are those who deserve thanks as well.

All Hebrew spellings used in this book are from *Godwin's Cabalistic Encyclopedia* by David Godwin, and the magic squares, seals, and sigils of the planets are as corrected by Donald Tyson in his edition of Henry Cornelius Agrippa's *Three Books of Occult Philosophy*. Both these books belong on the shelf of any serious Cabalistic magician.

The method of evocation presented in Chapter 11 is based on techniques found in John Hamill's collection of the magical papers of Frederick Hockley, *The Rosicrucian Seer*, and in the Dr. Rudd manuscripts edited by Adam McLean as *A Treatise on Angel Magic*, as well as other works of Renaissance magic.

Much of the material in this book has been presented in one form or another to my friends and students over the last ten years, and their responses have been a constant source of help to me. I would like to particularly thank the members of Emerald Lodge, who received the first drafts of several chapters as instructional lectures. Special thanks are owed to Carl Hood Jr., who has illuminated many aspects of the Golden Dawn system for me, and to my wife Sara, who has contributed to this and my previous book in more ways than I can name.

Finally, it's necessary to mention the issue (if it is an issue) of spelling. It's been suggested that in the magical community nowadays, a tradition consists of any three people who all spell the words "Cabala" and "magic" the same way. A great deal of importance has been attached to one or another variation; different spellings have been used as something not far from battle flags in squabbles between groups. Be that as it may, like *Paths of Wisdom*, *Circles of Power* uses the standard dictionary spellings of both these words. Both are (or were) common English terms, and it seems reasonable to treat them as such.

Part I

Principles of Ritual Magic

CHAPTER 1

THE NATURE OF RITUAL MAGIC

The magical traditions of the world contain a dizzying array of different methods, practices, and procedures. At first glance, there may seem to be very little in common between the pounding drums and bright colors of a Voudon ceremony under way in Haiti and the perfect meditative silence of an esoteric Buddhist magician at work in a temple in Japan, or for that matter between either of these and the ornate working tools and flowing robes, stylized gestures and chanted words of power of a magician working in the Golden Dawn tradition. Still, despite the visible differences, a deeper thread of connection joins each of these practitioners and their work. That thread is the thread of ritual.

Even to those with no magical background at all, the idea of ritual is central to any notion of what magic is or what magicians do. To many modern Americans, whose closest approach to magical thought comes from caricatures in Saturday morning cartoons or the even sillier caricatures condemned from church pulpits on Sunday mornings, magic is still a matter of gestures and words, special objects, and strange actions. This habit of thought is grounded in the realities of magic, for although there is more to magic than ritual, the art of ritual makes up the heart of magical technique in nearly all of the world's traditions.

We can define ritual as *symbolic action*. A symbol—this word opens up half the major issues of philosophy, but those will have to wait—is a thing that means something else; it defines a relationship, the relationship of

3

meaning, between the symbol itself and the thing symbolized. A finger that points to the moon isn't the same as the moon itself, but equally, it isn't the same as a finger that points to nothing at all. So, too, a symbol is neither the thing it symbolizes, nor simply the thing it is in itself. It has another dimension, the dimension of meaning, which exists in what (for now) we can call the realm, or world, of consciousness.

Human beings are symbolizing creatures; our languages, our social structures, the images and ideas that make up our understanding of the world, are all symbols. Our perceptions of the world itself, as they filter through our senses, our brain structures, and our thought processes, are themselves nothing more than symbols of the reality outside us. If ritual is symbolic action, the great majority of all human activity is ritual—and this is in fact true, as a little time spent watching human beings will show.

Most of the time, of course, the rituals of everyday life go on in a habitual, half-conscious fashion. We talk without thinking about the abstract, symbolic nature of the links between sound and idea, and we shake hands without remembering that this gesture once proved that neither party had a weapon ready to use. Still, the subtle connections between symbol and meaning often remain in place and shape human experience and behavior in a whole range of unexpected ways.

When ritual and the relationships of meaning that underlie it are studied and used deliberately, though, a whole range of possibilities opens up. These possibilities include most of the methods of magic. While the world's traditions of magic contain an enormous array of different tools, techniques, and approaches, symbolism and symbolic action—that is, ritual—form the most important elements of the magician's toolkit.

The mastery of ritual thus offers what is probably the single most important way to begin to make use of the immense hidden potentials of human consciousness, potentials that go far beyond the limits most people nowadays place on what it means to be human.

Models of Experience

In beginning the study of ritual magic, there's at least one major obstacle that has to be overcome before anything useful can be done. That obstacle is built out of some of the most basic elements of the modern way of thinking about the world. Unlike the students of magic in many non-Western cultures, who have grown up thinking in ways that include magic as a matter of course, the beginning magician in the modern West has been taught to perceive the world in ways that leave very little room for magic at all.

Over the last few centuries, a good deal of ingenuity has been put into the project of finding some way to wedge magic into the cracks and odd corners of the modern Western world view. One popular approach to this project reinterprets magic as a kind of psychology, usually along the lines of Carl Jung's archetypal theories; another, once more popular than it is now, postulates some not-yet-discovered energy or substance as a medium for magical action. This kind of theorizing has a valid place. At the same time, there's much to be said for a different approach: learning to think about the world in another way—the magician's way.

In order to do this, it's necessary to remember that the models we use to understand the world are exactly that: models. They are maps of a reality, not the reality itself. The model of scientific materialism is a very good map for understanding how physical matter and energy interact, but a very poor map for many other purposes. To use it as a basis for understanding magic, or for that matter much of the rest of life, is like trying to use a highway map to figure out topography or vegetation patterns. Nor is this simply a weakness in this one particular map; the universe of human experience is more complex than any single map, any one set of interpretations, can possibly be.

It's also important, in beginning to think about the world of experience from the magician's viewpoint, to recognize that changing from one map to another can be a disquieting experience, sometimes a deeply disturbing one. Much of the appeal of the various extreme belief systems currently being marketed as absolute truth in our society comes from this fact. Faced with the stark vision of a universe no map can contain— a universe that is, in its fullness, incomprehensible to the human mind— it can be all too easy to flee into some comforting belief system that promises certainty, whether that system be the abstract materialism of modern science or the arbitrary commandments of some religious dogma. Ultimately, though, the promise of certainty is a lie, and one that lessens those who embrace it.

In the same way, the model of the world we'll be examining here is simply a model, applicable to certain areas of human experience and less applicable to others. It is not itself the truth, in any real sense, and to take it as such is to waste most of its potential. Similarly, the wide range of things and beings that play a role in that model—levels of being and modes of action, elements and worlds, Spheres and Paths, spirits and angels, and Names of Power—are no more real than, say, electrons or the Gross National Product; they are simply ways of speaking about subtle aspects of the universe we experience each day. This, in turn, is their strength, for whether they exist or not, as Aleister Crowley was fond of pointing out, the universe does indeed appear to work as if they do.

With these points in mind, then, we can begin to venture across the debatable lands separating the familiar countryside of our culture's current image of the world from the forbidden realms where magic has its home. In doing so, we'll be straying onto ground that the founders and adepts of the Golden Dawn itself rarely touched. The excellence of the Golden Dawn system is in its practical methods; the theory and philosophy of magic behind these methods was rarely discussed in the Order, and few of the successor groups have much to offer in this field. It's in the traditions of magic from which the Golden Dawn arose— traditions reaching back through the great magical revival of the Renaissance into ancient times—that the meaning and context of magical practice can be found.

One way to explore the model of the world that underlies Golden Dawn magic, then, would involve a journey through the work of Cabalistic, Hermetic, and Neo-Platonic philosophers and mystics. This could easily fill a book by itself, though, and much of what would be covered has little direct relevance to the practice of ritual magic. Fortunately, it's possible to approach the magical model of the universe by a different route: one that begins not from ancient traditions or systems of thought, but from the simple realities of the way we experience the universe at each moment.

The Worlds We Perceive

One of the most important parts of the map of the universe that dominates modern Western culture is the idea that the "real world" is made up entirely of matter and energy, while consciousness is simply an odd phenomenon that goes on inside certain lumps of meat called human brains. This notion, which seems like plain common sense to most modern people, actually rises from a highly arbitrary set of beliefs about the universe; it has to be taught, and it makes sense only if some quite common aspects of human experience are ignored.

We'll need to leave behind, for a moment, the usual assumptions about what is "real" and what is not, and start from a more basic question. What kinds of perceptions do human beings have about this complicated thing we call the universe? What, at the most basic level, do we perceive?

First of all, there are perceptions that appear to come into consciousness through the senses of sight, hearing, taste, touch, and smell. These are the things modern thought classifies as information about the "real world."

Second, there are perceptions, hard to discuss in modern English but highly familiar to members of many other cultures, which seem to come through subtle forms of the ordinary senses. If you shake your hands thoroughly, then cup them before you as if you were holding a ball and, while breathing slowly and deeply, move your hands gently closer and farther apart from each other, you're likely to perceive one example of this kind of experience.

These perceptions seem to be closely related to those of the material senses in certain ways, for many of the things perceived by these more elusive senses—though not all—are related to things in the realm of physical experience; a given object, a particular place, a certain person, will tend to have a consistent "feel" or "energy" just as they have a consistent physical appearance.

Third, there are perceptions that take more or less sensory forms—spoken or written words, images, and so on—but which seem to be independent of the world perceived by the senses. These perceptions go on more or less constantly, as a kind of running monologue in awareness. Our modern way of looking at the world classifies these perceptions as thoughts, feelings, memories, daydreams, and so on.

Fourth, there are perceptions that do not take sensory forms, are independent of the world the senses perceive, and yet seem to have a role in structuring that world. These might best be described as perceptions of pattern—for example, the perception that things equal to the same thing are equal to each other. What modern thought calls the laws of logic, mathematics, and (to some extent) nature, are included in this category.

Fifth and finally, there are perceptions of the kind that are sometimes called "mystical." These are completely independent of the senses or sensory forms, or for that matter of the patterns of any of the previous kinds of experience; they seem to involve perception of the universe as a unity, and of the individual self in relation to that unity.

It's possible to divide the spectrum of possible human experience in other ways, of course, but this fivefold division offers a useful perspective on the modern "common sense" mentioned above. In the terms we've just explored, the modern way of thinking takes one of these kinds of experiences—the kind that comes through the senses—and sets it up as the only "real" kind, claiming that it reflects a "real" world of matter and energy, and dismissing all other kinds of experience as nothing more than byproducts of this world. Logically speaking, this is hard to justify.

It's been claimed that the world of sensory experience is real because it is objective—that is, experienced the same way by different people—while all other kinds of experience are subjective—experienced differently by different people. Common though the claim is, this simply isn't true.

First of all, there are plenty of experiences of the non-sensory kind that are as "objective" as anything material can be: the basic rules of mathematics, to give only one obvious example, are the same no matter who uses them, and the effectiveness of many martial arts depends on the concrete reality of experiences of the second kind we've examined above. Nor are all physical experiences necessarily perceived in the same way by everyone involved; the taste of a particular wine or the events of a traffic accident are likely to be perceived and described by different people in very different ways.

It's been claimed, many times, that this last factor simply represents inaccurate human perceptions of an objective fact. This argument might have some merit, except for the awkward point that these same inaccurate perceptions are the only evidence there is that the supposed "objective fact" exists at all. *Human perception is the only thing we can actually know.*

The realm of "objective fact" is no more than a mental construct, pieced together in our minds out of certain kinds of human experience according to certain fairly arbitrary rules. The only world we can know directly at all is the world of human perception, of human consciousness, and everything else comes to us only as shadows cast into this world.

It's reasonable to assume, though it can't be proved logically, that some of these shadows are cast by something outside of human consciousness. It's reasonable, too, to create mental models of that "something outside," and to treat these models as rough representations of a universe in which we exist. It's not reasonable, on the other hand, to dismiss most kinds of human experience as possible evidence on which such models can be based, and to use only one narrow set of perceptions to judge all the others—but this is precisely what the modern notion of reality does.

Levels of Experience

The traditions of Western magic, drawing from an older way of looking at the universe, have always taken a broader view. In the magical philosophy of the Cabala, on which Golden Dawn magic is based, the universe around us is seen as a continuum that reaches from spirit to matter without a break, passing through every level of human experience in between.

The most important model for this continuum is the diagram of the Tree of Life, which describes it in terms of ten fundamental stages or levels of existence. For our present purposes, though, a different model may be more useful, one based on the same fivefold division of experience we examined above. This model can be pictured as a pair of intersecting triangles, one representing matter, the other spirit, as shown in Diagram 1 on page 10.

The realms of intersection between matter and spirit can be divided into five levels, and these in turn can be related to the five elements of traditional magical symbolism, which we'll be exploring in more detail later. These levels are as follows.

1. *Physical*. The physical level is experienced through the five ordinary senses. It can be seen in terms of physical matter and energy, more or less as these are understood by modern scientific thought. Older traditions describe it as made by the interactions of four elements— fire, air, water, and earth—which correspond to the modern concepts of energy, gases, liquids, and solids. Symbolically, this level corresponds to the solid and unyielding element of Earth.

2. *Etheric*. The etheric level is experienced through a different set of senses, more or less paralleling ordinary sight and touch. It can be

thought of as a level of immaterial substance, which shares some qualities with both energy and matter, but which is closely connected to biological life. This "ether," as it is sometimes called, can be identified with the prana of Hindu yoga or the *ch'i* or *ki* of East Asian martial arts. In magical philosophy, it is seen as the underlying basis of the material level, an ocean of subtle substance providing patterns along which matter and energy take shape. Symbolically, it corresponds to the fluid and receptive element of Water.

3. *Astral.* The astral level, or level of concrete consciousness, is experienced through what we normally think of as the mind—that is, the faculties of intellect, emotion, imagination, will, and memory. It's important to understand that, from the magician's perspective, these can function as senses and instruments of action, and neither of these functions is limited to the inside of any one person's head. The astral level can be thought of as a realm of flowing energies

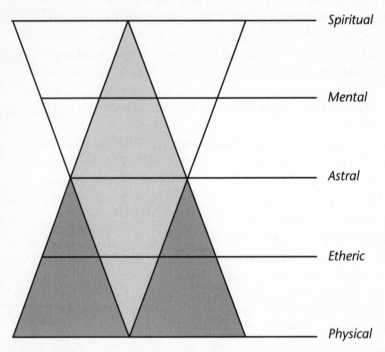

Spiritual

Mental

Astral

Etheric

Physical

Diagram 1—
Levels of Being

linking mind to mind, moving through ever-changing patterns that appear to our awareness as thoughts, feelings, images, and the like, and that are shaped by our own consciousness and that of others. Symbolically, this level corresponds to the energetic and transforming element of Fire.

4. *Mental.* The mental level, or level of abstract consciousness, is experienced through the innate capacities of awareness itself. It can be thought of as a realm of abstract patterns that exist beyond space and time, and that provide the organizing principles on which the first three levels are based. These patterns appear to our awareness as basic insights into the nature of things. Symbolically, this level corresponds to the transparent and intangible element of Air.

5. *Spiritual.* The spiritual level is experienced through the essential core of the self, which is also the source of consciousness. It can be thought of as pure being, beyond any other definition, and it is reflected in human awareness in a class of experiences difficult to define, which relate the self to the unity of all things. Symbolically, this level corresponds to the unifying and transcendent element of Spirit.

These five levels can be seen as parts of a single spectrum reaching from spirit to matter, or (to say the same thing in a different way) from complete potential to complete manifestation. The different regions of this spectrum, though, are distinct from each other in a number of ways. Notably, the rules that govern one often don't hold up in the others; you can't drive a nail into an idea, for instance, or think your way through a solid wall. Each realm, in effect, must be faced on its own terms.

There are certain underlying patterns that connect these five levels of experience, though, and a clear sense of these patterns will help make the principles of ritual magic a good deal clearer. Two of the levels, the physical and etheric, have to do with things that happen within the familiar context of space and time. The things we experience on these levels appear to take up space and change over time; they are subject to growth and decay, expansion and contraction. In the language of Platonic philosophy, these two levels can be thought of as the realm of Becoming.

Two other levels, the spiritual and the mental, have to do with things that are entirely outside space and time, and do not undergo change. These two levels, in turn, can be thought of as the realm of pure Being.

At the same time, there's an important parallel in the relationships between the two levels contained in each realm. The physical and mental levels are both levels where things exist in multiplicity—that is, there are many different things to be experienced, and each seems largely separate from the things around it. The book in your hands right now is distinct from the hands that hold it, the air around it, and so on. In the same way, the various patterns of the mental level are separate from one another, and can be experienced separately. A sudden insight into one abstract truth doesn't necessarily lead to equal insights into others. By contrast, the etheric and spiritual levels are levels of unity, where what's experienced is perceived as an aspect of a whole. There are few dividing lines in the ocean of ether, and none at all in the transcendent unity of the spirit.

And what of the astral level, standing between the realms of Being and Becoming? The movements of concrete consciousness we usually call thoughts and feelings aren't subject to the limits of ordinary time and space; equally, though, they don't exist in the changelessness of eternity. Rather, they take place in a space and time of their own, one that is flexible to a degree that ordinary space and time are not, and that relates more clearly to the realms of Being than ordinary space and time do.

The experience of dreaming, which is the deepest that most people ever get into the astral level, shows this clearly. In dreams, space exists and time passes, but they do so in a complex multileveled way almost impossible to define or describe. Things that are completely impossible in ordinary space and time take place constantly; time stretches, stops, or flows backward, an event takes place in two different places at once, and so on. The same is true of ordinary thinking, and dramatically true also of the more intensive kinds of astral experience, which magicians know how to enter.

In magical theory, the astral level has these special properties because it is the interface between the realms of Being and Becoming, the point of overlap where time meets eternity and change borders on the changeless. It's by way of concrete consciousness, in other words, that the two realms communicate. As we'll see shortly, this communication is the key to the process by which the universe comes into being, and it's also, critically, the key to the effective use of ritual magic.

Macrocosm and Microcosm

Here one of the prejudices of modern thought mentioned above becomes an obstacle to understanding. We've had it so thoroughly drummed into our heads that the experiences of consciousness are "subjective"—that is, unreal in a scientific sense—that the idea that consciousness has any role at all outside our own skulls is a radical one at present. Nonetheless, there's good reason to suspect that this idea, strange as it may seem, may be more useful as a model for experience than our culture's current belief systems might suggest.

The philosophers of an earlier time, free from the limitations of our models of the universe, saw the interaction between consciousness and matter in a very different light. They knew from their own experience, as we do if we pay attention, that in the human being movements of matter are caused by movements of consciousness. This happens on obvious levels, as when someone decides to raise his or her arm and then does so.

It also happens on less obvious levels. Careful attention to the phenomena of consciousness will reveal an entire range of processes that go on automatically, usually without being noticed, and control such things as the beating of the heart and the contraction of "involuntary" muscles in the digestive tract. (It's by learning to perceive these processes, in fact, that advanced practitioners of yoga are able accomplish their astonishing feats of physical control.) These automatic processes interact closely with the etheric level, and one way to conceptualize the whole process is to see events in consciousness causing changes in the ether, which then bring about changes in the realm of physical matter.

The idea that change in consciousness precedes change in matter, though, had broader implications, which thinkers in ancient times were not slow to explore. If this is true of human beings and other living things, they reasoned, might it be true of other things as well? Might it, in fact, be a general rule that all physical happenings have their cause in consciousness? Might this explain, for example, the ability of oracles and diviners to foretell the future before it happens? Such ideas, explored and tested over time, became central to the magical model of the universe.

There is, in that model, a complete set of levels on each side of the barrier between the self and the universe, a barrier that is simply the most deeply seated of all the habits of human thought. Physical, etheric, astral, mental, and spiritual experiences all relate to "inner" and "outer" phenomena alike, and the relationship between the levels—a relationship in which the astral mediates between time and the timeless, and sets patterns in motion that descend the levels into physical manifestation—works the same way in both. The parallel is extensive enough that the founders of the Western magical tradition, drawing on ancient images out of myth, spoke of the universe and the human individual as reflections of each other: the universe a vast human being, the individual a small universe.

This is the idea at the heart of the *principle of macrocosm and microcosm*, one of the central elements of the magical model of the world. These two words are much used in magical writings in the Western world; *macrocosm* comes from the Greek words *makros kosmos*—literally, "great universe"—and means the cosmos around us, while *microcosm* is from *mikros kosmos*, "little universe," and means the totality of the human individual. The principle of macrocosm and microcosm is that the two are in a certain sense equivalent.

This principle can be, and often has been, taken in directions it wasn't meant to go. It doesn't mean that there is a one-to-one correspondence between the physical universe and the physical human body; the universe, as Plato pointed out, doesn't have feet. Nor is this same sort of one-to-one link to be found on other levels. The point the principle makes, and it is an important one, is that the essential patterns of our experience of the universe and the essential patterns of our experience of ourselves are one and the same.

There's a deeper point at work here, one that ties into troubling issues of perception and reality. The patterns just mentioned are, ultimately, patterns of our experience, and are shaped by the particular set of equipment for perceiving and thinking we each inherit as members of the human race. Our perceptions are human perceptions, and as a result our universe is a human universe, made in our own image by the very structure of the means by which we perceive it.

Magic and the Process of Creation

In the philosophy of magic, the principle of macrocosm and microcosm is the basis of a perception hinted at above, one that has a central part in explaining the universe and the role of magic within it. Just as each individual human being exists on all levels of experience, it's held that every other thing we can perceive also exists on all these levels.

If you look at an object—a rock, for example—you see the physical rock, made of some particular kind of stone. The same rock, according to magical teaching, also exists on the etheric level, as a wave-pattern of stresses in the ether; on the astral level, as a concrete form in consciousness, a presence in the constant flow of perceptions; on the mental level, as an abstract and timeless idea, an essential quality of "rockness;" and on the spiritual level, as a revelation of the primal unity from which the rock, and everything else, ultimately derive.

From one point of view, these different levels of the rock's existence are simply different ways of looking at the same rock, using the powers of perception human beings possess on each of the levels. In the magical model of the universe, though, the five aspects of the rock—and of everything else—are linked by a process of reflection that is also a chain of cause and effect. The spiritual rock, in effect, is reflected on the mental level, and thus causes a mental rock to come into being; similarly, the mental rock is reflected on the astral, the astral on the etheric, and the etheric on the physical. To put it in another way, the same essential pattern descends this ladder of being, step by step, taking shape at each level in that level's manner.

This, in magical terms, is the secret of creation. In contrast to the orthodox religions of the West, which have usually seen creation as a once-for-all event at the beginning of time, the magical philosophy of the Cabala understands creation as an ongoing process in which all things and all beings are active participants. In this vision, everything we experience comes into being through a process that reaches up to the heights of the spiritual level and cascades downward level by level to the realm of matter and of sensory perception. Everything we experience, in turn, has a presence and an effect on all levels of being.

In this process of creation, the astral level is in many ways the critical factor. It's on the level of concrete consciousness that the eternal patterns of the spiritual and mental levels are reflected into specific forms within space and time—*this* rock, *this* tree, *this* human being. The astral level is the cutting edge of creation, and because of this it's also the place where magic is born.

A pattern that is established on the astral by human consciousness will tend to move down the levels into manifestation in the same way as any other astral pattern. This is the central insight of the traditional philosophy of magic, and it provides the key to magical practice. The entire complicated apparatus of ritual magic is ultimately nothing more than a collection of methods for building patterns in concrete consciousness.

This makes magic sound simple, and it is. "Simple," though, is not the same thing as "easy." There is a range of obstacles to the simple act of building a pattern on the astral level, and these obstacles and the ways to get around them will take up much of this book.

The Universe as Energy

The descent of the patterns of creation from spirit to matter can be understood in another way, one that provides a useful way of talking about the nature of magic. Each of the descending patterns we've discussed can also be seen as a flow or current of energy: an energy of a particular kind, with particular effects, which takes specific forms on each of the levels as it passes through. Each energy flow first emerges on the astral level, drawing on the mental and spiritual levels as its energy source, and finally grounds on the material level; during its descent, it interacts with other energies.

The language of energy is a metaphor, of course—the kind of energy discussed here won't fry eggs or show up on a voltmeter—and it's a modern metaphor at that; older books on magical theory generally speak of influences and effluvia, or of the ideal forms and receptive substance of Neoplatonist metaphysics. Still, the metaphor communicates the nature of the creative process effectively to modern minds. Like the more familiar kinds of energy, the metaphorical energy of creation has its sources and channels, its polarities and patterns of flow, its local imbalances and turbulence, within an overall balance.

From this perspective, then, the universe takes on the image of a vast and intricate pattern of energies that dance and surge through the levels of being, giving rise to everything we experience in the process. A human being is a single current of energy within that dance, shaped and influenced by many others, but capable of shaping and influencing as well. A magician is a current of this creative energy who has learned to put those capabilities into action.

As one small center of energy in a universe awash with tides of power, the magician is far from omnipotent. One of the most important rules of practical magic is that magical workings sometimes fail. Still, a human being who sets out to learn how to perceive and act on all levels of experience will find that he or she has possibilities for action that are closed to those who are satisfied with a purely physical approach to life. Since the patterns on each level cause and organize their equivalents beneath, too, the magician has the power to shape even the most material kinds of experience by influencing the equivalent patterns on a higher level. There are limits to this power, and we'll be discussing these later on, but the combined experience of magicians over centuries has shown that the power itself unquestionably exists.

The level of most magical practice, as we've seen, is the level of concrete consciousness. The magician thus stands, so to speak, on the astral level of experience, bringing down the timeless patterns of the higher levels and channeling them into manifestation on the lower. There are thus two dynamics at work in any magical training worth the name. On the one hand, the novice magician must look upward, toward the higher levels, and learn how to align himself or herself with the sources of the energies of creation; on the other, he or she must look downward, toward the lower levels, and learn how to direct those energies into manifestation.

The first of these dynamics defines the branch of magic called *theurgy* or *high magic*, which aims at transforming and balancing the self on all its levels; the second defines the branch called *thaumaturgy* or *practical magic*, which aims at reshaping the universe of experience in accordance with will. These two, the Janus faces of magic, make up between them the path of the ritual magician in the Golden Dawn tradition, and they will both need to be studied and practiced if skill in the art of magic is to be attained.

CHAPTER 2

THE MAGICAL MACROCOSM

THE WORLD OF THE MAGICIAN is a world of many levels, and these levels will appear in many different forms as you work with the ritual magic of the Golden Dawn tradition. In their purest sense, the five levels of the model outlined in the last chapter are simply particular kinds of human experience, and in philosophical contexts it may well be best to think of them purely in this way, without going into the largely unanswerable questions about what reality might lie behind these experiences. Human beings find it easiest to think in concrete terms, however, and whatever the deeper reality behind our experience may be, it's convenient to speak of the different kinds of experience concretely, as things we can know in some kind of objective sense.

Each of the five kinds of experience we've examined can therefore be treated as a distinct realm or level of reality: an aspect of the macrocosm or "great universe," the totality of the cosmos of which we inhabit one small part. Each level—physical, etheric, astral, mental, spiritual—is then seen as a realm of existence as well as a kind of experience. Through each of these realms in turn, the process of creation sends patterns of energy, shaping the substance of the levels as they pass and finally taking physical form on the level of matter to bring about the solid realities of our daily lives.

Everything in the universe, in turn, can be seen as having a spiritual, mental, astral, and etheric form, as well as a physical one, and the physical form we experience with our ordinary senses can best be seen, in magical terms, as a shadow cast in the realm of matter by the higher levels of existence. Each of these forms obeys the principles, laws, and habits of the level on which it exists, and the magician who seeks to work with any of these forms must keep this last point solidly in mind.

Clearly, a single mental model of the macrocosm won't be enough to handle this kind of complexity. In the Western magical tradition, there are three primary models of existence or—to say the same thing in different words—three main ways of talking about the universe in magical terms, and all three play a significant part in the work of the Golden Dawn magician.

The first of them, and the most important, sees the universe as a pattern in consciousness, an immense structure of ideas that are expressed in symbolic form. The second sees the universe as a vast assembly of beings of many different types and levels. The third, which is closest to the modern Western view of reality, sees the universe as a realm of substances of many kinds through which tides and patterns of movement ebb and flow. Each of these models of the universe has its place in magical theory and practice, and each has to be understood and used appropriately by the magician.

Levels of the Macrocosm

A look through the system of levels discussed in Chapter 1 will offer some help in all this complexity. We can take a first glance over the macrocosm, as the Golden Dawn tradition understands it, by looking at each level in terms of the ideas, the entities, or the substances that exist and function there.

On the spiritual level, the Golden Dawn tradition, drawing on the Cabalistic philosophy at its core, posits a unity of absolute being and absolute power, the ultimate source of the whole process of creation, and thus of all the levels of the universe of our experience. Older writings on magic typically use the same term for this unity that the dogmatic religions of the West use for their supreme deity—God—and this term can be a convenient label. It needs to be remembered, though, that most of the connotations the word usually carries simply don't apply here. Just to begin with, the unity at the highest level of existence in magical thought isn't seen as male, or as having any gender at all; it is not seen as human, or humanlike, in any imaginable sense, or as possessing human sentiments such as anger or jealousy—or for that matter, love. It cannot be categorized, defined, or even effectively described, by any human words whatsoever.

A concept this abstract may sound as though it has little usefulness for a magician, or anyone else. For practical purposes, however, a series of symbolic titles or formulae—the traditional Names of God—are used to represent this primal unity of power, expressing it in terms of the most basic manifestations of its creative force on lower levels of being. These Names are anything but meaningless in practical terms; they provide one of the main channels by which the magician summons and shapes the energies of the nonphysical levels of being.

On the mental level, the creative energies descending from the realm of absolute unity take shape as abstract patterns in consciousness, existing beyond space and time. These patterns can be seen as the fundamental ideas of existence, and collectively form a kind of blueprint of the universe on all its levels: the cosmos as pure information. The patterns of the mental level are also at the root of all perception, and they provide the deep structure that underlies systems of symbolic meaning such as mathematics and language—and magical imagery.

In magical teaching, the patterns of the mental level can also be seen as conscious beings, and can thus be dealt with as entities as well as ideas. They are traditionally equated with the archangels of Judeo-Christian mythology, and seen as powers of cosmic scale generated by the energy of the spiritual level: in theological language, the first and mightiest beings created by God. In ritual practice in the Golden Dawn tradition, it is often these archangelic forms that are used to contact the forces of the mental level.

On the astral level, the creative patterns descending from the mental realm interact, multiply, and give rise to an immense diversity of powers, which can be seen in three ways: as concrete patterns in consciousness, present within space and time; as conscious and active entities; or as a subtle substance pervaded by energies and motion. The astral level is at one and the same time the level on which most human awareness normally works, and the level at which ritual magic most often has its direct effects, and it should come as no surprise that this level has therefore been the focus of enormous amounts of attention in magical tradition.

Seen as a realm of concrete patterns in consciousness, the astral level is the medium for the whole range of processes we usually term "mental." The familiar part of this consists of individual mental actions—thoughts, feelings, acts of imagination and will, memories—all of which radiate outward through the boundaries of the self and can produce various kinds of telepathic and empathic communication.

Another part, less familiar, consists of the activities of collective consciousness, the subtle but powerful influence that gives groups and cultures "personalities" of their own, generates crowd phenomena, and transmits panics and fads. Yet another part, less familiar still, consists of factors from sources outside humanity, which can cause strange effects, sometimes powerfully healing and sometimes highly destructive, in those human beings open to them.

Seen as a realm of entities, the astral level is home to an immense number of beings of many different kinds, whom we may as well call by the traditional term "spirits." In the traditional lore, these range from angelic powers who reflect the primary creative patterns of the mental level, and who are generally beneficial to human beings, through a vast array of intermediate forms and stages, to malign entities born of imbalance and decay who appear to regard humanity as the astral equivalent of food—and to still other kinds of spirits, for whom human beings are simply irrelevant. Magical writings in and out of the Golden Dawn tradition offer various classifications of these beings, but there are severe limits to all of these schemes, and the Golden Dawn papers warn that there are countless spirits who do not fit into any classification at all.

Seen as a realm of subtle substance, the astral level is a context through which tides of energy ebb and flow in cyclical patterns and rhythms, influencing the levels below in ways that can often be predicted. Movements of the Earth relative to the Sun, the other bodies of the solar system, and the background of stars, affect these tides—an insight that forms the basis for the magical understanding of astrology.

On the etheric level, the complicated dance of forces that descend from the astral level takes on progressively more concrete forms, and comes within range of physical matter and energy. The processes of the etheric level can't effectively be modeled as interactions of ideas, but the remaining two models both have value here.

The entities identified with the etheric level in magical tradition are those who have direct contact with the world we experience through our ordinary senses. These include elemental spirits, who personify much of what we might call the forces of nature, and many other kinds of entities as well. Like the spirits of the astral level, these differ widely in their response to human beings, from friendly to hostile to wholly indifferent; unlike astral spirits, who normally affect consciousness alone, the denizens of the etheric level are said to be able to shape life-energies and raw matter as well, a power that has given material to many of the traditions of folklore.

The substance identified with the etheric level, as we saw earlier, is an immaterial but tangible presence deeply involved with biological life. Most of the world's languages have familiar terms for it—ours is apparently one of the few exceptions—and many Western people nowadays have encountered it by way of Eastern terms such as *prana* or *ch'i*. The magical traditions of the West have used a wide range of names for it, but "ether"—a term borrowed from nineteenth-century physics—is the most common. Like the substance of the astral level (or of the physical, for that matter), the ether has its tides and cycles, its periods of high and low intensity, and in the case of the ether, these are most strongly influenced by the daily and yearly cycles of the Earth and by the phases of the Moon.

On the physical level, finally, the forms descending from the etheric level take shape in the realm of matter and energy we perceive through our five physical senses. The physical level is best understood simply in terms of substance; it is essentially the world as known to modern science, and to what could be termed "common sense." Here fire burns, diseases kill, and the attempt to walk through a solid wall will simply result in a bruised nose unless you have a bulldozer go through first. The physical level interacts with higher levels, and some of these interactions are of substantial importance in magical practice, but it's important to remember that the world of matter has its own existence and its own laws, which cannot simply be ignored.

Three Realms of Magic

This system of levels interacts in a predictable way with the three models of the universe we've discussed, and this interaction has practical implications that can be predicted as well. Generally speaking, the universe can be understood as a pattern in consciousness from the spiritual, mental, and astral levels; it can be understood as a concourse of entities from the mental, astral, and etheric levels; and it can be understood as a structure of substances in motion from the astral, etheric, and physical levels.

Many traditions of folk magic from around the world focus on the third of these three approaches, working with the subtle effects of physical and nonphysical substances. The magical uses of herbs and stones make up one branch of this kind of lore that has been retained in Western magical practice. Medieval traditions of Western magic, by contrast, tended to make the second of the models the most important; the grimoires of the Middle Ages are very little more than collections of lore concerning the nature and uses of different kinds of spirits. Certain of this lore, too, has remained in use in many systems of Western magic.

In the Golden Dawn tradition, on the other hand, the first of these three models is far and away the most important. It alone functions effectively on the highest of the five levels, and for this reason it is best suited to the work of self-transformation at the heart of the theurgic side of Golden Dawn magic. In some ways, though, it is less effective for the practical work of the thaumaturgic side, since it has little applicability to the etheric and physical levels where so much of thaumaturgic magic is aimed. Because of this, both the other models do have a place in the original teachings of the Golden Dawn and its successor orders, and in the work of this book. We will examine them one at a time.

The Way of Symbolism

The spiritual and mental levels of experience, for reasons we'll examine in Chapter 3, are difficult for most people to perceive consciously. Because of this, the most commonly used ways of thinking about the forces of these levels, and putting them to work in ritual magic, make use of their reflections on the astral level of experience. These reflections are the symbols of magic.

As mentioned earlier, the questions brought up by symbolism include many of the major conundrums of philosophy. Most of those have no direct bearing on ritual magic, in or out of the Golden Dawn tradition, and so can be passed over here. It's important, though, to get a sense of the magical understanding of the nature of symbols and symbolism, because much of the lore of modern Western magic is symbolic in nature, and much of it—precisely because it is symbolic—has been subject to a certain amount of misunderstanding in recent years.

What is a symbol? At the most basic level, as we saw in the previous chapter, it's simply something that means something. In magical terms, on the other hand, a symbol is a pattern at the astral level, the level of concrete consciousness, where the act of meaning—in the usual sense of that word—takes place. Everything perceived on the astral level has meaning, and is thus a symbol of one kind or another.

If you take a moment to examine your thoughts and feelings, you'll soon see that everything that passes through your mind—that is, your awareness when it's focused on the astral level—is a word, an image, or some other kind of symbolic experience, with some kind of meaning attached to it that goes beyond what it itself is. Even the impressions taken in by the senses are symbolic in nature, since what we perceive when we look at, listen to, smell, taste, or touch something is not the thing itself, but rather the patterns produced in our awareness by a long chain of physical, neural, and psychological processes.

Each one of the infinity of symbols that passes through our awareness on the astral level is part of a pattern of creation that has its roots on the spiritual level and its completion on the physical. (Even a wandering thought has some physical manifestation, if only in the firing of nerve cells in the brain.) Certain of the symbols that we can perceive on the astral, though, sum up one of the primary patterns of the mental level with more clarity than others.

When a set of symbols related to a single pattern of the mental level is brought together in awareness, the creative energies of that pattern—and those of its root in the unity of the spiritual level—comes through more forcefully into the astral. There, these energies can catalyze changes in concrete consciousness, or they can be channeled further down the system of levels, to manifest on the etheric or physical levels. From the point of view of traditional magical philosophy, this is how ritual magic works.

The specific ways of using symbolism in ritual magic, and in esoteric work as a whole, are almost numberless—much of the rest of this book will be taken up with the ways in which symbols are put to work in a ritual context—but all derive from the way symbols represent higher-level forces in the realms of concrete consciousness. It may be useful, because of this, to think of symbols primarily as "handles" by which the forces of the astral, mental, and spiritual levels can be grasped and directed.

There are three major sets of symbols that are used for this purpose in Western magic, and these should be committed to memory early on in magical training, as all ritual work in the Golden Dawn tradition is based squarely on them. The first of them, the ten Spheres of the Tree of Life, are used to represent patterns that have their main effect on levels above the astral. These represent the primary creative powers of the universe, and are central to the practice of theurgic magic and the work of spiritual transformation on the highest and deepest levels of the self.

Table 1: The Spheres of the Tree of Life

Number	Name	Meaning	Power
1	Kether	Crown	Primal unity
2	Chokmah	Wisdom	Primal energy
3	Binah	Understanding	Primal form
4	Chesed	Mercy	Expansion, order, construction
5	Geburah	Severity	Limitation, chaos, destruction
6	Tiphareth	Beauty	Harmony, balance
7	Netzach	Victory	Interaction, love
8	Hod	Glory	Differentiation, intelligence
9	Yesod	Foundation	Combination of forces, power
10	Malkuth	Kingdom	Solidity, the world of ordinary experience

The second, the seven planets of traditional astrology, are used to represent patterns that have their major effect on the astral level itself, and thus represent the primary influences on what we can call, for want of a better word, psychology. These are central to those kinds of magic, both theurgic and thaumaturgic, that have the goal of changing mental and emotional processes in the magician as well as others. They can also be applied to etheric and material matters in certain situations, but this is a secondary use.

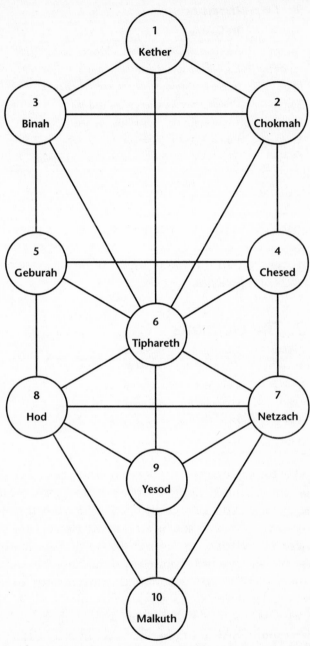

Diagram 2—
The Spheres

Table 2: The Planets

Symbol	Name	Rulership
♄	Saturn	Limitations, agriculture, old age, death
♃	Jupiter	Expansion, prosperity, aspiration
♂	Mars	Self-expression, violence, radical change
☉	Sun	Power, creative energy, individuality
♀	Venus	Love, emotions, sexuality, the arts
☿	Mercury	Intellect, craft, business affairs
☽	Moon	The body, the unconscious, the unknown

The third, the five elements of alchemy and natural magic, are used to represent patterns that have their major effect on levels below the astral, and thus shape the etheric realm of life energy and the physical realm of dense matter. These are thus central to the practice of any thaumaturgic magic that seeks to transform some aspect of the universe on the most material levels of experience.

Table 3: The Elements

Symbol	Name	Qualities	Nature
▽	Earth	Cold and dry	Stability
▽	Water	Cold and wet	Union
△	Fire	Hot and dry	Energy
△	Air	Hot and wet	Separation
⊕	Spirit	Union of all	Harmony

Each of these three broad systems of symbolism has its own patterns of interaction and meaning, and to a large extent its own ritual forms as well. There is a certain amount of overlap between them; thus, for instance, each of the planets and Spheres has an element associated with it. Still, these interrelations are far from exact—they are similarities, not identities—and the systems themselves should not be confused. The fact that the planet Mercury is traditionally linked with the element of Air does not make Mercury and Air the same thing in magical practice. Mercury, it's worth noting, is also linked with Hod, the eighth Sphere, which corresponds to Water rather than Air. In magic, things equal to the same thing are not always equal to each other!

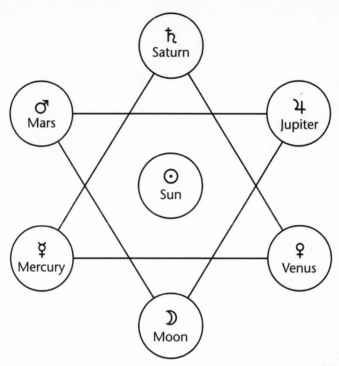

Diagram 3—
The Planets

Further details of each of the three systems can be found in the tables of correspondences in the Appendix, and throughout this book. As much of this material as possible should be committed to memory by the magician in training. This is not only a matter of convenience, although it is certainly that—you can't always be sure of having tables of correspondences at hand every time they will be needed—for the effort of learning these symbols will help to awaken and energize them in your consciousness and in certain levels of the subtle body. The work of memorization may be tedious, but it's a necessary part of magical training, and it should never be neglected.

Spirits in Ritual Magic

The second of the three models of the macrocosm used in the Golden Dawn tradition's approach to magic sees the universe as a vast dance of

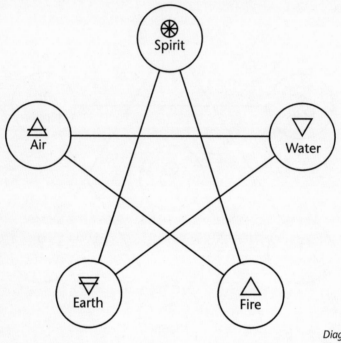

Diagram 4—
The Elements

relationships between conscious beings. Of all the models, this is probably the one hardest for the modern Western student of magic to understand or use; it runs headlong into some of the strongest prejudices of our current ways of thought. Plenty of people who have no difficulty at all coping with the idea of nonphysical realities draw back sharply at the notion that some of those realities might have a life and a consciousness of their own.

A good part of the difficulty, though, is purely a matter of terminology. The modern way of thinking about the world has generated its own descriptive language, in which everything comes down ultimately to material objects in motion, bouncing from place to place at random like so many billiard balls. The older, magical way, with its very different view of things, produced a very different language: a language in which consciousness plays a defining role, and conscious, personalized beings have a special role in the dance of forces that shape the universe, uniting a realm of abstract ideas with the more familiar realm of matter and energy.

The most striking product of this way of speaking is the vast array of gods and angels, spirits and demons, who throng the cosmologies of nearly all the world's cultures outside the modern West. From one perspective, these are simply other ways to talk about the same forces that modern scientific thought describes in its own impersonal terms. To speak, as the ancients did, of an angel or a goddess who guides the planet Venus in its course through the sky is in this sense simply to give another Name to the balance of kinetic and gravitational forces that keep that planet in its orbit.

It's an easy step, and one commonly made nowadays, to go from this to the notion that talk of angels is merely an unclear way of speaking about the physics of planetary motion. Making this last step is a mistake because the ancient terminology of angels and gods was not developed solely for the purpose of talking about celestial mechanics. The magicians and sages of the past, more pragmatic in some ways than our modern scientists, were at least as concerned with the effects of Venus on the world of human experience as they were with the abstract laws of its motion.

Those effects can be traced in specific areas of human life, and tend to take broadly predictable forms; they have particular power over personality, and in many ways can best be dealt with as though they have a personality of their own. Over time, this perception gave rise to precisely shaped images, names, and myths concerning a being who represented the forces of Venus, for images, names, and myths are the technical language of ancient magic and science.

This same language has become, in its turn, an important part of the terminology of Western magic, particularly in those branches that have stressed the value of preserving ancient approaches to the magical art. The Golden Dawn tradition is one of these, and as a result, descriptions of the universe found in the Order's materials, and in other writings in the tradition, often use the old terminology.

We'll be using the same terminology here, and not just because it has an old and honorable place in traditional lore. In practice, when working with certain kinds of human experience, a terminology of angels and spirits is a more effective way of communicating what appears to be going on in the universe than a terminology of matter and motion. In magical terms, every energy is also an entity, and the line between "subjective" and "objective" realities can rarely be drawn in a useful fashion;

if these principles are kept in mind, some of the deep places of magical tradition become a great deal less murky.

A Field Guide to Spirits

The magical lore of the Western world contains an enormous amount of material, much of it confused or contradictory, about the various kinds of beings that inhabit the magician's universe. The fine points of classification have little relevance to the practical work of magic, and tend to differ sharply from one source to another; still, it's possible to sketch in broad outline some of the lore concerning the types of spirits that play important roles in Golden Dawn magic.

Angels

The angels of magical tradition have little in common with the mass-marketed and rather saccharine winged beings that seem to be becoming the unicorns of the 1990s. Angels, in magical philosophy, are expressions of the primal unity of the spiritual level of existence; in theological language, they can accurately be called the servants of God, while from another perspective they can be seen simply as personifications of the primary creative powers of the universe acting within space and time.

Traditional lore has it that each individual angel has a specific, tightly defined purpose in the universe, and can be contacted by magical means in matters touching on this purpose. As expressions of primal creative power, though, they act in accordance with their own will, which is identical with the will of the absolute unity; they can be invoked, therefore, but they cannot be commanded or bound by any human power whatsoever.

Intelligences

This term is used for two related classes of spirits, both of whom function principally as sources of information in magical workings. The first class is made up of the Intelligences of the seven traditional planets, who play an important role in talismanic and evocatory magic. The second class is composed of the Intelligences governing certain methods of divination, who are thought to be the source of the information gathered through divinatory means. The planetary Intelligences can be summoned by magical means, and commanded within the limits of their nature.

Spirits

The modern English language has a very poor vocabulary for nonphysical beings, and so this general term has had to be pressed into use for a particular class of beings as well. These are beings that are roughly comparable to humanity in their level of development, differing mainly in that they lack physical and, often, etheric bodies. The planetary and Olympic spirits of magical tradition belong to this class, as do the entities listed in many of the medieval grimoires.

Spirits vary widely in their powers and their attitude toward human beings, just as human beings do, and they should be faced with the same qualities of courtesy and caution one would use in the company of human strangers. They can be commanded and bound by magic, and this can sometimes be a useful mode of magical working. By human standards, however, they are often evasive and dishonest, and information they provide should be checked and double-checked by ordinary and magical means before being taken at face value.

Elementals

These are the living beings who inhabit and structure the four elements of the physical world. They differ from spirits in that they have highly developed etheric bodies, and can therefore act directly on physical matter. They are divided into four types, assigned to the four elements: gnomes, corresponding to Earth; undines, to Water; sylphs, to Air, and salamanders, to Fire. (The last type shares its name with a class of small cold-blooded animals, also known as newts, because the latter often live in decaying logs and could be seen now and again crawling out from the midst of burning wood.)

Elementals of each type are said to be ruled by a king, who is essentially the collective consciousness of the element itself. They are somewhat less developed than human beings, approximating the level of the more intelligent animals. Their relationship to humanity is complex, and the subject of a great deal of rather odd theorizing in some of the tradition's writings, but it's generally agreed that they welcome interaction with us and, in some sense, benefit from it. They can be commanded and bound by magic, and if their needs and natures are respected they will follow simple instructions willingly.

Nature Spirits

Far more ambivalent are those entities we can call nature spirits, non-physical beings who have etheric bodies like those of elementals but have more specialized roles in the natural world. These include such entities as the dryads and oreads of ancient myth, as well as the complex beings described in the world's faery legends, which are called fays and arch-fays in the Golden Dawn material.

It's critical to remember that these are not the prettified flower-fairies of Victorian sentimentality; authentic faery-lore, as well as the records of modern magicians who have dealt with these beings, makes it clear that nature spirits are potentially highly dangerous, especially to the arrogant. They can and, under the right circumstances, should be contacted by the magician, but attempts to bind or command them are likely to backfire in very unpleasant ways.

Larvae

Much further down the scale of development are larvae, nearly mindless entities who function as scavengers on the etheric level. Under normal circumstances, they feed on the cast-off etheric bodies of dead humans and animals, and a range of other kinds of etheric debris. If the etheric body of a living person becomes weak or damaged, though, it can attract larvae, and this is said to play an important role in certain kinds of human illness. Larvae are of no valid use to the magician—there are methods of magical attack that involve sending larvae to feed on the etheric body of the victim, but like all forms of destructive magic, these inevitably rebound on the sender—but problems with larvae are not uncommon in the squalid etheric environment of modern cities. Ways of dealing with larvae will be covered later in this chapter, and in Chapter 11 as well.

Demons

This much-misused term is unfortunately the only word in modern English for nonphysical entities that are hostile or destructive to human beings. In the Cabalistic philosophy that underlies Golden Dawn magic, these are identified with the *Qlippoth* or Negative Powers, creatures of unbalanced force from the universe that preceded our own.

Each of the Negative Powers is an expression of some aspect of the universe in a totally pure and totally unbalanced form, and although they are not evil in any absolute sense—they have a place and a necessary purpose in the scheme of things, and therefore a right to exist—their nature (and ours) makes them utterly inimical to human beings. They can be commanded or bound by magic, under certain circumstances, but it's almost always wisest simply to banish them and let matters rest there.

The Tides of Magic

The third model of the universe in magical tradition portrays the world of our experience through the much more familiar image of substances in motion. On the physical level, this model blends into the vision of reality traced out by modern scientific thought. Unlike that vision, though, the third model sees two higher levels of substance—astral and etheric—which have some similarities to the physical level, but which also have laws and processes of their own.

The substance of the astral level can be thought of as a subtle energy extended throughout space. The movements of the planets in the solar system set up tides in the astral, and these influence our thoughts and feelings—themselves astral phenomena—in ways that can be tracked by the cycles of astrology. (In fact, it's the connection between these energies and astrology that led to this level of existence being named "astral" in the first place.)

In many kinds of ritual magic, particularly those involving planetary energies, these tides are of great importance. It's standard practice, for example, to face toward the actual position of a planet in space when invoking its powers, because this allows the astral energies of the planet to be drawn on most effectively.

During the Renaissance, a great deal of lore existed on the connections between ritual magic and astrology, and books such as Agrippa's *Three Books of Occult Philosophy* devote many chapters to the ways in which rituals can be strengthened by performing them at the astrologically correct time. The adepts of the Golden Dawn seem to have paid less attention to such matters, but my own experience suggests that certain kinds of Golden Dawn magic can be given a substantial boost through these older techniques, and some of the details involved are covered in the chapters ahead.

The influence of the etheric level and its tides is more certain, and for the beginning magician, more important. The substance of the etheric level has been described as a subtle fluid that permeates and flows through all things. Like matter in some ways, like energy in others, ether can be concentrated or dispersed by a number of means, and it can also take and hold patterns. These patterns form the templates on which the particles of physical matter collect to form the objects we perceive with our five ordinary senses; they also make up the organizing principle behind biological life and define the physical bodies of all living beings.

Like the astral or, for that matter, the physical oceans, the ocean of ether that surrounds us has its tides and currents, its patterns of movement, and cycles of energy, and these play an important role in nearly all kinds of magical practice. Various complex systems have been used to track these tides, in and out of the Golden Dawn tradition, but the major influences on the ether's ebb and flow are a much simpler matter and follow patterns that are fairly well known even in our present culture.

The most important of these derives from the phases of the Moon. The Moon dominates the etheric tides as it does the physical ones of the Earth's oceans, and the cycle of lunar phases thus has a potent influence on all magical work directed at or through the etheric level. Etheric energies are at their strongest at the Full Moon and their weakest at the New; when the Moon is waxing—growing from new to full—those energies support increased and upward motion, while the waning Moon—shrinking from full to new—marks a time of decrease and downward motion.

In magical practice, correspondingly, workings intended to bring growth and increase on any level are done while the Moon is waxing, while workings designed to cleanse, purify, and decrease are done while the Moon is waning. The last few days before the Full or New Moon are the strongest for either purpose; the latter period, called the dark or eld of the Moon, was once greatly feared, as it is the most effective time for destructive magic.

These lunar cycles are paralleled by another set of patterns based on the daily and yearly positions of the Sun. As the primary source of every kind of energy in the solar system, the Sun floods the Earth with a constant stream of ether, and this stream can effectively drown out other patterns in the etheric ocean; this is why, for example, ghosts and other etheric phenomena not connected to physical matter are rarely seen while the Sun is above the horizon. Similarly, objects charged with etheric patterns will gradually lose their charge if exposed to unfiltered sunlight.

Where the lunar tides govern the way that individual things relate to energy, the solar tides govern the way that they relate to unity. Workings intended to balance, to heal, to unify, and to dissolve are more effective when done in daylight, while those intended to create, to define, or to separate are better done at night.

The broader cycle of the year has its own tides, which relate to the cycle of the seasons and of the agricultural year; the same etheric patterns that influence magic also shape the life of the natural world, a point that many traditions of folk magic have learned to use with a high degree of exactness.

The fine details vary according to latitude and other local factors, but in general, the time between the spring equinox and the summer solstice (March 21 to June 21, approximately, in the northern hemisphere) is a time of beginnings and of growth; that between the summer solstice and the fall equinox (June 21 to September 23), a time of completion and fruitfulness; that between the fall equinox and the winter solstice (September 23 to December 23), a time of preservation and taking stock; and that between the winter solstice and the spring equinox (December 23 to March 21), a time of destruction and purification. These four times have been called, respectively, the Tide of Sowing, the Tide of Reaping, the Tide of Planning, and the Tide of Destruction, and these names sum up their nature fairly well.

The spring and fall equinoxes are points of special importance in the Golden Dawn tradition and are celebrated with special ceremonies in Golden Dawn temples. During the forty-eight hours to each side of the actual moment of equinox—the moment when the Sun crosses the celestial equator—Sun and Earth stand in a relationship that allows a much more intense flow of energy between them, and the etheric body of the Earth is charged and renewed. The details of this process, as well as an Equinox ceremony adapted for the solitary magician, will be covered in Chapter 14.

All these tides are affected, in turn, by the rotation of the Earth; the same movement that makes the Sun appear to move in an arc from east to west across the sky makes many of these tides seem to cycle in the same direction. This defines some of the standard patterns of movement in ritual. Moving in a circle in the same direction as the Sun—in the northern hemisphere, clockwise—your body flows with these cycles, and so tends to build up energy, while moving in the other direction tends to disperse energy. Most movement in a ritual context, therefore, moves with the Sun, but movement against the Sun is used in specific situations when it's useful to disperse forces that have been gathered.

The influence of the Earth is also a matter of importance in this third model of the magical universe. The "Gaia Hypothesis" recently proposed by James Lovelock, which holds that the entire Earth can be understood as a single living organism, is in many ways simply a restatement of a much older principle of magical philosophy. Traditional writings on magic, alchemy, and similar subjects often speak of the *anima mundi*, the soul of the world, and the *spiritus mundi*, the spirit or life-force of the world, as the inner aspects of the world we inhabit.

In terms of the system of levels we've been using, the anima mundi is the astral level of the Earth, its manifestation on the level of concrete consciousness. It can best be understood, perhaps, as the innate intelligence of Nature, the guiding power that holds natural processes in balance. The spiritus mundi, in turn, is the etheric level of the Earth, and can be thought of as a life pervading and including all other lives on the planet and shaping physical matter in accordance with the patterns that are established by the anima mundi. These same phenomena were also expressed in a different way by the concepts of elementals and Elemental Kings discussed earlier; the elementals represent the active power of the spiritus mundi in the four elements, the Elemental Kings the guiding presence of the anima mundi directing them.

Like the magical applications of astrology, the practical uses of these two subtler aspects of the Earth were better understood in earlier times than they were when the Golden Dawn system was put together. Patterns in the spiritus mundi play a significant part in the practice of transformation, discussed in Chapter 12, and both the anima mundi and the spiritus mundi have a role in the Ceremony of the Equinox and the workings derived from it, which will be explored in Chapter 14. On the whole, though, this area of magical lore requires a great deal of study and further development before it can be applied in practice in Golden Dawn magic.

Natural Magic

The presence of astral and etheric forces in the very substance of the world we inhabit opens up other possibilities to the magician, though. The patterns of these levels interact with the matter and energy of the physical level; different kinds of matter, however, interact in different ways. Some materials hold etheric charges well, others poorly, while still others will erase such charges, and still other substances affect the etheric realm in more specialized ways.

These effects are the basis for what Hermetic and Cabalistic magicians of an earlier time called *natural magic*. Like many systems of folk magic, the natural magic of the Western tradition relies not on the inner powers of the magician but on the subtle relationships between physical substances and nonphysical energies. Natural magic and ritual magic are thus two different ways of accomplishing magical work, and although they are not incompatible—in fact, properly used, they reinforce each other—they follow different laws and use different approaches.

Many of the magical systems of the Renaissance contained a great deal of natural magic and combined this with ritual magic in a wide range of ways, some of them highly effective. In the original Golden Dawn system, on the other hand, only a small part of this lore was used. Other applications of natural magic were introduced by the Order's successor groups or by writers involved in the current magical renaissance, but the total amount of natural magic technique in the tradition is as yet fairly small.

The use of crystals and metals as etheric condensers is one application that has been developed to some extent. The term "etheric condenser" will not be found in the Golden Dawn papers, but the ability of crystalline substances and pure metals to take up and hold an etheric charge—which is what the term refers to—was well known to the adepts of the Golden Dawn and its successor orders. An etheric condenser is like a battery, which can be charged with ether and then used as a source of power for etheric workings. Pure mineral crystals do this better than anything else. Pure metals also hold charges well; each metal corresponds, in magical lore, with one of the seven traditional planets, and will efficiently hold charges that are harmonious with that planet's nature.

Water, on the other hand, is an etheric eraser. A charged object immersed in running water will quickly be stripped of its charge; the purer and colder the water is, the stronger the effect. The old tradition that ghosts and evil magic cannot cross running water has its origin in this principle.

The use of Holy Water, which is water that has had consecrated salt dissolved in it, is a further application of the same principle. Holy Water is typically flicked from the fingers, and the fine spray of droplets this produces has a double effect. First, it sends water through any etheric patterns present in the area; second, as the smallest droplets evaporate in midflight, they produce tiny salt crystals, which like any other crystal will soak up whatever ether happens to be present. The combination makes Holy Water one of the more effective tools for magically cleansing a space, and a method for preparing and consecrating it will be given in Chapter 5.

A subtler effect with similar uses involves evaporated acids. A shallow bowl half full of vinegar left out in a room will cause the ether present in the air to gradually lose any patterns it may contain. Stronger acids do the same thing more forcefully, although they should be diluted with water to prevent accidents. This can be valuable to know in the case of a haunting, or when a space previously used for magical work is to be put to other uses.

Another far more extensive field of natural magic touched on by the Golden Dawn system involves the use of volatile aromatics from plant sources. Most often used in the form of incense, these substances have a vast range of effects, and their most common use in modern magic—as an aide in the invocation of corresponding elemental or planetary forces—is only one of many possible applications. The space available here does not permit anything like an adequate discussion of this side of natural magic, but a few examples may be worth mentioning.

Frankincense, an aromatic resin traditionally associated with the Sun, has a powerful purifying and harmonizing effect. It can be used in any ritual working where no more specialized incense is needed.

Dittany of Crete, a relative of oregano associated with Venus, has long been the standard incense to use when evoking spirits to physical manifestation. It has a powerful materializing effect and allows nonphysical entities to take on etheric forms dense enough that, under the right conditions, they can be seen with ordinary vision. (On the other hand, it's generally easier and at least as effective to use a scrying mirror or some similar device as a focus for evocation, and to do without the dittany.

The rituals for evoking spirits presented in Chapter 11 are designed around this latter procedure.)

Asafoetida, a vile-smelling herb associated with Saturn, is perhaps the most effective means of banishing known in Western magic. Used as incense, it strips etheric charges from whatever its smoke touches, and will drive away spirits when other methods fail; a small airtight container of asafoetida is a wise thing to have on hand when performing evocations, exorcisms, or any other relatively high-risk procedure. (On the other hand, it smells unbelievably foul when burned. For this reason, not to mention the annoyance of having to reconsecrate all one's working tools after using it, it's best used only in serious emergencies.)

The following easily available incenses, corresponding to the elements and planets, can be used in the rituals given in this book; stick or cone incense may be used, or the substance itself may be burned over disks of self-lighting charcoal (available from incense suppliers and most occult bookstores). The list of incenses isn't an exhaustive one, and there are many disagreements among the systems of attribution. The sets of correspondences given in books on magical herbalism may be worth consulting as well.

Elements

Air: sandalwood
Fire: cinnamon
Water: lily

Earth: patchouli
Spirit: frankincense

Planets

Saturn: myrrh
Jupiter: cedar
Mars: basil
Sun: frankincense

Venus: rose
Mercury: lavender
Moon: jasmine

One final element of natural magic that is used in Golden Dawn magic derives from the special etheric effects of iron. It's commonplace in folklore that sharp iron will dispel hostile magic and drive off or destroy certain kinds of spirits, and this is quite accurate: a knife, a nail, a sword, or anything similar, thrust into a concentration of etheric energy, will cause something not unlike an etheric short-circuit, dispersing the ether and obliterating whatever patterns may have been present in it.

This effect is the basis for the magician's sword, one of the chief working tools of the Golden Dawn magician, which is described in detail in Chapter 9. It also provides one of the simplest and most effective ways of dealing with larvae, the sometimes dangerous scavenger-entities mentioned earlier. A piece of sharp iron that is moved in brief jabbing motions all around the outer edge of the aura—an egg-shaped zone of forces extending two to three feet out from the physical body, which will be discussed in more detail in the next chapter—will drive off or destroy any larvae who may have attached themselves to the person in question. The handle of the iron instrument must be insulated, however, or the exorcist may receive the etheric equivalent of an electric shock!

Other aspects of natural magic could easily be worked into the Golden Dawn system; some steps in this direction have been taken in the "Green Ray" work of some of the Golden Dawn's successor groups, but there's an immense body of magical knowledge from other cultures and from older elements in the Western tradition that could be integrated here.

CHAPTER 3

THE MAGICAL MICROCOSM

THE SAME LEVELS OF EXPERIENCE found in the universe as a whole can be found within the human self as well. This realization is central not merely to the art of ritual magic, but to the entire structure of Cabalistic thought and practice, of which the Golden Dawn's ritual magic is only one part. The principle of macrocosm and microcosm, which represents this mirroring of levels, is the foundation for all the practical work of the Golden Dawn tradition. It is also a reminder that, however strange the universe may seem to us, we and it share one nature and one life.

The individual human being, then, is understood in magical terms as a reflection of the whole of the universe, and the same levels we've traced in the universe as a whole can be traced in the self as well. Just as the levels of experience in the universe can be treated in practice as distinct levels or realms of existence, the levels in the self can be treated, for practical use, as separate though interrelated aspects, each playing a part in the whole structure of the self.

In keeping with this approach, the levels in their human expression are generally called "bodies" in the Golden Dawn tradition. Along with the biological or *physical body*, we can speak of the *etheric body*, which is made up of ether or life-energy; the *astral body*, which is the body of concrete consciousness shaped by thoughts and feelings, and part of which can be detached from the physical and etheric bodies under certain conditions; the *mental body*, the body of abstract consciousness perceived by pure

43

awareness, which opens on realms of experience not bounded by space and time; and the *spiritual body*, the root of consciousness and the inner-most essence of the self. As with the levels of the macrocosm, each body can be seen as governing the body "below" it—that is, denser or more material than it; thus, for example, the astral body is shaped and directed by the mental body, and in turn shapes and directs the etheric body.

Each of these parts of the self has its own nature and functions, and its own role in the practice of magical ritual. The physical body, for its part, is the body known to medical and biological science. It serves as the material foundation and instrument of the other parts of the self, enabling the whole self to perceive and act in the realm of material experience. Traditional lore assigns each of its parts to one or another part of the symbolism of magic; thus, for instance, each of the five fingers is assigned to one of the five elements. In the technical Hebrew termi-nology of the Cabala, the physical body is called the *guph*.

The etheric body is usually divided, for clarity, into two parts. The first of these is the *etheric double*; this closely resembles the ordinary body of matter, extending out perhaps an inch beyond the surface of the skin, and provides the framework of subtle formative energies on which the material body is built. It contains a series of channels (the meridians of Oriental medicine) and energy centers, which have an important role in many classes of magical work.

The second part of the etheric body is called the *aura* or, in another context, the *Sphere of Sensation*. This is a roughly egg-shaped field of energies surrounding the etheric double, extending out several feet from the physical body. It serves as the interface between the etheric body of the individual and that of the cosmos, and all the forces of the universe are reflected on its surface. In Cabalistic terms, the etheric body as a whole is called the *nephesh*.

The astral body cannot be so easily mapped out in this kind of spatial language. A body of consciousness, it comes closer to the modern idea of "mind" than to that of "body," although neither of these too-rigid cate-gories fits well anywhere in the magical view of the self. The astral body can be thought of as a field of energy occupying roughly the same space as the aura, but constantly shaped and reshaped by patterns of thought and feeling. All images, words, and sensations affect this body, and are affected by it in turn; it interacts freely with the astral level of the cosmos, and with the astral bodies of other human and nonhuman beings. It contains most of those parts of the self we normally think of as "mental" or "inner"—intellect, emotion, imagination, will, and memory, the instruments of concrete consciousness—and it is also the basis for the individual personality. In Cabalistic language, it is called the *ruach*.

The mental body can be thought of as the essential pattern of the self; it can be described as a "body" only in a highly metaphorical sense, and cannot be located in a spatial sense at all. This body is the instrument of abstract consciousness—that is, thought that does not involve forms and images of the sort we perceive with our senses—and thus makes it possible to perceive the core ideas or structures of experience, which exist outside of space and time. In Cabalistic language, it is called the *neshamah*.

The spiritual body, finally, is the root of the self, the essence or "divine spark" around which all the other layers of the self are built up; it represents the point of contact between the human microcosm and that unity of being that, in theological terms, we may as well call God. It can best be imagined as pure being, without any other definition or quality. In Cabalistic terminology, it is called the *yechidah*.

In practicing magic in the Golden Dawn tradition, each of these levels of the self comes into play in one way or another, and specific aspects of these levels provide the principal tools by which the powers of the macrocosm are directed by the magician. The tools and their applications are covered in detail in Chapter 4, and their specific uses in ritual will be explored more fully throughout the rituals in Part Two. In order to make sense of this material, it's necessary to get a clearer sense of the magical understanding and the hidden potentials of this complex and beautiful thing each of us calls "I."

It's also necessary to realize, as we study the nature of the human microcosm, that the information covered isn't simply abstract knowledge. The traditional understanding of humanity is also the basis for the way of transformation that is central to the Golden Dawn system. As we consider the levels of the self, then, we will increasingly have to deal with the possibilities for intentional change within the self—possibilities that can be summed up within the magical idea of *initiation*.

The Body as Talisman

Many of the traditions of Western spirituality have had a highly negative view of the physical body, and of matter and the material side of the universe in general. Ideas and imagery of the sort that see the body as a trap and a burden to the soul, and matter as the enemy of spirit, have a long history in the West, both in the orthodox religions and in heretical and magical schools of thought as well. Like all one-sided viewpoints, this one has often given rise to its opposite, the equally unbalanced notion that anything outside the purely physical level is evil or, more often, simply nonexistent.

The traditions that gave rise to the Golden Dawn system tended toward a more balanced approach. To this third way of thinking, the physical body is neither the enemy of the subtler levels of the self, nor the only real part of the self, but the natural expression of the higher levels on the level of matter. The teachings of Cabalistic philosophy, in keeping with this approach, came to see each part of the human body as a representation in matter of the powers of the higher realms of being.

The Five Fingers

The five fingers of each hand, for example, were linked with the five elements according to a particular pattern. The published Golden Dawn material on this link has been garbled, but other documents make the correct attributions plain.

Spirit: thumb

Air: little finger   Water: index finger
Earth: third finger   Fire: middle finger

This symbolism relates to the elemental attributions of the pentagram, which will be explored in the next chapter; the fingertips of the right hand, held palm up and thumb above palm, mark the points of a pentagram with the correct elemental attributions.

The Seven Openings of the Head

Similarly, the seven openings of the head have been assigned to the seven traditional planets as follows:

Right ear: Saturn   Left ear: Jupiter
Right eye: Sun   Left eye: Moon
Right nostril: Mars   Left nostril: Venus
Mouth: Mercury

The Ten Spheres of the Tree of Life

In the same way, the ten Spheres of the Tree of Life, along with Daath, a quasi-Sphere located below Chokmah and Binah, correspond to eleven parts of the entire body in the following way:

Kether: above crown of head

Binah: right side of head   Chokmah: left side of head

Daath: throat

Geburah: right shoulder   Chesed: left shoulder

Tiphareth: heart

Hod: right hip   Netzach: left hip

Yesod: genitals

Malkuth: feet

Most of the attributions given here are based on a more or less arbitrary symbolism—that is, the right ear does not seem to have any greater connection to Saturnian forces than, say, the left one does—and there are alternative sets of attributions to be found in other systems of magic. Still, the fact that a given symbolism is arbitrary doesn't make it useless; the connection between the sounds of English and the letters you're reading at this moment is equally arbitrary. In both cases, meaning can be applied to the symbolism, and once applied it can be used in practical ways.

There are also certain parts of the symbolism of the body that are not arbitrary in nature, but relate to some of the subtler aspects of the physical body—and, in turn, to the links between this level of the self and the etheric body. The most significant of these are the centers along the midline of the body that correspond to the Spheres Kether, Tiphareth, Yesod, Malkuth, and the quasi-Sphere Daath. Like all material things, the physical body vibrates according to a complex pattern of rhythms; the movements of blood, lymph, and cerebrospinal fluid, the contractions of various groups of muscles, and a wide range of similar processes make the human body as much a structure of vibrations as one of flesh and bone.

The midline of the body is the axis on which these vibratory patterns interact, and at certain points on that line—determined by the same mathematics that define the notes on a violin string—the patterns of vibration come into focus and link to subtler patterns on the etheric level. Five of these points are used in Golden Dawn magic: the crown of the head, the middle of the throat, the heart, the genital area, and a point between the soles of the feet. These are primary points of contact between the levels of the self, and a special method of working with them through ritual, the Middle Pillar exercise, plays a central role in magical training in the Golden Dawn tradition.

These patterns of symbolism and energy have a role in a wide range of magical practices. One of the most basic and yet most useful effects of these symbolic links, though, is that through them the body of the magician comes to be understood as a talisman. In the jargon of magic, a talisman is a material object charged with the creative energies of the higher levels of experience and directed toward a particular purpose.

The making of talismans is one of the more useful branches of practical magic and will be covered in detail later on in this book; at least as important, though, is the use of the talisman each of us was born with. That talisman, as a microcosm of the macrocosm, is charged with every aspect and type of power present in the universe, and it can be directed to any imaginable purpose, from simple day-to-day survival up to the highest reaches of magical and spiritual attainment. Keeping this in mind is one way to begin facing life as a magician.

The Magical Mirror of the Universe

Just as the physical body serves as a representation of the higher levels of experience, the next higher body—the etheric body—reflects the powers of the levels above it as well. The inner layer of the etheric body, the etheric double, does this in essentially the same way as the physical body, since these two are closely interconnected. The outer layer of the etheric body, the aura or Sphere of Sensation, has a different function, and from this derive some of the keys to the Golden Dawn tradition's understanding of magic.

The Sphere of Sensation is also called "the magical mirror of the Universe," and this is a good description of the way it works. An Indian legend incorporated into the Buddhist Garland Sutra puts the matter with great clarity. The god Indra was said to have a magical net, infinitely large, in which each knot held a pearl. Each pearl reflected all of the others, so that the whole net was present in each individual pearl. The net is the universe, and the pearls—to return to our present terminology—are the Spheres of Sensation of everything in the universe, from planets and stars to motes of dust, each mirroring all the others.

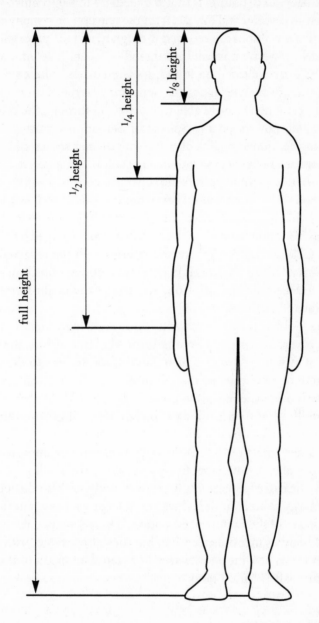

Diagram 5—
Proportions of the Middle Pillar

The Sphere of Sensation is thus the medium through which we and all other beings perceive and interact with the universe on nonphysical levels. All etheric perceptions are received through it, and the perceptions of the astral level—what we normally call thoughts, feelings, dreams, memories, and so on—are reflected on it and, to some extent, filtered through it. Under ordinary circumstances, the same thing is true of those mental and spiritual perceptions we are able to receive. It's through the reflection of macrocosmic powers on the Sphere of Sensation that the scryer sees images of the hidden realms of being, the diviner senses and reads patterns that have not yet come into manifestation on the physical level, and the magician calls those powers into operation in ritual work.

The Sphere of Sensation reflects what is inside as well as what is outside, and this is at once one of its great strengths and its most serious weakness. Forms generated on the astral level and charged by emotion or will are mirrored on the Sphere and interact with the reflected energies there. Done deliberately, this is magic; done unintentionally, it's a fruitful source of deception and delusion, and one of the major factors behind many kinds of madness.

In the Golden Dawn documents, there are detailed charts and tables that apply various systems of symbolism—the Tree of Life, the signs and planets of astrology, the Enochian Tablets, and so on—to the surface of the Sphere of Sensation, so that it's possible to work out precisely what influence is present at any given point in the aura. These charts have little direct application to ritual magic, but they are of great importance in certain other kinds of work within the tradition.

One other aspect of the etheric body is of extreme importance in the ritual work ahead. The same five points along the midline of the body, which we discussed as part of the physical body, are also the locations of major energy centers in the etheric double, as well as anchoring points for the forces of the Sphere of Sensation. These centers interact with the physical body, as mentioned earlier, but they also interact with the astral body, and thus provide an interface between the aspects of the self that our culture labels "mind" and "body."

The Veil of the Sanctuary and the Higher Self

Like the physical and etheric bodies, the astral body, or body of concrete consciousness, reflects the universe on its own level, and also reflects the influences of the levels above it. Both of these reflections are mediated, as we've seen, through the Sphere of Sensation. In the Golden Dawn teachings, it's the movement of awareness over the astral images reflected on the Sphere that constitutes what we call thought.

The concrete consciousness of the human microcosm can be divided, for convenience as well as symbolic reasons, into five faculties: intellect, emotion, imagination, will, and memory. Intellect is the faculty that reasons and communicates, while emotion is the faculty that assesses and responds. Imagination, which is so often discounted in our culture, is actually the most important faculty of all; it assembles the things we experience into meaningful patterns, and in this way quite literally creates the world in which each of us lives. Will is the faculty that chooses and directs action; memory, finally, is the faculty that records, and gives the world of our experience continuity over time.

Each of these faculties can also be seen, in magical terms, as a way in which human awareness interacts with the images of concrete consciousness reflected on the Sphere of Sensation. Intellect, the thinking faculty, is the ability of awareness to move in an ordered way from reflection to reflection on the Sphere; emotion is the ability to synthesize reflections into a perception of their overall nature; imagination, the ability to organize, create, and project reflections onto the Sphere; will, the ability to energize a specific reflection and direct various forms of action toward it; memory, the ability to relate a series of reflections to each other and to time.

So far, so good; but our ability to experience all five of these powers is uneven, to say the least. Most human beings are aware of their thoughts and feelings, although those who have learned to think competently too often don't know how to handle their feelings, and those who have learned to feel honestly too often don't know how to manage their thoughts. Imagination, will, and memory, by contrast, are present in most people only to a highly limited degree.

This last statement may seem extreme, but it needs to be understood in context. We all experience the capacity to imagine, to will, and to remember, as these words are usually understood. In the magical philosophy of Cabalism, though, the forms of these three faculties normally available to human awareness are seen as dim reflections of the full potential they (and we) possess.

We marvel at the imaginative brilliance of great artists, writers, and musicians, at the willpower of people who have overcome tremendous obstacles, at the mnemonic abilities of those who can recall and synthesize vast amounts of information at will. And yet most of us, most of the time, are content to use the imaginations of others to define the world around us, however poorly these may fit our own experiences and needs; most of us, most of the time, spend our lives reacting to feelings, whims, and biological cravings rather than acting on the basis of conscious choice; most of us, most of the time, remember things so poorly that entire industries have come into existence to make up for the failures and inaccuracies of memory.

It's usual and comforting to dismiss the higher reaches of human possibility as some kind of inborn gift unavailable to most human beings. Most of us, though, have experienced the sudden flash of imagination that shows the entire world in a new light; most of us have committed ourselves to some goal in an act of will, and found strengths we did not know we possessed; most of us have stumbled across some trigger to memory and found ourselves recalling the smallest details of some distant time with perfect clarity. These quite common experiences show something of the potential we each have inside us, and they suggest that the same possibilities that our culture's map of reality calls "genius" are in fact open to every human being.

This is the perspective of Cabalistic philosophy. In the symbolic language of that philosophy, a barrier—the Veil of the Sanctuary—divides the astral level of the self in two, separating our ordinary consciousness from the part of ourselves that contains imagination, will, and memory, and that links upward to the mental and spiritual levels of the self. The barrier is not complete; as the image of the veil implies, it lets through dim glimpses of what is beyond it. These glimpses include the limited forms of the three higher faculties we ordinarily experience, and they also provide what contact we have, under ordinary conditions, with the levels of the self above the astral. The barrier may be more or less transparent in different people, and this difference in transparency lies behind the wide variations in imagination, will, and memory we see around us.

Cabalistic tradition contains a substantial amount of lore, speculation, and mythology concerning the Veil of the Sanctuary, but for our present purposes it can be seen simply as the boundary between the potentials that have been made real in the course of human evolution and those that have not yet been achieved in our species as a whole. In the traditional lore, it's suggested that the evolutionary process itself will bring about the opening of the Veil in time. Where the entire species will go in the future, though, the individual can go in the present. Using certain intensive methods—the methods of ritual magic among them—the processes of evolution can be accelerated and the Veil opened on an individual basis.

The process of opening the Veil is the highest task of theurgic ritual magic in the Golden Dawn system, and forms the culmination of an extended process of magical self-development. A range of symbols and metaphors are used to represent it in the teaching documents of the tradition. Some of these, like the phrase "opening of the Veil" itself, are taken from Cabalistic imagery; others, such as "the Great Work," are taken from the language of alchemy; still others, such as the well-known "knowledge and conversation of the Holy Guardian Angel," come from specific magical practices that are intended to bring it about—in this case, the process of intensive invocation described in a medieval grimoire, *The Sacred Magic of Abramelin the Mage*, and borrowed by Aleister Crowley and a number of other modern magicians.

It's worth remembering that all of these terms refer to the same experience: the union of the known part of the magician's self with another part, unknown or very poorly known, resulting in an expansion of awareness and the awakening of a range of uncommon powers. The known part of the self, in Golden Dawn terminology, is called the Lower Self; the less known, the Higher Self, or, for reasons we'll examine shortly, the Lower Genius. This experience and its effects correspond, in turn, to the process known in many Eastern traditions as "enlightenment."

The Abyss and the Higher Genius

As both Eastern and Western teachings recognize, the opening of the Veil does not complete the work of awakening the possibilities of the self. The transformations brought about by the Veil's opening unify the astral level of the self, but beyond that level are the aspects of the human microcosm that function on the mental and spiritual levels of experience. At the present stage of human evolution, these two higher levels are almost entirely closed to our awareness. In the language of Cabala, this closure is a function of a second barrier, which is called the Abyss.

In its most basic sense, the Abyss is the difference between the realm of space and time, change and differentiation, that we experience as the universe, and the timeless realm of essential being and unity that is the source of the universe we know. This second realm has been much discussed by philosophers, and some of the ways in which it's understood in magical tradition have roots in these discussions, particularly those of Plato and his successors. The realm above the Abyss, however, is not really subject to discussion; it transcends not only space and time, but the most basic categories of human thought.

Nonetheless, as we've seen, each human being is a mirror of the universe, and every level of experience and being that can be traced in the universe can be traced in each of us as well. The realms above the Abyss are thus not wholly foreign territory to us. Our ordinary ways of perceiving the world range no higher than the astral level of concrete consciousness, and it's as useless to try to experience the mental or spiritual levels with the astral self as it would be to try to catch a thought or a feeling in one's fingers. Still, the powers and perceptions of the mental and spiritual bodies offer ways to function on these levels. These powers and perceptions are closed to us at present, but they can be opened.

The crossing of the Abyss, to give this process of opening its most usual name, is not a matter of ritual magic, although ritual work can lay some of the foundations for it. It properly belongs to mysticism, not to magic, and can be taken up only once the Veil has been opened and the powers of the higher astral faculties gained; the teaching documents of the Golden Dawn tradition thus quite sensibly have little concrete to say about it. It remains, though, the summit of the path of theurgy in the tradition.

The levels of the self above the Abyss also have another function in magical thought, one that is easy to misunderstand but that plays an important role in theory and practice alike. These levels cannot be experienced by the self in its ordinary state, but this does not make them nonexistent—or powerless. Quite the contrary; as aspects of the self beyond space and time, they continue to function in their own way, whatever the limitations of the levels below them.

It's as an expression of this sense that the highest part of the self is called the Higher Genius in Golden Dawn terminology. (The word "genius" meant guardian spirit before it took on its modern meaning of a person with unusual talent.) Another term sometimes used for the Higher Genius in the tradition, the *Augoeides*, comes from a Greek word meaning "shining one," and has similar implications. The point made by both these terms, and by the teachings behind them, is that until the Abyss is crossed, the highest part of the human self behaves more like a separate being than like a part of what we usually call ourselves.

In traditional lore, in fact, the Higher Genius is sometimes described as the god of the self, and this is a valid description if it's understood correctly. The Higher Genius has much the same relationship to the rest of the human microcosm as the primal creative unity of the spiritual level, which we can call God in theological language, has to the macrocosm as a whole. The Higher Genius overshadows and sustains the lower levels of the self, but those lower levels still have the capacity for independent action in their own realm of space and time, a capacity we call "free will." It's when this lesser will enters into harmony with the timeless patterns of the Higher Genius that the magician enters into the highest realms of power and the ultimate attainment of his or her art.

Initiation

The immense possibilities open to the magician are measured at least in part by the amount of work needed to attain them. Theurgy, like any other branch of magic, is work: sometimes tedious, sometimes difficult, occasionally dangerous, but never effortless. The details of this work will take up much of the rest of this book. One of the major processes involved in the magical way of transformation, though, will need to be discussed at this point: the process of initiation.

An enormous amount has been written and said about initiation over the last several centuries, in and out of Western magical circles. Quite a remarkable percentage of that total, unfortunately, is thorough nonsense. With the possible exception of lost continents of the Atlantis variety, no single topic in the whole field of esoteric study has been burdened with so much pompous gibberish, and the resulting mess makes it difficult even to bring up the subject without inviting confusion. Still, the attempt has to be made, as the process of initiation lies close to the heart of the way of magical attainment.

What, then, is initiation? We can begin at the most basic level. The word "initiation" comes from Latin, and means, simply, "beginning." A long and murky history lies behind the word's more complex meanings in magical circles, but that is of little importance here. In an important sense, an initiation is still exactly that, a beginning: the start of a process that the initiate himself or herself must complete.

In a magical initiation, the candidate (the person who is being initiated) is placed at the focus of a ceremonial working in which specific magical energies are called up by the initiators. The goal of the ceremony is to use these energies to awaken the corresponding factors in the Sphere of Sensation of the candidate. If this takes place—which does not always happen—the initiation has succeeded, the candidate becomes an initiate, and he or she can then begin to make use of the forces that have been awakened in the ceremony. If those forces represent a single narrowly focused factor, the initiation can help bring specific magical or personal abilities into being; if the forces represent a balanced array of factors, the initiation can guide the self toward harmony and balance on many different levels; if the forces represent the higher, hidden aspects of the self, the initiation can help lay the foundation for the opening of the Veil.

The process is rendered more complex by the fact that most initiatory systems in the West make use of a series of initiation ceremonies, which are patterned according to the various models of the process of inner development. In the Golden Dawn tradition, the standard model is based on the Cabalistic Tree of Life. As shown in Table 4 on page 57, this model assigns one initiation to each of the ten Spheres, along with two additional ceremonies: the Neophyte Grade, which begins the entire sequence, and the Portal Grade, which symbolically opens the way through the Veil.

Table 4: Grades of Initiation

Number	Grade	Meaning	Sphere
0=0	Neophyte	"New Plant," Novice	(none)
1=10	Zelator	Zealous One	Malkuth
2=9	Theoricus	Theoretical Student	Yesod
3=8	Practicus	Practical Student	Hod
4=7	Philosophus	Philosophical Student	Netzach
——	Portal	——	(Veil of the Sanctuary)
5=6	Adeptus Minor	Lesser Adept	Tiphareth
6=5	Adeptus Major	Greater Adept	Geburah
7=4	Adeptus Exemptus	Exempt Adept	Chesed
8=3	Magister Templi	Master of the Temple	Binah
9=2	Magus	Magician	Chokmah
10=1	Ipsissimus	"Most Oneself"	Kether

Reasonable as this system looks, it has proven to be a potent source of confusion over the years, and there are some solid arguments against using it in its traditional form as a framework for understanding the initiatory process. The heart of the problem comes out of the distinction between these ceremonies and the actual attainment of the Spheres in question. The Practicus Grade, for example, can help the initiate grasp and use the powers of Hod, the Sphere of the intellect. It cannot, by itself, grant those powers. This is even more true in the case of Grades that correspond to the Spheres beyond the Veil. The Golden Dawn's Adeptus Minor Grade is a beautiful and powerful ceremony, but it does not and cannot bring about the far-reaching transformation of the self involved in the attainment of the Tiphareth level of consciousness. Only personal work and inner growth can do that.

In place of the Golden Dawn model, then, we'll be using an older and simpler model of initiation in this book, one that has left traces in the Order's ceremonies and underlies most of the existing systems of initiatory ritual in the Western world. This model divides the process of initiation into three stages, or as they're more usually called, degrees. The First Degree of this older system corresponds primarily to the Golden Dawn Neophyte Grade, and to a lesser extent the Zelator, Theoricus, Practicus, and Philosophus Grades; its imagery is based on the symbolism of light in darkness. The Second Degree corresponds to the Golden Dawn Portal Grade and is based on the symbolism of ascent, while the Third Degree corresponds to the Golden Dawn Adeptus Minor Grade and the higher Grades of adeptship, and uses a symbolism of loss and restoration.

These three degrees also have a specific practical meaning, and for this reason they play a substantial role in much of the material we'll be covering in this book. The initiation of the First Degree establishes an etheric link, symbolized as light, between the candidate and the balanced energies of the macrocosm. The initiation of the Second Degree uses that link to rise up the levels of experience, helping the candidate to come into more direct contact with the higher levels of the universe and of his or her own self. The initiation of the Third Degree turns the process around and brings these higher potencies down through every level of the self, including the physical body, bringing each level into harmony with the others.

The First Degree links higher and lower, defining a formula of Connection; the Second Degree rises from lower to higher, defining a formula of Ascension; the Third Degree descends from higher to lower, defining a formula of Regeneration. Any form of magical work that does one of these three things—and any magical ritual, done for any purpose, can be understood in at least one of these ways—can be performed using a formula derived from one of the three degrees. This is true of thaumaturgic and theurgic magic alike, and these same formulae are thus the basis for what is unquestionably the most important subject we'll be discussing in this book: the way of self-initiation.

Self-Initiation

The process of initiation as it was practiced in the Golden Dawn and similar orders has certain limits, some theoretical, some practical. One of the most severe of the latter is that it takes a group of trained magicians to perform a ritual initiation effectively, and few magicians nowadays belong to a magical lodge capable of performing these complex ceremonies as they should be done. Fortunately, there are other options.

The most useful of these, and the one this book will be stressing, is the path of self-initiation. The same results that can be produced by a team of skilled adepts in an hour-long ritual can also be produced, if a good deal more slowly, by a solitary magician working alone. The process involved is essentially the same: a balanced set of energies are brought into play through ritual means and used to awaken their equivalents in the Sphere of Sensation of the magician. Since a novice magician initiating himself or herself is unlikely to be able to bring through energies at high intensity, at least at first, the rituals of self-initiation are repeated, often many times. The end result, however, is identical.

This last point has been a subject of quite a bit of dispute over the years, and there are those who claim that self-initiation is, at best, a poor substitute for the initiatory rituals offered in the lodge setting. It's certainly true that working within a lodge has other advantages, beyond access to the method of initiation outlined above. Still, the basic process remains the same, and some of the special features of lodge work can prove double-edged in practice.

A magical lodge, like any other group of people, develops a pattern of energies on the astral and etheric levels that functions as a kind of collective personality. This pattern, which is called an *egregor* in magical jargon, can be deliberately charged with power and used as a tool in ritual, and its energies can be transmitted to new members who are initiated into the lodge. It's the presence of a charged and magically active egregor that makes a true magical lodge something more than a working group of magicians, something with a life and a power of its own.

The egregor of a lodge, on the other hand, is a tool, not an end in itself. It has value in a magical setting because, and only because, it enables individual magicians to develop their own inner powers and perceptions more quickly than they could on their own. The potentials within each human being are all that's needed for the magical path, and it's entirely possible to rise to the summit of magical attainment without the help of a lodge egregor; it simply takes somewhat longer.

There are also certain risks involved in work with a lodge egregor. The egregor of a magical lodge takes its tone and character from the individuals who make up the lodge, and from the specific kinds of magical work the lodge does. That tone and character, in turn, influences the individual members in the same way that two people who live together will tend to influence each other. If the members of the lodge are men and women of integrity and understanding, and if the ritual work done in the lodge is competently handled and calls on balanced energies, the egregor will become a potent positive influence on every member.

If the lodge falls short of this ideal, so will the egregor, and so will the influence the egregor exerts on the lodge's members. In extreme cases—which are not as rare as one might wish—a tainted egregor can take on the lineaments of a collective psychosis and lead to any number of destructive actions. A glance at the history of Nazi Germany will show the same process at work on a somewhat larger scale.

None of these points should be taken as a blanket condemnation of magical lodge work. There are many aspects of magical practice in the Golden Dawn tradition that can't be done outside of a lodge setting, and these include some of the most powerful and interesting elements of the tradition; furthermore, the support and direction that a lodge can provide to the magician in training can smooth out many of the rough places on the path. For the beginning magician, though, membership in a lodge is in no way a requirement, and in some situations can be a liability. The way of self-initiation, in turn, has its disadvantages—primarily, as mentioned before, the fact that it's somewhat slower—but it offers an effective path to magical attainment that anyone can take.

The system of three grades of initiation mentioned above provides a model we can use for the process of self-initiation as well. In this model, the three grades become three tasks, each of which must be accomplished by the magician-in-training.

The first thing that must be done in the work of self-initiation is that the fundamental direction of consciousness needs to be changed. Most of the time, our awareness reacts to the events and experiences of the physical level to the exclusion of almost everything else. Being intensely aware of the physical level is a good idea in some situations—for example, when driving a car—but it represents only a small portion of the total range of experience open to human beings; as a result of it, most of us know more about the small details of our physical surroundings than we do about our own thoughts and feelings. We also remain turned away from the higher faculties of the astral self, and the capacities of the levels above the astral, by sheer lack of attention.

This is more than metaphor; to a significant extent, the magician learns to imagine, will, and remember in the true sense of these words simply and precisely by paying attention to these things, and doing them as effectively as he or she can. This can be done only by facing the world of consciousness with as much attention and as much persistence as we face the physical one. It is in this way that the powers of the higher levels of the self can be recognized, and the foundation for the opening of the Veil established.

The magician, therefore, must learn to focus awareness on any level of experience he or she can perceive, and in particular must become attentive to the glimpses that come through from the levels he or she cannot yet reach. This corresponds to the First Degree of the system described above, and thus to the formula of Connection.

The second of the tasks of self-initiation is that unbalanced factors in the self have to be brought into harmony. The sum total of these unbalanced factors, taken together, make up what the Golden Dawn tradition calls the Negative Persona, and this forms the chief source of opposition faced by the novice magician. To a large extent, this opposition is purely a matter of inertia; the various levels and aspects of the self have grown up doing things in a particular way, however ineffective that way might be, and it takes effort to break them out of their rut.

In a deeper sense, the Negative Persona is the reflection in the microcosm of the Negative Powers, the primal energies of unbalanced force mentioned in Chapter 2. It includes all the unreconciled conflicts and unhealed wounds of the self, and dealing with it requires the magician to come to terms with exactly those aspects of the self he or she least wants to think about.

It also requires the magician to deal with certain factors that affect the interactions between the different levels of the self. In most people who have no magical or mystical training, the centers of consciousness on the astral level are deeply enmeshed with the centers of the etheric body. This entanglement, a product of the incomplete development of the astral level, causes the connections between these two levels of the self to become garbled. It results in a confusion of levels in which astral thoughts and feelings have unwanted etheric and physical effects, including psychosomatic illnesses, and etheric and physical experiences come to dominate the attention of the astral self.

In the Golden Dawn papers, this entanglement of levels is described as the descent of the human consciousness of the astral level into the automatic consciousness of the etheric, and the work of repairing it is thus an ascent back to the human. The magician must accomplish this ascent, reshape the relationships between the levels and reorganize ways of dealing with the self that are all but inborn. This process of balancing and inner clarification corresponds to the Second Degree of initiation, and to the formula of Ascension.

The third task of self-initiation, finally, involves calling the energies of the Higher Genius into manifestation down through the levels of the self. This process ends in the transformation that Cabalistic imagery describes as the rending of the Veil. In most cases, this is a gradual process brought about by years of work, and the brief glimpses of the higher levels that come through in the course of this work—tremblings of the Veil, as they have been called—are less important than the slow and steady opening up of the higher levels of perception and power, and the growth of the ability to focus those higher levels on any part of life, including the most material. This task corresponds to the Third Degree of initiation, and to the formula of Regeneration.

Each of these three tasks of the magician in training can be fostered through a range of different practical methods, and many of the basic techniques of magical training work on more than one at the same time. The work of reorienting the awareness is in large part simply a matter of learning to observe one's own inner life clearly and honestly, but it can be helped along through ritual techniques that call on energies of balance and harmony, or that waken unused portions of the self. The work of balancing the self makes use of many different kinds of magical and psychophysical techniques, a number of which will be covered at various points in this book. The work of invoking the Higher Genius, finally, is most commonly carried out through ritual invocations, as few other methods provide a more effective way to orient the self toward its own highest aspect.

These three phases of self-initiation, in turn, establish a basis from which the higher reaches of magical attainment and the crossing of the Abyss can be carried out effectively. It's important to remember that all any kind of initiation can do is bring the magician to the doorstep of the highest levels of the work, and this is as true of the most complex form of lodge initiation as it is of self-initiation. The rest of the road must be walked by each magician alone.

CHAPTER 4

THE TOOLS OF RITUAL MAGIC

ANY KIND OF WORK REQUIRES TOOLS, and magic is no exception. One of the advantages of ritual magic is that the essential tools needed to perform it are all to be found within the magician. All the various devices and hardware of the magical arts—the weapons and talismans, the circles and lamens, the herbs and stones and incenses, all the objects that clutter up the old grimoires and keep dozens of modern craftspeople and mail-order merchants gainfully employed—are simply ways to help the ritual magician make use of the abilities that are already contained in the treasure house of human consciousness.

At first glance, the Golden Dawn tradition may look as though it takes the opposite view. Pound for pound, the published Order rituals probably make use of more magical hardware than any other Western system of magic, and the full kit of a Golden Dawn adept rivals that of magicians anywhere in the world. Still, appearances deceive, and habits established during the Victorian period are not necessarily a valid test for the whole tradition. Many of these devices are useful, and instructions for making and consecrating some of them will be covered later on in this book; none of them are necessary. Everything a Golden Dawn magician needs for his or her work is contained within the complex and beautiful structure of matter, energy, mind, and spirit that is the human microcosm.

It should come as no surprise that the different tools used in ritual work can be classified according to the same five categories of experience we've used elsewhere. While each of these basic tools of magical practice can work with several different levels of experience, it's useful to divide them into five categories based on the specific level of the self they involve most intensely. Thus:

Posture and gesture correspond to the physical body;
Breathing and vibration correspond to the etheric body;
Visualization corresponds to the astral body;
Geometry and number correspond to the mental body;
Contemplation corresponds to the spiritual body.

These are the "handles," so to speak, by which the energies of macrocosm and microcosm alike are grasped, and a thorough grounding in their use is an essential part of a Golden Dawn magician's training. Some of the specific techniques belonging to these categories will be explored later in the context of actual ceremonies, but the nature and the basic applications of each of these tools is best covered here at the outset.

Posture and Gesture

The role of posture and gesture in magical work is easy to misunderstand, and some perceptive writers on magic have been misled into seeing such things as a matter of arbitrary symbolism. The placement and movement of the physical body can affect the other levels of human experience in ways that have little to do with the realm of symbols. Since the etheric double is closely linked to the physical body, changes in physical posture can bring certain etheric centers into contact, for example when the hand (an important energy focus) is brought close to other parts of the body. Furthermore, posture and movement powerfully influence the way the energies of the microcosm interact with those of the macrocosm, and this has an important role in defining certain aspects of physical position in magic.

In many of the world's traditions of magic and mysticism, the subtle connections between the physical body and the subtler levels of the human organism have been explored deeply. Eastern systems such as yoga or the martial arts may offer some idea of the potential power of these connections. The spiritual traditions of the West have a great deal to learn from some of these systems, and one place to begin this learning process is with the physical aspects of Western magic itself.

Relaxation

Before this can be done, it's necessary to learn how to relax. Most people in the modern West carry around a startling amount of unnecessary muscular tension in their bodies. This interferes with the magical uses of the physical body, just as it does with wider issues of health and function, and at least some of these tensions need to be cleared away as a first step in the physical work of magic.

One of the most effective ways to learn relaxation is also one of the simplest. Lie down on your back on a hard surface, such as an uncarpeted floor. In a very short time you'll be aware, with uncomfortable clarity, just how tense your body actually is! Take a few deep slow breaths, allowing your body to sag against the floor with each outbreath, and then begin to systematically relax your body, starting with your head and working your way down to your feet.

When you get down to your feet, turn your attention back to your scalp. Odds are that you'll find the tensions there have reestablished themselves. Relax them again, and try to keep your whole body in a state of relaxation at once. This probably won't come without some practice, but five or ten minutes each day spent on this exercise will lead to success in time.

The Golden Dawn papers contain another useful exercise for releasing habitual tensions. Sitting in a comfortable chair, draw in a deep breath, filling your lungs to their full capacity. Hold the breath, and then tense your abdominal muscles; relax them; tense them again, and relax; tense them, and relax. On the third relaxation, allow your whole body to go limp and breathe out all the air in your lungs, to the last gasp. Repeat this whole process three times. This exercise should also be done once a day; it works with the solar plexus, which plays an important role in both the nervous system and the energy channels of the etheric double.

Posture

The most basic postures in the Golden Dawn system of magic are the sitting and standing postures. These are designed around a common set of principles. In both, the spine is straight without being rigid, allowing free energy to flow up and down the major channels along the body's midline; the feet and legs are in contact, bringing the earth centers in the feet into contact and balance; the palms rest against the thighs, closing the hand centers to the forces of the macrocosm.

The *sitting posture* requires a chair with a straight back and a seat raised to a level so that, when you are seated, your thighs are parallel to the floor. Sit down, legs and feet together, lower legs vertical; your hips and knees should each form a right angle. Straighten the spine gently, with a feeling as though the top of your head is suspended from above. Allow the upper arms to fall vertically from the shoulders; your elbows should be at your sides, and your hands rest palms down on top of your thighs, fingers together. Your body should be neither tense nor limp; "poised" is a description that has been used, and it's a fairly good one.

To take the *standing posture*, place your feet together side by side, or as close to this as the shape of your body will allow, and stand straight, with the same feeling of having the top of your head suspended from above. Your weight should be on both feet equally. If you're like most Americans, you tend to stand with your buttocks and belly protruding; to correct this, tuck your tailbone slightly down and forward, and lower your chin slightly. Your arms should hang vertically from your shoulders, palms flat against the sides of your thighs and fingers together; your legs should be touching each other along as much of their length as you can comfortably manage. Again, a "poised" feeling is the proper mean between tension and slackness.

A variant of the standing posture is used when tracing symbols in the air or otherwise projecting energy. In this variation, the right foot points ahead, but the left foot is behind it and at right angles, toe pointing left, as if forming an upside-down letter T. The rest of the posture is the same. This posture centers the energies of the body on many levels and makes it easier to direct those energies into magical action. It can be instructive to stand in each of the two standing postures for a time, and notice the different effects they have on your body and your awareness.

Like the elements of every system of inner training, these will seem awkward when you first start using them, and they are likely to become more awkward rather than less in the early stages of practice, as your normal habits of posture try to reassert themselves. Here, as with all of magic, perseverance is the key; once these early difficulties have been mastered, you'll begin to learn the advantages of balanced posture in magical work.

Gesture

Like many other spiritual traditions, the Golden Dawn system makes use of the subtle energy effects of hand position in its ritual work. The most important use of these effects is in the Signs, which we'll be examining shortly, but there are also several simpler patterns of gesture that are used often in ritual work and that should be explored first.

The *open position* is the first of these. Starting from the standing posture, raise your arms out to your sides in the form of a cross, with your palms facing forward and your fingers together. The arms should be straight but not stiff, and the joints should not be locked or overextended. The rest of your body remains in the standing posture.

The *closed position* also begins from the ordinary standing posture. Bring your hands up to the center of your chest and press the palms together, fingers together and pointing upward, elbows out to the sides. Your forearms should be parallel to the ground, forming a single line from elbow to elbow, with the hands rising at right angles. Again, the rest of your body remains in the standing posture. Both these positions are shown in Diagram 6.

Closed Position   Open Position

Diagram 6—
Closed and Open Positions

These two gestures play a role in many of the ritual processes of Golden Dawn magic, and will appear again and again in Part Two of this book. They can also be used as postures for standing meditation and energy work, especially when combined with rhythmic breathing. The open posture, as the name suggests, opens the subtle levels of the body to outside energies; the closed posture seals the aura and concentrates the energies of the self inward.

Another kind of gesture uses the hand to trace symbols in the air. In general practice, such symbols are drawn with the first two fingers of the right hand; the other fingers and the thumb are folded into the palm, making what is called the "sword hand." (See Diagram 7.) There is, however, a more advanced use of the hand, which is based on the link between the fingers and the elements discussed in the last chapter.

Using this symbolism, each of the fingers can act as a symbol or working tool of its corresponding element, and can be used in ritual to trace symbols of that element. The right hand in this context is used to project force, the left hand to absorb it—as in the Sign of Silence described later. Thus, a symbol of the element of Spirit intended to project force could be traced in the air with the right thumb.

This way of working with the hand can be usefully combined with the Rituals of the Pentagram and Hexagram and other ritual patterns, which we'll be covering later on.

Diagram 7—
The Sword Hand

The Signs

The Golden Dawn magician also has a set of specific gestures, or Signs, that correspond to particular magical energies and actions, and are used constantly in ritual. The basic concept of such Signs derives from the traditional body of lodge technique, and was borrowed and adapted by the Golden Dawn's founders from the practices of fraternal orders such as Freemasonry. The specific Signs used in the Golden Dawn tradition, on the other hand, were mostly taken from gestures that appear in Egyptian art, but have been substantially reworked to fit them to the needs of the practicing magician.

Like the gestures described above, the Signs have uses that go substantially beyond their applications in ritual. They can be used as positions for standing meditation, especially when combined with the Fourfold Breath described in the next section of this chapter. If this is done, each Sign will be found to charge the aura with particular energies, and this offers a starting point to a whole range of possible developments.

There are a number of versions of these Signs in common use; there seems to have been different ways of making them even in the original Hermetic Order of the Golden Dawn. The descriptions of the Signs given here are taken in part from a set of Order papers that differ somewhat from those used by Israel Regardie in assembling his collection of the Order's teachings, and so certain details vary. The basic principles, though, remain essentially the same between versions. All take the standing posture as their basis.

The Signs of the Enterer and of Silence

The first Signs we'll examine here were traditionally the ones taught at the very beginning of Golden Dawn training, but they are in some ways the most complex of all—as well as the most important to the practicing magician. The Sign of the Enterer and the Sign of Silence can be used whenever the magician wishes to direct energy toward an object, whether physical or not; the Sign of the Enterer is used to project force, the Sign of Silence to end the projection and close the link. Both of these Signs involve motions of the feet as well as the arms. Among the formulae of initiation, they relate to the First Degree.

To perform the Sign of the Enterer from the standing posture, bring your arms up and over your head, as though reaching for a ball that is a little above the top of your scalp. Raise up your left foot, and at the same time draw your hands down to the level of the ears, turning the palms forward and pointing the fingers up. Then stamp down with the left foot, placing the heel six inches forward of the place where the toe was in the standing posture. As your foot descends, bring your hands forward forcefully, palms down, fingers together and forward, as though projecting rays from your fingertips. Your gaze and your fingers should all be pointing at the same place; for practice, this should be directly in front of you and on a level with your throat. The whole process is shown in Diagram 8.

From this position, to make the Sign of Silence, raise the left foot again and stamp it back down in its original place; at the same time, lower the right hand to your side, and bring the left back up to your face, folding in all the fingers except the index finger to make the conventional gesture for silence.

These two Signs are also known as the Attacking or Projecting Sign and the Defending or Protecting Sign, which suggests one of their more advanced uses. They work with several of the energy centers of the etheric body, ranging from the crown center atop the head to the earth center at the feet, and when thoroughly practiced can become a precise and powerful tool for directing energy.

Sign of Silence   Sign of the Enterer

Diagram 8—
The Sign of Silence and the Sign of the Enterer

The Signs of the Elements

The next Signs we'll examine are the Signs of the four elements, which were used in Golden Dawn practice as ritual gestures in the elemental Grades—Zelator, Theoricus, Practicus, and Philosophus—between the First and Second Degrees. These corresponded, respectively, to Earth, Air, Water, and Fire, and their Signs can be used in invoking and working with the energies of these elements.

To make the Sign of Fire, raise your hands to your forehead, palms out, making an upward-pointing triangle with your fingers and thumbs. The Sign of Water is the opposite of this; place your hands a little below your navel, palms in, making a downward-pointing triangle with your fingers and thumbs.

To make the Sign of Air, raise your hands to the level of the top of your head, elbows out to the sides, palms up and flat, fingers pointing inward. Raise your chin slightly, as if looking upward.

The Sign of Earth is a little different, as it involves a change in the position of the feet. Move your right foot forward about six inches, and then to the right the same distance. At the same time, raise your right hand up in an arc from your side until it rises at a forty-five-degree angle. The palm is forward, and the fingers are together and pointing straight up, as shown in Diagram 9 on page 72.

This last Sign was done differently in original Golden Dawn practice, and the story behind the change is of some interest. The older version of this Sign had the hand in line with the arm; this forms what everyone since the 1930s recognizes at once as the salute of Adolf Hitler's Nazi Party. If you've ever seen a picture of Hitler receiving salutes at a Nazi rally, though, you may have noticed that he responded to this gesture with an entirely different salute: elbow out, hand near the head, and palm up, a gesture very similar to a one-sided Sign of Air. Hitler devoted much of his youth to the study of occultism, and it's quite possible that he found the Signs, or something like them, in the course of his studies and put them to his own corrupt uses.

The old Sign of Earth—like the swastika, another symbol of Earth in Golden Dawn usage—thus has connotations that make it inappropriate for use nowadays. The alternative version given here avoids these, while keeping the same basic movement and energy pattern.

Diagram 9—
The Signs of Fire, Water, Air, and Earth

These four Signs work primarily with the major elemental regions of the physical body—the head, attributed to Fire; the belly, to Water; the chest, to Air; the limbs, to Earth—and the first three focus energy on these primarily by way of the etheric centers in the hands.

The Signs of the Rending and Closing of the Veil

The next two Signs we'll examine, which are assigned to the element of Spirit and the Second Degree, use the same technique but focus instead on the important energy center in the heart region. They also make use of the open and closed positions described earlier, but place them in the context of movement. These gestures are called the Signs of the Rending and the Closing of the Veil.

To make the Sign of the Rending of the Veil, from the standing posture, place your hands in the closed position described above. Turn your hands so that the fingers point forward, as though you were slipping them through the opening in a curtain. Then pull the Veil open, extending your arms out to the sides to form the open position. This Sign symbolically opens the "veil" of matter, reorienting the awareness of the magician toward the higher levels of being.

The Sign of the Closing of the Veil is the reverse of this; starting with your arms in the open position, as described above, pull the Veil closed, bringing your palms together at the center of your chest and returning to the closed position. This sign symbolically closes the veil opened by the first Sign, returning consciousness to its ordinary state. Both of these Signs are shown in Diagram 10 on page 74.

The Signs of Isis, Apophis, and Osiris

The next set of Signs work primarily with the energy center located in the throat, rather than the heart center. The throat center is linked with the mental level of experience, and is crucial in magical work with a theurgic focus. These Signs thus have a special place in the mystical side of Golden Dawn ritual. They are called the Signs of Isis, Apophis, and Osiris, or the IAO Signs for short; these figures from Egyptian legend were adopted as symbols for a particular relation of energies, central to the Golden Dawn development of the Third Degree formula, which is also central to a series of ritual processes we'll be covering in later chapters.

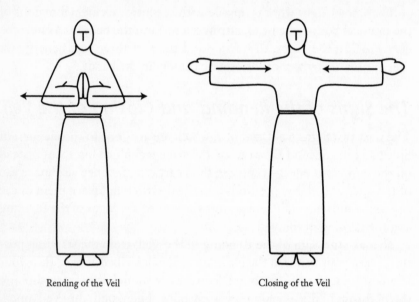

Rending of the Veil   Closing of the Veil

Diagram 10—
The Rending of the Veil and the Closing of the Veil

These Signs also have a link, a subtle one, with the transformations of solar energy mentioned in Chapter 2 and discussed in more detail in Chapter 14. The first Sign symbolizes the Sun at the equinoxes, the point of balance between light and darkness. The second symbolizes the Sun at the summer solstice, the period of maximum daylight; the third symbolizes the Sun at the winter solstice, the point of maximum darkness. The fourth, mediating between them, represents the cycle of the year joining these two opposing factors into a constantly changing whole.

The Sign of Osiris Slain is made simply by extending the arms out to the sides in the open posture and bowing the head. It represents sacrifice, balance, and transformation.

The Sign of Isis is made by raising the right arm straight up, extending the left arm out to the side and down—traced on an imaginary clock face, the hands would be at twelve o'clock and eight o'clock respectively—and bowing the head. It represents the energies of Nature in their bright aspect, the forces of life, and the bright half of the year.

The Sign of Apophis is made by raising both arms up and out to ten o'clock and two o'clock on our imaginary clock face—forming the shape of the letter "V"—and throwing back the head. It represents the energies of Nature in their dark aspect, the forces of suffering and death, and the dark half of the year.

The Sign of Osiris Risen is made by crossing the arms across the chest, right over left, elbows down and palms toward the body, the fingers of each hand touching the front of the opposite shoulder. It represents resurrection and transcendence, and the synthesis of light and darkness, life and death. All these Signs are shown in Diagram 11 on page 76.

Breathing and Sound

In many spiritual traditions around the world, practical exercises using the breath are central to the training process. Few Westerners with an interest in esoteric teachings could have missed learning something about *pranayama*, the rhythmic breathing exercises practiced by students of yoga, or about the role of breath in many Asian martial arts. Many of the words for spirit or related concepts in the world's languages literally mean "breath" or "air"—including "spirit" itself, from the Latin *spiritus*, also the root of our word "respiration." Behind this, according to magical theory, is the fact that breathing is one of the most effective ways to influence the human etheric body and, through it, the currents of life energy in the world as a whole.

The magical traditions of the West make use of this effect in certain ways. Breathing techniques are not, though, as important in Golden Dawn magic as in some other traditions, and it's worth taking a moment to understand why this is so.

The central reason is historical. Breathing techniques have potent effects on the human etheric body; by the same token, they can disrupt that body all too effectively if mishandled. In many Eastern countries, this risk has been dealt with effectively by passing on these techniques in the context of personal instruction by a skilled teacher who can detect problems and correct them before any permanent damage is done. This sort of instruction requires a social setting in which esoteric schools can exist unmolested—a setting that did not exist in the West until quite recently. In the Western world, by contrast, magical techniques long had to be taught in secret, and the methods used in Western magic thus tended to be those that could be passed on quickly and developed through unsupervised individual practice.

Sign of Osiris Slain

Sign of the
Mourning of Isis

Sign of Apophis and Typhon

Sign of Osiris Risen

Diagram 11—
The Signs of Isis, Apophis, and Osiris

This limitation no longer holds—at least for now. Still, the techniques of Western magic have been evolved along their specific lines over a good many centuries, and it will take time and experimentation before more intensive forms of breathwork are fully absorbed into the magician's toolkit. In the meantime, the methods that have been put to use in the tradition are powerful in their own way, and can be used with good effect.

One breathing exercise that has been absorbed into the Golden Dawn system of magic is the so-called "Fourfold Breath." This is done in either the sitting or standing posture. To do it, draw in a breath through the nose, mentally counting to four slowly; hold the breath for the same count; breathe out, also through the nose, to the same count; hold the breath out for the same count, and repeat. The breath should be held with the muscles of the chest and diaphragm, not the throat; a sharp tap on the chest should be able to drive out air. The rhythm should be as slow as you can manage comfortably without gasping.

The Fourfold Breath is an essential skill in the practice of magical meditation, as described in *Paths of Wisdom*. It also has a role in ritual work, for it stabilizes the etheric body and centers the mind. In any ritual where energies are unstable and threaten to get out of control, the Fourfold Breath can prove a valuable anchor.

At least as important is the use of breath as a vehicle for moving energy into or out of the body. In many kinds of ritual work, a visualized force is drawn into the body with an inbreath, or sent out of the body with an outbreath. More subtle energy work, in which energy is circulated along special channels in the etheric body, is also keyed to the breath. This technique is central to the Middle Pillar exercises, among many other kinds of work. In certain rituals, finally, the magician uses breath as a way of charging physical objects with etheric force; in consecration rituals for talismans, in particular, this can play an important part.

Vibration

Perhaps the most important way of using the breath in Golden Dawn magic is as the instrument of vibration, a method of chanting or speaking words that awakens their full magical potential. Most often used with the Names of God, vibration is one of the most important skills the novice magician can learn; there are few more effective ways to waken and direct energy.

To begin working with vibration, it's often useful to practice with a simple vowel tone like "ah" or "oh." Draw in a deep breath and chant the sound, stretching it out until you run out of breath. As you make the sound, try changing the shape of your mouth and the quality of the tone. You're seeking a way of shaping the sound that will set up a buzzing or tingling feeling in your throat and chest, or elsewhere in your body. The effect may be slight at first, so it's wisest not to worry if you feel little. Vibration is used constantly in the rituals of Golden Dawn magic, so you'll have plenty of opportunity to develop the skill.

Practice will make the effect stronger and more reliable. It will also bring the ability to focus the vibration at various points of the body, and in time to focus it outside the body as well. This ability is important in many kinds of magical work because vibration energizes. To vibrate a Name of God in an energy center is to awaken that center; to vibrate the Name in a symbol drawn in the air is to bring the symbol to life; to vibrate the Name in a talisman during its consecration is to charge that talisman with a precise and powerful energy.

Each of the techniques we're discussing interacts with all the others, of course, and learning how those interactions combine in ritual is part of the work of becoming a magician. Vibration has a particular connection with posture and gesture because both are primarily done through the medium of the physical body. The practice of vibration will soon make it clear why the sitting and standing postures both hold the spine vertical but not stiff; neither a slumped position nor a rigid one will allow vibration to be done effectively. The Signs, too, combine with vibration in important ways. The joining of vibration with the Sign of the Enterer allows energy to be projected at very high intensities, high enough that, done properly, one performance of the technique can leave the magician exhausted.

Vibration also has a healing effect on the physical body, at least in part because it strengthens the etheric body in which the life of the physical body is based. As more of the ancient knowledge of the etheric body's structure is recovered, this effect may be one foundation for a system of magical healing, of the sort once practiced in many traditions of Western magic.

The Names of God

The primary use of vibration in ritual work, as mentioned above, is the energized pronunciation of the traditional Names of God. These Names have been the subject of a certain amount of confusion through the years, so it's worth taking a moment to look at them and grasp their role in ritual practice.

What are the Names of God? Originally, they were a set of titles of the tribal god of the ancient Hebrews, preserved in the collection of legends that later became the Old Testament of the modern Bible. The development of mystical traditions within Judaism led to a great deal of speculation and study of these titles, and to the rise of interpretations that saw each of them as the highest expression of some aspect of the Infinite. These interpretations, gathered and systematized by the early Jewish Cabalists, were then borrowed by the scholars and magicians of the Renaissance who created the magical Cabala as a tradition outside of Judaism.

Central to this development was the rise of a language of symbolism based on the letters of the Hebrew alphabet. The twenty-two letters took on a series of symbolic meanings over the years, drawing on astrology, philosophy, Tarot, and many other sources, including the ancient pictographs from which the Hebrew alphabet itself descends. The result of this was the transformation of the Names of God into expressions of a kind of mathematics of symbolism, where each Name (like a mathematical formula) denotes a set of specific images and energies combined in specific ways.

In the modern magical Cabala, each of the Names of God is therefore seen as a formula of power, representing the ultimate spiritual essence of some aspect of the universe. The letters making up each of the Names can be read, through the symbolic language of Cabala, as the elements of its formula, and can be explored through meditation to open up the inner secrets of the Name and its power. In magical ritual, in turn, each Name can be used to attune the self to some aspect of the Infinite, drawing through that same power in order to shape the universe of our experience.

The Names of God are thus the primary sources of power for magical work, and they are used in every aspect of the ritual work we'll be covering in this book.

The essential meaning and some of the applications of the Names have been explored in *Paths of Wisdom* and similar books on the magical

Cabala, and can be studied there. For our present purposes, it's enough to understand something about two Names that play a central role in Golden Dawn magic, and to examine the correspondences between the Names and the patterns of symbolism examined in Chapter 2.

The Tetragrammaton

The most important of all the Names of God used in Cabalistic magic is the Tetragrammaton, the Name of Four Letters. It's spelled ה ו ה י , YHVH, and is apparently an archaic form of the Hebrew verb "to be." The Cabala sees this Name accordingly as the essential pattern of the entire process of creation. In mythological language, it is the creative Word before which the darkness rolled back at the beginning of time.

The inner meaning of the Tetragrammaton is linked to the elemental and sexual symbolism of its four letters. י , Yod, is called the Father, and corresponds to the element of Fire and to pure creative energy; ה , Heh, is called the Mother, and corresponds to the element of Water and to the form that receives the creative force. Their interaction is ו , Vau, the Son, which corresponds to the element of Air and the union of force and form, and produces ה , Heh final, the Daughter, which corresponds to the element of Earth and to the result of the union, form transformed through its interaction with force. From these symbols and their interactions, in turn, a large part of the whole body of Cabalistic philosophy and practice can be derived.

The pronunciation of this Name has been a matter for some dispute, in and out of magical circles. Jewish tradition holds that the Tetragrammaton is so holy that it must never be spoken aloud, and in synagogues to this day it's replaced with another Name, Adonai, whenever it occurs in readings from the scriptures. In fact, since written biblical Hebrew uses "vowel points"—small markings around the letters—to indicate vowels, the Tetragrammaton is usually written with the vowel points for Adonai, in order to remind readers to make the switch.

Philologists and biblical scholars nowadays generally assert, on linguistic grounds, that the correct pronunciation of the Tetragrammaton is "Yahweh." In magical tradition, though, another pronunciation was standard until the modern period. This is the Latin transliteration of the Tetragrammaton, Jehovah, which in classical Latin is pronounced "Yehowah." This form of the Tetragrammaton, for example, was used by Jacob Boehme and the Rosicrucian writers of the seventeenth and eighteenth centuries.

It's often been claimed that this spelling and pronunciation are the result of a simple-minded mistake made by early biblical translators who simply read the Tetragrammaton with the vowel points for Adonai and came up with a mangled hybrid of the two. Still, this "mistake" may well have been less accidental than it looks. There's a whole family of divine names and words of power used in ancient cultures that sound suspiciously like "Yehowah." For example, Iao and Iahu, which were Gnostic names for God; Evoe, a word of power used in the Dionysian mysteries in Greece; or Jove, a Roman name of Jupiter, which in old Latin was pronounced "Yoweh." Behind these and the many similar names lies an almost forgotten system, at one time practiced all over the ancient world, which used chanted vowel sounds in various patterns to invoke spiritual energies.

In the Golden Dawn itself, the Jewish prohibition against pronouncing the Tetragrammaton was taken seriously enough that members were taught simply to pronounce the letters of the Name—"Yod Heh Vau Heh"—when using the Tetragrammaton in ritual. This works after a fashion, but it produces none of the deeper effects of the original vowel pattern. For this reason, I have followed the lead of several other writers in the Golden Dawn tradition and used the pronunciation "Yehowah" throughout this book. This way of speaking the Name has a clear and strongly focused effect, and works well in the whole range of ritual processes we'll be exploring.

The Pentagrammaton

Many of the same magical circles in the West that developed the pronunciation of the Tetragrammaton used in this book were also involved in the development of another Name of great importance to the Golden Dawn tradition. This is the Pentagrammaton, or Name of Five Letters. A magical adaptation of the name of Jesus, borrowing the Christian form of the myth and formula of the Dying God, it consists of the Tetragrammaton with the letter ש, Shin, added. Shin corresponds to the element of Spirit, and the Pentagrammaton therefore symbolizes the redemptive presence of Spirit in the realm of the elements.

There are two ways to spell the Pentagrammaton, each with its own pronunciation and meaning. The first is ה ו שה י, YHShVH, pronounced

"Yeheshuah"; the second is יהושה, YHVShH, pronounced "Yehowashah." These are normally used together in ritual work, for they express the two sides of a single magical energy.

In order to understand that energy, it's necessary to note the relationship between this Name and the Tetragrammaton, from which it derives. In the first form of the Pentagrammaton, the letter Shin is placed in the middle of the Tetragrammaton, and is symbolically "enthroned" upon Vau, the letter of Air. (This may be clearer if you imagine the Name written in a vertical line downward.) In the second form, by contrast, the letter Shin is "enthroned" upon Heh final, the letter of Earth.

In the language of Christian mythology, then, the Name Yeheshuah corresponds to Jesus' existence as a heavenly power in eternity. The Name Yehowashah corresponds to his earthly birth, life, and death. To say the same thing in magical terms, the formula of YHShVH represents transcendent Spirit beyond the realm of physical matter, while that of YHVShH represents immanent Spirit present within physical matter. The first, in magical practice, attunes the magician to the presence of the Higher, while the second opens a pathway for the descent of the Higher through the levels of being into manifestation. These Names are therefore deeply linked to the formula of the Third Degree, and appear in most workings based on that formula.

This use of Christian symbolism in magical practice may seem strange to modern eyes, but Gnostic and heretical Christian teachings have been an important element of the Western magical tradition since ancient times. While the actions of some modern versions of Christianity have succeeded in giving many magicians a bad case of "Jesus allergy," it's important to remember that the meaning and value of a symbol is independent of the theology built around it or the atrocities committed in its name.

Other Names of God

There are many other Names used in magical work, of course, and each has a symbolism and meaning worth exploring. For our present purposes, they can simply be listed according to their correspondences in the symbol systems of Golden Dawn magic. The pronunciations given here are standard in the Golden Dawn tradition in English-speaking countries. The literal meanings of the Names have been included in parentheses; these are approximations, since Hebrew permits shades of meaning that can't easily be converted into English. (For example, the Name Elohim is made of the word *elohe*, "goddess," a feminine noun, with the masculine plural *-im* added to it, implying an image of the divine with multiple aspects of both genders; "Gods and Goddesses" is a very rough way of translating this.)

Elements

Air—ה ו ה י, YHVH, "ye-ho-wah" (That-Which-Is)

Fire—ם י ה ל א, ALHIM, "ell-o-heem" (Gods and Goddesses)

Water—ל א, AL, "ell" (God)

Earth—י נ ד א, ADNI, "ah-dough-nye" (Lord)

Spirit (active)—ה י ה א, AHIH, "eh-heh-yeh" (I Am)

Spirit (passive)—א ל ג א, AGLA, "ah-geh-la" (the initials of the Hebrew sentence *Ateh gibor le-olam, Adonai*, "Thou art mighty forever, Lord")

Planets

Saturn—ם י ה ל א ה ו ה י, YHVH ALHIM, "yeh-ho-wah ell-o-heem" (That-Which-Is, the Gods and Goddesses)

Jupiter—ל א, AL, "ell" (God)

Mars—ר ו ב ג ם י ה ל א, ALHIM GBVR, "ell-o-heem gih-boor" (Mighty Gods and Goddesses)

Sun—ת ע ד ו ה ו ל א ה ו ה י, YHVH ALVH VDAaTh, "yeh-ho-wah ell-o-ah vah da-ath" (That-Which-Is, God of Knowledge)

Venus—ת ו א ב צ ה ו ה י, YHVH TzBAVTh, "yeh-ho-wah tza-ba-oth" (That-Which-Is of Armies)

Mercury—ת ו א ב צ ם י ה ל א, ALHIM TzBAVTh, "ell-o-heem tza-ba-oth" (Gods and Goddesses of Armies)

Moon—י ח ל א י ד ש, ShDI AL ChI, "shah-dye ell chye," with the "ch" pronounced as in the Scottish word "loch" (Almighty Living God)

Spheres

Kether—ה י ה א, AHIH, "eh-heh-yeh" (I Am)

Chokmah—ה י, YH, "yah" (Be)

Binah—ם י ה ל א ה ו ה י, YHVH ALHIM, "yeh-ho-wah ell-o-heem" (That-Which-Is, the Gods and Goddesses)

Chesed—ל א, AL, "ell" (God)

Geburah—ר ו ב ג ם י ה ל א, ALHIM GBVR, "ell-o-heem gih-boor" (Mighty Gods and Goddesses)

Tiphareth—ת ע ד ו ה ו ל א ה ו ה י, YHVH ALVH VDAaTh, "yeh-ho-wah ell-o-ah vah da-ath" (That-Which-Is, God of Knowledge)

Netzach—ת ו א ב צ ה ו ה י, YHVH TzBAVTh, "yeh-ho-wah tza-ba-oth" (That-Which-Is of Armies)

Hod—ת ו א ב צ ם י ה ל א, ALHIM TzBAVTh, "ell-o-heem tza-ba-oth" (Gods and Goddesses of Armies)

Yesod—י ח ל א י ד ש, ShDI AL ChI, "shah-dye ell chye," with the "ch" pronounced as in the Scottish word "loch" (Almighty Living God)

Malkuth—ץ ר א ה י נ ד א, ADNI HARTz, "ah-dough-nye ha ah-retz" (Lord of Earth)

Symbolic Imagery

Visualization is probably the best known of the contents of the magician's toolkit; books on "creative visualization" and the like have made the role of mental imagery in inner work familiar to most people interested in alternative spirituality nowadays. In traditional Western magic, that role is central. Most ritual techniques make use of extensive visualizations, and any major ceremony will involve a whole series of them crafted into an interlocking pattern that defines and develops the energies of the rite, creating the forms through which power works in ritual.

There's at least one critical difference between magical visualization and the kind most often used outside magical circles, however. In magical work, imagery is almost always built up according to detailed traditional symbolism. Where the "creative visualizer" who wants to "manifest" something will as often as not simply visualize that thing, the magician creates an abstract symbol representing the thing desired and then uses that symbol as the focus for his or her ritual work. There are a number of reasons for this, but one of the more important is purely practical, having to do with differences in the innate ability to visualize. The talent for making mental images is something that varies from person to person, and it's not always possible for a magician to be able to call up images of movie-screen intensity even after a great deal of training. The best way around this difficulty is the use of relatively simple symbolic images as a focus for magical action. These images can be visualized much more easily than the object or concept they represent, and are at least as effective.

On a deeper level, the use of a formal alphabet of abstract symbols allows the magician to move outside of the limits of a purely microcosmic approach to magic. As we've seen, the theory of Western magic holds that the symbols used in magical work are reflections of actual powers of the macrocosm and link with forces that are not limited to the human mind. The symbolic correspondences of any of the traditional magical systems have been used and tested over generations, and have an impact and an effectiveness that purely personal symbols or simple images of concrete goals often can't begin to equal.

The symbols most commonly used in Cabalistic magic, then, are usually abstract, clear, and uncomplicated. They include geometrical figures such as the pentagram and hexagram, which will be discussed a little later in this chapter; planetary and elemental signs also are used, as well as the letters of the Hebrew alphabet. One of the most important elements of symbolic imagery is color. Lines, forms, currents, and areas are visualized in various colors to represent the different energies used in Cabalistic ritual. While the fine points of this kind of work tie into the complicated fourfold color scales that Golden Dawn lore assigns to the Spheres and Paths of the Tree of Life, most practical magic uses the following simpler elemental, planetary, and Sphere color scales.

Elements

Spirit—white

Air—yellow   Water—blue
Earth—green   Fire—red

Planets

Saturn—indigo   Jupiter—blue
Mars—red   Sun—yellow
Venus—green   Mercury—orange
Moon—violet

Spheres

Kether: white

Binah—black   Chokmah—gray
Geburah—red   Chesed—blue
Tiphareth—yellow
Hod—orange   Netzach—green
Yesod—violet
Malkuth—citrine, olive, russet, black

Since the symbolisms of Spheres, planets, and elements are not normally used together in the same ritual, the overlap between the two systems is rarely a difficulty; furthermore, the assignment of colors to these scales is not random, and symbolic categories in each system that share a color will be found to share other factors as well.

Flashing Colors

The application of color in magical practice was a focal interest of several of the Golden Dawn's adepts, and at least one other discovery they made has a practical use in ritual work. This is the system of flashing colors. Certain colors placed side by side will produce a visual effect of flickering or flashing if they are looked at steadily for a time; in the Golden Dawn papers, this was said to be the result of an etheric current drawn into a vortex by the combination of colors. The use of flashing colors thus serves to heighten the etheric charge of talismans and other magical devices, and a specific class of talismanic device—the flashing tablet—was devised to make the fullest use of the effect.

The flashing colors used by the Golden Dawn were as follows:

White with black or gray
Red with green
Blue with orange
Yellow with violet
Olive with red-orange
Blue-green with russet
Violet with citrine
Reddish orange with green-blue
Deep amber with indigo
Lemon yellow with red-violet
Yellow-green with crimson

As a general rule, any two colors from opposite points on the color wheel used by designers will flash if placed together. The colors should be bright and clear in order to produce the best effect.

A more complex way of using flashing colors is often useful in planetary talismans or devices. Here, the colors are related to the heptagram, as shown in Diagram 12 on page 87.

Starting with the color of the planet you wish to invoke, simply follow the lines of the heptagram to the two colors most nearly opposite, and use both of these together with the planetary color in the device. Thus a talisman of Venus, for example, would use the colors green, red, and violet. This produces a subtly different flashing effect and a more balanced energy; it's often worth doing when a magical device is to be made with maximum power.

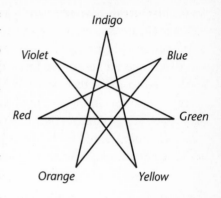

Diagram 12
The Heptagram of Colors

Telesmatic Images

At the higher levels of magical work, the basic color visualizations are supplemented and energized by the much more complex art of telesmatic imagery—the construction of symbolic beings as representations and containers of magical force. Telesmatic images have a long history in the magical traditions of the West, with origins that can be traced back to Greek and Roman times. Old magical writings such as the *Picatrix* give lists of images designed for specific purposes, and the bizarre images of evil spirits listed in the grimoires of the Middle Ages may well be garbled remnants of the same tradition. In Golden Dawn magic, on the other hand, lists of set images are rarely used; rather, it's been found to be more useful to teach the way in which these images are constructed, and to allow the student to learn to devise his or her own.

The basic framework is founded on the correspondences of the Hebrew alphabet and the symbolic structures of the magical Cabala, as listed in the Appendix at the end of this book. From these, several special sets of correspondences have been devised, which can be used to put together the image of a symbolic being.

The essential rules are these. The image used in most kinds of telesmatic magic is a conventional angel, humanlike and winged, as beautiful as the imagination will allow; coarse or ugly images tend to produce muddled energy and are less effective. The letters of a name, either taken from the traditional lore or devised according to a method that will be discussed in Chapter 10, are converted into the correspondences in Table 5 and applied to the image. The first letter determines the head, and the following letters determine the rest of the form, down to the feet. Skin and hair colors are limited to those that occur in human beings. Gender and build are averaged out among the letters of the name. Colors of garments and the like, which are taken from the table of Hebrew letters in the Appendix, are to some extent treated in the same way; transitions in all cases should be smooth, not abrupt, to avoid confusion of energies.

Table 5: Correspondences for Telesmatic Imagery

Alphabet	Correspondences
Aleph	Slender, winged, radiant. Androgyne, more male than female.
Beth	Active, lightly built and colored. Male.
Gimel	Gray, full build, round-faced. Changeable. Female.
Daleth	Very attractive, full build. Female.
Heh	Fierce, strong, fiery. Red hair and brilliant eyes. Female.
Vau	Steady and strong. Heavy, massive build. Dark colors in general. Male.
Zayin	Tall, thin, intelligent. Many colors. Male.
Cheth	Full face, not much expression. Withdrawn. Female.
Teth	Strong, fiery, beautiful. Female.
Yod	Very white and rather delicate; translucent, as if not quite material. Female.
Kaph	Tall, muscular and strong. Male.
Lamed	Well-proportioned, medium build. Female.
Mem	Reflective, dreamy, lightly colored. Medium build. Androgyne, more female than male.
Nun	Square and determined, sinewy, dark. Male.
Samech	Thin, expressive and mobile. Male.
Ayin	Expressionless, almost mechanical. Full build. Male.
Peh	Strong and resolute, solidly built. Female.
Tzaddi	Thoughtful, intellectual, light build. Dark hair and eyes, dark colors generally. Female.
Qoph	Round-faced, full figure. Figure half-defined, as though through mist. Male.
Resh	Proud and dominant, dark. Male.
Shin	Fierce and constantly active. Bright colors. Androgyne, more male than female.
Tau	Dark, gray, heavy. Androgyne, more male than female.

An example will show how this is to be done. Imagine that we need to produce a telesmatic image of the name of Nakhiel, the traditional Intelligence of the Sun. This name is Hebrew and is spelled נ כ י א ל, NKIAL. Almost all Hebrew angelic names end in either AL or IAH, and these endings can largely be disregarded in making telesmatic images; the one effect they have is that the ending AL denotes a standing figure wearing a sword, and the ending IAH denotes a figure seated on a throne.

The letters NKI, Nun, Kaph, and Yod, should be looked up in Table 5. Two male letters to one female means that the figure will be male; the average of the build makes Nakhiel strong and powerful, but not heavy. Nun gives him dark hair and a square, determined face; Kaph gives him great sweeping wings and a strong chest; Yod gives him graceful hips and legs, with a sense of translucency. If he wears a garment, it will be dark blue-green at the upper end, lightening to a pale turquoise at the lower, and he will certainly wear a belt with a sword on it. Since he symbolizes a power of the Sun, he wears a golden solar disk in the center of his chest, and a halo of golden light surrounds him.

This figure may be built up in the imagination and visualized intensely at the appropriate place in certain kinds of ritual work—for example, the consecration of a talisman of the Sun. It then becomes a container for the forces that have been invoked in the ritual, and those forces may be focused through it in ways we'll examine later.

There are several other kinds of telesmatic images besides the one described above. The most useful of these for the practicing magician is the elemental form, which is constructed using the correspondences in Table 6 on page 90. This form uses animal and zodiacal symbolism, and colors the body according to the ordinary color scale attributions.

In the case of Nakhiel, the elemental form of the telesmatic image differs sharply from the angelic form. Nun gives the image an eagle's head; Kaph gives it an eagle's wings and feathers on the upper body; Yod gives it a woman's body from breasts to feet. The head is dark blue-green, the wings and body feathers blue, the rest of the body pale translucent yellow-green. The solar disk in the center of the chest, and the solar halo around the whole body, are common to both forms.

This form has sharply increased power in the elemental world—that is, the realm of ordinary experience and of physical matter—but tends to be difficult to handle in ritual; it's best to begin working with it only after the method using the angelic form has been practiced and mastered.

Table 6: Elemental Correspondences for Telesmatic Imagery

Alphabet	Correspondences
Aleph	Winged and feathered, birdlike, shining. Androgyne. Pale yellow.
Beth	Humanlike, male, long and agile. Yellow.
Gimel	Shimmering and changing form, humanlike, female, full-bodied. Blue.
Daleth	Beautiful, humanlike, female. Emerald green.
Heh	Fierce, strong, fiery. Thick red hair, curling ram's horns, animal face, cloven hooves. Red.
Vau	Massive build with immense strength. Dark colors in general. Horns and hooves. Red-orange, brown.
Zayin	Tall, thin, humanlike, but winged. Combines male and female attributes. Many colors, orange predominating.
Cheth	Expressionless, pale and still. Clad in armor. Amber or silver.
Teth	Lion's features, fierce and energetic. Golden, as though glowing from inner heat.
Yod	Very delicate; translucent, as if not quite material. Humanlike, and female. Yellow-green, as of new spring growth.
Kaph	Eagle's wings and head. Very strong and shining. Violet or blue.
Lamed	Humanlike, female. Tends to moderate extreme features of other letters. Emerald green.
Mem	Skin covered with fishes' scales, shimmering with all colors. Androgyne. Blue.
Nun	Dark, intense, with blazing eyes. Eagle's feathers and wings, serpent's scales. Blue-green.
Samech	Centaur's form, strong and wild. Combines male and female attributes. Blue.
Ayin	Curling goat's horns, hooves, animal hair. Dark, shadowy. Indigo or brown.
Peh	Humanlike, female, very strong. Red.
Tzaddi	Humanlike, female, light build. Dark hair and eyes, darkens colors generally. Violet.
Qoph	Figure half-defined, as though seen through mist. Luminous, humanlike. Magenta.
Resh	Blazing like the Sun, humanlike. Male. Orange or golden.
Shin	Fierce, animal features, constantly moving, clad in flames. Androgyne. Red, like flame.
Tau	Dark, gray, heavy. Humanlike, but as though made of stone or earth. Androgyne. Indigo, brown or black.

Godforms

A final application of visualization to practical magic is the art of creating godforms. In Golden Dawn practice, these were detailed images of Egyptian gods and goddesses, which were built up through visualization and used as containers for energies in lodge ritual.

Some magicians and groups in the Golden Dawn tradition have put godforms of various kinds to use in personal ritual work as well, but this has certain drawbacks, especially for the solitary magician working without the guidance of an experienced teacher. Godforms focus and bring through energies of a very high intensity, and unless the aura has been balanced and strengthened by a good deal of preliminary work, they can cause damage or imbalance at various levels of the self. For this reason, the methods used to create and work with godforms aren't covered in this book. Those who have done the preparatory work and are willing to take the risks involved will find the details of the Golden Dawn use of godforms in the published collections of the Order's papers.

Geometrical Forms

Few people realize nowadays that the art and science of sacred geometry was once one of the central elements of Western esoteric tradition. Along with magic and alchemy, it provided one of the core approaches to thinking about the universe and the self; in the interactions of geometrical shapes and proportions lay a symbolism and a philosophy, and from these grew traditions of art and architecture, music, healing, and martial arts that are all but forgotten at the present time.

Much of this tradition has been lost through the years, although enough of the foundations remain to point the way for future students. The ideas of sacred geometry entered into Western magical ritual at an early stage, as they offered a useful and exact way to symbolize the abstract relationships of the mental level of experience. Some of the most commonly used symbols in Golden Dawn magic derive from this contact. Four of these will be discussed here in detail: the cross, the pentagram, the hexagram, and the circle.

The Cross

In most magical circles today, the cross is treated as an exclusively Christian symbol, and some people have gone to remarkable lengths to eliminate it from traditional rituals. The "Jesus allergy" common to so many magicians nowadays has brought a hypersensitivity to such things. The cross was an ancient symbol long before Jesus of Nazareth was born, however, and it has meanings that go far beyond anything Christian orthodoxy has been willing to tolerate.

A cross is formed by two lines that meet at ninety-degree angles. These lines may or may not be the same length, and may or may not cross at their centers; each variation expresses a different concept, but all derive from the essential abstract meaning of the cross, which is contact between opposites.

The most common form of the cross used in Golden Dawn magic is the equal-armed or Greek cross. The two lines forming this cross can be seen as male and female, active and receptive, spirit and matter, equal and equally participating in union. This cross can also be seen as a fourfold symbol, standing for the balance of the four directions and four elements in the world, and is thus a symbol of the macrocosm, the universe we perceive around us. When used in ritual, it stabilizes and extends energy.

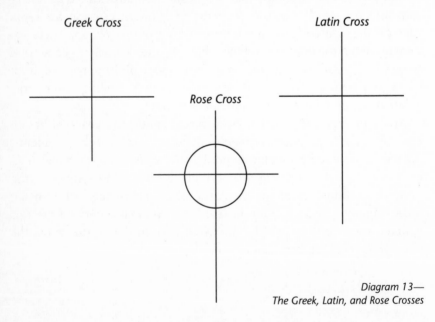

Greek Cross

Latin Cross

Rose Cross

Diagram 13—
The Greek, Latin, and Rose Crosses

Another form of the cross commonly used in the magician's work is the Latin or Calvary cross, in which the lower arm is twice as long as the others. Here the symbolism is not one of equal union and balance, but of extension, dynamism. This cross is a symbol of spirit taking matter up into itself, and thus of redemption and transcendence; its role in Christian symbolism in the West develops from this. In ritual, it is used to raise energy from a lower to a higher level of experience.

A variation of the Latin cross is the so-called Rose Cross symbol. This symbol is used in ritual work as a symbol of Tiphareth, the sixth Sphere of the Tree of Life. It combines the meanings of the Latin cross with those of the circle to produce an image of hidden spiritual power, one that has deep connections with the Rosicrucian myths central to the Golden Dawn developments of the Third Degree.

The Pentagram

The pentagram is based on a more complex geometry. The relationship between the sides of a pentagram and the sides of the pentagon in which it is traced forms the proportion known as ϕ (the Greek letter phi) or the Golden Section—the geometrical symbol of harmony and reconciliation, and one of the most important proportions in traditional sacred geometry. The five points also correspond to the five elements and the head and four limbs of the human body. The pentagram thus stands for the rulership of Spirit over the elements, and for the microcosm, the individual human being.

For practical use in ritual, each point of the pentagram is assigned to one of the elements, and the pentagram may be traced in specific ways to concentrate or disperse—in magical terms, "invoke" and "banish" are the words used—elemental energies. In most cases, one begins toward the point of the element to invoke, and away from it to banish. The complete attributions are given in Diagram 15 on page 94.

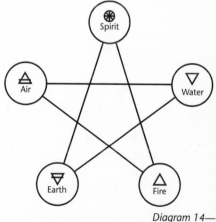

Diagram 14—
Attributions of the Pentagram

Invoking Earth

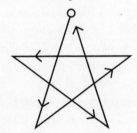

Invoking Water

Invoking Air

Invoking Fire

Invoking Spirit (Active)

Invoking Spirit (Passive)

Diagram 15—
Attributions of the Invoking Pentagrams

Banishing Earth

Banishing Water

Banishing Air

Banishing Fire

Banishing Spirit (Active)

Banishing Spirit (Passive)

Diagram 16—
Attributions of the Banishing Pentagrams

symbolizes the balance between two whole systems in interaction—often, between macrocosm and microcosm. Its geometry, based on the square root of 3, is also the geometry behind the Cabalistic Tree of Life, and the same geometry also governs the important figure called the *vesica piscis*, which is the most common form for the magician's lamen.

In practical magic, the hexagram is used to work with the
energies of the seven traditional
planets in the same way that the
pentagram is used with the elements. Here, though, both banishing and invoking begin with
the point of the planet; banishing
goes counterclockwise, invoking
clockwise. The attributions are
shown in Diagram 17.

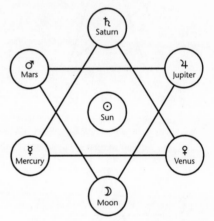

Diagram 17—
Attributions of the Hexagram

There are two complicating
factors in the use of the hexagram. One is that the form of the
hexagram given here, in which
the two triangles interpenetrate, is only one of four forms used in Golden
Dawn magic. These four forms relate to the four elements and reflect the
presence of the seven planetary powers in the realm of the elements;
they are given in Diagram 20 on page 99.

The connections between these forms and the elements are not difficult to work out if it's remembered that the upward-pointing triangle
represents the energies of Fire and the downward pointing one the
energies of Water. The Earth form is the balanced union of these two,
which corresponds well to the stability of Earth. The two triangles of
the Water form point toward each other, with the Water triangle above,
while those of the Air form point away from each other, with Fire
above; this represents the tendency of Water, both physically and symbolically, to join things together, and that of Air to disperse things and
separate them. The Fire form, finally, with the Water triangle turned
upward, represents Fire's capacity to convert all things into itself.

The second complication has to do with the attribution of the Sun. As
there are only six points on the hexagram, the Sun has generally been
assigned to the center, and it's hard to trace the ordinary hexagram starting

Invoking Saturn

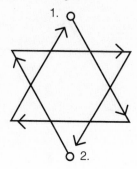

Invoking Jupiter

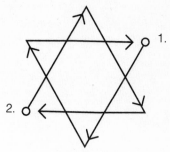

Invoking Mars

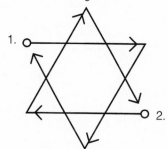

Invoking Venus

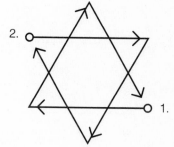

Invoking Mercury

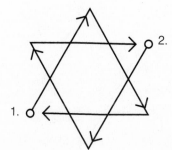

Invoking Moon

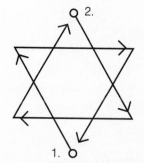

Diagram 18—
Attributions of the Invoking Hexagrams

Banishing Saturn

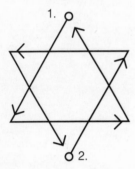

Banishing Jupiter

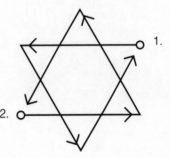

Banishing Mars

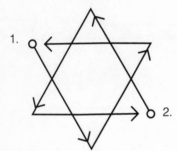

Banishing Venus

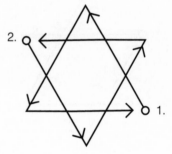

Banishing Mercury

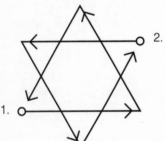

Banishing Moon

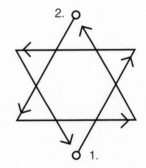

Diagram 19—
Attributions of the Banishing Hexagrams

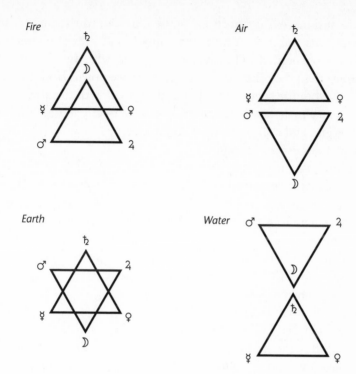

Fire

Air

Earth

Water

Diagram 20—
The Elemental Forms of the Hexafram

from that point! The traditional way to invoke or banish the Sun in Golden Dawn magic is to trace each of the planetary hexagrams—one each of Saturn, Jupiter, Mars, Venus, Mercury, and the Moon, in that order—in the same space. This works well, as the Sun in magical terms is the balance point of the planets, but the process is slow for modern tastes.

Some magicians have taken to using the hexangle or pseudohexagram (the so-called "unicursal hexagram") as a way out of this problem, giving it the same attributions as the hexagram. While this provides an easy way of invoking and banishing the Sun, the pseudohexagram has a different geometry, and Golden Dawn teachings give it a different attribution—the two large points symbolizing the Sun and Moon, the four smaller ones the elements, and the central point Spirit.

This is more than a quibble, because the traditional philosophy of magic holds that symbols such as this are not simply arbitrary signs;

they have an inherent connection, subtle but real, to the powers they represent. This point is of particular importance where geometrical symbols are concerned. The pseudohexagram, with two points very much larger than the other four, calls much more power from the large points than from the small ones. To use it in ritual with the attributions of the ordinary planetary hexagram is to risk an overload of Saturn and Moon energies and a shortage of anything else.

Perhaps the best way around these is to use the pseudo-hexagram on its own terms for solar (and, where appropriate, lunar and elemental) invocations and banishings, using a ritual designed for the purpose; an example of such a ritual will be given in a later chapter. The attributions will then be as given as in Diagrams 21, 22, and 23. The pseudohexagram invokes and banishes the Sun as source and ruler of the elemental world. The hexagram, on the other

Diagram 21—
Attributions of the Pseudohexagram

hand, invokes and banishes the Sun as ruler of the planetary powers, and should be used when this quality is more appropriate.

The Circle

The circle, one of the simplest of geometrical forms, has a vast array of meanings in sacred geometry. In ritual work, though, it nearly always serves only one function—as a boundary or limiting factor. In the banishing rituals that begin and end ceremonial work, a circle is drawn around the ritual space, defining the area in which the rite will take place; in consecration rituals, a circle is drawn over the talisman, and invoking pentagrams or hexagrams are traced in it, symbolically binding the invoked powers to the talisman's material basis. The protective circles used in the summoning of spirits are a more extensive development of the same theme.

Invoking Sun

Invoking Moon

Invoking Fire

Invoking Water

Invoking Air

Invoking Earth

Invoking Spirit (active)

Invoking Spirit (passive)

Diagram 22—
Attributions of the Invoking Pseudohexagrams

Banishing Sun

Banishing Moon

Banishing Fire

Banishing Water

Banishing Air

Banishing Earth

Banishing Spirit (active)

Banishing Spirit (passive)

Diagram 22—
Attributions of the Banishing Pseudohexagrams

Other Geometrical Figures

The traditional lore of Western magic makes use of other geometrical figures, besides the four we've examined here. The regular polygons and polygrams—those figures made with equal lines and angles—are far and away the most important. A summary of these, up to the decagon and decagrams, is included in the appendix.

Numbers

Geometry and arithmetic go together in magical mathematics, just as in the ordinary kind, and there is a complex system of Cabalistic number symbolism to go along with the traditional lore of sacred geometry. Much of this has been lost or obscured in recent centuries, and most of what remains has little practical relevance to ritual magic. One part of number symbolism that does have relevance here is the role of certain numerical keys in magical work with the energies of the seven traditional planets.

In its simplest form, this symbolism assigns a number to each of the planets, as follows:

Saturn—3	Jupiter—4
Mars—5	Sun—6
Venus—7	Mercury—8
Moon—9	

Students of the Cabala will recognize these at once as the numbers of the Spheres to which the seven traditional planets are assigned. In many contexts, similarly, the Spheres themselves can be represented by their numbers. As for the elements, Earth, Water, Fire, and Air all relate to the number four, while the element of Spirit corresponds to five, the number of the pentagram and the human microcosm.

From the planetary attributions, though, a more complex set of number symbols develops. These are the magic squares of the seven planets, which are shown in Diagrams 24 and 25 on pages 104 and 105.

A magic square—in older books, the word *kamea* is also used for these diagrams—is a pattern of numbers so arranged that each column, each row, and the diagonals connecting opposite corners all add up to the same number. Since ancient times, these patterns have been used as matrices to represent different aspects of planetary energy.

Kamea of Saturn

4	9	2
3	5	7
8	1	6

Kamea of Jupiter

4	14	15	1
9	7	6	12
5	11	10	8
16	2	3	13

Kamea of Mars

11	24	7	20	3
4	12	25	8	16
17	5	13	21	9
10	18	1	14	22
23	6	19	2	15

Kamea of the Sun

6	32	3	34	35	1
7	11	27	28	8	30
19	14	16	15	23	24
18	20	22	21	17	13
25	29	10	9	26	12
36	5	33	4	2	31

Kamea of Venus

22	47	16	41	10	35	4
5	23	48	17	42	11	29
30	6	24	49	18	36	12
13	31	7	25	43	19	37
38	14	32	1	26	44	20
21	39	8	33	2	27	45
46	15	40	9	34	3	28

Kamea of Mercury

8	58	59	5	4	62	63	1
49	15	14	52	53	11	10	56
41	23	22	44	45	19	18	48
32	34	35	29	28	38	39	25
40	26	27	37	36	30	31	33
17	47	46	20	21	43	42	24
9	55	54	12	13	51	50	16
64	2	3	61	60	6	7	57

Diagram 24—
Magic Squares of the Planets

Each of the planetary squares has certain numbers that derive from it and represent the planetary influence in different forms. One of these is the root of the square, the number of "boxes" or spaces for numbers on each side of the square. (The magic square of Saturn, for example, is a root 3 square.) Another is the total number of "boxes" or spaces making up the square; another is the sum of the numbers in any row or column of the square; and the last is the sum of all the numbers in the square. (For the square of Saturn, these are respectively 9, 15, and 45.)

Kamea of the Moon

37	78	29	70	21	62	13	54	5
6	38	79	30	71	22	63	14	46
47	7	39	80	31	72	23	55	15
16	48	8	40	81	32	64	24	56
57	17	49	9	41	73	33	65	25
26	58	18	50	1	42	74	34	66
67	27	59	10	51	2	43	75	35
36	68	19	60	11	52	3	44	76
77	28	69	20	61	12	53	4	45

Diagram 25—
Magic Squares of the Planets

With typical Cabalistic complexity, these numbers then serve as the beginning of a chain of transformations involving numbers, letters, and geometrical forms. The letters of the Hebrew alphabet stand for numbers as well as sounds, as shown in the tables in the Appendix, and so any of these planetary numbers can be represented by a name made up of letters that, taken and added together, add up to the number. So, for example, the name Zazel, in Hebrew, ל ז א ז or ZAZL, adds up to 45: Z = 7, A = 1, L = 30, and 7 + 1 + 7 + 30 = 45. The name Zazel is thus associated with Saturn, as the traditional Spirit of that planet.

That name, in turn, can be traced on the square by taking the number of each individual letter in the name and locating that number on the square, dividing the number by 10 or 100 if necessary to find an equivalent. (In the case of Zazel, for instance, there is no 30 in the square of Saturn to correspond to the letter L, so L is placed on 3 instead.) The points thus marked are then connected by lines in order, and made into a sigil—a visual representation of the name, which can be traced in the air in ritual or drawn upon a talisman. The whole rather complex process is displayed with the name Zazel in Diagram 26 on page 106.

Seals derived from the numerical structure of the squares are added to these sigils to produce the full set of planetary symbols shown in the following diagrams.

4	9	2
3	5	7
8	1	6

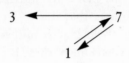

Diagram 26—
Tracing the Sigil of Zazel

Seal of Planet   Sigil of Intelligence   Sigil of Spirit

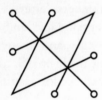   

Diagram 27—
The Seal and Sigils of Saturn

Seal of Planet   Sigil of Intelligence   Sigil of Spirit

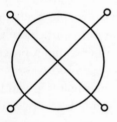   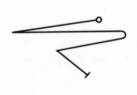   

Diagram 28—
The Seal and Sigils of Jupiter

Seal of Planet   Sigil of Intelligence   Sigil of Spirit

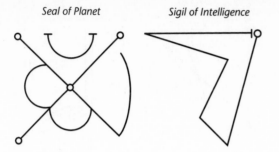

Diagram 29—
The Seal and Sigils of Mars

Seal of Planet   Sigil of Intelligence   Sigil of Spirit

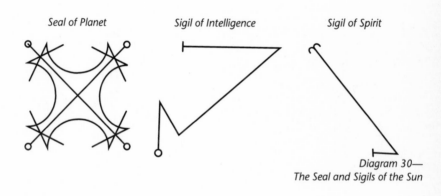

Diagram 30—
The Seal and Sigils of the Sun

Seal of Planet   Sigil of Intelligence   Sigil of Spirit

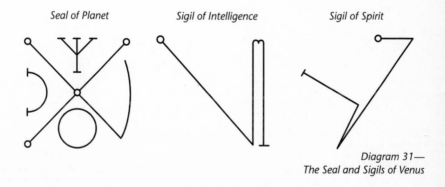

Diagram 31—
The Seal and Sigils of Venus

Seal of Planet

Sigil of Intelligence

Sigil of Spirit

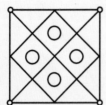

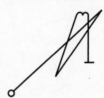

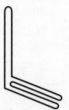

Diagram 32—
The Seal and Sigils of Mercury

Seal of Planet

Sigil of Spirit of Spirits

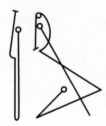

Sigil of Spirit

Sigil of Intelligence of Intelligences

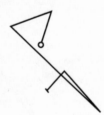

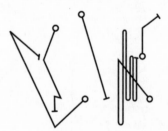

Diagram 33—
The Seal and Sigils of the Moon

Contemplation

Beyond the Signs and gestures, the energized breaths and words of power, the colors and telesmatic images, the circles and stars that make up the toolkit of the Cabalistic magician, lies another factor, simpler and more basic, which may be called contemplation: the turning of the awareness toward what Western magicians, impatient with doctrinal quibbles, have often simply termed "the Higher." In an important sense, this turning is the most important element of the magical art, and all of the tools and techniques we've discussed are primarily of value as ways to help the cluttered and chattering mind set aside its concerns for a moment and accomplish this one necessary act.

The central factor in contemplation, and the only aspect of it that can be called a "technique" at all, is bare intention. At certain points in ritual work, when the Higher is invoked, the magician turns his or her awareness upward—physically upward, making use of one of the oldest of symbolisms, but also "upward" in the sense this term is usually given in magical philosophy: away from the realm of matter, division, and definition, and toward the realm of spirit and unity. This focus is maintained through each invocation.

In Cabalistic teachings, each human being is a center of consciousness on the border between individuality, the experience of being a separate being among other beings, and unity, the experience of oneness with all things. In an abstract sense, we are capable of entering into both of these experiences freely, but between this capability and its use stands most of what we think of, incorrectly, as ourselves. That capability is also the root of magic and the source of power, and the more sharply we define ourselves as separate, limited beings set apart from the universe, the more effectively we choke off our capacity to take part in the dance of creative energies by which the universe is constantly created and preserved, destroyed and renewed.

The practice of contemplation in ritual is one way—in Golden Dawn magic, a central way—to begin to undo this self-imposed straitjacket. By learning to see himself or herself as a small part of an immeasurable whole, by sensing the acts of ritual as acts of participation in a wider realm, by allowing the words of the traditional invocations to turn consciousness upward toward its root in unity, the magician begins to take part in the realm of oneness and to outgrow the fear that is at the core of our human egotism. All magic, whether theurgic or thaumaturgic, ultimately works by way of this fusion of the energies of microcosm and macrocosm. The spiritual development of the magician depends on opening up to the realm where these two become one; so, too, does the ability to shape experienced reality by magical means.

CHAPTER 5

THE PRACTICE OF
RITUAL MAGIC

T HE MATERIAL WE'VE COVERED SO FAR provides the essential framework for ritual magic in the Golden Dawn tradition—the understanding
of the nature of magic that underlies ritual work, the vision of the universe and the self that makes sense of ritual techniques, and the tools that
are put to work in a ritual context. In this chapter, it's time to draw all
these things together in the context of practical magical work. Magic
differs from many kinds of philosophy and most kinds of religion in that
its central focus is on practice, not belief; you can be an existentialist or a
Christian simply by believing something, but in order to be a magician,
you must *do* something—which is a very different matter.

Magic is a way of doing things, and the first requirement of any magical working is that the magician must decide exactly what he or she
intends it to do. A magical ceremony may be aimed at consecrating a
wand, healing an illness, summoning a spirit, taking on a transformation
body, invoking the Higher Self, or any number of other things, but it
needs a purpose of some sort, and it will be most effective if this purpose
is single, specific, and carefully defined. The selection of a purpose is
thus the first and most necessary step in any kind of magical work.

It is important to remember that magic is not omnipotent, especially
in bringing about change on the physical level. There are some goals
that, practically speaking, are impossible to achieve by magical means,
and others that are at best extremely difficult. History has thrown a

111

number of roadblocks in the way of clarity here; shifting cultural fashions, rather than any more relevant factor, have tended to determine common beliefs in what (if anything) magical methods are able to do. Still, despite the burdens of history, it's possible to trace several limitations that seem to hold good in practice.

Some of these limitations rise out of the nature of the process by which magic works, others depend on what it is the magician is trying to affect by his or her work, while still others come from factors internal to the magician. All of these need to be examined if magic is to be used effectively.

The Limits of Magic I: The Way of Nature

The clearest of these limits can be seen in the way in which magical methods get results in the first place. As we saw in Chapter 1, the key to magic is the natural process of creation, by which patterns of energy move down the levels of experience to take shape on the physical level. By interacting with that process higher up, on the astral and etheric levels, the magician shapes the descending patterns or establishes new ones that follow the currents of energy down into manifestation. It's critical to remember, though, that this whole process is a natural one; the changes it sets in motion are natural changes, and follow natural patterns. Trying to violate those patterns breaks with the very process by which magic operates.

As an example, let's examine magical levitation, a standard notion in the sort of magic that appears in fantasy fiction and an ability claimed (if not demonstrated) by quite a number of figures in the current "New Age" scene. Consider, for example, a magical working intended to make a fist-sized rock fly up into the air. Under normal circumstances, of course, rocks don't fly; barring some outside factor, such as an explosion or a small child, they sit where they are. Such is the nature of rocks. To try to make a rock violate its nature and go flying up in the air by itself is to go against the entire momentum of the creative process that makes rocks what they are, and it is—to say the least—unlikely to succeed.

On the other hand, a ritual of this sort, seriously and competently performed, may achieve its effect in an unexpected way. It may not be natural for rocks to fly by themselves, but it's entirely natural for them to fly if propelled by another force, and if any such force is available, it may be brought into play. The next child who passes the rock, for example, is quite likely to pick it up and throw it, accomplishing the purpose of the ritual by what we normally call "coincidence"—the subtle combination of natural factors which is, most of the time, the way the results of magic show up on the physical level.

These same patterns can be traced equally well on other levels. A common etheric application of magic, one with an extremely long history, is to improve the fertility of crops. Workings of this sort quite often produce measurable results because they work in harmony with the natural process; it's the nature of plants to grow and flourish, unless outside factors intervene. No amount of ritual work, though, will make tomato plants bear apples. In the same way, magical methods of healing and etheric balancing can be used to maintain human health, and given decent heredity and a sensible lifestyle, these practices can help ensure a long and relatively healthy life. They cannot stop the aging process completely, though, or bring about physical immortality. It's the nature of human beings to grow old and die, and the use of magic isn't going to change that fact.

On the astral level, the highest level that can be contacted magically by anyone who hasn't yet crossed the Abyss, the same is true. Many of the old grimoires, for example, include magical methods for learning various branches of knowledge; an entire branch of medieval magic, the *Ars Notoria* or Notory Art, existed for this purpose. In a certain sense, this can be done, for work on the astral level can produce what might be called a "talent" for some particular field of study, and can even draw on the constant flow of information on the astral level, which links what we normally think of as separate minds. Still, the abilities thus gained will have to be integrated and fostered through ordinary study and practice—even Mozart had to start out by learning scales and fingerings—because this is the way the faculties of human concrete consciousness naturally develop.

These considerations give rise to the first principle the practicing magician needs to keep in mind when contemplating a magical working: *magic follows nature*. Trying to ignore the natural flows and patterns of experience while doing magic is as pointless, and at times as risky, as trying to ignore the winds and currents while sailing a small boat. The reason is the same in both cases; the forces surrounding the magician, like those surrounding the sailor, form the environment and provide the power through which the process is done.

The Limits of Magic II: Questions of Scale

A second set of difficulties that need to be taken into account when considering the purposes of magic have to do with the extent of the change the magician seeks to make in the experienced world. There are purposes that do not violate the patterns of nature, but which are out of reach by magical means because of the sheer scale of the transformations involved or the opposition to be overcome.

Consider, for example, a well-intentioned magician who sets out to bring about world peace by magical means. It's by no means unnatural for human beings to live peaceably with one another—most people do, the vast majority of the time—so this goal is not necessarily a violation of the first principle we've discussed. On the other hand, the elimination of war through magic would involve shaping the possible behavior of more than five billion people. Many of those people believe that there are valid reasons to go to war, and—when those reasons come into play—our hypothetical magician may find that his magic has to counter the emotions and the deeply held beliefs of millions of people at once. At the same time, there are deeper issues involved, and forces at work in the life of nations that go far beyond the scale of the individual; these, too, have to be overcome by our magician. To put it mildly, this isn't likely to be easy.

Moving from the hypothetical to the historical, there's a similar lesson to be learned from the fate of Anna Kingsford, an important figure in the English magical scene in the years just before the emergence of the Golden Dawn. A devout vegetarian and a leading proponent of what we would now call animal rights, she was sufficiently infuriated by the use of animals in medical research to attempt to kill several such researchers by magical means.

Whatever the ethical issues involved here—a point we'll be discussing shortly—she was apparently competent in her magical work; her first two targets, both relatively minor figures, both died abruptly within a short time. For her third target, though, she chose Louis Pasteur, who was not a minor figure. One of the founders of modern microbiology and the inventor of what is still the only effective treatment for rabies,

Pasteur was a French national hero at the time. Protected by the prayers and good wishes of most of a nation, he was untouched by Kingsford's attack—and it was thus Kingsford who took the brunt of the energies she had summoned, and who died suddenly a short time later.

Here as elsewhere, it must be remembered that the process by which magic works isn't anything exotic; the universe we experience is itself the product of magic, and the effects any individual magician (or any group of magicians) can produce are small stuff indeed compared to the larger, transpersonal processes that go on around us every day. The great creative acts of nature function by magical means, and so do patterns in human collective consciousness and in the consciousness of nonhuman realms of being. All these operate at levels of power that the actions of individual magicians cannot begin to touch, and that even the most powerful magical lodges and working groups can rarely attain.

It's for this reason that many magicians use methods of divination to explore potential magical workings in advance, turning to the stars and planets, the cards of the Tarot, or the figures of geomancy to test the waters, so to speak, and to get some sense of the matrix of wider forces at work in the situation. On a simpler level, though, it's possible to formulate another principle: *magic is sensitive to scale*. What works on one person may not work on ten people, and is almost certain not to work on ten thousand; what can affect the natural world over a few days or a few square miles will probably do little on the wider scale of years and continents. The lesson for the beginning magician is straightforward: start small and take on larger projects only when you've succeeded with the smaller ones.

The Limits of Magic III: Unity of Purpose

A third and somewhat more complex set of limitations on magic has to do with obstacles in the magician that can stand in the way of success in a magical operation, even when the goal of the working is in harmony with the order of nature and of an appropriate scale. These limits take many forms, but they can all be seen as functions of a single cause.

In order to effectively shape the process of creation, the magician must be able to build up patterns on the higher levels with clarity and strength; a weak, muddled, or inconsistent pattern will produce little or nothing in the way of results. To do this, though, all the different aspects of the magician's self must work together. He or she must meet the universe of power as a unity—and this is considerably less easy than it may sound.

This is a particularly intense problem in some kinds of magical work done on the self. One significant use of magic is the transformation of the personality using magical processes and energies to eliminate weaknesses from the self and replace them with corresponding strengths. Sometimes this kind of work is quick and effective; sometimes, it gets no results at all, or even appears to backfire, worsening the problem it was intended to solve. Similar difficulties show up when a magician seeks to change some situation in which he or she has heavy emotional involvement. It's a common experience of magicians that the most difficult and least successful workings are the ones in which the magician most wants to succeed, or in which he or she has the most at stake.

The problem in both of these cases is that the magician cannot act from a basis of unity. In magic meant to change the self, the efforts of the magician are placed in opposition to some part of his or her own inner structure, and when that part is strong—or ties into unexpected sources of energy, such as unresolved conflicts in the self—the resulting division within the magician sharply lessens his or her ability to bring the whole of his or her potential power to bear. In magic aimed at a subject of personal concern, every bit of the self's energy that is caught up in worrying about the situation, hoping for some outcomes or fearing others, is energy that is not available for magical action.

There are, of course, certain ways around this difficulty. The practice of theurgic magic, which has the unification of the self as one of its major goals, is one good way to overcome some of these problems, especially in working with the self. It's often the case that regular work with rituals of spiritual development will heal weaknesses in the self even when they are not dealt with directly. In working with issues of personal importance, the hard but effective art of inner detachment is one of the oldest and most traditional responses; involvement in a magical lodge or working group of magicians, in which it's possible to ask for help in cases of this kind, offers another option.

In general, though, we can define a third principle for the practicing magician: *magic depends on unity*. Any purpose you choose for magical work should be one toward which you feel, after serious thought, you can direct every ounce of energy you possess, without doubts, worries, or second thoughts.

One other factor is worth mentioning in this context. A very effective way to become emotionally involved in a situation you're trying to shape by magical means is to tell other people what you're doing. Human nature being what it is, you're likely to end up with at least some of your ego invested in succeeding—and this is perhaps the most effective of all ways to divert energy from the actual work at hand. It's far wiser and far more useful to act in silence and leave your ego out of the picture. There are other reasons for the tradition of magical secrecy, of course, but this is an important one, and one well worth keeping in mind.

Ethical Issues in Magic

Beyond these questions of what purposes magic can serve is another equally important issue. Like any other tool, magic can be used for a wide range of purposes, some of them constructive, others less so. It can be used to help and heal; it can also be used to harm and dominate. The question of what purposes magic *should* serve—that is, of magical ethics—is one that needs to be dealt with.

Here, too, history has loaded the question with rather more confusion than it deserves. The same fashions that have shaped beliefs about the powers of magic have also had their effect on beliefs about the ethics of magic, and the claims of various kinds of moral philosophy have been played out in the realm of magic as in other aspects of Western culture. Some magicians, heavily influenced by orthodox religious opinion on the subject, have claimed that any use of magic for purposes that are less than perfectly spiritual is a fall from grace of the most dreadful kind; others, reacting against this, have insisted that the whole point of magic is the personal attainment of godlike powers and the fulfillment of all one's worldly cravings. Still others have taken up positions here and there in the vast open space in between.

One of the major factors contributing to the confusion has been the typical dualist habit, fostered by the structure of Jewish and Christian mythology, of assuming that the opposite of a bad thing must be, by definition, a good thing. Those who are appalled by the excesses of self-glorification common to one extreme kind of magic have too often turned to the excesses of self-abnegation common to the other—and vice versa. It's as though people thought the only alternative to stuffing oneself to the point of sickness was fasting to the point of starvation. This may seem silly—and it is—but for two thousand years, most moral disputes in the West have been carried out on exactly these lines.

The key to a resolution of these squabbles, of course, is the idea of moderation: the realization, common in pre-Christian and non-Christian ethical thought, that a virtue is not the opposite of one vice but the balanced midpoint between two. By avoiding selfishness, which respects the self but not others, as well as self-abnegation, which respects others but not the self, the way is open to a position of shared respect—the position of justice. Courage, similarly, is neither cowardly nor rash, prudence is neither penny-pinching nor wasteful, and so on through the catalog of virtues. In magical ethics, the same principles can be usefully applied.

There is another factor at work in magic, which is less ethical than practical in nature, but which tends to reinforce the value of ethical principles. This is the tendency of magic to rebound on the magician. It has been loaded down with a great deal of moral and mythological baggage, but the essence of the matter is based on the same process of creation we examined earlier in this book.

Consider, for example, an attempt to destroy another person by magic. As the earlier discussion of Anna Kingsford's activities may suggest, this can certainly be done; the same powers that allow magic to heal mental and physical damage can equally be used to produce such damage. Ancient records of many cultures, and archeological finds like the leaden cursing tablets unearthed in hundreds of Greek and Roman sites, show that this has been quite a common goal of magic throughout history, and the events involving Anna Kingsford are evidence that it was far from unknown in the context from which the Golden Dawn arose.

There are a wide range of methods used, but the most common involves patterns of despair, pain, or sickness that are built up on the astral level and directed at a target. These then work their way down the levels of experience like any other astral pattern, and unless they are countered by magic, by other astral patterns, or by sheer strength of will, they take shape on the material level in the form of suicide, severe illness, or sudden death.

The problem with this kind of magical work is that the magician who calls on these energies links them to himself or herself at least as tightly as to the target of the working. The same process that brings these patterns down the levels into the target's life does exactly the same thing to the magician. There are ways to delay or interfere with the consequences, but sooner or later those ways are likely to fail, and the more often such workings are done, the more likely and more drastic failure becomes.

Additionally, if the target of the working uses effective magical defenses or simply proves too resistant, the energies called up by the working have only one place to go. The result, again, is backlash. Here, too, there are ways to stave this off—Anna Kingsford apparently did not know them, which may have been just as well—but they are far from foolproof.

The same kinds of difficulties tend to show up in any kind of magic that seeks to dominate another person's will, thoughts, or feelings (most so-called love spells are examples of this), or to get something at another person's expense. The forces that allow others to be used in these ways have their effect on the magician as well, making the dominator vulnerable to domination, the thief to theft. On the other hand, the same process works in the opposite direction with equal force. This is one of the advantages of the constructive use of magic, when it is handled properly; the initiator and the healer receive many of the same benefits as the initiate or the one who is healed.

There is, of course, a substantial gray area to be found in this issue as well, an area made up of uses of magic that don't fall obviously on either side of the ethical boundary. There are certain rules of thumb, however, which may be worth following here. It's generally a bad idea to do things to other people by magic without asking their permission first. It's almost always a bad idea to do things to other people by magic that you wouldn't wish someone to do to you.

Also, many situations that seem to require the use of magic on other people can actually be handled more effectively, as well as more safely, by magic directed at the self. For example, instead of using magic to force a love relationship with some particular person, one might well use ritual and personal work to remove the less than loveable features from one's own character: a slightly slower process, maybe, but one far more likely to produce worthwhile results.

The habit of using destructive magic, like most kinds of cruelty, usually rises out of fear and weakness. The path of the true magician, on the other hand, requires that fear be replaced by knowledge and compassion, and weakness by openness to the sources of power. If these are the landmarks of your own quest in magic, you're unlikely to go too far off the track.

Formulating the Purpose

All these considerations, ethical and practical, go into the choice of a purpose for magical working. That choice is the first and, in many ways, the most important step in the process of ritual magic. The second step, which is nearly as important, is the exact formulation of the purpose.

Nearly everyone knows the joke in which a man finds a bottle on the beach, uncorks it, and releases the genie inside. The genie offers him a wish; thirsty, the man says, "Make me a milkshake." A moment later, there are three things on the beach: a milkshake, the genie's bottle, and the genie, shaking his head, wondering why anyone would want to be turned into a milkshake.

There are a vast number of stories of this kind from around the world, and a good many of them have roots in authentic magical tradition. There's a good reason for this: the entities and energies that participate in magic function according to a logic of symbols, not of language, and make no allowances for linguistic ambiguity. In a magical operation, in other words, what you ask for is precisely and literally what you get, whether or not what you ask for is what you actually want.

The purpose of any magical working, then, must be clearly and precisely formulated. A good rule of thumb is that it should be able to be stated in a single sentence, without figures of speech or phrases that allow more than one meaning. This helps to avoid vagueness or excess complexity, and it also makes it easier to explore the project you're considering in terms of the practical and ethical points covered earlier in this chapter.

It's often wisest, especially in the early and intermediate phases of magical training, to put a good deal of time into this process of formulation—to spend days or weeks thinking about the subject, and listening to feelings and intuitions as well, until the right formulation of your purpose becomes clear. This has an added advantage—it tends to discourage the use of magic for trivial purposes or whims. Although there is a space, and even a necessity, for humor in the life of the magician, magic itself is a serious business; in a very real sense, any magical act redefines who the magician is and how he or she relates to the universe. In magic, as in life, there's no such thing as an act without consequences, and it's usually a good idea to keep this in mind.

Formulating the Symbolism

In magical work in the Golden Dawn tradition, as mentioned in Chapter 2, patterns of symbolism make up the primary model used to understand and shape the powers of the universe. Once a purpose has been chosen and formulated, it must be translated into an appropriate symbolic form. There are, as we've seen, three main sets of symbols used in this context: the Spheres of the Tree of Life, the planets of traditional astrology, and the elements of alchemy and natural magic. Each of these has its own use in magical terms according to a traditional system of rulerships that assigns the different events and activities of life to different symbolic categories.

The Elements

As mentioned before, the elements are used primarily for magic that affects the physical and etheric levels, although they also have a good deal of effect on the denser aspects of the astral level—for example, the sides of human thought and feeling that are most closely linked with biology. The traditional rulerships of the elements are as follows:

Earth governs solid physical matter and all things connected with it; agriculture, mining, and all that relates to the ground and what lies under it; the solid parts of the physical body, such as bones and muscles, and the sense of touch. It also governs employment, money, and physical property.

Water governs liquid physical matter and all related things; oceans, lakes, rivers, and streams; fertility and reproduction; the liquid parts of the physical body, such as blood and lymph; the emotions and the sense of taste. It also rules social and sexual interactions between people, and is generally associated with happiness.

Fire governs physical energy and all things related to it; heat, light, electricity, and radioactivity; the energetic aspects of the body, such as movement and body heat, the will, and the sense of sight. It also governs activity of all kinds, leadership, and personal and organizational power.

Air governs gaseous physical matter and all associated things; the atmosphere, the winds, and weather; the gaseous parts of the physical body, such as air in the lungs, the nervous system, the intellect, and the sense of smell. In the social realm it governs communication, but also conflict, violence, and pain, and it is generally associated with suffering.

Spirit governs all those aspects of the universe that are entirely above the physical level; it is associated with consciousness and the sense of hearing, and also with spiritual development and initiation.

The Planets

The planets are used primarily for magic that affects the astral level, the realm of concrete consciousness, although they have a strong influence on the subtler aspects of the etheric realm and can tap into the more concrete aspects of the mental realm as well. Each planet has its own traditional rulership, as follows:

Saturn governs all things concerning sorrow, death, old age, the past, limitation, stability, agriculture, abstract thought, and philosophy.

Jupiter governs all things concerning good fortune, growth and expansion, formal ceremonies and rites of passage, charity, feasting, and advancement in one's profession or in bureaucratic contexts.

Mars governs aggression, destruction, conflict, and violence, in all their forms, as well as male sexuality and—oddly enough—all matters connected with livestock.

The Sun governs power, leadership, and all positions of authority, success of any kind, balance and reconciliation, and also sports and games involving physical exertion.

Venus governs music, dance, and all the arts, social occasions and enjoyments, all pleasures, love, the emotions, and female sexuality.

Mercury governs learning and intellectual pursuits, messages and communications of all kinds, gambling, medicine and healing, commerce and economic matters, but also trickery, deception, and theft.

The Moon governs journeys, the sea, hunting and fishing, biological cycles, reproduction and childbirth, psychic phenomena, dreams, visions, the unconscious, and the unknown.

The Spheres

The spheres are used primarily for magic that works with the mental and spiritual levels—that is, theurgic and initiatory magic—and form a specific initiatory sequence of their own from the tenth Sphere, Malkuth, to the first, Kether. Any significant use of the Spheres in ritual should be done in conjunction with regular study and meditation on the Tree of Life, as outlined in *Paths of Wisdom* or similar books. The specific natures and applications of the individual Spheres can be found in these sources, and should be studied there.

The traditional system of rulerships given here may seem somewhat strange to modern eyes—almost a random assortment of topics—but there is a precise symbolic logic undergirding the system, and experience shows that it works well. Once the specific category that most closely fits the purpose you have in mind has been chosen, the Names and symbols that correspond to that category can be found in the Appendix or in any number of magical reference books. These are then combined with a *formula*—a basic ritual pattern—to generate a specific ritual for bringing about what you have chosen to accomplish.

The Formulae of Magic

In many ways, it's the use of formulae in the ritual work of the Golden Dawn tradition that sets it apart from most of the other schools of Western magic. In magic, as in most other things, practice makes perfect; the more often you perform a given ritual, the stronger and more focused the effect you are likely to be able to get with it. The more advanced applications of ritual magic depend on a level of mastery that can be achieved only by years of regular practice with a given set of ritual forms.

Many of the medieval grimoires deal with this issue by a simple if restrictive tactic. They each present one fixed ritual that is used for every purpose, a ritual that is varied only in specific (and fairly minor) ways— for example, by changing the name and seal of the spirit summoned. This approach is probably the quickest route to mastery of ritual, but its inflexibility creates a problem: no one ritual can possibly handle the whole range of goals a magician may choose to seek through ritual work. Other Western magical systems offer a series of set rituals for different purposes, or present a theory upon which rituals can be built, and then the student to designs his or her own.

The Golden Dawn approach is different, and subtler. While it's true that different magical purposes demand different types of ritual, any magical ceremony contains certain actions—opening and closing ritual space, summoning or dispersing energy, establishing symbolic patterns, and so on—which can be done in the same way. In Golden Dawn ritual magic, therefore, there are a series of basic rituals to carry out these necessary tasks, which can be varied to fit the different symbolisms and energies that may be needed, and which are then assembled together like prefabricated parts to form a complete magical ceremony. As a result, each of these basic rituals becomes highly familiar to the Golden Dawn magician, and he or she can construct new rituals out of thoroughly practiced elements. It doesn't greatly matter if one has never done a ritual of invisibility before when every part of that ritual is familiar from other contexts.

The framework on which these building blocks of ritual are set is called, in Golden Dawn terminology, a formula, and the formulae of Golden Dawn ritual are at once one of the most important and one of the least studied parts of the Order's system. Very little attention was paid to this aspect of the tradition in most of the Order's successor groups. In the Golden Dawn itself, by contrast, a great deal of attention went into the formulae of the great initiatory rituals, and an important collection of papers discussing the formula of the Neophyte Grade and its application to a wide range of magical operations can be found in the published collections of Order documents.

This focus on ritual formulae derived from lodge workings has a great deal to teach, and in Chapter 14 we'll be discussing the use of a formula derived from one of these rituals, the Ceremony of the Equinox. Even much less complicated rituals, though, make use of simple formulae, many of which can be adapted for a wide range of uses.

The easiest and most effective way to learn the uses of formulae is to see them applied in actual ritual work, and the collection of ceremonies that makes up Part II of this book is in part designed to do just that. While ceremonies that can be used for a wide range of purposes have been included, it's important that these aren't used simply like recipes in a cookbook. Instead, they should be studied and practiced, and then used as a resource for the design of new rituals and—at a more advanced stage of mastery—of new ritual formulae as well.

Putting Magic into Practice I: Space

The selection and formulation of a purpose, the choice of appropriate symbolism, and the construction of a ritual around a workable formula make up the "homework" of magic, the necessary preparation that comes before the actual performance of magical ritual. This preparation forms one crucial requirement for ritual magic in the Golden Dawn tradition. There are several other requirements to be met, which have to do with the practice of ritual itself.

The first of these defines the space needed for ritual work. The romantic image of magic as something that needs to be performed in disused abbeys, ancient temples, or caverns far beneath the earth is a notion of fantasy fiction, not a rule for the practicing magician; at the same time, ritual magic does require a certain amount of physical space. It's not necessary, although it is useful, to have a room that can be set aside entirely for magical purposes.

The minimum that's needed is a space large enough and empty enough that a simple altar can be set up in the middle and still leave clear space for movement on all sides. An ordinary bedroom is often quite adequate. It's useful to have as little decoration or clutter as possible, as either of these can distract the mind during ritual and make it harder to build up images and mental states. Crucially, though, the space needs to provide privacy. Opaque curtains and a lock on the door are often useful, although good relations with family or housemates also play their part here.

Within this space, the most important factors are the directions. You'll want to determine the location of true north, south, east, and west in your working space, and orient yourself to these in ritual work. East is always the primary direction, to take advantage of the energy currents set up by the Earth's rotation, but different symbolic patterns of energy are associated with different directions.

In elemental ritual, each element corresponds to a quarter of the compass, and is invoked from that direction. In this scheme—the *terrestrial system*, which is based on the seasons and the winds—Air is assigned to the east, Fire to the south, Water to the west, Earth to the north, and Spirit to the center.

Another system—*the celestial system*, based on the signs of the zodiac— is used for workings in which the magician enters the elemental realms by astral projection, scrying, Pathworking, or the like; it is also used for certain kinds of ritual work that use elemental symbolism in a planetary context. In this scheme, Fire is assigned to the east, Earth to the south, Air to the west, and Water to the north, while Spirit remains in the center.

In planetary ritual, matters can become a good deal more complex. Planetary energies are linked with the actual position of the planets in Earth's sky, and the most effective direction for invocation or visionary travel is the point on the horizon corresponding to the planet's position. This can be found by erecting an astrological chart for the time the ritual is to start, pointing the ascendant to due east, and treating the center of your space as the center of the chart, as Diagram 34 shows. There are many good astrology books that explain the procedure for erecting a horoscope, and the computer-equipped also have accurate horoscope programs to choose from.

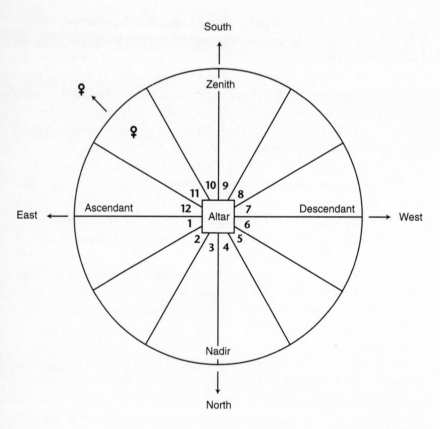

Diagram 34—
The Horoscope as a Map of Ritual Space

There's a simpler method, though, for the astrologically challenged, or for situations in which there's no time to erect a chart. Each planet is assigned to one of the elements according to symbolism based on the zodiac; it's possible, though not quite as effective, to invoke a planet's energies from the direction of its corresponding element in the celestial order. The Sun and Jupiter thus can be invoked from the east, the Moon and Venus from the south, Mercury and Saturn from the west, and Mars from the north. Visionary travel to the astral realms of planetary energy can be aimed in the same directions.

In Sphere ritual, on the other hand, directional issues are utterly simple. For invocation and visionary travel alike, the Spheres of the Tree of Life can be treated as being in the east.

Putting Magic into Practice II: Time

Time factors also influence the practice of ritual magic. The tides of energy discussed in Chapter 2 rise and fall in complex patterns, and these can have a great deal of influence on the outcome of a magical operation. There's a substantial body of material on such tides and patterns in Western magical lore, and some of this was adopted into the Golden Dawn system.

Much of this material was garbled long before the Golden Dawn came to it, and a good deal of it is based on arbitrary symbolism with little practical effect on ritual work. The complicated system of Tattvic tides, which the Golden Dawn's founders borrowed from Theosophical literature, falls into this category; so does the medieval lore of planetary hours found in grimoires such as the Key of Solomon. Both of these systems can be used quite effectively as purely symbolic ways of patterning time, but for the present purpose they simply make matters more complicated for the practicing magician.

Astrology is another matter. Movements of the planets do seem to correlate to astral and etheric energy tides to a large degree, and many of the more useful grimoires of the Middle Ages and the Renaissance relied on astrological factors as a way of timing rituals, noting that a given ceremony should be done when the Moon was in particular signs, or when it and the planet governing the working were well placed and in good aspect. This approach works well, but it demands a good basic knowledge of the lore of electional astrology and its interactions with magic—a subject that could easily fill a book all by itself.

In many ways, the influence of the Moon provides the single best guide to timing, and this can be tracked easily, even by magicians without a background in astrology. Most ordinary calendars give the dates of the lunar quarters, and the discussion of lunar phases in Chapter 2 can serve as a guide for practical work.

Certain mundane factors also affect the timing of ritual magic. Generally, it's not a good idea to perform ritual within an hour or two of eating a meal; the early stages of digestion tend to hold awareness close to the physical level, and many people find that vibrating Names on a full stomach is a good way to induce nausea. It's also best to wait an hour or so after lovemaking before doing the kind of ritual work covered in this book, due to certain effects of sex on the etheric body. Finally, the social and physical worlds we inhabit will place time restrictions of their own on magical work.

Putting Magic into Practice III: Materials

There are a number of material objects that have a place in the practice of ritual magic. Different rituals require different kinds of equipment; many of the simplest rituals require nothing at all, while some of the more complex kinds of ceremonial working call on a range of magical working tools. (These will be covered in detail in Chapter 9.)

Certain things are common to most of the rituals in this book. One of these is an altar on which working tools and other ritual equipment will sit during ceremonies. The standard Golden Dawn altar is square-topped, three feet high and one and a half feet across, and has solid sides; one can be made quite easily from plywood. It's also possible to use any small table of roughly the right dimensions as long as it's stable, can be used without stooping over, and doesn't take up too much room. In either case, it should be either painted black or draped with a black cloth.

The altar should be furnished with two candlesticks, an incense burner, and a cup for Holy Water. Brass furnishings of this sort can be picked up at import stores for very little money. The candlesticks represent, on a small scale, the two pillars that play such an important part in Golden Dawn lodge work; one (on the north side of the altar) will hold a black candle, the other (on the south) a white one. The incense burner may be of any convenient type. The cup for Holy Water is not the same as the cup that is the elemental working tool of Water; a simple container, it has a role in the most common opening and closing rituals. An altar with furnishings is shown in Diagram 35.

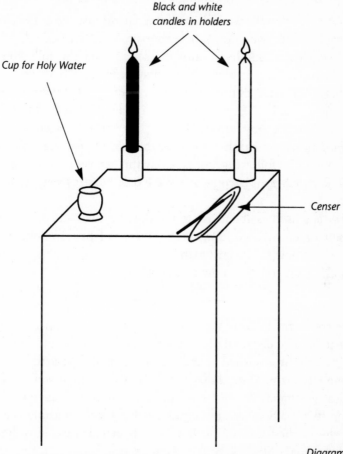

Black and white candles in holders

Cup for Holy Water

Censer

Diagram 35—
The Altar with Furnishings

Holy Water itself is used in a range of ritual contexts and can be useful in other ways as well. It's prepared with a simple ritual.

First, place the following things on your altar:
- The cup, half full of pure water;
- A small dish, or a piece of paper, holding a little salt;
- Another just like it, holding a little incense ash.

Second, stand at the west of your altar, facing east across the altar. Hold your right hand, palm down, over the salt. Visualize white light streaming down from your hand onto the salt, saying the following words: "May wisdom abide in this salt and may it preserve body and soul from all corruption. May all phantoms depart from it so that it may become a heavenly salt, salt of Earth, and Earth of salt. May it feed the threshing ox and strengthen my hope with the horns of the Winged Bull."

Third, move your right hand over the ash. Repeat the same visualization, saying the following words: "May this ash return unto the fount of living Water. May it become a fertile Earth. May it bring forth the Tree of Life."

Fourth, add the salt and ash to the water at the same time, saying: "In the salt of eternal wisdom, in the Water of preparation, in the ash whence the new Earth springeth, may all be accomplished unto the Age of Ages." This completes the consecration.

Being consecrated, Holy Water should be treated as a magical substance. If it needs to be disposed of, it should be poured onto the soil so that its energies will be absorbed by the etheric body of the Earth.

One last material item that can be useful in ritual work is a robe or magical vestment. It can be as simple or as ornate as you wish. The notion that magic needs to be practiced in exotic clothing is a modern one; the medieval grimoires have the magician dress in ordinary garments for magical work. Still, the connection between magic and robes is strong enough in our culture's mental furniture that there's a case to be made for going along with it on that basis alone.

The simplest form of magical vestment is a tabard, a shoulder-wide strip of cloth with a neck hole in the middle and a cord belt, long enough to fall to your ankles in front and back. The basic tau robe, which nearly anyone can make, is simply the same thing with the sides stitched up and sleeves added on; it should be made loose for freedom of movement. Anything beyond this is a luxury, if a pleasant one.

Tabards, robes, or ornate vestments should be white, since other colors have more focused symbolic meanings in the Golden Dawn system. Colored tabards over a white robe can be a useful addition for elemental or planetary rituals.

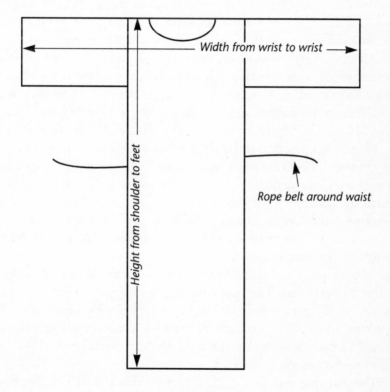

Width from wrist to wrist

Height from shoulder to feet

Rope belt around waist

Diagram 36—
The Tau Robe

The Performance of Ritual

Beyond the preparations discussed above is the actual practice of ritual, and about this there's not a great deal that can be said here. No other human activity is quite like magical ritual, and the best introduction to it—in point of fact, the *only* introduction to it—is the personal experience of setting up the altar, lighting the incense, drawing in a deep breath, and doing it. Like falling in love or facing death, it's something that doesn't translate well into words.

A few points can be made, though, to guide the novice in the art of ritual magic. First of all, the more thoroughly you know the ritual you're doing, the better you're likely to do it. "Cookbook magic"—doing a ritual out of a book, as written, without any prior study or preparation—is one of the best ways there is to guarantee failure. Before you begin a magical working, read through the text of the ceremony several times at least, until you have a solid grasp of the ceremony's formula and structure. Commonly used elements such as the Pentagram and Hexagram Rituals and the First Degree Opening and Closing should be learned by heart as soon as possible and done from memory.

Magic takes practice, and practice is the single most important teacher any magician has. This point has been made before in these pages, but it deserves making again, for it's the willingness to take up regular practice that's the difference between the magician and the "wannabe." Daily work with the Lesser Ritual of the Pentagram and the Middle Pillar exercise, and regular practice with more extensive ceremonial workings, will build the foundation for mastery of Golden Dawn ritual magic, just as daily practice and regular performance are the keys to mastering a musical instrument. The comparison is exact; few people would expect to become concert violinists by getting together with friends once every few months to play a few tunes out of a book. It's surprising how many would-be magicians seem to think that the same scale of effort will bring them to the summit of their art.

The old rule that you get out of something what you put into it applies constantly in magical work. The more of yourself you put into a magical ceremony, the more impressive the results are likely to be. Part of the discipline of magic involves learning to control thought, so that the whole mind focuses on the work to be done—the visualizations, words, gestures, and the deeper patterns of meaning underlying them—rather than chasing off after every notion that comes wandering through. This isn't a quick process, but even the first steps toward mental focus have a substantial payback in and out of ritual.

Another thing that's good to remember is that things will go wrong. Candles may go out or fall over, the phone you forgot to unhook may ring, the upstairs neighbors may turn on loud music just as you come to the critical part of the ceremony. Then again, the problems may be internal: your mind may keep wandering, your bladder may fill up unexpectedly, or—perhaps the most frustrating of all—the ritual will go perfectly, except that you get no response whatsoever. These things happen. If you respond to them calmly and keep going, there's a good chance the ritual may still be salvaged. If it fails, try again later. Persistence and a sense of humor are necessary parts of the magician's toolkit.

Finally, it's a standard practice in the Golden Dawn system of magic to keep a magical journal, a detailed record of what you've done and what the results were. Each practice and each ritual should be written up in your journal as soon as possible after you finish, with the date, time, lunar phase, and any other relevant factor noted down. Over time, your magical journal will become a valuable resource, a tool for finding out what works for you and what doesn't in magical terms. Any convenient blank book or notebook will do.

Part II

Practice
of
Ritual
Magic

CHAPTER 6

INVOKING AND BANISHING

I N THE WORK OF THE CEREMONIAL MAGICIAN, like that of the electrician, there are two requirements that must be met before anything can be put to practical use. The first of these requirements is the ability to turn the power on; the second, no less important, is the ability to turn it off again when it's no longer needed. Electricians manage this with switches of various kinds. Magicians do the same thing with invoking and banishing rituals.

These rituals are by far the most important of the practical foundations of ceremonial magic, and they should be practiced and mastered at an early stage in magical training. The need for them is as real as the need for switches in electrical work. Very little experience with magic will show that the states of awareness that bring insight and power in magic are not necessarily the same ones that allow one to pay one's bills or drive a car safely! On a deeper level, there are realms of consciousness reachable by magic that border very closely on madness, and at times it's only the ability to enter and leave these realms at will that distinguishes the magician from the lunatic.

There are any number of ways to open and close the "switches" of magical power. In the Golden Dawn system of Cabalistic magic, certain specific rituals are used for this purpose most of the time. These are among the most skillfully designed ceremonies in all of Western magical tradition. They allow the particular energy needed for the ritual to be identified by symbols, which are fitted into a standard formula and text. They also require a certain amount of practice before they will call up any significant amount of power. This may not seem like an advantage, but it is one, and an important one at that: it means that the ability to raise power develops at roughly the same rate as the ability to control it.

Invoking, Evoking, Banishing

The word *invoke* comes from a Latin word meaning "call in." In magical terms, that is precisely what an invoking ritual does; it calls a specific energy into manifestation within the self. Another word, similar in form but representing a different concept, is *evoke*; this comes from the Latin for "call forth," and in magical terms, to evoke means to call a specific energy into appearance outside oneself. It's been said that a magician invokes God (or the gods) and evokes spirits; while this doesn't do justice to the full potential of either concept, the basic idea is sound. More broadly, what you evoke, you perceive; but what you invoke, you become.

To *banish*, by contrast, is to send away, and banishing is used in magical writings as the opposite of invoking and evoking alike. This is more than a matter of words; the same symbols, as we'll show shortly, will do both equally well once they have been mastered. Each major ceremony ends with a banishing, which sends away the powers that have been invoked or evoked and returns both the magician and the place to a more normal condition. Equally, each major ceremony begins with a banishing, which clears away conflicting patterns of energy from the magician and the place, so that the specific patterns of the ritual can take shape in the clearest possible form.

Between these two banishings comes the rest of the ceremony, and an invoking ritual is normally part of this—in most cases, a critical part. These three, between them, define the basic structure of ceremony in Golden Dawn magic: a banishing, followed by an invocation, followed by a banishing. This structure can be made almost infinitely complicated, with multiple banishings at beginning and end, a whole series of invocations in between, and other kinds of magical work taking place in the intervals between all of these. Still, the essential form remains, and nearly every major ceremony in the tradition makes use of it.

The Cabalistic Cross

Just as each major ceremony begins and ends with a banishing, the banishing and invoking rituals used in Golden Dawn magic begin and end with a brief but important ritual action called the Cabalistic Cross. This has a certain outward similarity to the orthodox Christian habit of making the sign of the cross over the body, and indeed it may have been evolved from this; Western traditions of magic have never been shy about borrowing and adapting useful habits from other sources. Still, the Cabalistic Cross is not Christian, and its symbolism and purpose lead in directions that are quite foreign to those of any Western orthodoxy.

The Cabalistic Cross is performed as follows.

First, stand straight, feet together, arms at sides, facing east. Pause, clear your mind, and then visualize yourself expanding upward and outward, through the air and through space, until your body is so large that your feet rest on the Earth as though on a ball a foot across. Raise your right hand above your head; draw it down, palm toward your face, visualizing a beam of light descending from far above your head. Touch your fingers to your forehead, and visualize the descending light forming a sphere of light, the same size as the Earth beneath your feet, just above the crown of your head. Vibrate the word ATEH (pronounced "ah-teh").

Second, draw your hand down to touch your solar plexus, just below the lower point of the breastbone, and visualize a shaft of light descending from the sphere above your head to the visualized Earth beneath your feet. Vibrate MALKUTH (pronounced "mahl-kooth").

Third, bring your hand back to the center of your chest, and then over to the right shoulder; visualize a beam of light extending from the vertical shaft to a point just past your shoulder, where it forms a sphere of brilliant red light, the same size as the others. Vibrate VE-GEBURAH (pronounced "veh geh-boo-rah").

Fourth, bring your hand straight across from your right shoulder to your left shoulder; visualize a beam of light extending from the vertical shaft to a point just past your left shoulder, where it forms a sphere of brilliant blue light the same size as the others. (At this point, you have visualized a cross of light within your body, with each of its ends forming a sphere.) Vibrate VE-GEDULAH (pronounced "veh geh-dyoo-lah").

Fifth, join the hands in front of the center of the chest, fingers together and pointed upwards, palms together and flat. Visualize the Earth and the three spheres of energy joined by the cross of light. Vibrate LE-OLAM, AMEN (pronounced "leh o-lahm, ah-men"). This completes the rite.

———

The symbolism of this little ritual derives from some of the deeper teachings of the Cabala. All human beings, in the traditional lore, are in some sense parts of Adam Cadmon, the androgynous Primordial Human—who in another sense is the image of God in which all human beings are said to be created. The body of Adam Cadmon is the Tree of Life; Malkuth, the world of our ordinary experience, is at Adam Cadmon's feet, and Kether, the primal Sphere of absolute unity, is the crown upon his/her head; Geburah, the Sphere of Severity, and Chesed or Gedulah, the Sphere of Mercy, form his/her arms, the powers by which he/she shapes the universe.

In the Cabalistic Cross, the magician affirms his or her identity with this vast figure. This is the point of the expansion of the self to cosmic scale, and also of the tracing out of the core structure of the Tree of Life—the twin polarities of Kether-Malkuth and Chesed-Geburah—on the self. At the same time, the Cabalistic Cross also places Adam Cadmon in the context of the greater powers from which he/she emanates. To use theological language briefly, Adam Cadmon is not God, but rather the image of God; this is the point of the visualization of descending light from above.

This is also expressed by the words that are vibrated in the rite, an ancient Hebrew invocation also borrowed by the first Christians. *Ateh* means "to thee;" *malkuth*, "the kingdom;" *ve-geburah*, "and the power;" *ve-gedulah*, "and the glory;" *le-olam*, either "forever" or "throughout the universe," as biblical Hebrew (like most ancient languages) makes no distinction between infinity in space and in time. *Amen*, which is little more than a kind of verbal punctuation in modern prayers, was in earlier times one of the most important words of power, related by sound to the Hindu *Aum* and the Celtic *awen*.

The Lesser Ritual of the Pentagram

The Cabalistic Cross may be practiced and used on its own; like most of the seemingly simple elements of Cabalistic magic, it contains a much greater wealth of potential than appears at first glance. Most often, though, it serves as the opening and closing of one or another of the basic rituals of invocation and banishing.

Of these, the one usually taught first to beginners is the Lesser Ritual of the Pentagram. There is good reason for this; the basic form of the Pentagram ritual is both simple and, when practiced regularly, highly effective. It can be done in one of two ways, invoking and banishing, and the only difference between them is the way in which the pentagram is traced. The ritual is performed as follows.

First, stand in the center of your practice space, facing east. Clear your mind, and then perform the Cabalistic Cross.

Second, step to the eastern edge of the space. With the first two fingers of your right hand (the "sword hand" position), and the arm itself held straight, trace a pentagram some three feet across in the air before you. In an invoking ritual, trace the invoking pentagram in Diagram 37; in a banishing, trace the banishing pentagram. These should be made as even and exact as possible. As you trace them, visualize the line drawn by your fingers shining with blue-white light.

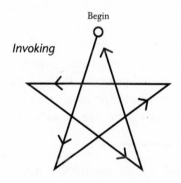

Diagram 37—
The Invoking and Banishing Pentagrams

When you have finished tracing the pentagram, point to the center of the pentagram and vibrate the Name YHVH (pronounced "yeh-ho-wah").

Third, holding your arm extended, trace a line around a quarter circle to the southern edge of the space, visualizing that line in the same blue-white light. Trace the same type of pentagram in the south, with the same visualization; point to the center, and vibrate the Name ADNI (pronounced "ah-dough-nye").

Fourth, trace the line around a quarter circle to the western edge of the space and repeat the process, this time vibrating the Name AHIH (pronounced "eh-heh-yeh"). Then trace the line around a quarter circle to the north and repeat, this time vibrating the Name AGLA (pronounced "ah-geh-lah").

Fifth, trace the line back around to the east, completing the circle. You are now standing inside a ring drawn in visualized light, with a pentagram shining in each of the four quarters. Return to the center and face east, as you were at the opening, but raise your arms to the sides in the open position. Say aloud:

"Before me, Raphael (pronounced "ra-fa-ell"); behind me, Gabriel ("gah-bree-ell"); to my right hand, Michael ("mee-ka-ell"); to my left hand, Auriel ("oh-ree-ell"). For about me flame the pentagrams, and upon me shines the six-rayed star!"

While naming the archangels, visualize them as conventional winged angelic figures, larger than human height and blazing with light. Raphael wears yellow and violet, and carries a sword; Gabriel wears blue and orange, and carries a goblet; Michael wears red and green and carries a staff; Auriel wears every shade of earth and green growth, and carries a disk bearing a pentagram. When the pentagrams are mentioned, visualize them as clearly as possible. When the six-rayed star is named, visualize a hexagram on the front of your body, about two feet across, the upward-pointing triangle red, the downward-pointing triangle blue.

Sixth, repeat the Cabalistic Cross. This completes the ritual.

———

The Lesser Ritual of the Pentagram is built around a simple but powerful structure. In that structure, a space (both physical and symbolic) is defined, first at the four quarters, then at the center, with symbols and symbolic powers representing the power of unity over the level of experience being shaped. The pentagram represents the power of Spirit over the four material elements, while the four Archangels are the powers of the Infinite present throughout the elemental realm. In the midst of this process, the hexagram—a symbol of the higher, planetary powers—is introduced. Symbolically, the magician establishes the system of elemental powers, and then rises above it. This same pattern of outward movement followed by upward movement is the key to the formula on which all the basic invoking and banishing rituals are constructed.

The Greater Ritual of the Pentagram

The Lesser Ritual of the Pentagram directs power toward the establishment of balance, whether by bringing balanced power into a situation or by removing unbalanced power from it. It's possible to define the power being used more exactly, and to bring it to bear on a specific element—or on all four—at a higher level of potency. This is the purpose of the Greater Ritual of the Pentagram.

The Lesser Ritual uses the pentagrams of Earth, since in Cabalistic theory Earth represents the fusion of the three primary elements—Fire, Water, and Air—and serves as a general banishing or invoking of elemental force. In the Greater Ritual, by contrast, any or all of the four sets of elemental pentagrams may be used, and these are combined with the pentagrams of Spirit and the elemental and redemptive Signs to give additional focus and strength to the work.

The most complete form of the Greater Ritual of the Pentagram invokes or banishes Spirit by working with all four of the elements, each in its proper quarter. It is done as follows.

First, stand in the center of your practice space, facing east. Clear your mind, and then perform the Cabalistic Cross.

Second, step to the eastern edge of the space. With your right hand in the sword hand position, and the arm itself held straight, trace the pentagram of active Spirit (invoking or banishing, depending on the purpose of the ritual) in the air before you. The pentagram should be made as even and exact as possible. As you trace it, visualize the line drawn by your fingers shining with blue-white light.

When you have finished tracing the pentagram, point to the center of the pentagram and vibrate the Name AHIH (pronounced "eh-heh-yeh"). Then make the Signs of Isis, Apophis, and Osiris.

Third, trace the pentagram of Air (again, invoking or banishing) in the air before you, in the same space as the pentagram of Spirit, but visualize the line drawn in brilliant yellow light. Then point to the center of the pentagram and vibrate the Name YHVH (pronounced "yeh-ho-wah"). Then make the Sign of Air.

Fourth, point to the center of the pentagrams again, and holding your arm extended, trace a line around a quarter circle to the southern edge of the space, visualizing that line in blue-white light. Trace the active pentagram of Spirit in the south, with the same visualization; point to the center and vibrate the Name AHIH again; then make the IAO Signs. Trace the pentagram of Fire, visualizing it in brilliant red light; point to the center, vibrate the Name ALHIM (pronounced "ell-oh-heem"), and make the Sign of Fire.

Fifth, trace the line around a quarter circle to the western edge of the space and trace the passive pentagram of Spirit. Then point to the center of the pentagram and vibrate the Name AGLA (pronounced "ah-geh-lah"), and make the IAO Signs. Then trace the pentagram of Water, visualizing it in brilliant blue light; point to the center, vibrate the Name AL (pronounced "Ell"), and make the Sign of Water.

Sixth, trace the line around a quarter circle to the north and again trace the passive pentagram of Spirit; point to the center of the pentagram, vibrate the Name AGLA, and make the IAO Signs. Then trace the pentagram of Earth, visualizing it in brilliant green light; point to the center, vibrate the Name ADNI (pronounced "ah-dough-nye"), and make the Sign of Earth.

Seventh, trace the line back around to the east, completing the circle. You are now standing inside a visualized ring made of blue-white light with a pentagram shining in each of the four quarters. Return to the center and face east, as you were at the opening, but raise your arms to the sides like the arms of a cross, palms forward. Say aloud, as in the Lesser Ritual:

"Before me, Raphael; behind me, Gabriel; to my right hand, Michael; to my left hand, Auriel. For about me flame the pentagrams, and upon me shines the six-rayed star!"

While naming the archangels, visualize them as conventional winged angelic figures, larger than human height, and blazing with light. Raphael wears yellow and violet, and carries a sword; Gabriel wears blue and orange, and carries a goblet; Michael wears red and green, and carries a staff; Auriel wears every shade of earth and green growth, and carries a disk bearing a pentagram. When the pentagrams are mentioned, visualize them as clearly as possible. When the six-rayed star is named, visualize a hexagram on the front of your body, about two feet across, the upward-pointing triangle red, the downward-pointing triangle blue.

Eighth, repeat the Cabalistic Cross. This completes the ritual.

———

The Greater Ritual of the Pentagram of Spirit can be used as a template for Pentagram Rituals working with a single element. Simply use the words, pentagrams, and signs of the element you wish to invoke or banish, as given in the ritual above, in all four quarters. The rest of the ritual remains exactly the same.

A few fairly simple principles will help prevent confusion. Invoking and banishing pentagrams should never be mixed within the same pentagram ritual, nor should two or three elements be invoked or banished at the same time; do one at a time, or all four at once. The pentagram and sign of any given element are always used together. The passive pentagrams of Spirit are used with the passive elements, Water and Earth; the active pentagrams of Spirit are used with the active elements, Fire and Air. The Signs of Isis, Apophis, and Osiris are used with all.

Thus, for example, in a Greater Invoking Ritual of the Pentagram done to invoke the element of Air, the magician traces the active invoking pentagram of Spirit and vibrates the Divine Name governing Spirit in its active form, which is AHIH, Eheieh, and then makes the three redemptive IAO Signs. He or she then traces the invoking pentagram of Air and vibrates the Divine Name governing Air, the Tetragrammaton, and then makes the Sign of Air. This is done in each of the four quarters. The rest of the Pentagram Ritual remains the same in every case.

The Lesser Ritual of the Hexagram

The Ritual of the Pentagram allows the Cabalistic magician to invoke or banish any of the powers of the elements at will. In many of the practical applications of magic, though, the energies assigned to the seven traditional planets are more useful than those of the elements, and for these, a different ritual is used to invoke and banish: the Ritual of the Hexagram.

Like the Ritual of the Pentagram, the Ritual of the Hexagram has Lesser and Greater forms—the Lesser for the general banishing or invoking of energy, the Greater for specific work with the forces of a given planet. The basic formula, as mentioned above, is the same. There are two important differences between the Pentagram and Hexagram Rituals.

The first difference is that the Hexagram Ritual uses a different set of correspondences for the directions. The same difference between terrestrial and celestial systems of directions mentioned in Chapter 5 affects these rituals as well. The Ritual of the Pentagram uses the terrestrial order, based on the seasons and the winds; the Ritual of the Hexagram, on the other hand, uses the celestial order, based on the zodiac.

The second major difference is that the Hexagram ritual replaces the calling of the archangels and the visualization of the hexagram with a Cabalistic invocation based on the IAO Signs, calling on the energies of the sixth Sphere of the Tree of Life, Tiphareth. This difference comes out of the needs of the basic formula of invoking and banishing. The upward shift in awareness that completes the formula requires a shift in symbolism, from the elements to the planets, or from the planets to the Tree of Life. The transition from elemental to planetary levels is an easy one for most people; it corresponds to the shift, one we all make hundreds of times a day, from awareness of the outer senses to awareness of our inner life of thoughts and feelings. Making the transition to the realm of the Spheres, though, is less easy, and requires a more powerful ritual process.

Some of the symbolism used in this invocation of Tiphareth derives from Gnostic traditions of Christianity, another of the sources used by the Golden Dawn as a mine of ideas. Other portions are taken from ideas about Egyptian mythology that went into circulation in Western magic during the Renaissance. Some students of magic have objected to both of these borrowings. As yet, though, no one has come up with a better version, and the existing ritual works extremely well. It is performed as follows.

First, standing in the center of your practice space, perform the Cabalistic Cross. (If this ritual is being performed immediately after a Lesser Banishing Ritual of the Pentagram, make the Signs of Isis, Apophis, and Osiris Risen, slowly and in silence, as the first step; you'll have just completed a Cabalistic Cross, and there's no point in doing another one immediately thereafter.)

Second, go to the eastern edge of the space, and with the first two fingers of your right hand trace the Banishing Hexagram of Fire as given in Diagram 38 (the invoking form, used much less often, starts from the same points but goes clockwise) in the air before you. It should be about three feet tall. Visualize the upper triangle in red, the lower in blue. Point to the center and vibrate the Name ARARITA (pronounced "ah-rah-ree-ta").

Fire (in East)

Earth (in South)

Air (in West)

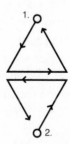

Water (in North)

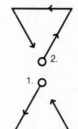

Diagram 38—
The Banishing Hexagrams of Fire, Earth, Air, and Water

Third, with your arm extended, trace a line around to the southern edge of the space, visualizing it as drawn in pure white light. There, draw the Hexagram of Earth, about the same size as that of Fire, with the upward-pointing triangle visualized red and the downward-pointing one blue. Point to the center and again vibrate the Name ARARITA.

Fourth, repeat the process, tracing a line around to the west, and there draw the Hexagram of Air, about the same size, upper triangle red and lower blue. Point to the center and vibrate ARARITA. Repeat the process once more, around to the north, and there trace the Hexagram of Water, again about the same size; here the upper triangle, which is drawn second, is blue, and the lower one is red. Once again, point to the center and vibrate ARARITA.

Fifth, trace a line around to the East, completing the circle, and return to the center. Stand, facing east, and say the following aloud:

"I, N, R, I.

"Yod, Nun, Resh, Yod.

"Virgo, Isis, mighty mother. Scorpio, Apophis, the destroyer. Sol, Osiris, slain and risen.

"Isis, Apophis, Osiris.

"I, A, O."

Vibrate, as forcefully as possible:

"IAO!" (pronounced Eee-Aaa-Oh!)

Sixth, raise your arms out to your sides, making the Sign of Osiris Slain. Say: "The Sign of Osiris Slain!" Make the Sign of Isis, and say: "The Sign of the Mourning of Isis!" Make the Sign of Apophis, and say: "The Sign of Apophis and Typhon!" Make the Sign of Osiris Risen, and say: "The Sign of Osiris Risen!" Then repeat the Signs of Isis, Apophis, and Osiris, saying: "L, V, X." Lower your arms to your sides, and say: "Lux—Light—the Light of the Cross." Raising your arms up above your head, as though reaching out, say: "Let the Divine Light descend!"

Seventh, at this point visualize a shaft of brilliant white light, wide enough to encompass the entire space within the circle you have traced, shining on you from far above. Hold the image for a time, and then release the image and perform the Cabalistic Cross. This completes the ritual.

The formula of the Ritual of the Hexagram draws on much of the symbolism of Tiphareth, a topic large and complex enough that it can only be reviewed here. Briefly, Tiphareth combines the imagery of king and sacrificial victim; to it correspond all gods who die and rise again, such as Jesus and Osiris. The meaning, or one of the meanings, of this symbolism rises from Tiphareth's role in the energy dynamics of the Tree. As the center and balance point of the Tree's polarities, it both rules and is ruled by every other Sphere, and it forms the central point of a hexagram of powers on the Tree.

The central invocation, which is called the *Analysis of INRI*, builds on these points in a dizzying play of symbols. The letters traditionally written on the cross of Jesus—INRI, standing for the Latin *Iesus Nazarethus Rex Iudaeorum*, "Jesus of Nazareth, King of the Jews"—are turned into their Hebrew equivalents, ` י ר נ י `. The letter ` י `, Yod, corresponds to Virgo, ` נ `, Nun, to Scorpio, ` ר `, Resh, to the Sun, and again, Yod to Virgo; and to these correspond the deities central to the most important Egyptian version of the dying-god myth.

From their names, in turn, comes the Gnostic Name of God IAO, and from the Signs attributed to them comes the Latin word *lux*, "light," and the conclusion of the invocation. The whole pattern symbolizes the death and rebirth of the Sun and of the self, the two central manifestations of the power of Tiphareth in the realms of human experience.

The Greater Ritual of the Hexagram

The Greater Ritual of the Hexagram makes use of the same pattern, in almost exactly the same way. The only differences are that, in place of the four forms of the hexagram of Saturn used in the Lesser Ritual, the normal or Earth form of the desired planetary hexagram is used in the Greater; the hexagrams are visualized in the planetary color rather than red and blue; the Name of God governing the planet is vibrated while tracing the hexagram; and the Name ARARITA is vibrated afterward, while pointing at its center.

The Greater Ritual of the Hexagram is also used in theurgic ritual to invoke or banish the energies of the ten Spheres of the Tree of Life. It's not entirely clear why the Spheres don't have an invoking and banishing ritual of their own—the Ritual of the Decagram, perhaps, using a ten-pointed star—but the magical effects of planets and Spheres are close enough in practice that the Hexagram Ritual can be used for the Spheres with great effectiveness. The correspondences between Spheres and planets, which are given in the Appendix, provide the key to this application. A twist that needs to be kept in mind is that all three Spheres of the Supernal Triad, Kether, Chokmah, and Binah use the Saturn hexagram, but their own Names of God; similarly, Yesod and Malkuth both use the hexagram of the Moon, but their own Names.

The Greater Ritual of the Hexagram of the Sun (or of Tiphareth), in which all six planetary hexagrams are traced, plays roughly the same role in the planetary realm as the Greater Ritual of the Pentagram of Spirit does in the elemental realm. It can be used as a model for other forms of the Greater Hexagram Ritual. In its invoking form, it is performed as follows.

———

First, standing in the center of your practice space, perform the Cabalistic Cross.

Second, go to the eastern edge of the space, and with the first two fingers of your right hand, trace the Earth forms of all six of the invoking planetary hexagrams in their traditional order—Saturn, Jupiter, Mars, Venus, Mercury, and Moon—in the air before you. They should all be the same size, about three feet tall, and in exactly the same space. Visualize each in its planetary color as you draw it, and slowly vibrate the Name of God YHVH ALVH VDAaTh (pronounced "yeh-ho-wah ell-o-ah vah da-ath") while tracing the lines. Point to the center, and vibrate the Name ARARITA; as you do this, visualize the colors blending into solar gold.

Third, with your arm extended, trace a line around to the southern edge of the space, visualizing it as drawn in pure golden light. There, repeat the entire process, tracing the Earth forms of the planetary hexagrams and vibrating the Name. Finish by again vibrating ARARITA.

Fourth, repeat the process, tracing a line around to the west, where you draw the planetary hexagrams and vibrate the Name, and then to the north, where you do the same.

Fifth, trace a line around to the East, completing the circle, and return to the center. Stand, facing east, and repeat the entire Analysis of INRI as in the fifth and sixth steps of the Lesser Ritual of the Hexagram.

Sixth, visualize the descending light, hold the image for a time, and then release the image and perform the Cabalistic Cross. This completes the ritual.

Other Invoking and Banishing Rituals

The same principles that govern the Rituals of the Pentagram and Hexagram can be used to construct invoking and banishing rituals that make use of other geometric figures and their symbolism. While the elemental and planetary powers will answer for most magical needs, there are certain kinds of work in which other symbolic systems are more appropriate. For example, an alchemically based working may make use of the Three Principles—Mercury, Sulfur, and Salt—as its basic categories, and some way to invoke and banish the energies that correspond to these would then be needed. A ritual using the triangle as its basic symbol would be one way to do this.

Similarly, one form of the enneagram, or nine-pointed star, represents the seven planets along with the north and south nodes of the Moon; the lunar nodes are the powers governing eclipses, and certain kinds of ceremonial work based on this could make use of a ritual of the enneagram.

These are relatively advanced magical practices, but two points about such workings are worth considering here. First of all, the pentagram and hexagram draw strength from use as well as geometry; both of them have had important roles in Western magic for centuries, and the egregors that have built up around them in that time give them much of their force. Rituals using other geometric patterns will not have that advantage. It's probably wisest to banish with the Lesser Ritual of the Pentagram before and after any such working, whatever the geometries you use within it.

Secondly, the difference between elemental and planetary powers, as described earlier, should determine whether you use the invocations of the Pentagram or Hexagram Ritual as the model for any alternative rite. When working primarily with material forces, invoke the archangels; when working with subtler powers, invoke Tiphareth through the IAO

Formula. Thus the Ritual of the Triangle mentioned above would be performed like the Pentagram Ritual, while the Ritual of the Enneangle would be done like that of the Hexagram.

For the sake of example, here is the text for a Ritual of the Hexangle. As mentioned earlier, this figure symbolizes the power of the Sun and Moon in the realm of the elements, governed by Spirit; in particular, it represents a less time-consuming way to invoke or banish the energies of the Sun than the hexagram allows. The ritual will be especially useful for consecrating solar or lunar talismans, for workings involving fertility, and for ceremonies connected to alchemy. The form given here is an invoking ritual of the Sun.

First, stand in the center of your practice space, facing east. Clear your mind and then perform the Cabalistic Cross.

Second, go to the eastern edge of the space. With the first two fingers of your right hand, trace the hexangle, beginning at the topmost point and moving clockwise, as shown in Diagram 39. Make it as even and exact as possible, and visualize the line drawn by your fingers shining with golden light. Then point to the center of the hexangle and vibrate the Name YHVH ALVH VDAaTh (pronounced "yeh-ho-wah ell-o-ah vah da-ath").

Third, holding your arm extended, trace a line around to the southern edge of your practice space and draw a second hexangle like the first,

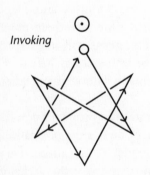

Invoking

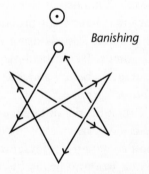

Banishing

Diagram 39—
The Invoking and Banishing Hexangles of the Sun

vibrating the same name at the center. Repeat the process to the west, and then to the north.

Fourth, trace the line back around to the east, completing the circle. You are now standing inside a visualized ring made of golden light with a hexangle shining in each of the four quarters. Return to the center and face east, as you were at the opening, but raise your arms to the sides like the arms of a cross, palms forward. Say aloud, as in the Ritual of the Pentagram:

"Before me, Raphael; behind me, Gabriel; to my right hand, Michael; to my left hand, Auriel. The Sun and Moon above me; the Earth below me; for about me and upon me shine the six-rayed stars!"

The same visualizations are to be used for the archangels as in the Pentagram Ritual. When the Sun and Moon are named, visualize them as though above the space, Sun a little to your right, Moon a little to your left; when the Earth is named, be aware of the Earth beneath your feet. The "six-rayed stars" around you are the hexangles, but the one upon you is a hexagram, visualized as in the Pentagram Ritual.

Fifth, repeat the Cabalistic Cross. This completes the ritual.

The Ritual of the Rose Cross

The invoking and banishing rituals covered so far are the chief rites based on the formula we've explored in this chapter, but there is one other ritual built on the same lines that is well worth learning and practicing. This is called the Ritual of the Rose Cross. It is rarely if ever used as an element of larger ceremonies; rather, it serves as a specialized rite of invocation for a limited, but valuable, purpose. It invokes the energies of Tiphareth directly for healing and protection.

The Ritual of the Rose Cross requires a stick of incense—frankincense, or some other astringent scent, is best—along with the usual requirements of ritual work. It is performed as follows.

First, standing in the middle of your practice space, facing east and holding the lit stick of incense, perform the Cabalistic Cross.

Second, go to the southeast corner of your space. There, with the
incense, trace the symbol of the
Rose Cross in the air before you, as
shown in Diagram 40. The symbol
should be about three feet high,
with the upper end of the cross at
the level of the top of your head,
and it should be visualized in white
light. Point the lit end of the
incense at the center of the cross
and vibrate the Name YHShVH
(pronounced "yeh-heh-shu-ah").

Third, trace and visualize a line
around to the southwest corner of
the space, and repeat the same process, tracing the symbol and vibrating the same Name. Then trace
the line around to the northwest
corner, repeating the process there,
and do the same to the northeast
corner, repeating the process there.

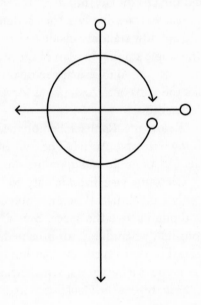

Diagram 40—
The Rose Cross

Fourth, trace the line back around to the southeast, completing the
circle. Then draw a line with the incense up and over your head, diagonally across toward the northwest corner of the space. At the center of
the room, stop, trace the symbol of the Rose Cross directly above you,
point to its center and vibrate the Name.

Then continue to the northwest corner. From there, trace the line
down and across the floor, diagonally across to the southeast corner; stop
in the middle of the room, draw the symbol of the Rose Cross just above
the floor, point to its center and vibrate the Name. Then finish tracing
the line back to the southeast.

Fifth, retrace the line from the symbol in the southeast corner to the
one in the southwest corner, and then trace another line up over your
head, across to the symbol in the center of the ceiling, across and down
to the northeast corner, down and across to the symbol in the center of
the floor, and back across and up to the southwest corner again. Then

retrace the line back around to the southeast. (The result of all this tracing is shown in Diagram 41.) There, draw the symbol of the Rose Cross again, over the first one, but somewhat larger; while tracing the lower half of the circle, vibrate YHShVH; while tracing the upper half of the circle, vibrate YHVShH (pronounced "yeh-ho-wah-shah").

Sixth, return to the center. Stand, facing east, and say the Analysis of INRI aloud:

"I, N, R, I.

"Yod, Nun, Resh, Yod.

"Virgo, Isis, mighty mother. Scorpio, Apophis, the destroyer. Sol, Osiris, slain and risen.

"Isis, Apophis, Osiris.

"I, A, O."

Vibrate, as forcefully as possible:

"IAO!" (pronounced Eee-Aaa-Oh!)

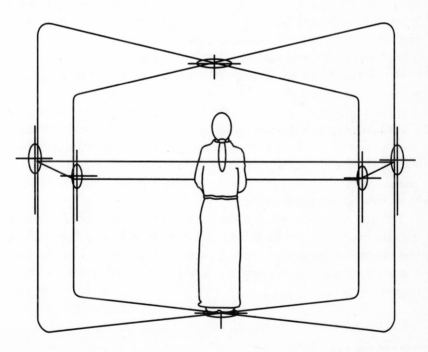

Diagram 41—
The Rose Cross Ritual

Seventh, make the Sign of Osiris Slain. Say: "The Sign of Osiris Slain!" Make the Sign of Isis, and say: "The Sign of the Mourning of Isis!" Make the Sign of Apophis, and say: "The Sign of Apophis and Typhon!" Make the Sign of Osiris Risen, and say: "The Sign of Osiris Risen!" Then repeat the Signs of Isis, Apophis, and Osiris, saying: "L, V, X." Lower your arms to your sides, and say: "Lux—Light—the Light of the Cross." Raising your arms above your head, as though reaching out, say: "Let the Divine Light descend!"

Eighth, visualize a shaft of brilliant white light, wide enough to encompass the entire space within the lines you have traced, shining on you from far above. Hold the image for a time, and then release it and perform the Cabalistic Cross. This completes the ritual.

———

In this ritual, the invocation of Tiphareth is combined with a different way of defining symbolic space. The result is a different effect; the energies of balance and harmony associated with Tiphareth focus inward, into the subtle bodies of the magician, rather than outward into the realms of being the magician seeks to shape. It is thus well worth doing whenever one faces stress, pain, or illness.

The Ritual of the Rose Cross brings healing rather than power, but it has another effect that makes it particularly useful in magical train-ing—by bringing the aura into balance, it also brings protection against many kinds of magical disturbance. For this reason, it should be learned and performed regularly in the early stages of magical training to help clear away the common troubles with "astral static"—unexpected and unwanted etheric and astral presences, harmless but often annoying—that often bother the beginner.

It's been said, and truly, that there is a certain satisfaction in being hit over the head by a spirit whose existence one has previously doubted; still, this becomes tedious after a certain number of repetitions, and the Rose Cross Ritual is an effective way of bringing such annoyances to an end.

CHAPTER 7

THE MIDDLE PILLAR EXERCISES

An important part of magical training, and one that is too often neglected, is the opening and development of the energy centers in the subtle bodies of the magician. These centers link the powers of the human microcosm to their sources in the macrocosm; to continue the electrical metaphor used in the last chapter, they serve as the connections through which current is drawn in ritual, and in most other kinds of magical work. The process of awakening and balancing these centers is thus central to the process of your development as a magician.

Any form of magical training develops the centers to some extent. Just as muscles are strengthened by using them, the less physical parts of the self are energized and developed through magical practice involving them. The ordinary disciplines of magical training, then, will bring about the development of the centers in time. If this phase of training is undertaken deliberately, on the other hand, the same work can be accomplished more quickly and, depending on the specific magical practices being performed, in a more balanced way.

There has been a great deal of unnecessary confusion about these centers among Western occultists in the last century or so. Much of this came about because several Western esoteric groups borrowed and actively promoted the Hindu system of seven spinal vortices, or *chakras*, as the only valid way of thinking about subtle-body centers. Connected with this is the common habit of identifying the goal of all mystical work with the raising of *kundalini*—the coiled energy at the base of the spine—through the chakras to the "thousand-petaled lotus" center at the crown of the head.

This system is a perfectly valid one, and it can certainly be adapted successfully for use in Western magic. At the same time, despite the claims of some of its more fervent partisans, it's not the only game in town. There are esoteric systems that use only one energy center; there are others that use as many as several hundred. Certain areas of the body—the navel, the region around the heart, the crown of the head—tend to be fairly common sites for energy center development, but no one area is used by all systems, and specific locations within these areas vary widely.

Nor is the so-called "kundalini experience" the only possible result of the awakening of these centers. It does happen, and not only to those who set out to make it happen; still, it's only one of a whole range of possible transformative experiences that can result from this particular kind of spiritual practice.

It may be useful here to turn to a different perspective on these matters. Some magical writings from the Renaissance liken the human body to the string of a musical instrument, which can be pressed against the fretboard at different places to make different notes. No one combination of these notes is the right one for every kind of music; major scales, minor scales, blues scales, and the traditional modes each use some of the possible notes and leave others out.

In the same way, the energies coursing through the human body can be focused or "fretted" at many different points, and each combination of points has different uses and different effects. If the "music" you have in mind comes from Oriental martial-arts traditions, the energy center you'll want to use is the *hara* or *tan t'ien* two inches below the navel; if you would rather practice Tantra, it works better to tune the instrument of yourself to what might be called the "chakra scale." If your goal is the mastery of the Cabalistic magic of the Golden Dawn, you'll want to tune to a different set of notes: the five centers of the Middle Pillar.

The Spheres of the Middle Pillar

These centers correspond to the four Spheres on the central axis of the Tree of Life, along with Daath, the quasi-Sphere between Kether and Tiphareth. All, appropriately enough, are located on the midline of the body. Unlike the chakras, which are related to the major nerve plexi and ductless glands, these centers are not associated with a particular set of organs; their placement is determined by subtler factors.

The physical body is more than a lump of meat, as medical science is beginning, however reluctantly, to admit. Its more obvious structures— organs, bones, flesh—are in many ways governed by a deeper structure of rhythms and vibratory movements. Blood, lymph, cerebrospinal fluid, and other parts of the body pulse to a whole series of harmonic patterns that can be felt by anyone willing to become still enough to perceive them; these patterns have focal points, and as we saw in Chapter 3, the most important of these are along the midline of the body at the stations of the Middle Pillar.

At the etheric level, the level of life energy, similar factors apply. The human etheric body is very nearly as complicated as the physical one, and its own patterns of flow and vibration—the meridians of Oriental medicine—focus on a series of etheric centers, the organs of the subtle body. Of these, according to the Golden Dawn teachings, five major centers are located on the physical body's midline, at the same places as the focal points of physical vibration.

This overlapping of centers makes these five locations points of con- nection between the physical and etheric levels of the body. That con- nection can be strengthened through the subtle effects of sound and breath, and it can also be extended up into the astral, mental, and spiritual levels by linking visualizations, abstract concepts, and Names of God with the centers. This same combination of methods is used in nearly every system of energy center work, Eastern and Western, and it is the key to a wide range of mystical and magical practices.

Each of the centers of the Middle Pillar, when activated by this kind of work, has certain functions deriving from its relationship to the Tree of Life and the levels of magical experience. These can be outlined as follows.

The first, or Kether, center is just above the crown of the head; it repre- sents the contact point between the individual self and unity—in theo- logical language, the presence of God at the highest level of the self. It corresponds to the spiritual level of experience, and its activation is connected to the awakening of the self to unity with all things, the highest phase of mystical attainment.

The second, or Daath, center is at the midpoint of the neck, and includes the organs of speech. It represents the contact point between the self and the essential patterns underlying the world we experience. The Daath center corresponds to the mental level of experience, and its activation is connected to the understanding of universal pattern and the expansion of awareness beyond the limits of space and time.

The third, or Tiphareth, center is at the heart. Here, too, there has been a certain amount of confusion, as the version of the Middle Pillar work most common in the magical community nowadays places this center several inches lower, at the solar plexus. Like the chakra system, this is entirely valid on its own terms. At the same time, different centers produce different effects, and as we'll show a little later in this chapter, the energies that focus at the heart center are of great importance in the major traditions of Western mysticism and occultism.

The Tiphareth center represents the contact point between the self and the realm of concrete consciousness, the realm in which most magical work takes place. It corresponds to the astral level of experience, and its activation is connected to self-knowledge, the awakening of compassion, and the ability to shape consciousness—one's own, as well as that of others—by the power of will.

The fourth, or Yesod, center is at the genitals. It represents the contact point between the self and the fundamental energies of life, the subtle forces that shape and unify the physical universe. It corresponds to the etheric level of experience, and its activation is connected to heightened vitality, the gift of healing, and the ability to consciously direct the life force in oneself and others.

The fifth, or Malkuth, center is at the soles of the feet. It represents the contact point between the self and the world of physical matter. It thus corresponds to the physical level of experience, and its activation is connected to the ability to bring magical forces to bear directly on matter.

The whole system is shown in Diagram 42 on page 161. The line connecting the centers is the Middle Pillar itself, the axis and main energy channel of the body. If you've performed any of the ritual work from the last chapter, this pattern may seem somewhat familiar, and it should: the vertical line of the cross in the Cabalistic Cross, with the sphere of light above and the image of Earth below, is another way of symbolizing the same channel of energies, and provides a different but

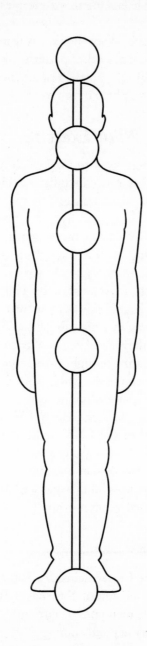

Diagram 42—
The Centers of the Middle Pillar

related way of shaping and balancing these energies in the various levels of the body.

This main channel, though, is not the only way in which energies pass from center to center. There are other patterns of linkage between the spheres of energy; as you'll see shortly, one of these has a particularly important role to play in this phase of the work.

The Lesser Middle Pillar Exercise

The simplest of the practices used to awaken these centers in Golden Dawn magic is called the Lesser Middle Pillar exercise. This is a common part of many systems of magical training. The version of this exercise in general use at present was developed from the teachings of one of the Golden Dawn's successor Orders by Israel Regardie, one of this century's major occultists. In working out his version of the exercise, Regardie made several changes in the work, some of them far from minor.

One of these changes—the movement of the Tiphareth center from the heart to the solar plexus—has already been mentioned. Another equally significant change is the way in which Regardie's version circulates the energies of the Pillar once they have been awakened. Drawing on Jungian psychological thought, Regardie thought it best to restructure this Circulation of the Light to pass around the whole Sphere of Sensation in three different patterns. In the traditional method, by contrast, the Circulation followed one pattern linking the Tiphareth and Malkuth centers only.

None of these points makes Regardie's method worthless; it remains an effective way of opening and directing energy centers in the body. The traditional method, however, has certain possibilities for development that Regardie's method does not, possibilities that we'll be examining shortly.

A more traditionally based version of the Middle Pillar exercise may be performed as follows.

First, perform the complete Lesser Banishing Ritual of the Pentagram.

Second, standing in the center of the space, facing east, with legs together and arms at sides, turn your attention to a point infinitely far above your head. Visualize the point shining with light, like a star. Next, drawing in a breath, visualize a stream of light descending from that point to the area just above your head, where it forms a sphere of intense white light about eight inches across. The bottom of the sphere is just above the crown of your head. Concentrate on the sphere, thinking of the first, or Kether, center and its functions, while you breathe in; on the outbreath, vibrate the Name AHIH (pronounced "eh-heh-yeh"). Repeat this process three more times, focusing on Kether on the inbreath, vibrating the Name on the outbreath. Try to make the vibration resonate within the sphere of light itself.

Third, with the next inbreath, bring the stream of light down to the middle of your throat, and there form another sphere of light of the same size, this one a soft gray color. Concentrate on it, thinking of the second, or Daath, center and its functions, while you breathe in slowly and deeply; on the outbreath, vibrate the Name YHVH ALHIM (pronounced "yeh-ho-wah ell-o-heem"). Repeat three times and try to make the vibration resonate in the sphere itself.

Fourth, in the same way, establish the golden sphere of Tiphareth at the level of the heart, and vibrate the Name YHVH ALVH VDAaTh ("yeh-ho-wah ell-o-ah vah da-ath") four times; the violet sphere of Yesod at the genitals, and vibrate the Name ShDI AL ChI ("shah-die ell chye") four times; and the black or dark green sphere of Malkuth at the soles of the feet, and vibrate the Name ADNI HARTz ("ah-dough-nye ha ah-retz") four times.

Fifth, pause, and then direct your attention upward again toward the Kether center above your head. Draw in a breath and visualize a shaft of brilliant light descending with the inbreath to the Tiphareth center at your heart; visualize the Tiphareth center shining more brightly as you breathe out. Repeat this process four times; on the last outbreath, the Tiphareth center should blaze like the sun.

Sixth, slowly draw a breath in, feeling the air pass through your nostrils and down your windpipe. Visualize it passing into the Tiphareth center at your heart and from there out to your left side, down the left flank and leg, to the Malkuth center at the feet. Hold the breath there for the same amount of time you took to breathe in, then breathe out at the same pace, visualizing the breath passing up the right leg and flank, into the Tiphareth center, and then up and out the windpipe and nostrils; hold the outbreath for the same amount of time. (It's helpful to use the Fourfold Breath during these four phases to get the rhythm.) Make the visualization of the moving breath as concrete as possible, so that you feel the path of the breath down and up again as though it were a physical movement. Repeat this whole process four times.

Seventh, pause, and perform the Cabalistic Cross. This completes the exercise.

This rite is the most important of the basic practices of Golden Dawn magic, and serious students of the tradition should perform it every day. For the beginning magician, there is no better way to spend fifteen minutes. The initial banishing ritual clears the space and helps bring the magician into a state of balance; not incidentally, it also offers an opportunity to practice this important ritual and its formula. The formulation of the centers of the Pillar follows. After this, energies are drawn into the system of centers and circulated in a special way, one designed to bring two of the centers—the Tiphareth center at the heart and the Malkuth center at the feet—into a new relationship. To understand the nature and purpose of that relationship, though, it will be necessary to look at the heart center and its potentials a little more closely.

The Way of the Heart

In many ways, this center has been—well, the heart, for lack of a better term—of Western culture since the latter emerged out of the chaos of the Dark Ages and the wreckage of the classical world. Cultures, like magical traditions, have their favorite energy centers; many of the cultures of East Asia, for example, locate the core of the self in the belly, and some of the ways these cultures differ from those of other parts of the world can be understood most clearly by comparing the subtle powers and functions of the navel area to those of other centers. In the West, by contrast, the heart was always considered the essential focus of the self until a kind of revolt of the brain-center at the time of the Scientific Revolution ushered in the ruinous split between head and heart that afflicts our culture at present.

The heart has also been central to Western spirituality, in both orthodox and esoteric forms. Catholic devotions to the Sacred Heart of Jesus are one manifestation of this; another is the potent system of meditative prayer called *hesychasm* practiced in Eastern Orthodox monasteries for centuries, in which controlled breathing and the constant repetition of a short prayer bring the awareness into focus at the heart center and open the door to mystical experience. In the occult traditions of the West, the role of the heart center has often been veiled by the use of symbolism as a way of concealment, but it can be clearly traced, especially in the Rosicrucian tradition of the late Renaissance, one of the major sources used by the founders of the Golden Dawn. The heart itself is one of the primary Rosicrucian symbols. Other images used constantly in the tradition—the heart identified with the Sun; the phoenix in flames; the pelican wounding its own breast; the central image of the Rose blooming on the Cross— are exact and powerful symbols of the experiences of energy and transformation that occur during the opening of the heart center.

These experiences vary somewhat from person to person, but typically begin with a sense of warmth in the heart region. Occasional at first, this gradually becomes more stable with time and further work, and grows in intensity as well. At the same time, balancing processes start to take place in the emotions and mind; they are usually not very pleasant, for the conscious self must awaken to full self-knowledge, and that generally involves coming to terms with a great many things one has tried very hard to avoid noticing!

This stage, the *nigredo* or "black phase" in the language of alchemy, eventually gives way to the *albedo* or "white phase," marked by clarity of mind and a change from the experience of heat to that of brilliant light radiating from the heart region. As the heart center reaches full activation, this phase gives way in turn to the *rubedo* or "red phase," in which the experience of light transforms into that of unity with the transcendent power most Western traditions call God, and the higher and lower phases of the self fuse into one, transforming the self on every level.

There are—it needs to be said at once—more ways than one to reach this last stage. Work with the heart center is one way out of many, even in the traditions of Western magic. Nor is it the end of the path of magic; in the language of Cabalistic theory, it accomplishes the opening of the Veil, but the passage across the Abyss still remains. At the same time, work aimed in this direction is perhaps the most useful of the transformative processes open to the Golden Dawn magician; it is highly effective, on the one hand, and relatively safe to use (even without the personal guidance of a teacher) on the other.

It is in this context, then, that the last phases of the Lesser Middle Pillar exercise can be understood. The energies of the higher levels of the macrocosm are brought into focus in the heart, and established there; this is the essential technique of the opening of the heart center. At this point, with the aid of ether drawn in with the breath, the energies of the heart center are circulated down to the Malkuth or ground center at the soles of the feet, anchoring them to the physical substance of the body and helping to stabilize the process by grounding it in the material realm. Cabalistic writings, using some of the traditional symbolism of Tiphareth and Malkuth, describe this process as the marriage of the Son and Daughter of Tetragrammaton, or of the King and his Bride. This process is repeated four times, and then the energy system of the whole body is rebalanced by the closing Cabalistic Cross.

The Vibratory Formula of the Middle Pillar

The patterns of energy the Middle Pillar exercise sets up in the magician's subtle body, as mentioned above, are crucial to the development of magical power and to the ability to shape the forces of the macrocosm. There's an even more direct application of the Middle Pillar formula to the work of the ritual magician. This is a technique called the Vibratory Formula of the Middle Pillar.

The Vibratory Formula is a method of invoking force through the vibration of a single Name in the context of the energy channels of the Middle Pillar. It is typically used in a ritual working in place of, or along with, the more standard methods of invoking force. It is done as follows.

———————

First, stand in the open position with your arms out to your sides. Then, as in the basic form of the Middle Pillar exercise, turn your attention toward a point of light infinitely far above your head and, holding that image, breathe in, visualizing a current of white light descending from above into your heart center. As you breathe out, visualize the Name of God you intend to invoke taking shape in Hebrew letters of white flame in your heart center, and speak the Name silently, imagining it sounding in the same place. Repeat this whole process until you've done it as many times as the symbolic number of the force you seek to invoke. This establishes what is called the Invoking Whirl in the heart.

Second, breathe in again, and be aware of the Name in your heart. Then, holding the breath, visualize the Name descending the Middle Pillar to the ground center at your feet; speak it silently there also, then bring it up again to the heart and out with the breath as you vibrate the Name aloud. At the same moment, make the Sign of the Enterer in the direction of the force you are invoking. Imagine the Name turning into a bolt of energy that shoots away into infinite distance.

Third, remain in the Sign of the Enterer until your focus begins to weaken. When this happens, make the Sign of Silence and breathe in, opening yourself to the returning current of energy. Visualize the energy in the form of colored light and allow it to fill your Sphere of Sensation. This establishes what is called the Expanding Whirl in the aura, and completes the technique.

In practice, the Vibratory Formula of the Middle Pillar is usually followed by the Four Revolutions of the Breath, which are done as follows:

Fourth, pause for a time, contemplating the force you have invoked, and lower your left hand. At this point, circulate the force with the breath, as in the Middle Pillar exercise: drawing it in with the inbreath to the heart, out to the left side, down the flank and leg to the ground center at the feet; holding it there with the breath; bringing it up the right side with the outbreath, back to the heart and out; holding it out with the breath; each phase taking the same amount of time. As in the Middle Pillar exercise, it's helpful to use the Fourfold Breath to establish the rhythm. Circulate the energy with the breath a total of four times.

This process allows the energy awakened by the Vibratory Formula of the Middle Pillar to be brought down fully into manifestation, using the energy pathways of the magician's own body as a channel. Together, these two techniques can bring through a much higher intensity of power than the standard methods of invocation, and they also help develop the energy centers of the subtle body, reinforcing the work done in the Middle Pillar exercise.

The Greater Middle Pillar Exercise

The two applications of the Middle Pillar formula covered above provide a fully functional way of beginning the process of opening the energy centers of the body, and they can be practiced for years with good effect. The Golden Dawn material, though, contains the outlines of a more powerful development of the same exercise, making use of certain additional techniques from the toolkit of Golden Dawn ritual and organizing the whole within the formula of the Neophyte Grade.

This exercise is one of the most intensive of all the methods of magical work we'll be examining in this book. It's recommended that at least two years of daily practice with the Lesser Exercise *in the version given in this book*—working with the heart center, in other words, rather than the solar plexus, and circulating the energy through the Tiphareth-Malkuth cycle—should be done before taking up the more advanced exercise on a daily basis. On the other hand, an occasional performance of the advanced exercise will strengthen the effect of the basic form, and help speed the development of the energy centers.

As mentioned above, this exercise is based on the formula of the Neophyte Grade, and many of the details of the process can be found in the Golden Dawn papers on that grade ritual. It is performed as follows.

———

First, perform the Lesser Banishing Ritual of the Pentagram.

Second, establish the five centers of the Middle Pillar exactly as in the second, third, and fourth parts of the Lesser Exercise, descending from Kether to Malkuth, vibrating the appropriate Name of God four times in each Sphere.

Third, turn your attention upward again to the point of light far above your head. Extend your arms to either side in the open position. Breathing in, visualize a shaft of white light streaming down from high above you into the heart center, where it forms the Name יהשוה, YHShVH, in white Hebrew letters. Vibrate the Name (pronouncing it "yeh-heh-shoo-ah") on the outbreath. Repeat this process, drawing down the light with the inbreath and vibrating with the outbreath, until you have vibrated the Name six times. This establishes the Invoking Whirl in the heart. The vibrations should be felt as though they echo outward to the ends of the universe.

Fourth, still holding your arms out to your sides in the open position, draw in a breath and visualize the echoes of the Name you have vibrated being drawn with it from all sides into the heart center. There, pronounce it once silently. Then, holding the breath, visualize the Name descending the Middle Pillar to the ground center at the soles of the feet, and pronounce it silently there.

Fifth, bring your arms up and forward, making the Sign of the Enterer, and as this is done bring the Name up to the heart center and out, sending it forward with the hands and the gaze. As you do this, vibrate the second form of the Name, YHVShH (pronounced "yeh-ho-wah-shah"), with all your strength; this need not be done loudly, but should involve maximum intensity and maximum focus. Hold the Sign for as long as you can maintain your mental focus on the Name, and then make the Sign of Silence to call the response. Remain still, and be aware of any returning flow of energy you may perceive; this may be slight in the early phases of work on this exercise. Allow the returning flow to fill your Sphere of Sensation; this establishes the Expanding Whirl in the aura.

Sixth, lower the left hand to the side, draw in energy from your aura with the breath and circulate it four times as you did the energy in the Lesser Exercise: from the nostrils to the heart center and down the left side of the body to the ground center on the inbreath; holding at the ground center; up the right side of the body to the heart center and back out through the nostrils with the outbreath; holding while focusing on the heart center. This should be done to the Fourfold Breath as before.

Seventh, direct the attention to the ground center. With the inbreath, visualize a shaft of green light (representing the energies of the Earth) rising up from the center of the Earth far below you to the ground center at your feet. With the outbreath, feel the earth energy establishing itself in that center. With the next inbreath, draw down a shaft of white light from far above your head and send it down the Middle Pillar to the Malkuth center, establishing it there on the outbreath; visualize the two energies in the ground center, white and green, blending together. This fusion is called the Lesser Conjunction.

Eighth, draw in more earth energy with the breath and circulate it four times: from deep within the earth to the ground center and up the right side of the body to the heart center on the inbreath; holding at the Tiphareth center; down the left side of the body to the Malkuth center and back out into the earth on the outbreath; holding while focusing on the ground center. This circulation should also be done to the Fourfold Breath.

Ninth, when these circulations are completed, draw a shaft of green earth energy with the inbreath straight up the Middle Pillar to the heart center, and establish it on the outbreath. Then draw down a shaft of white light from the Higher with the next inbreath, straight down the Middle Pillar to the heart center, and establish it on the outbreath. Then draw in the energy called by the Name YHVShH, which remains in the aura, through the nostrils to the heart center; on the inbreath, the three energies fuse into a center of golden light blazing like the Sun; this fusion of energies is called the Greater Conjunction. On the outbreath, vibrate both Names, YHShVH YHVShH, the inner and the outer, and visualize the golden light radiating out through the body, the Sphere of Sensation, and the universe. At the same time, the green earth energy sinks back to the ground center, while the descent of light from the Higher to the heart center continues.

Tenth, hold the awareness of the golden light at the heart center for a time. Then draw in energy from the aura with the inbreath, and circulate it in reverse four times: from the nostrils to the heart center, and then down the right side of the body to the ground center; hold it at the ground center; then circulate it up the left side of the body to the heart center, and back out through the nostrils; holding while focusing on the heart center. This should be done to the Fourfold Breath, as with the other circulations.

Eleventh, when this is completed, perform the Cabalistic Cross. This completes the exercise.

———

Like all the applications of the Neophyte formula, this exercise uses repeated patterns of circular movement as a means of bringing energies of lower and higher levels into harmony. Here, though, the magician's body itself becomes the ritual space in which the formula is enacted and the play of subtle energies takes place. Spiritual forces from the higher levels of the macrocosm and etheric substance from the etheric body of the Earth are drawn into the self, combined in an alchemy of energies, and used to energize and strengthen the corresponding energy centers of the microcosm.

CHAPTER 8

OPENING AND CLOSING

T HE RITUALS OF INVOKING AND BANISHING, and the exercises of the Middle Pillar, are the core training practices of Golden Dawn ceremonial work, and form the foundation on which the full-scale ceremonies of the tradition are built. Between these two levels is an intermediate kind of ritual work: rites in which the Pentagram and Hexagram Rituals are imbedded for working purposes, and in which the centers awakened in the Middle Pillar exercises are put to work in a variety of ways. There are a number of these intermediate rituals in the Golden Dawn tradition; the most common, most useful, and in many ways the most interesting of these are the Rituals of Opening and Closing.

A banishing ritual, as we've mentioned, clears a physical and symbolic space for ceremonial work; an invoking ritual calls power into that space. These two, alone, can be used to begin a magical working. A third element, though, has an important place in most major ceremonies: the building up of a framework and a pattern of energies that will provide context and background for the invoked power.

There are at least two ways to do this. The first way is to use ritual elements that deal specifically with the energies to be invoked; for example, Saturnian symbolism for a ritual using the energies traditionally assigned to Saturn. This is perfectly workable, but it requires a different rite for every one of the traditional symbolic categories. The second way, more subtle in its design, is to use a ritual structure that includes the entire magical image of the universe, with all its powers. This second approach provides the framework for a wide range of different symbolism in ceremonial work with just one ritual. It also, importantly, helps bring the invoked energies through in balance with the wider context of the energies of the universe.

The second approach is more common in magic in the Golden Dawn tradition, and is the one we'll be studying here. In the three Rituals of Opening and Closing, which are based on this pattern, the whole structure of the universe as understood by the Golden Dawn's Cabalistic philosophy is contained in a kind of outline form, organized around the framework of the formulae of the three degrees discussed earlier. The same principles that govern other applications of these formulae shape these ceremonies; here, though, the initiatory aspect of the three degrees plays a more important part. In point of fact, regular practice of these ceremonies will have much the same effect on the subtle bodies of the magician as actually passing through the initiation rituals on which the formulae are based.

The First Degree Ritual of Opening and Closing: Basic Form

This rite will require, along with the usual needs of ritual, an altar, a stick of incense in a holder, and a cup or goblet of water. It's traditional to bless the water before the ritual, using the rite for the consecration of Holy Water given in Chapter 9. The Ritual of Opening and Closing itself is performed as follows.

———————

First, standing at the west of the altar facing east, say: "Hekas, hekas esti bebeloi!" (These words form the ancient proclamation of the Mysteries, and mean "Begone, profane ones.") Then perform the Lesser Banishing Ritual of the Pentagram. The parts of this ritual usually done at the center—for instance, the Cabalistic Cross—should be done standing at the west of the altar.

Second, pause, and then take the cup of Water in both hands, raising it above the level of your head. Say: "And so therefore first that priest who governeth the works of Fire must sprinkle with the lustral waters of the loud-resounding Sea." Lower the cup, and take it to the eastern point of the space. With the cup, draw an equal-armed cross in the air to the east;

this should be about the same size, and in the same position, as the pentagram drawn in the banishing, and should be visualized in deep blue. Then dip the fingers of your left hand into the cup, and flick Water three times to the east.

Third, go around to the south—without tracing a circle around the arc, as is done in the Pentagram Ritual—and repeat the process in the south, tracing the cross and sprinkling the Water. Do the same to the west, and then to the north. Finally, return to the east, raise the cup high, and say, "I purify with Water." Return to the west side of the altar and put the cup back in its place.

Fourth, take the stick of incense from its holder and, holding it in both hands, raise it above the level of your head. Say: "And when, after all the phantoms are banished, thou shalt see that holy formless Fire which darts and flashes at the hidden depths of the universe, hear thou the voice of Fire." Lower the stick of incense and go to the east; trace an equal-armed cross, like the one you made with the cup, and wave the incense three times to the east. The cross should be visualized as brilliant red. Go around in the same way to south, west, and north, repeating the action, and then return to the east; raise the stick of incense high, and say, "I consecrate with Fire." Return to the altar and put the stick back in its holder.

Fifth, go around the left of the altar to the east, and then slowly circle clockwise around the space three times. As you circle, imagine yourself climbing a spiral stair, while the altar and its implements, the pentagrams and crosses traced around you, and the floor beneath you all rise with you. Each time you pass the eastern quarter of the space, including the first time, perform the Sign of the Enterer in the direction of your movement. As you reach the east at the end of the third circuit, imagine yourself reaching the top of the stair.

Sixth, return to the west side of the altar and face east. Make the Sign of the Enterer and say: "Holy art thou, Lord of the Universe." Repeat the Sign and say, "Holy art thou, whom nature has not formed." Repeat the Sign and say, "Holy art thou, the vast and the mighty one, Lord of the Light and of the Darkness." As you finish, make the Sign of Silence, timing it so that your finger reaches your lips as you say the word "darkness."

This completes the opening stage of the ritual; in a larger ceremony, the invoking ritual and the rest of the working follow. The closing stage of the ceremony is performed as follows.

First, perform the purification by Water and consecration by Fire again, exactly as in the second, third, and fourth parts of the opening phase.

Second, go around the right side of the altar to the east and slowly circle counterclockwise around the space three times. As you are circling, visualize yourself descending the spiral staircase you climbed in the opening, and see the altar and implements, the crosses and pentagrams, and the floor itself descending with you. Each time you pass the eastern quarter of the space, including the first time, make the Sign of Silence in the direction of your movement.

Third, at the end of the third circuit, return to the west side of the altar, face east, and extend your arms to your sides in the form of a cross. Say, "In the great Name of strength through sacrifice, YHShVH YHVShH (pronounced 'yeh-heh-shu-wah yeh-ho-wa-shah'), I now release any spirit that may have been imprisoned by this ceremony. Depart in peace unto your habitations, and peace be between us, now and in time to come."

Fourth, perform the Lesser Banishing Ritual of the Pentagram. This completes the ceremony.

———————

The symbolism of the Ritual of Opening and Closing sums up most of the major themes of Cabalistic thought in a skillfully woven pattern of images and movements. The three speeches included in the ritual are drawn from ancient sources, the first two from the *Chaldean Oracles*, a handbook of magic dating to Roman times, and the last from a Gnostic magical prayer.

The Lesser Ritual of the Pentagram, opening it, establishes the basic fourfold structure of space that is used in most Cabalistic ceremonies. The purification by Water and consecration by Fire that follow build on this, but they also do two other things.

First of all, these actions establish the equal-armed cross upon the pentagram; these two symbols, which represent macrocosm and microcosm, are resolved by the "six-rayed star" or hexagram already established in the banishing ritual. The magician, standing at the center of the ritual space, is symbolically—and practically—the point of balance between macrocosm and microcosm, the place where these two realms enter into harmony.

Secondly, the purification and consecration link the forces of the ritual to the great polarities of the macrocosm, represented by Fire and Water. These polarized forces are brought into relation with the structure of ritual space already established in such a way that the center of the space becomes the natural point of balance. Here again, during the core elements of the ritual, the magician is standing at the place of harmony, uniting both sides of the balance.

Once the space has been purified and consecrated, the magician circles around the altar three times with the sun. Like all circumambulations, these interact with the subtle energies of the Earth, again linking the ritual with the forces of the macrocosm. The three circumambulations also have a specific function in terms of the First Degree formula, as explained in an earlier chapter. The Sign of the Enterer is used here in order to project the magician's own energy along the course of the circumambulation.

The final phase of the Ritual of Opening is the Gnostic invocation of God as Lord of all things—"of the Light and of the Darkness." The point to this is twofold. On the one hand, the magician recognizes the existence of a Power that resolves all polarities eternally, a Power in which all lesser powers participate. On the other hand, the magician identifies his or her own acts in ritual space with the actions of that Power in the universe as a whole; like God, the magician stands at the meeting place of contending forces, and the pattern of balance that structures ritual space is a model and a reflection of the eternal pattern of balance in the mind of the Infinite.

The Ritual of Closing is essentially the same as that of Opening. The same patterns of purification and consecration are used in order to confirm the symbolic balance of the space, and of the acts performed within it. The reverse circumambulation, against the Sun, is used so that energy is dispersed rather than concentrated, and the Sign of Silence helps the magician absorb the energies he or she projected in the opening. Finally, the spiritual forces of the macrocosm that were summoned in the ritual are commanded to depart and are then banished, so that ritual space is resolved into ordinary space. The same themes of fourfold orientation, of polarity and its resolution, and of the interplay between macrocosm and microcosm, are repeated in the Closing, again formulating the most basic elements of the magical universe.

The Ritual of Opening and Closing can be used as an exercise on its own; in fact, it should be practiced in this manner a number of times before you attempt to use it in even the most minor ceremony. It provides a useful bridge between the simpler ritual forms shown in, for example, the Pentagram ritual, and the more advanced ceremonies of practical magic that will be explored in the following chapters.

The First Degree Ritual of Opening and Closing: Expanded Form

The First Degree Ritual of Opening and Closing also has certain links to the Elemental Grades of the Golden Dawn tradition, the four ceremonies that open the powers and realms of the four elements to the initiate and form the bridge between the First and Second Degrees. The Grade ceremonies delve much more deeply into the traditional symbolism of the Cabala than the Neophyte ceremony does, and the texts and images they use may seem strange to the modern magician; nevertheless, these are well worth using, as even very little practical experience will show. In ceremonies that work with the elemental powers, it can sometimes be useful to incorporate the symbolism of these Grades into the opening and closing ritual; at the same time, the ritual expanded in this way makes a valuable practice for developing ritual skill and carrying on the work of self-initiation.

This expanded ritual has the same requirements as the ordinary First Degree Opening and Closing. It is performed as follows.

First, standing at the west of the altar facing east, say: "Hekas, hekas esti bebeloi!" Then perform the Lesser Banishing Ritual of the Pentagram, followed by the Lesser Banishing Ritual of the Hexagram.

Second, perform the purification by Water as before, in the four quarters of the space, and return to the altar.

Third, perform the consecration by Fire as before, in the four quarters of the space, and return to the altar.

Fourth, go to the east. With the first two fingers of your right hand, draw an invoking pentagram of Air. Say: "And the Elohim said, 'Let us make Adam in our image, after our likeness, and let them have dominion over the birds of the Air.'" Make the Sign of Air, and vibrate the Name YHVH (pronounced "yeh-ho-wah"). Say: "In the Great Name that ruleth over the element of Air; in the name of Raphael, great Archangel of Air; and in the sign of the head of the Man—spirits of Air, adore your Creator."

Fifth, go to the south and draw an invoking pentagram of Fire. Say: "And the Elohim said, 'Let us make Adam in our image, after our like-ness, and let them have dominion over the beasts of the field.'" Make the Sign of Fire, and vibrate the Name ALHIM (pronounced "ell-oh-heem"). Say: "In the Great Name that ruleth over the element of Fire; in the name of Michael, great Archangel of Fire; and in the sign of the head of the Lion spirits of Fire, adore your Creator."

Sixth, go to the west and draw an invoking pentagram of Water. Say: "And the Elohim said, 'Let us make Adam in our image, after our like-ness, and let them have dominion over the fishes of the sea.'" Make the Sign of Water, and vibrate the Name AL (pronounced "ell"). Say: "In the Great Name that ruleth over the element of Water; and in the name of Gabriel, great Archangel of Water; and in the sign of the head of the Eagle—spirits of Water, adore your Creator."

Seventh, go to the north and draw an invoking pentagram of Earth. Say: "And the Elohim said, 'Let us make Adam in our image, after our likeness and let them have dominion over every creeping thing that creepeth on the Earth.'" Make the Sign of Earth, and vibrate the Name ADNI (pronounced "ah-dough-nye"). Say: "In the Great Name which ruleth over the element of Earth; and in the name of Auriel, great Archangel of Earth; and in the sign of the head of the Ox—spirits of Earth, adore your Creator." Go around to the east, and then return to the west side of the altar and face east.

Eighth, go around the left of the altar to the east, and then slowly cir-cumambulate clockwise three times, visualizing yourself climbing a spiral stair as before, and making the Sign of the Enterer each time you pass the east. Finishing, return to the west side of the altar.

Ninth, look up and to the east. Make the Sign of the Enterer, saying: "Holy art thou, Lord of the Universe." Make the same Sign again, say-ing: "Holy art thou, whom nature has not formed." Make the Sign a third time, saying: "Holy art thou, the vast and the mighty one, Lord of the Light and of the Darkness." At the word "darkness" make the Sign of Silence.

This completes the opening phase of the ritual. The closing phase is performed as follows:

First, perform the purification by Water and consecration by Fire, exactly as in the second and third parts of the opening.

Second, go around the right side of the altar to the east, and slowly circumambulate counterclockwise three times, visualizing yourself descending the spiral staircase you climbed in the opening, and making the Sign of Silence each time you pass the east. Finishing, return to the west side of the altar and face east.

Third, go to the east. Say: "Tetragrammaton, Lord of Air, blessed be thy Name to countless ages." Make the Sign of Air, and vibrate the Name YHVH. Say: "Let us rehearse the prayer of the sylphs, or Air spirits.

"Spirit of life! Spirit of wisdom! Whose breath giveth forth and withdraweth the form of all things; thou, before whom the form of all beings is like a shadow which changeth, and a vapor which passeth; thou who mountest upon the clouds and walkest upon the wings of the wind; thou who breathest forth thy breath, and endless space is peopled; thou who drawest in thy breath, and all that cometh from thee, returneth unto thee.

"Ceaseless motion in eternal stability, be thou eternally blessed! We praise thee and we bless thee in the changeless empire of created light, of shades, of reflections, and of images, and we aspire without cessation to thy immutable and imperishable brilliance.

"Let the ray of thy intelligence and the warmth of thy love penetrate even unto us! Then the volatile shall be fixed; the shadow shall be a body; the spirit of Air shall be a soul; the dream shall be a thought. And no more shall we be swept away by the tempest, but we shall hold the bridles of the winged steeds of dawn, and we shall direct the course of the evening breeze to fly before thee.

"O spirit of spirits! O eternal soul of souls! O imperishable breath of life! O creative sigh! O mouth which breathest forth and withdrawest the life of all beings, in the flux and reflux of thine eternal Word, which is the divine ocean of spirit and of truth."

Draw a banishing pentagram of Air, and say: "Depart in peace unto your habitations. May the blessing of Tetragrammaton rest with you, and peace be between us."

Fourth, go to the south. Say: "Elohim, Lord of Fire, blessed be thy Name to countless ages." Make the Sign of Fire, and vibrate the Name ALHIM. Say: "Let us rehearse the prayer of the salamanders, or Fire spirits.

"Immortal, eternal, ineffable, and uncreated father of all, borne upon the chariot of worlds which ever roll in caseless motion; ruler over the ethereal vastness where the throne of thy power is raised, from the summit of which thine eyes behold all, and thy pure and holy ears hear all—help us, thy children, whom thou hast loved since the birth of the ages of time. Thy majesty, golden, vast, and eternal, shineth above the heaven of stars. Above them art thou exalted.

"O thou flashing Fire, there thou illuminatest all things with thine insupportable glory, whence flow the ceaseless streams of splendor which nourisheth thine infinite spirit. This infinite spirit nourisheth all, and maketh that inexhaustible treasure of generation which ever encompasseth thee, replete with the numberless forms wherewith thou hast filled it from the beginning. From this spirit arise those most holy kings who are around thy throne and who compose thy court.

"O universal father, one and alone! Father alike of immortals and mortals. Thou hast specially created powers similar unto thy thought eternal and to thy venerable essence. Thou hast established them above the angels who announce thy will to the world!

"Lastly, thou hast created us as a third order in our elemental empire. There our continual exercise is to praise and adore thy desires; there we ceaselessly burn in eternal aspiration unto thee. O father! O mother of mothers! O archetype eternal of maternity and love! O son, flower of all sons! Form of all forms! Soul, spirit, harmony, and numeral of all things!"

Draw a banishing pentagram of Fire. Say: "Depart in peace unto your habitations. May the blessing of Elohim rest with you, and peace be between us."

Fifth, go to the West. Say: "El, Lord of Water. Blessed be thy Name unto the countless ages." Make the Sign of Water, and vibrate the Name AL. Say: "Let us rehearse the prayer of the undines, or water spirits.

"Terrible king of the sea, thou who holdest the keys of the cataracts of heaven, and who holdest the subterranean waters in the cavernous hollows of Earth; king of the deluge and of the rains of spring; thou who openest the sources of the rivers and of the fountains; thou who commandest moisture, which is the blood of the Earth, to become the sap of the plants: we adore thee and we invoke thee. Speak to us, thy mobile and changeful creatures, in the great tempests and we shall tremble before thee. Speak to us also in the murmur of the limpid waters and we shall desire thy love.

"O vastness wherein all the rivers of being seek to lose themselves—which renew themselves ever in thee! O thou ocean of infinite perfection! O height which reflectest thyself in the depth! O depth which exhalest into the height! Lead us into the true life, through intelligence, through love! Lead us into immortality through sacrifice, that we may be found worthy to offer one day unto thee, the water, the blood, and the tears for the remission of sins."

Draw a banishing pentagram of Water. Say: "Depart in peace unto your habitations. May the blessing of El rest with you, and peace be between us."

Sixth, go to the North. Say: "Adonai, Lord of Earth. Blessed be thy name unto the countless ages." Make the Sign of Earth and vibrate the Name ADNI. Say: "Let us rehearse the prayer of the gnomes, or Earth spirits.

"O invisible king who, taking the Earth for foundation, didst hollow its depths to fill them with thy almighty power; thou whose name shaketh the arches of the world, thou who causest the seven metals to flow in the veins of the rocks, king of the seven lights, rewarder of the subterranean workers, lead us into the desirable air and into the realm of splendor. We watch and we labor unceasingly, we seek and we hope, by the twelve stones of the holy city, by the buried talismans, by the axis of the lodestone which passes through the center of the Earth—O Lord, O Lord, O Lord! Have pity upon those who suffer. Expand our hearts, unbind and upraise our minds, enlarge our natures.

"O stability and motion! O darkness veiled in brilliance! O day clothed in night! O master who never dost withhold the wages of thy workmen! O silver whiteness! O golden splendor! O crown of living and harmonious diamond! Thou who wearest the heavens upon thy finger like a ring of sapphire! Thou who hidest beneath the Earth, in the kingdom of gems, the marvelous seed of the stars! Live, reign, and be thou the eternal dispenser of the treasures whereof thou hast made us the wardens."

Draw a banishing pentagram of Earth. Say: "Depart in peace unto your habitations. May the blessing of Adonai rest with you, and peace be between us."

Seventh, go around to the east, and then return to the altar. Say: "I now release any spirit who may have been imprisoned by this ceremony.

Depart in peace unto your habitations, and peace be between us now and in time to come."

Eighth, perform the Lesser Banishing Ritual of the Hexagram, and then the Lesser Banishing Ritual of the Pentagram. This completes the ceremony.

———————

The rather baroque language used in this expansion of the Ritual of Opening and Closing comes, like much of the traditional material used in Golden Dawn ceremonies, from a wide range of sources. The biblical passages in the Opening are held, in Cabalistic tradition, to proclaim the right of the magician to command the spirits of the elements, and the invocation that follows uses the Names of God, archangels, and Kerubic or astrological emblems—Aquarius the Man, Leo the Lion, three-formed Scorpio with the Eagle as its highest aspect, and Taurus the Ox—in a fairly straightforward manner.

The elemental prayers in the Closing are seen as expressions of the elements themselves; speaking them, the magician gives voice to the aspirations of matter and takes his or her place as the bond between heaven and earth, spirit and matter. While they make for a somewhat longer ritual, they strengthen the balancing and harmonizing effect of the whole rite and should not be neglected.

A Magical Eucharist

The fully expanded form of the First Degree Ritual of Opening and Closing is a useful ceremony in its own right for personal spiritual development; the work of balancing the elements in ritual space leads, with practice, to the balancing of the elements within the self. This effect can be heightened by including a rite based on the formula of the Eucharist between the opening and closing phases.

Best known, perhaps, in its Catholic form, the formula of the Eucharist is one used in many traditions around the world. In it, food and drink are consecrated by the descent of a spiritual force, and then consumed by the participants in the rite. As what is eaten becomes part of the body, so the invoked force within the consecrated food and drink is absorbed into the body and can catalyze deep transformations at all levels, including that of the physical body itself.

In the Golden Dawn tradition, a eucharistic rite formed part of every performance of the Neophyte Grade and the Ceremony of the Equinox. This rite, which we'll be using here, makes use of the symbolism and energies of the four elements. To perform it, you'll need a cup partly full of wine, a plate with a small piece of bread and some salt, a rose, and a red lamp or votive candle, as well as the other requirements for the First Degree Ritual of Opening and Closing. Either the basic or the expanded form of the ceremony may be augmented in this way, although the elemental symbolism of the expanded form has a stronger effect. The rose should be at the east of the altar, the lamp at the south, the wine at the west, and the bread and salt at the north.

In Golden Dawn ritual, this rite took place as the final act of the closing ceremony after the four elements of the eucharist had absorbed the full force of the ritual working. In individual work, it's best to make the eucharistic work the center of a ceremony of its own, and to begin it just after the opening is completed. It is performed as follows.

———————

First, standing at the west of the altar and facing east, raise your hands above the altar, palms down and fingers outspread in a gesture of blessing. Say:

"For Osiris Onnophris, who is found perfect before the Gods, hath said: These are the elements of my body, perfected through suffering, glorified through trial. For the scent of the dying Rose is as the sigh of my suffering; and the flaming Fire is as the energy of mine undaunted will; and the cup of Wine is as the pouring out of the blood of my heart, sacrificed unto regeneration, unto the newer life; and the Bread and Salt are as the foundations of my body, which I destroy that they may be renewed.

"For I am Osiris triumphant, Osiris Onnophris, the Justified; I am he who is clothed with the body of flesh, but in whom is the spirit of the great Gods. I am the Lord of life, triumphant over death. He who partaketh with me shall arise with me. I am the manifestor in matter of those whose abode is the invisible; I am purified; I stand upon the universe; I am its reconciler with the eternal Gods. I am the perfector of matter, and without me, the Universe is not."

Second, lower your hands, and then lift up the rose. Say: "I therefore invite all beings here present to inhale with me the perfume of this rose, as a symbol of Air." Smell the rose and return it to its place. Lift up the lamp. "To feel with me the warmth of this sacred Fire." Pass your hand over it, and then return it to its place. Lift up the plate with bread and salt. "To taste with me this bread and salt, as types of earth." Dip the bread in the salt, and eat, then return the plate to its place. Lift up the cup of wine. "And to drink with me this wine, the emblem of Water." Drink, then return the cup to its place.

Third, say: "May that which we have partaken maintain us in our search for the quintessence, the Stone of the Philosophers: true wisdom, perfect happiness, the *summum bonum*." Pause, and then proceed with the Closing.

———

Here the symbols of the elements are identified with the human body as well as the elements, and related to the symbolism of Tiphareth, which is both the Sun and the essence of the individual self, and which is represented by a symbolism combining the imagery of self-sacrifice and transcendent attainment. The words of Osiris in the prayer of consecration also define, fairly exactly, the magical understanding of the inner nature of every human being. Also suggested here is the transformation of the self on every level, which is the goal of Golden Dawn magic, and which is fostered as well as symbolized by the Eucharistic ceremony.

The Second Degree Ritual of Opening and Closing

In workings based on the Second Degree formula, the context for magic is defined in somewhat different terms. Here, as we've seen, the vertical dimension enters into the picture and the play of energies in ritual becomes the basis for movement from a lower level to a higher one.

This ritual has the same requirements as the First Degree Opening and Closing, plus a set of symbols for the four elements. A set of elemental working tools, made and consecrated as described in the next chapter, can be used for this purpose, but simpler objects will serve if these are not available: a lamp or votive candle for Fire, a cup for Water, a folding fan or a flower for Air, and a stone for Earth might be one approach. These are placed on the altar in their proper directions. The cup and incense for purifying and consecrating the space should be separate from these symbols of the elements, and should be placed in the center of the altar.

The ritual is performed as follows.

———————

First, standing at the west of the altar facing east, say: "Hekas, hekas esti bebeloi!" Then perform the Lesser Banishing Ritual of the Pentagram, followed by the Lesser Banishing Ritual of the Hexagram, ending west of the Altar facing east.

Second, perform the purification by Water and Consecration by Fire, exactly as in the First Degree opening. When this is done, stand at the west of the altar facing east; make the Sign of the Enterer toward the east, followed by the Sign of Silence. Say: "The light shineth in darkness, but the darkness comprehendeth it not. The Dukes of Edom ruled in Chaos, lords of unbalanced force. By the equated forces of the four elements, banished be the power of the Dukes of Edom, and let the power of the cross of the elements be established."

Third, perform the Greater Banishing Ritual of the Pentagram of Spirit, beginning and ending west of the Altar facing east.

Fourth, say clearly and slowly: "Peh. Resh. Kaph. Tau. The Word is Paroketh, which is the Veil of the Sanctuary." Make the Sign of the Rending of the Veil, and then say: "In and by that Word, I open the Veil." Then perform the Cabalistic Cross.

Fifth, go to the east of the altar, take up the symbol of Air, and go to the eastern quarter of the space. Raise the symbol high, and then trace an invoking pentagram of Air with it. Hold the symbol at the center of the pentagram and vibrate YHVH (pronounced "yeh-ho-wah"). Say: "By the Great Holy Name which governs the kingdoms of the East, I invoke ye, ye angels and spirits of Air."

Sixth, return the symbol of Air to the east of the altar; take the symbol of Fire from the south of the altar and go to the southern quarter of the space. Repeat the invocation of the last step, substituting the Name ALHIM (pronounced "ell-oh-heem") and the words "south" and "fire" where appropriate. Return the symbol of Fire to the altar. In the same way, invoke the angels and spirits of Water in the west by the Name AL (pronounced "ell"), and those of Earth in the north by the Name ADNI (pronounced "ah-dough-nye").

Seventh, return to the west of the altar and face east. Trace the active invoking pentagram of Spirit over the altar, and vibrate the Name AHIH (pronounced "eh-heh-yeh"); then trace the passive invoking pentagram of Spirit in the same place and vibrate the Name AGLA (pronounced "ah-geh-lah"). Say: "By the Great Holy Names which govern the kingdoms of the Unseen, I invoke ye, ye angels and spirits of Spirit."

Eighth, return to the west of the altar, face east, and say:

"Holy art thou, Lord of the Universe. Holy art thou, whom Nature hath not formed. Holy art thou, the vast and the mighty one, Lord of the Light and of the Darkness."

As in the First Degree Opening, make the Sign of the Enterer to the East each time you say "Holy art thou," and make the Sign of Silence at the word "Darkness."

This completes the Opening. The Closing is performed as follows.

First, say clearly and slowly: "Peh. Resh. Kaph. Tau. The Word is Paroketh, which is the Veil of the Tabernacle." Make the Sign of the Closing of the Veil, and then say: "In and by that Word, I close the Veil."

Second, go to the east of the altar, take up the symbol of Air, and go to the eastern quarter of the space. Raise the symbol high, and vibrate the Name YHVH. Say: "By the Great Holy Name which governs the kingdoms of the East, I release ye, ye angels and spirits of Air. Depart to your habitations in peace, and peace be between us." Then trace the banishing pentagram of Air with the symbol of Air.

Third, return the symbol of Air to the east of the altar; take the symbol of Fire from the south of the altar and go to the southern quarter of the space. Repeat the words and actions of the last step, substituting the Name ALHIM and the words "south" and "fire" where appropriate. Return the symbol of Fire to the altar. In the same way, banish the angels and spirits of Water in the west by the Name AL, and those of Earth in the north by the Name ADNI.

Fourth, return to the west of the altar and face east. Vibrate the Names AHIH and AGLA, and say: "By the Great Holy Names which govern the kingdoms of the Unseen, I release ye, ye angels and spirits of Spirit. Depart to your habitations in peace, and peace be between us." Then trace both banishing pentagrams of Spirit.

Fifth, say: "In the great Name of strength through sacrifice, YHShVH YHVShH (pronounced "yeh-heh-shu-ah yeh-ho-wah-shah"), I now set free any spirits who may have been imprisoned by this ceremony. Spirits of the five elements, adore your Creator!"

Sixth, purify with Water and consecrate with Fire as in the Opening.

Seventh, perform the Lesser Banishing Rituals of the Hexagram and Pentagram. This completes the ritual.

The Opening phase of this ritual is a good deal more complex symbolically than most of the rituals we've explored so far. Symbols from Cabalistic mythology—the Dukes of Edom, who represent the *Qlippoth* or Negative Powers, the primal worlds of unbalanced force that are said to have existed before the creation of the universe—appear here as images of the unruly energies that are to be balanced, transformed, and sublimated through the Second Degree formula. The "cross of the elements" referred to a little later refers, among other things, to the four letters of the Tetragrammaton, the great creative Name by which the universe was and is symbolically created.

The creation of the world, in fact, is the core symbolism of this ritual, and the reason for this is not hard to find. In the Cabala, the traditional philosophy of Western magic, the universe comes into being out of unity and returns to unity, in a cycle as vast as all of time and as minute as the space between one moment and the next. This root in unity is also the foundation of balance—it is the fact that "all things are from one, by the meditation of one," as the Emerald Tablet puts it, that makes it possible for different things to be brought together into harmony with each other.

At the same time, this potential for balance is just a potential until it is brought into manifestation by way of a conscious act. The mythology of the Cabala represents this as the defeat of the Dukes of Edom by the power of the Tetragrammaton, the "breaking forth of the light" that brought our universe into being. That same symbolism governs the Second Degree Opening, from the initial polarity between light and darkness, through the opening of the Veil between levels, to the invocation and establishment of the elemental powers in an ordered array.

Another significant feature of the ritual is the role of Spirit, the fifth of the elements, as a balancing force uniting the other four. In one of its senses, Spirit simply means the whole matrix of powers on levels above any particular level being considered, and the connection of this symbolism to the Second Degree formula is clear. The pentagrams and Names assigned to Spirit help focus this symbolism in the ritual.

It's worth noting, finally, that some of the basic symbolism of the First Degree plays a part in this Second Degree Opening, where one might expect it—at the beginning. The purification by Water and consecration by Fire were not used in the Golden Dawn's Portal ritual, but because of their positive effects, they should not be neglected in personal ritual practice. The Signs of Entering and Silence, on the other hand, do appear in the Portal ritual at this point, and serve—in a wide range of magical applications as well as in initiation—to link the work of this Degree with that of the one before it.

The Closing portion of this ritual, in contrast to the complexities of the Opening, is a relatively straightforward banishing of the forces invoked earlier in the ceremony. The constant focus on balance during the Opening has a payoff of sorts at this point; where the momentum generated by the First Degree opening has to be carefully neutralized to keep it from influencing everything in reach, the balance fostered by the Second Degree has far less potential for unintended effects.

The Third Degree Ritual of Opening and Closing

Like the formulae of the First and Second Degrees, the Third Degree formula gives rise to a ritual method for opening and closing. Roughly the first half of this method, under the title of "The Watchtower Ritual," has been used fairly widely by magicians in and out of the Golden Dawn tradition for some years. Like so many other treasures of the Golden Dawn, the complete method has been largely neglected.

One of the reasons behind this particular act of neglect is that the second half of the Third Degree Opening, as it was practiced in the initiation ceremonies of the Golden Dawn, focused on the specific structure and symbolism of the Vault of Christian Rosencreutz, the heart (in several senses) of the Order's Adeptus Minor ceremony. In Golden Dawn practice, the actual opening ceremony was done once a year, or when a Vault needed to be set up after a period in storage; it remained open and in use for various magical activities until, and unless, it had to be taken down or moved.

This allowed for an enormous intensity of energy to be gathered and used by the adepts of the Order. A full-scale Vault made to the Order's specifications, though, would be an appallingly difficult project for most magicians nowadays, even given the space necessary to store one and set it up; as a result there has been little interest in a ritual that requires one.

Here again, a too-concrete approach to the Golden Dawn's traditions has had its usual effect. The formula of the Third Degree requires the use of *some* specific symbolism, and this is as true in the Rituals of Opening and Closing as it is elsewhere. Still, that symbolism can be based on whatever the details of any specific magical working require; it does not have to duplicate the Order's Vault imagery, or even refer to the Vault at all, as long as it harmonizes with the core purpose of the Third Degree formula—regeneration through the descent of energies from higher levels to lower ones. The following Third Degree Ritual of Opening and Closing has been designed with this sort of flexibility in mind.

In order to make use of this ritual, you'll need to prepare yourself by making sure you have a thorough grasp of the symbolism of the working you have in mind—of the element in an elemental working, the planet in a planetary working, and so on. A written list set unobtrusively on the altar is a good idea until you've gained some familiarity with the ritual, and with magical symbolism as well. When this ritual is used to open and close a ceremony for the consecration of a working tool, a talisman, or some other physical object, every symbol on the object and every correspondence relating to it should be included on the list.

In terms of physical requirements, you will need the same things as in the Second Degree Opening and Closing: an altar, a cup of water, a stick of incense in a holder, and a set of elemental symbols or working tools, as well as the basic requirements of ritual. The elemental symbols are placed on the altar in their terrestrial directions, with the incense and cup in the center. The ritual itself is performed as follows.

———————

First, standing at the west of the altar facing east, say: "Hekas, hekas esti bebeloi!" Then perform the Lesser Banishing Ritual of the Pentagram, followed by the Lesser Banishing Ritual of the Hexagram, ending west of the altar facing east. Then perform the purification with Water and consecration with Fire, as in the First and Second Degree Openings, but in silence.

Second, go to the south of the altar and take up the elemental symbol of Fire. Go to the south of the space and circumambulate clockwise once, saying: "And when, after all the phantoms are banished, thou shalt see that holy and formless Fire, that Fire which darts and flashes through the hidden depths of the universe, hear thou the voice of Fire." Returning to the south at the end of the circumambulation, face south. Vibrate the Name ALHIM (pronounced "ell-o-heem") and trace the invoking pentagram of Fire with the symbol of Fire. Then say: "In the Name which governeth all the realms of Fire, I summon ye, ye angels and spirits of the south."

Third, replace the symbol of Fire on the south of the altar; go to the west of the altar and take up the symbol of Water. Go to the west of the space, and circumambulate clockwise once, saying: "So therefore first the priest who governeth the works of Fire must sprinkle with the lustral Water of the loud-resounding sea." Returning to the west at the end of the circumambulation, face west. Vibrate the Name AL (pronounced "ell") and trace the invoking pentagram of Water with the symbol. Then say: "In the Name which governeth all the realms of Water, I summon ye, ye angels and spirits of the west."

Fourth, return the symbol of Water to the west of the altar; go to the east of the altar and take up the elemental symbol of Air. Go to the east of the space and circumambulate clockwise once, saying: "Such a Fire existeth extending through the rushings of Air, or even a Fire formless whence cometh the image of a voice, or even a flashing light, abounding, revolving, whirling forth, crying aloud." Returning to the east at the end of the circumambulation, face east. Vibrate the Name YHVH and trace the invoking pentagram of Air with the symbol of Air. Then say: "In the Name which governeth all the realms of Air, I summon ye, ye angels and spirits of the east."

Fifth, return the symbol of Air to the east of the altar; go to the north of the altar, and take up the elemental symbol of Earth. Go to the north of the space and circumambulate clockwise once, saying: "Stoop not down into that darkly splendid world wherein lieth continually a faithless depth and Hades wrapped in gloom, delighting in unintelligible images, precipitous, winding, a black ever-rolling abyss, ever espousing a body unluminous, formless, and void." Returning to the north at the end of the circumambulation, face north. Vibrate the Name ADNI (pronounced "ah-dough-nye") and trace the invoking pentagram of Earth with the symbol of Earth. Then say: "In the Name which governeth all the realms of Earth, I summon ye, ye angels and spirits of the north."

Sixth, return the symbol of Earth to the north of the altar, and return to the west of the altar, facing east. Take up the incense, vibrate the Name AHIH (pronounced "eh-heh-yeh"), and trace the active invoking pentagram of Spirit; then vibrate the Name AGLA (pronounced "ah-geh-lah") and trace the passive invoking pentagram of Spirit. Then say: "In the Names which govern all the realms of Spirit, I invoke ye, ye divine forces of the Spirit of Life. I summon ye, ye angels of the celestial sphere, whose dwelling is in the invisible. Ye are the guardians of the gates of the universe; be ye also the watchers of this rite. Keep far removed the evil and unbalanced; strengthen and inspire me, that I may preserve unsullied this abode of the mysteries of the eternal gods. Let this place be made pure and holy, so that standing herein I may become a partaker of the secrets of the divine light."

Seventh, return the incense to its place, go to the east, and circumambulate clockwise three times as in the First Degree Opening and Closing, except that the Signs of Isis, Apophis, and Osiris Risen are made each time you pass the east. After the third circumambulation is completed, return to the west of the altar, face east, make the Sign of Osiris Slain, and say: "Holy art thou, Lord of the Universe. Holy art thou, whom Nature hath not formed. Holy art thou, the vast and the mighty one, Lord of the Light and of the Darkness."

Do not make the Signs of Entering or Silence while repeating this invocation.

Eighth, lower your arms, and say slowly and clearly: "Peh. Resh. Kaph. Tau. The Word is Paroketh, which is the Veil of the Sanctuary." Make the Sign of the Rending of the Veil and say: "In and by that Word, I open the Veil." Then perform the Cabalistic Cross.

Ninth, say slowly: "The Great Name which governeth this working is (Name). The archangel who governeth this working is (name). The angel who (or angelic host which) governeth this working is (name). The (Sphere, planet, or element) which governeth this working is (name)."

Proceed in the same way, one at a time, through the full list of correspondences you have prepared.

Tenth, pause, and then say: "I. N. R. I. Yod. Nun. Resh. Yod. Virgo, Isis, mighty mother. Scorpio, Apophis, the destroyer. Sol, Osiris, slain and risen. Isis, Apophis, Osiris. I, A, O."

Then vibrate, as forcefully as possible, the Name IAO (pronounced "eee-aaa-oh").

Eleventh, make the Sign of Osiris Slain and say: "The Sign of Osiris Slain." Make the Sign of Isis and say: "L. The Sign of the mourning of Isis." Make the Sign of Apophis and say: "V. The Sign of Apophis and Typhon." Make the Sign of Osiris Risen and say: "X. The Sign of Osiris Risen." Then say: "L. V. X.," repeating the IAO Signs as you do so. Lower your arms to your sides and say: "Lux. Light. The Light of the Rose Cross. Let the light descend!"

Twelfth, visualize a shaft of brilliant white light, wide enough to contain the whole area within the circle traced by the initial banishing rituals, shining down on the space from far above. Hold this visualization for a time, and then release the image and perform the Cabalistic Cross.

This completes the Opening phase of the ritual. The Closing is performed as follows.

First, standing at the west of the altar, facing east in silence, make the IAO Signs.

Second, say clearly and slowly: "Peh. Resh. Kaph. Tau. The Word is Paroketh, which is the Veil of the Sanctuary." Make the Sign of the Closing of the Veil, and then say: "In and by that Word, I close the Veil."

Third, perform the purification with Water and consecration with Fire in silence, as in the Opening. Then go to the east and circumambulate counterclockwise three times, making the IAO Signs each time you pass the east. At the end of the last circuit, return to the west of the altar and face east. Say: "In the great Name of strength through sacrifice, YHShVH YHVShH (pronounced "yeh-heh-shu-ah yeh-ho-wah-shah"), I now permit any spirits not intentionally bound in this ceremony to depart. Go in peace to your habitations, and peace be between us."

Fourth, perform the Lesser Banishing Rituals of the Hexagram and Pentagram. This completes the ritual.

In the Third Degree Opening and Closing, some of the same patterns we saw in the Second Degree version of the ritual are repeated, although both the focus and the application are different. Once again, the symbolism of an earlier Degree enters into the ritual, with the Veil of the Sanctuary from the Second Degree playing a role here in the Third;

once again, the symbols of the four elements have a critical part, one linked to the Cabalistic symbolism of the Tetragrammaton.

Here, though, the order in which the elements are invoked is the order of the Tetragrammaton itself. The elements are not present as balancing factors, as they are in the Second Degree and to some extent in the First; the process of crystallization central to the Third Degree formula ensures balance on its own if it is properly carried out. Rather, the elements in this ritual function as expressions of creative energy, the energy that enters into the crystallizing process. This also explains the simplicity of the Closing; the energies summoned in the Opening, and in the ceremony itself, are absorbed in the course of a Third Degree working, and only the most basic measures to balance stray forces and return to ordinary consciousness are needed to close down safely afterward.

CHAPTER 9

WORKING TOOLS

T HE ESSENTIAL TOOLS OF RITUAL MAGIC in the Golden Dawn tradition are found within the magician, as powers and capabilities that exist on the various levels of the human microcosm and can be used to shape the forces of the macrocosm around us. These powers and capabilities, not the hardware found in occult-supply stores, are what accomplish the work of magic, and their development is the chief task of the magician in training.

At the same time, these innate tools can be supplemented and strengthened by the use of a set of specially designed and consecrated objects. These objects have generally been called "magical weapons" in recent writings, but this term is unsatisfactory for a whole range of reasons, starting with the fact that most of the objects in question are not especially weaponlike in any ordinary sense. Here, a phrase from another branch of Western esoteric tradition will be borrowed, and these implements will be referred to as "working tools."

A magical working tool, in this sense, is an object that has been charged with a specific set of magical energies, and is then used to direct and shape those energies in ritual. The tool works through a kind of artificial form of the process of creation we traced in Chapter 1. Working tools are charged through a ceremony of consecration of the First Degree, which links the material form to patterns of energy on the higher levels of experience; a working tool thus becomes an expression of those patterns on the physical level, and it then functions in magical terms exactly as though it had been brought into being by those patterns in the natural course of the creative process.

The Cup, for example, the elemental working tool of Water in Golden Dawn usage, is a physical expression of the higher-level energies that are linked to Water, in much the same way that a lake is. The connection, however, is made through deliberately chosen astral symbolism and etheric patterns, rather than through the ordinary course of the creative process. In the case of the Cup, this is done simply because a solid object of modest size is more convenient to use in ritual work than, say, a physical lake would be. In the case of other kinds of working tools, the energies placed in the tool are often sufficiently abstract or sufficiently subtle that they have no direct physical expression, or none that is uncontaminated with other influences; a working tool in this situation allows the magician to handle energies that otherwise could not be ritually directed at all.

It's useful to trace out the interactions between a working tool and the five levels of experience in order to get a clearer sense of the way in which these devices are made, consecrated, and used.

On the spiritual level, a working tool is linked through contemplation and the use of appropriate Names of God to the highest aspect of the energy the tool represents. This is done in the consecration ceremony, above all, but it is also renewed each time the tool is used in ritual work. In the case of the Cup, for example, the energies of Water are invoked by means of vibration and contemplation of the Name אֵל, EL.

On the mental level, a working tool expresses the essential idea or concept of the pattern of energy it represents; its design may include geometrical or mathematical aspects that express that idea, and its consecration ceremony will certainly do so. In the case of the Cup, the essence of the element of Water in Cabalistic thought is seen as receptivity, which is symbolized very effectively by the basic form of the Cup. The proportions and shape of the Cup may be designed to heighten this symbolism, and the Cup will be consecrated in a ritual employing the invoking pentagram of Water and the number four, which relates to all the elements.

On the astral level, a working tool is the focus of a series of astral processes during its consecration, in which visualizations and other methods of astral work will be used to link the working tool with the appropriate kind of astral energy. This same process will be renewed each time the tool is used in ritual. In the case of the Cup, the names, symbols, sigils, and images of Water dominate the consecration ceremony, and are used in any ritual where the Cup takes an active role.

On the etheric level, a working tool is charged during its consecration with etheric substance, which serves as the link between the astral patterns shaped by the ceremony, on the one hand, and the physical form of the tool on the other. This etheric charge is carefully preserved and renewed through the regular practice of ritual. In the case of the Cup, a piece of silk or linen is used to wrap the Cup whenever it is not in use, and the Cup itself should not be touched by anyone other than the magician.

On the physical level, a working tool is the manifestation in matter of the levels already mentioned, and will be made with this in mind. It is normally made of a material that takes etheric charges well, and may bear Names, colors, sigils, and the like, corresponding to the spiritual, mental, and astral patterns it represents. It should also be conveniently sized and shaped for its role in ritual. In the case of the Cup, a medium-sized goblet is suitable—ceramic or metal should be used rather than glass, which does not hold etheric charges effectively—and it may be painted, etched, or otherwise decorated with the Names and symbols of Water.

These same levels can be traced in each of the applications of magic we'll be examining, but they are particularly important in the case of working tools, because they are the primary instruments by which energies are brought down the levels into manifestation by the Golden Dawn magician. It's a useful exercise to think through the presence of the different levels in each of the working tools described here, and an even more useful one to keep all the levels in mind during ritual work.

Making the Working Tools

Over the years there has been a great deal of dispute on the subject of procuring the working tools of magic, and some unintentional comedy of a very high order. The medieval grimoires or handbooks on magic typically hedged the process with a wide range of difficult requirements and called for unpleasant ingredients such as moles' blood in the consecration ceremonies. In more recent times, writers on magic of the type exemplified by Eliphas Levi tended to replace the moles' blood with an equally unnecessary mess composed largely of veiled hints and references to forbidden secrets, high on bombast and very low on practical information.

Compared to these, the Golden Dawn's instructional papers on working tools must have come as a pleasant shock to their original readers. The working tools of the Order were made from commonly available materials and consecrated by some of the best-designed short ceremonies in the Golden Dawn system. These basic principles of the Order's approach to working tools have become standard in much of the magical community, and will be used here.

The instructional papers also prescribed designs, highly elaborate ones, for each of the working tools. These designs are effective, and it's possible to make a case for retaining them as standard. At the same time, the Order's tendency to follow Victorian standards of taste has made these designs unnecessarily cluttered, to a degree that occasionally borders on ugliness, and it's generally been found that plainer working tools are just as effective in actual use as the more ornate kind.

A simpler and more flexible approach has much to offer the student, and will be presented here. Those who wish to follow the Golden Dawn pattern for their working tools should certainly consult the Order's papers on the subject in Volume 3 of Regardie's *The Golden Dawn*, or Chic and Sandra Tabatha Cicero's excellent manual, *Secrets of a Golden Dawn Temple*.

It deserves to be stressed that the working tools should be made (when possible) and consecrated by the person who will be using them. Many of these objects can be made by anyone, given a modest amount of time and effort, and it's a commonplace of magic that even the plainest working tools handmade by the magician are often more effective than technically more perfect pieces purchased from someone else. Once consecrated, working tools should never be touched by anyone but the magician himself or herself. Each should be wrapped in its own silk or linen wrapper and kept in a secure place when not in use.

The Elemental Working Tools

In the Golden Dawn, the construction and consecration of working tools was reserved for members who had reached the Adeptus Minor grade, and the tools themselves were made and charged in an order based on a portion of the symbolism of that grade, with the elemental working tools coming last of all. For the magician working independently in the Golden

Dawn tradition, though, this isn't particularly useful. The consecration ceremony for the elemental working tools is in many ways the simplest of these rites, and as it is done four times—once for each of the elemental tools—it allows the novice magician to gain some skill with this kind of ritual work before moving on to more demanding ceremonies of the same type. At the same time, the work of making and consecrating the elemental working tools in a particular order can correspond to, and in some senses take the place of, the sequence of elemental initiations that laid the foundations of magical development in the Golden Dawn itself.

The first of the elemental working tools in the sequence followed here is the Pentacle, which corresponds to the element of Earth. This should be a disk of wood, ceramic, or wax, between four and six inches across, and between one-half inch and one inch thick. It may be left undecorated, or carved or painted with a symbol representing the universe in magical terms; a pentagram or a hexagram are among the more traditional designs. If it is colored, the colors of Earth—citrine (a brownish yellow), russet (a rusty red-brown), olive (a brownish green), and black—may be used, or alternatively, black or forest green.

The second elemental working tool is the Dagger, which corresponds to the element of Air. The Dagger should be a short, sharp, double-edged knife with a straight blade and a cross guard. A yellow hilt would be suitable for the sake of the elemental colors. It may be purchased or made from a piece of steel through grinding and filing.

The third elemental working tool is the Cup, which corresponds to the element of Water. The Cup should be a plain, medium-sized goblet of metal or ceramic—if metal, silver is preferable to brass; if ceramic, a blue glaze would be suitable.

The fourth elemental working tool is the Wand, which corresponds to the element of Fire. The Wand is a straight length of wooden dowel three-quarters of an inch to one inch thick and eight to twelve inches long. In Golden Dawn practice, the Wand had a thin magnetized steel rod running down its center and projecting one-sixteenth of an inch at each end; this is useful if it can be arranged, as it allows for a greater intensity of energy flow through the Wand, but it's entirely possible to make an effective Wand without it. If you wish to try the more complicated form, it's best to saw the dowel in half lengthwise with a fine saw, make a narrow channel for the rod, and then glue the whole assembly back together with wood glue, and sand to smoothness. The rod should be magnetized beforehand by stroking it from end to end with a bar magnet, taking care always to stroke it in the same direction, until the end of the rod will pick up iron filings.

All four of the elemental working tools are shown in Diagram 43.

Consecrating the Elemental Working Tools

The consecration ceremony for the elemental working tools given here is a slight adaptation of the Golden Dawn form. Before performing it, you'll want to familiarize yourself with the text and the elemental correspondences, and construct in your imagination the telesmatic images of the spirits and angels to be invoked. A brief written description of each of the images may be helpful as a memory aid during the ceremony, as there are a fair number of images to be remembered and used. The requirements of the ceremony are the same as those of the First Degree Opening and Closing; the working tool to be consecrated, the one addition, is to be placed at the center of the altar, with its silk or linen wrapping nearby. The ceremony is performed as follows.

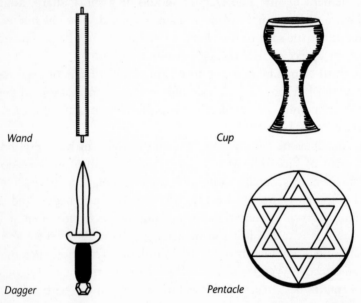

Wand

Cup

Dagger

Pentacle

Diagram 43—
The Elemental Working Tools

First, perform the complete First Degree Ritual of Opening as given in Chapter 6, in the expanded form.

Second, perform the Greater Invoking Ritual of the Pentagram of the element corresponding to the working tool you will be consecrating, beginning and ending at the west of the altar, facing east.

Third, move around the altar, if necessary, until you face the direction corresponding to that element, across the altar. (If you are consecrating the Pentacle, for example, move to the south of the altar and face north.) Then trace the invoking pentagram of the element in the air above the working tool, as though the pentagram were standing upon it.

Fourth, repeat the following invocation, using the appropriate elemental correspondences from the appendix at the end of this book. Names of God, but none of the other names, should be vibrated. While repeating the invocation, the various powers who are invoked should be visualized: the presence of Unity (represented by the Name of God) should be visualized as pure formless light, the archangel should be given the same form used in the Pentagram Ritual, while the angel and ruler should be visualized in the form of their telesmatic images, made according to the principles given in Chapter 4. Hebrew spellings of the names, which you'll need to make the images, are included in the tables.

"O thou who art from everlasting, thou who hast created all things, and doth clothe thyself with the forces of Nature as with a garment, by thy holy and divine Name (Name of God) whereby thou art known especially in that quarter we name (Hebrew name of direction), the (direction), I beseech thee to grant unto me strength and insight for my search after the hidden light and wisdom.

"I entreat thee to cause thy wonderful archangel (name of archangel), who governeth the works of (element), to guide me in the pathway; and furthermore to direct thine angel (name of angel) to watch over my footsteps therein.

"May the ruler of Earth, the powerful prince (name of ruler), by the gracious permission of the infinite Supreme, increase and strengthen the hidden forces and occult virtues of this (name of working tool) so that I may be enabled with it to perform aright those magical operations for which it has been fashioned. For which purpose I now perform this rite of consecration in the divine presence of (Name of God)."

Fifth, trace the invoking pentagram of the element again over the altar, and then repeat the following invocation of the Elemental King of the Element. Once again, the Names of God are to be vibrated. The elementals and their King are to be visualized as a great mass of the appropriate element, through which half-distinct forms move.

"And in and by the holy Names of God which govern all the powers of the (direction), I summon thee, thou great king of the (name of elementals), (name of Elemental King), to attend on this ceremony and by thy presence increase its effect, whereby I do now consecrate this magical (name of working tool). Confer upon it the utmost occult might and virtue of which thou judge it to be capable in all works of the nature of (element), so that in it I may find a strong defense and a powerful weapon wherewith to rule and direct the spirits of (element)."

Sixth, raise your hands over the working tool and say: "And command also thy subjects, the (name of elementals) of (element), that they shall place the energies of thy realm in this (name of working tool) of (element), that its outward and material form may remain a true symbol of the inward and spiritual force; and command also that they shall be obedient unto me in the work of the Magic of Light." While saying this, visualize the presence of the elemental spirits, with the King a looming presence above and behind them.

Seventh, pause, and then take up the working tool in both hands, raising it high. Say: "In the Name of (Name of God), I proclaim that this (name of working tool) of (element) has been truly consecrated!" Return with it to the west of the altar, face east, and perform the Greater Invoking Ritual of the Pentagram of the appropriate element, using the working tool to trace all lines and pentagrams. When this is done, wrap the working tool in its silk or linen wrapping.

Eighth, perform the full First Degree Ritual of Closing in the expanded form. This completes the ceremony.

The Lamen

The lamen, a consecrated symbol worn about the neck, is a specialized form of working tool, one that has a subtle but crucial role in magic in the Golden Dawn tradition. At first glance, it seems to be part of the magician's costume rather than one of his or her working tools, as it is worn rather than handled in ritual. Still, its function is an active one. It is designed to bring through the balancing and harmonizing energies of Tiphareth, the central, solar Sphere of the Tree of Life, in the course of ritual work, and it is made and consecrated with this goal in mind. It serves to link the magician's purpose in ritual work with the deeper goals of magical practice.

Wearing the lamen has two effects, both of them important. On the one hand, it offers protection against unbalanced energies and, in many situations, hostile entities as well; on the other, it helps direct the work of the magician himself or herself along those paths of balance that lead to the attainment of the Great Work.

The particular form of lamen used in the Golden Dawn, the Rose Cross Lamen, is highly effective for this purpose, but there are other issues involved that need to be considered. In Cabalistic teaching, Tiphareth represents the essential core of the individual as such, the point where each independent being comes into contact with its own root in Unity and its context amid the great impersonal powers of the cosmos. Different individuals will thus tend to perceive Tiphareth, or to reach toward it, in subtly different ways, and no one symbolism will fit the needs of all. This is particularly true in the case of a complex and highly developed system of symbols.

The Rose Cross is one of the major symbols of Tiphareth in the broad Western magical tradition, but the form used in the Golden Dawn's lamen is only one form of it, and different forms will connect more deeply with different people. There are also those to whom the Rose Cross does not speak at all, and who are better able to work with other symbols of Tiphareth—the Holy Grail, for example, or the alchemical Stone of the Wise, or for that matter, the Tiphareth imagery of another religious tradition.

For this reason it seems wiser to suggest that each magician design his or her own lamen, making use of any symbolism that links into the essential pattern of Tiphareth's energies and is personally appropriate as well. The Rose Cross, Golden Dawn-style or otherwise, is certainly one possibility here; so are other symbols of the Rosicrucian tradition, such as the phoenix or the flaming heart; so are the Grail, the Philosopher's

Stone, or for that matter, the Crucifixion or the Eye of Ra; so is a more straightforward use of solar imagery. In the course of designing a lamen, it can be useful to read books on symbolism and to study magical images from the traditional lore, and it's certainly a good idea to work through different drafts and allow the image you seek to show itself to you over time.

The lamen itself can be made of thin wood covered with artists' gesso, and supported by a fabric collar or a loop of gold-colored cloth ribbon fastened to the back. The imagery on it may be painted or drawn using any convenient method.

The design shown in Diagram 44 is one example of a possible lamen. Its overall shape is that of the *vesica piscis*, a shape that stands for the reconciliation of opposites in traditional sacred geometry, and it combines a form of the Rose Cross with the phoenix and words from the Emerald Tablet, an ancient text of alchemy.

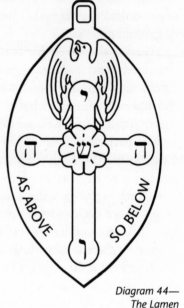

Diagram 44—
The Lamen

Consecrating the Lamen

The consecration ceremony for the lamen follows the same lines as that for the elemental working tools, but involves planetary as well as elemental energies. Like the ceremony just given, it has been adapted from the Golden Dawn version. Its requirements are the same, and the symbols and images of the ceremony should be learned beforehand in the same way. It is performed as follows.

———

First, perform the complete First Degree Ritual of Opening, using the expanded form.

Second, perform the Greater Invoking Ritual of the Hexagram of the Sun, using all six planetary hexagrams, beginning and ending at the west of the altar facing east.

Third, go to the east of the space and trace in the air the symbol of the Rose Cross, made as in the Rose Cross Ritual given in Chapter 6. This should be done slightly closer to the altar than the pentagrams you have traced. Point to the center of the Rose Cross and vibrate the Name YHShVH (pronounced "yeh-heh-shu-ah"). Go to the south, without tracing a connecting line, and repeat the process. Do the same in the west and north, and then return to the west of the altar and face east.

Fourth, trace another Rose Cross above the lamen, as if the Rose Cross were standing on it, and vibrate the Name YHVShH (pronounced "yeh-ho-wa-shah"). Raise both hands and repeat the following invocation. Names of God, but not other names, are to be vibrated; the archangel Michael should be visualized as a mighty angelic figure robed in gold and red, bearing a spear, while the angels, whose names are spelled PNIAL and PLIAL, should be visualized in the forms of their telesmatic images.

"O thou most glorious light which lighteneth every one who cometh into the world; thou who art in due season shadowed forth by Tiphareth, the Sun of Beauty; I invoke thee that thou mayest direct thy light upon this lamen, which I have fashioned in thy Name and for the furtherance of the Great Work. By the mighty Name YHVH (pronounced "yeh-ho-wah"), by thy Name of wisdom YHVH ALVH VDAaTh (pronounced "yeh-ho-wah ell-oh-wah vah da-ath"), permit I beseech thee thy shining archangel Michael, and the mighty angels Peniel and Pelial, so to influence this lamen that it may be mighty for all good, so that through the glorious sphere of Shemesh they may confer upon it such power and virtue that in wearing it, I may lose and so find myself in that light which I seek."

Fifth, lower your hands and say: "And a river, Nahar, went forth out of Eden to water the Garden, and from thence it was parted and came into four heads." Trace the active invoking pentagram of Spirit over the lamen, as if the pentagram stood upon it, and vibrate the Name AHIH (pronounced "eh-heh-yeh"); then trace the passive invoking pentagram of Spirit and vibrate the Name AGLA (pronounced "ah-geh-lah").

Then say: "And the name of the first river is Pison; it is that which compasseth the whole land of Havilah, where there is gold. And the gold of that land is good. There is bdellium and the onyx stone." Trace the invoking pentagram of Fire over the lamen, then make the Sign of Fire and vibrate the Name ALHIM (pronounced "ell-o-heem").

Then say: "And the name of the second river is Gihon, the same as that which compasseth the whole land of Ethiopia." Trace the invoking pentagram of Water over the lamen, then make the Sign of Water and vibrate the Name AL (pronounced "ell").

Then say: "And the name of the third river is Hiddekel, that is it which goeth forth to the east of Assyria." Trace the invoking pentagram of Air over the lamen, then make the Sign of Air and vibrate the Name YHVH.

Then say: "And the name of the fourth river is Euphrates." Trace the invoking pentagram of Earth over the lamen, then make the Sign of Earth and vibrate the Name ADNI (pronounced "ah-dough-nye").

Sixth, take up the lamen in both hands and raise it high. Say: "In the mighty Name YHShVH YHVShH, I proclaim that this lamen has been truly consecrated!" Then wrap it in a silk or linen wrapping.

Seventh, perform the full First Degree Ritual of Closing in the expanded form. This completes the ceremony.

The Magical Sword

There's a rather odd tendency, common among certain spiritual movements in the Western world, to assume that anything that lacks a physical body is by definition well disposed toward human beings. This rather naive notion has a long pedigree and is rooted in ancient ideas that see physical matter as the source of all evil. In recent years, too, the established religions' persistent habit of labeling any spiritual force that shows up outside church doors as "demonic" has led many people to the opposite folly of assuming that all spiritual forces—except, possibly, Christian ones—must be angelic instead.

It's worth noting that both these simplistic approaches clash sharply with the traditions of magic. While many of the nonphysical beings who populate the magician's universe are seen as helpful or at least harmless, much of the lore of magic from cultures around the world tells of spirits and energies that, for a wide range of reasons, are hostile or harmful to human beings. There's a huge and cross-cultural literature of demonology chronicling the names and natures of these wayward powers, their habits and weaknesses, and the best ways of coping with their activities when they impact the realms of human experience.

The Western magical traditions from which the Golden Dawn system descends have, as we've seen, a great deal of this kind of lore, much of it dating back to ancient times; the teachings of the Golden Dawn and its successor orders contain many references to hostile and destructive forces on the subtle levels of experience. Sensibly, they also contain effective means for coping with them both in and out of the context of ritual. Some of these methods—in particular, certain kinds of natural magic, and basic rituals such as the Banishing Ritual of the Pentagram and the Ritual of the Rose Cross—have already been discussed, and a good deal more will be covered in Chapter 11, where the evocation of spirits is discussed. One of the most important defenses against hostile nonphysicals, on the other hand, belongs here, as a working tool in the Golden Dawn tradition. This is the Magical Sword.

In the magic of the medieval grimoires, the sword had a special place as the chief instrument used to command and banish spirits. On the one hand, the role of the sword in common life as the weapon of chivalry and the most common tool of personal defense in a violent age made it an obvious symbol of protective force; on the other, the effects of sharp iron on etheric patterns, a function of natural magic, gave it a great deal of usefulness when hostile spirits had to be faced. Both of these considerations made the Magical Sword a natural addition to the armament of the adepts of the Golden Dawn.

In the original Golden Dawn system, the Magical Sword was designed and consecrated as an instrument of Geburah, the fifth Sphere of the Tree of Life, which corresponds to the element Fire and the planet Mars, and has the character of overwhelming power and severity. This is certainly a valid approach. Still, in important ways, it is a limiting one; there are more flexible ways to use power than sheer brute force, and a set of energies derived from a single Sphere can be unequal to all needs, particularly those involving powers derived from Spheres higher on the Tree. The ceremony of consecration for the Magical Sword given here takes a different approach, drawn from the Cabalistic symbolism of the Flaming Sword, and results in a working tool capable of a wider range of applications.

The physical form of the Magical Sword is also worth discussing. A century ago, when the Golden Dawn system was being designed, swords of reasonable quality were still quite easily come by, since the sword had not yet dropped out of use as a military sidearm; the Order papers could thus instruct the adept to use "any convenient sword" and leave it at that. Nowadays, a magician who does not have the time or resources to manufacture a sword out of raw materials often has to choose between shoddily fashioned replicas, many of which are made of cheap (and magically useless) pot-metal alloys, and competently made weapons costing hundreds of dollars.

One way out of this bind is to make use of the somewhat different Magical Sword developed in central European schools of magic, shown in Diagram 45, which can be made more easily than a full-sized sword of the more common type. The blade of this type of Magical Sword can be cut from sheet iron with a hacksaw; the hilt is made of wooden dowel, with a slit cut in one end to receive the blade, which is glued in place with a good all-purpose glue. The three points of the blade should be filed sharp.

The hilt of either type of sword should be made of, or covered with, an insulating substance—wood, leather, fabric, cord, or several coats of

Diagram 45—
The Magical Sword

enamel paint are examples. The sword may be decorated with pentagrams or other symbols, if you wish, or left plain; if the hilt is painted, it
should be black, rather than the red used in the Golden Dawn version.

Consecration Ceremony for the Magical Sword

This ceremony has the same requirements as the two already given in
this chapter. It is performed as follows.

First, perform the complete First Degree Ritual of Opening in the
expanded form.

Second, perform the Greater Invoking Ritual of the Pentagram of Spirit.

Third, standing at the west of the altar facing east, the sword upon the
altar with its hilt to the east and its point to the west, raise your hands,
palms down, above the altar. Visualize darkness surrounding you and say
slowly, in a low voice: "The realm of chaos and old night, before ever the
Aeons were, when there was neither heaven nor earth, nor was there any
sea, when nothing was save the shape unluminous, formless, and void. To
and fro in the deeps swayed the coils of the dragon with eight heads and
eleven horns. Eleven were the curses of Mount Ebal, eleven the rulers of
the Primal Powers, and at their head the two Contending Forces."

Fourth, take the hilt of the sword in both hands and raise the sword
above the altar, point down and hilt up. Say: "Then in darkness was
spoken the Word!" Then, pausing after each one, vibrate the following
Names of God of the ten Spheres in order: AHIH (pronounced "eh-
heh-yeh"); YH ("yah"); YHVH ALHIM ("yeh-ho-wah ell-o-heem");
AL ("ell"); ALHIM GBVR ("ell-o-heem gih-boor"); YHVH ALVH
VDAaTh ("yeh-ho-wah ell-o-wah vah da-ath"); YHVH TzBAVTh
("yeh-ho-wah tza-ba-oth"); ALHIM TzBAVTh ("ell-o-heem tza-ba-
oth"); ShDI AL ChI ("shah-dye ell chye"); ADNI HARTz ("ah-dough-
nye ha ah-retz").

Then turn the sword so that the point is up and the hilt down; lower
the hilt to the level of your heart, and say: "And the Elohim said, "Let
there be light, and there was light." As you say this, visualize light
descending and banishing the darkness; then set the sword upon the altar,
point to the east, and make the Signs of Isis, Apophis, and Osiris Risen.

Fifth, recite the following invocation: "In the ten great and holy Names of God before which the darkness rolled asunder in the morning of time, I invoke thee, Metatron, Prince of Countenances, and thee, Sandalphon, who art the Reconciler for Earth. As the Flaming Sword of the creative Light cast down the powers of the Primal Worlds, so grant that this sword, which I have made in its image and do now consecrate to the service of the Infinite, may banish and dispell every baleful spirit and every hostile current of force against which it may be wielded."

While reciting this, visualize the two archangels Metatron and Sandalphon in the east. Metatron is on the right, a winged male figure in white robes, shining with light so brilliant his form can scarcely be made out. Sandalphon is on the left, a winged female figure in black robes, shining with a subtle and gentle light.

Sixth, take the cup of Water and sprinkle the sword thrice, saying, "I purify with Water." Then cense the sword three times with the incense, saying, "I consecrate with Fire." Then raise up the sword in both hands and say: "In the mighty Name YHShVH YHVShH, I proclaim that this Sword has been duly consecrated!"

Seventh, perform the complete First Degree Ritual of Closing in the expanded form. The banishing rituals should be performed using the Magical Sword to trace the pentagrams. This concludes the ceremony.

This ritual is based on some of the deeper levels of Cabalistic symbolism and mythology. The Primal Worlds were realms of unbalanced force that, in the traditional lore, are said to have existed before the birth of the universe we experience. The Flaming Sword that shattered them is made up of the ten Spheres of the Tree of Life, and is also—under a slightly different symbolism—known as the Lightning Flash. The Magical Sword is thus charged, in this ritual, with energy drawn from all ten Spheres in balanced array, and this balance is also invoked by way of Metatron and Sandalphon, the archangels of the first and last Spheres of the Tree and the rulers of polarity and polar forces in Cabalistic teaching. A more complete account of the whole symbolism may be found in Chapters 3 and 5 of *Paths of Wisdom*.

In ritual practice, the Magical Sword is used to trace all banishing pentagrams, hexagrams, and other symbols, and to command hostile spirits in ceremonies of evocation and exorcism. Outside of ritual, it may also be used to dispell unwanted energies, particularly those with a strong etheric component. The most effective way to do this is to find the location of the energy by feel or astral vision, and then make a series of short thrusts with the point (or points) of the sword through the area, as though you were poking something soft. Depending on your sensitivity, you may see or feel the discharge as the sharp iron comes into contact with the etheric patterns you are dispelling.

The Lotus Wand

In legend, as in reality, the wand or staff has long been the generic working tool of the magician in the Western world. There are a range of reasons this is the case, but central among them is an entirely practical one. A long, straight piece of wood, or some other suitable substance, offers a convenient and easily handled form with which linear currents of energy can be raised and directed.

Most people are familiar with the short and slender wands that stage magicians, those professional imitators of the occult, use in their illusions; the working tool of the ritual magician, though, is a more substantial object. Medieval traditions sometimes called for wands on the scale of Robin Hood's six-foot quarterstaff, which is perhaps too large for indoor use! In the Golden Dawn tradition, on the other hand, the proportions chosen were a little less awkward. The wand for general ritual use, the Lotus Wand, was between twenty-four and forty inches long.

Actually, two different wands were part of the working tools of the Golden Dawn adept, but the quite small Wand of Fire served less as an instrument for shaping energies in general work than as a vessel for elemental power. The Lotus Wand had a far more important role in ritual. It was topped with a stylized lotus blossom of twenty-six petals and had bands of fourteen different colors painted on it, marking the places by which it was held to invoke and banish different forces.

The blossom seems to have a positive effect in certain of the wand's applications, and at the very least does not get in the way during use. The same cannot be said for the system of colored bands, and they can be abandoned without any significant loss of effectiveness. Lacking the bands, the Lotus Wand may be toward the shorter end of the range—

perhaps two to two and one half feet long—and between one-half and one inch in diameter. A piece of doweling will make a serviceable shaft; it should be sanded smooth, and may be painted white. The blossom may be made of thin cardboard or sheet metal, in four whorls as shown, curving in slightly at the tips; the whorls can be fixed to the shaft with a brass screw. The complete wand is shown in Diagram 46.

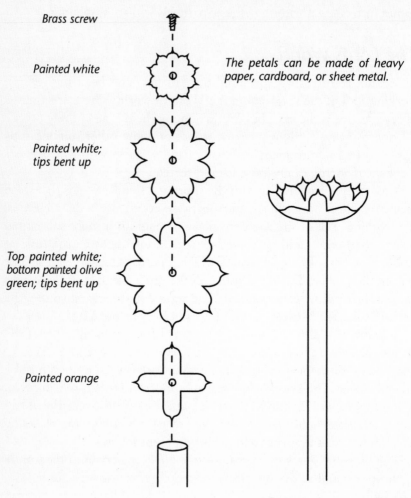

Brass screw

Painted white

The petals can be made of heavy paper, cardboard, or sheet metal.

Painted white; tips bent up

Top painted white; bottom painted olive green; tips bent up

Painted orange

Diagram 46—
The Lotus Wand

Consecration Ceremony for the Lotus Wand

This ceremony has the same requirements as the others in this chapter. It has been adapted slightly from the Golden Dawn version to adjust for the absence of the colored bands. It is performed as follows.

―――――――

First, perform the complete First Degree Ritual of Opening, banishing with the Lesser Ritual of the Pentagram. Either the basic or the expanded version of the Opening may be used.

Second, perform the Greater Invoking Ritual of the Pentagram of Spirit.

Third, standing west of the altar, facing east, make the Signs of Isis, Apophis, and Osiris Risen. Then take up the Lotus Wand in your right hand, raise it high, and say: "O Harpocrates, Lord of Silence, who art enthroned upon the lotus. Twenty-six are the petals of the lotus, flower of thy wand. O Lord of Creation, they are the number of thy Name. By the letters of the Great Name, Yod Heh Vau Heh, let the divine light arise!"

Then, one after another, speak the name of each of the letters of the Hebrew alphabet in order, from Aleph to Tau, and as you name each letter, visualize it, as though written in brilliant white light, just above the flower.

Fourth, say the following invocation of the elemental powers five times, once each for Air, Fire, Water, Earth, and Spirit, in that order, facing respectively east, south, west, north, and east as you do so, and holding the proper elemental working tool in the left hand while invoking the first four. Fill in the names and symbols of the invocation from memory or from the tables in the Appendix. As you begin each invocation, trace the invoking pentagram (for Spirit, use both pentagrams) of the element above the altar in the appropriate direction, using the Lotus Wand.

"Heaven is above and the Earth is beneath, and betwixt the light and the darkness the powers vibrate. I supplicate the powers and forces governing the nature, place, and authority of the element (name of element), to which is assigned the Letter (letter) of Tetragrammaton and the (direction) quarter of the world, by the majesty of the Divine Name (Name) and in the presence of the mighty archangel (name), to bestow, this present day and hour, and confirm their hidden and potent influence upon this Lotus Wand, which I hereby dedicate to the work of magic, and may its grasp strengthen me in the work of the character of (name of element) and its attributes."

While reciting each of these elemental invocations, visualize the archangel of the element using the same visualizations you use in the Pentagram Ritual for the first four elements, and both Metatron and Sandalphon, visualized as in the consecration ceremony of the sword, for the element of Spirit. Around each of these images, visualize countless other presences gathering, who relate to the same element and are robed in the same colors as the archangel. These presences should, as far as possible, be felt as well as seen.

Fifth, standing at the west of the altar facing east, lay the Lotus Wand on the altar, blossom to the east, and raise your hands over it. Say: "By the four letters of the Great Name, Yod Heh Vau Heh, may this Wand have rulership over all the forces of Nature, and may it be consecrated to the works of the Magic of Light." Then raise the wand up in both hands and say: "In the mighty Name YHShVH YHVShH, I proclaim that this Lotus Wand has been duly consecrated!" Finally, wrap it in a silk or linen covering.

Sixth, perform the complete First Degree Closing Ritual. This concludes the ceremony.

———

In contrast to the consecration ceremony for the Magical Sword, the consecration of the Lotus Wand is fairly simple and uses formulae that should be familiar to you from the ceremonies for the elemental working tools. At the same time, there is a subtle connection between sword and wand, one that ties into Cabalistic symbolism and is hinted at by those many legends in which a wand or staff is transformed into a serpent. The Flaming Sword, which represents the ten Spheres and the descending power of creation, is balanced in the traditional imagery by the Serpent, which represents the twenty-two Paths of the Tree of Life and the ascending path by which the promise of creation is fulfilled in each of us.

Where the Magical Sword is used to banish, then, the Lotus Wand is used to invoke, and invoking pentagrams, hexagrams, and other figures used in ritual work should be traced with the blossom end. That end should never be touched in working or pointed toward the ground. In theurgic workings, particularly when the highest spiritual influences have been invoked, the blossom is to be directed toward the forehead during periods of contemplation. This should also be done during the exercise of Rising on the Planes, which will be discussed in Chapter 12.

The Magical Mirror

The Lamen, the Sword, the Lotus Wand, and the four elemental working tools formed the basic toolkit of the adepts of the Golden Dawn, and they form, as well, the foundation for most of the magical rituals in this book. There is at least one other working tool that belongs in the set. The three major working tools correspond, in an important sense, with three of the four elemental tools; the Lotus Wand is an expansion of the Wand, the Sword of the Dagger, the Lamen of the Pentacle, and these correspondences can be traced in the function, as well as the form, of the devices in question. The Cup, however, is without an equivalent in the standard Golden Dawn set. Along with the Lotus Wand to invoke, the Sword to banish, and the Lamen to balance, then, there's a place for a working tool to receive.

In Western magical practice outside the Golden Dawn, the most common tool for this purpose has been the Magical Mirror. As a working tool, a consecrated mirror functions as a gateway to the astral level; it is used both in and outside of ritual to focus and extend astral perception or to communicate with spirits of various kinds. It can also be used to perceive the physical level clairvoyantly, bringing visions of distant places and times to the magician. In advanced practice, the mirror can become a gateway in another sense, and the magician can pass through it, either to the astral level, or across barriers of space and time.

The Magical Mirror and its close equivalent, the shewstone or scrying crystal, played an important part in many of the traditions that became part of the Golden Dawn. Its absence from the Order's own curriculum, though, is not hard to explain. In the years just before the Golden Dawn was founded, another magical order—the Hermetic Brotherhood of Luxor—was a major presence in the English occult scene. The teachings of the H. B. of L., as it was called, included some offbeat theorizing about past ages of Earth's history and a good deal of the sexual magic that Karl Kellner, an erstwhile H. B. of L. member, later incorporated into the teachings of the Ordo Templi Orientis. A central part of the H. B. of L.'s system was the use of the Magical Mirror, and the founders of the Golden Dawn would have had to avoid duplicating these methods in order to prevent charges of plagiarism.

The political concerns of the turn-of-the-century magical community, fortunately, need not influence choices made in the Golden Dawn tradition now, and the Magical Mirror is far too useful a device to leave out of the kit of working tools. To make one, you'll need a suitable piece of glass; a clock glass three to six inches in diameter, which can be bought at any clock repair shop, will work perfectly. The concave, or hollow, side is the one you will be looking into; the other side of the glass, the convex side, should be painted with at least three coats of flat black enamel paint to produce a dark reflective surface.

You'll also need a piece of black velvet, as wide as the clock glass, and twice as long, to make a cushion that will support the mirror. It should be folded in half, velvet side in. The edges can then be sewn up, leaving a small opening on one side. It should then be turned inside out, so that the velvet faces outward, by pulling the cloth from inside through the opening; stuffing can then be put in through the opening before it is sewn shut.

Since glass does not hold etheric charges well, the cushion will need to retain the bulk of the energy received in the consecration. It should be filled with a suitable natural-fiber stuffing—cotton batting will serve— and with several small pieces of quartz or moonstone as well. It can then be consecrated.

Consecration Ceremony for the Magical Mirror

First, perform the complete First Degree Ritual of Opening, banishing with the Lesser Ritual of the Pentagram. Either the basic or the expanded form may be used.

Second, perform the Greater Invoking Ritual of the Pentagram of Spirit.

Third, standing at the west of the altar, facing east, with the mirror on the altar before you, point to the heavens with your right hand and to the earth with your left. Say: "That which is below is as that which is above, and that which is above is as that which is below, to perform the miracles of the One Thing." Return your hands to your sides. "All things are reflected in all things. All things are contained in all things. All things are revealed in all things."

Fourth, raise your hands and say: "In the Name YHShVH YHVShH, I invoke the power of the Recording Angel. I adjure thee, O Light invisible and intangible, wherein all the thoughts and deeds of all creatures are written, wherein all the events of time past, time present, and time to come are reflected. By all the Names and symbols of power, I call thee from thy abodes to concentrate here in this mirror of Art. Fill it with thy secret virtue, that it may show me true images of hidden things. Let it become a sure guide and an instrument of vision in the works of the Magic of Light."

While repeating this invocation, visualize the form of the Recording Angel, a shining winged figure with a robe that shimmers with all colors. The Angel holds a mirror in both hands, and turns the mirror slightly as you finish the invocation, so that a ray of light shines from it onto the mirror you are consecrating.

Fifth, trace an invoking pentagram of active Spirit above the mirror, as though the pentagram stood over the mirror. Vibrate the Name AHIH and say, "Let this mirror of Art show me true images of hidden things in the realm of Spirit." In the same way, using the appropriate pentagrams, divine Names, and names of the elements, call upon Air, Fire, Water, and Earth; for the last three, face the direction of the element across the altar while invoking. Return to the west of the altar and trace an invoking pentagram of passive Spirit above the mirror; vibrate the Name AGLA and say, "Let this mirror of Art show me true images of hidden things in every quarter of the universe."

Sixth, raise the mirror, on its cushion, with both hands, being careful not to touch the glass, and say: "In the mighty Name YHShVH YHVShH, I proclaim that this Mirror has been duly consecrated!" Then wrap the mirror and its cushion in a silk or linen wrapper and close with the complete First Degree Ritual of Closing. This concludes the ceremony.

———————

Unlike the other working tools, the mirror can require a substantial amount of practice for the novice magician to become skilled in its use. To learn to see visions in the mirror, set up an altar in a private room and place the mirror and its cushion, in their wrapping, on the altar. Place a comfortable chair to the west of the altar. Perform the Lesser Banishing Ritual of the Pentagram, sit in the chair, unwrap the mirror and set it on the cushion, and say the following invocation.

"In the Divine Name IAO, I invoke thee, thou great angel HRU, who art set over the operations of this secret wisdom. Lay thine hand invisibly upon this mirror of Art, that thereby I may see true images of hidden things, to the glory of the Ineffable Name." (The angel HRU, who is invoked here and in certain other Golden Dawn rituals, is the angelic guardian over the entire Golden Dawn system of esoteric work, and has particular power over the art of divination.)

Then trace an invoking pentagram of Earth over the mirror and look into it, trying to keep your mind as clear as possible. In more advanced work, this can be replaced by any invoking symbol desired, and the corresponding banishing symbol is then used at the end. It often helps to focus your eyes as though you were looking through the mirror at something far away. Sooner or later—much depends on the personal equation here—you will see the image of clouds in the mirror. When this happens, formulate an image in your mind of the thing you wish to see: a symbol, if you seek a vision of some part of the astral level; a person or place, if you seek a vision of something on the physical level. The vision will then appear. When you have finished, wrap the mirror and cushion in their wrapping and trace a banishing pentagram of Earth over the altar to break the link; then perform the Cabalistic Cross to close.

Some people will find that it takes only a few practice sessions before they are seeing clear, detailed visions in the mirror; others need to work at it for a year or more before anything significant comes through. Given patience and the willingness to work, anyone can learn to use the mirror effectively, and it can then be put to use in some of the more advanced techniques that will be introduced later.

Other Magical Working Tools

The set of working tools described here will meet most of the needs of the practicing ritual magician. Now and again, though, it can be useful or even necessary to design and consecrate other kinds of working tools for certain kinds of magical operations, not all of them ritual in nature.

For example, Golden Dawn adepts of a certain rank made and used a device called the Ring and Disk, which worked rather like a modern divining pendulum. It was used outside of ritual as a means of divination, and in ritual as a means of communicating with certain classes of spirits. Either a standard Golden Dawn ring and disk, made according to the Order documents, or a pendulum of some other kind, could easily be made and consecrated as a working tool. The consecration ceremony used in the Order was based on the Zelator Grade ritual, but a simpler approach could easily be used as well.

Several more recent magicians in the Golden Dawn tradition, similarly, have proposed a set of working tools for geomantic divination, one of the three major kinds of divinatory work taught in the Order. A shallow box filled with sand, and a pointed stick, painted with colors and symbols representing the element of Earth, can be made and consecrated for this purpose; the simplest approach to the consecration might be a ritual derived from the ceremony for the elemental working tools, using the symbolism of Earth.

More advanced possibilities include a set of working tools corresponding to the seven traditional planets, which would be of great value to a magician who worked extensively with planetary energies. While tradition does not provide a specific set of tools for the planets, as it does for the elements, it's not hard to derive a set that would be easy to prepare and convenient to use, drawing on images from planetary mythology. For Saturn, then, a sickle would be suitable; for Jupiter and Mars, perhaps the crook and flail of the Egyptian kings, the one an emblem of compassion, the other of punishment; for the Sun, a lamp; for Venus, a hand mirror; for Mercury, a wand; and for the Moon, a crystal sphere. These tools could easily be consecrated using rituals based on those for the elemental working tools, adapted to planetary symbolism.

Other possibilities will occur to the working magician. In all such cases, the principles covered earlier in this chapter can be used as a guideline for construction and consecration. Working tools that correspond with one particular symbolic pattern—an element, a planet, a Sphere—can be made and consecrated in much the manner as the elemental working tools, while those with a wider applicability will require ceremonies less easily written to a formula; these may be modeled on the consecrations of the lamen, sword, Lotus Wand, and mirror, or put together along other lines entirely. Here as elsewhere in magic, there is a great deal of room for experimentation and the personal touch.

CHAPTER 10

TALISMANS

THE WORKING TOOLS covered in the last chapter make up one of the two major classes of consecrated physical objects put to use in Golden Dawn ritual magic. The other class, which provides the system with one of its most important practical methods, consists of talismans.

In modern magical usage, a talisman is a piece of some physical substance—metal, parchment, or paper are the most common materials—that bears symbols of a particular magical energy and has been charged with that energy by a ritual of consecration. Like a working tool, a talisman is a physical anchor for a pattern of nonphysical force, consecrated by a ritual formula and operating by way of the natural flow of power through the process of creation. Unlike a working tool, which functions as an instrument of power in any context the magician may choose, a talisman is intended to bring that force to bear on one specific and tightly focused purpose, and its energies continually seek that purpose until and unless it is ritually deconsecrated.

Talismans thus have a persistence of effect few other magical methods can equal, and this can be extraordinarily useful in the operations of practical magic. Once consecrated, a talisman continues to shape the energies of the creative process on its own, night and day, without any further action on the part of the magician. Like any force steadily applied, it builds momentum over time and combines with other energies moving in the same direction. As a result, most magical purposes that aim for a long-term or permanent change on any level of experience can be done more effectively by way of a talisman than by any other means.

There are, on the other hand, certain drawbacks to talismanic magic. The most important of them comes out of the need to charge a talisman with etheric substance. The most effective way to do this is to draw some of that substance from the etheric body of the magician, using it to set up a vortex that draws in more ether from the surrounding atmosphere. Ether is the life force, however, and the more effectively the talisman is consecrated, the more exhausted the magician is likely to be afterward. Food and rest will set this right in time, but it can be a definite hindrance.

Similar factors come into play when a large number of talismans are made by the same magician. Each talisman is charged by the magician's own etheric force, and this leaves a subtle connection. If the talisman's energies are placed under strain—if, for example, another magician attempts to counteract the talisman, or if its purpose is in opposition to some broader pattern in the macrocosm—the talisman will draw additional force from the consecrator's etheric body. With one or two talismans, this is rarely a problem; with a dozen, the loss of energy can be severe enough to damage one's health.

Finally, a talisman that has completed its work can't simply be thrown out; it must be formally deconsecrated and its energies released into the macrocosm so the energy link is closed off and the talisman itself deactivated. Until this is done, like the bunny in the commercial, it just keeps on going. A talisman that has passed out of your hands and can't be physically recovered can be deconsecrated at a distance—a method of doing this will be given later in this chapter—but it's not always an easy process.

To help clarify the way in which talismans work, we can map out the interactions between a talisman and the five levels of experience as follows.

On the spiritual level, a talisman connects with unity through one of the traditional Names of God, which is invoked in the consecration ceremony and in most cases written or engraved on the talisman as well. A talisman intended to bring stability to some situation, for example, might bear the Name ' ﬥ ﬧ א , ADNI, the Name governing the element of Earth.

On the mental level, a talisman bears geometric and numerical patterns that correspond to the essential idea of the energy it carries, and some of these same patterns will be used in the consecration ceremony. The talisman for stability, accordingly, might include a square or fourfold symmetry in its design, and patterns such as the invoking pentagram of Earth will certainly play a part in its consecration.

On the astral level, a talisman is the center of a set of concrete images and ideas symbolized in its color, form, and decoration, and energized in the context of its consecration ceremony. The talisman for stability will therefore have a series of appropriate names, sigils, and other traditional symbols written on it, and each of these will also play a part in the process of consecration.

On the etheric level, a talisman is a vortex of etheric force that comes partly from the descending impact of the astral patterns wakened in the consecration, and partly from the etheric body of the magician. Establishing this etheric vortex is the critical factor in the making of a talisman according to the Golden Dawn system; it provides both the link between the astral patterns and the physical level, and the energy through which the talisman shapes events on the etheric and physical levels. For this reason, the talisman for stability will be consecrated by a form of ritual that sets up the vortex, and it will be handled after consecration in a way that will minimize disruptions to the etheric structure.

On the physical level, a talisman is a physical expression of nonphysical force, and every part of it will be made with this in mind. Since it doesn't need to be handled in ritual, or in any other context—in fact, as we'll discuss a little later, it's best not to handle it at all once it's consecrated— the physical basis can be extremely simple, so long as it will hold an etheric charge well and can carry the appropriate symbolism.

Each of these levels, then, has a role in the consecrated talisman taken as a whole. The process of creating a talisman, on the other hand, divides more naturally into two practical phases. The first is making the talisman; the second, preparing and performing the consecration ceremony.

Making the Talisman I: The Physical Basis

Older books of magic tend to go on at great length about the proper material to use for a talisman of a given type. In many of these texts, the seven planetary metals form the basic stock in trade of the talismanist— quicksilver, the metal of Mercury, was generally replaced by brass for obvious reasons—and were quite often supplemented by a range of animal products of the mole's blood variety. The resulting farrago is at least as complex and messy as the instructions for making working tools, and in many cases prohibitively expensive as well; the cost of a disk of pure gold four inches in diameter and half an inch thick would put a talisman of the Sun out of reach of all but the wealthiest modern magicians!

Fortunately, this approach isn't necessary or even useful in magical workings today. Most of the magicians of the modern pagan revival have quite sensibly turned to plant substances for their talismans and amulets, and there are several excellent books available on the magical use of herbs, perfumes, and the like. By contrast, the Golden Dawn material, although it covers the making and use of talismans in detail, has surprisingly little to say about their material basis. To some extent, this is a reflection of the Order's tendency to stress astral rather than etheric technique—from an astral standpoint, a talisman can be made from anything that will allow the necessary names and symbols to be drawn, painted, or engraved on it. Another factor at work is the Order's use of the flashing colors, which produces an etheric current by itself.

At the same time, this also reflects an unexpected side of one of the great advantages the modern magician has over his or her medieval counterpart: the ready availability of paper. Paper itself has a modest capacity for etheric charges. If you've ever sniffed a newspaper after it's been read by someone who smokes, though, you'll know how well paper takes up volatile aromatics. Most consecration rituals use incense, and many use incense of specific kinds; after spending an hour or so being consecrated in a room full of incense smoke, a paper talisman will have absorbed quite enough of the incense to give it whatever etheric qualities the incense may have. If those qualities include the ability to pick up etheric charges—as many do—the results are as obvious as they are useful.

The etheric capacity of paper can also be increased substantially by a method taken from central European magical traditions, which have paid a great deal more attention to etheric workings than the Golden Dawn tradition ever did. A *fluid condenser* is a liquid that can hold etheric charges with a high degree of efficiency. If several coats of fluid condenser are painted onto a piece of paper, the paper can then be used as a talisman with nearly the same etheric storage capacity as pure metal.

There are many recipes for fluid condensers; examples can be looked up in Franz Bardon's useful book *Initiation into Hermetics*. The core ingredient of all of them is a small amount of metallic gold, and for the present purpose, this alone will be more than adequate.

To make a fluid condenser for talismanic use, you'll need a glass or ceramic-lined saucepan with a tight lid, a cup of distilled water, and a piece of gold or gold-plated jewelry. Put the gold and water in the pan, cover, bring to a boil, and then let the pan cool to room temperature while still covered. Repeat this process at least half a dozen times. (Cheap gold plating may break down under this treatment; be sure you haven't borrowed an heirloom before you start.) When this is finished, pour the water into a clean glass jar, seal it tightly, and store it in a dark place.

Next, you'll need one or more sheets of heavy watercolor paper, which can be bought at any art supply store. It's often more convenient to cut out the piece for the talisman before you apply the fluid condenser; a circle of paper four inches across will usually prove sufficient. Paint the paper with the fluid condenser using a soft watercolor brush and allow it to dry in a place where it will not be disturbed. Two or three coats of this etheric "paint" will normally be enough.

Once the paper has thoroughly dried, it should be cleansed of unwanted energies. This can be done by a simple ceremonial method. You'll need a piece of silk or linen, and your altar, as well as the paper. The ritual is performed as follows.

First, place the paper on the silk or linen atop the altar. Then perform the Lesser Banishing Ritual of the Pentagram and, if the talisman is to be consecrated with the energies of a planet or Sphere, the Lesser Banishing Ritual of the Hexagram as well.

Second, for an elemental talisman, trace the banishing pentagrams of active Spirit, Air, Fire, Water, Earth, and passive Spirit over the paper, as though the pentagrams stood upright atop the paper. For a talisman of a planet or Sphere, trace the banishing hexagrams of Saturn, Jupiter, Mars, Venus, Mercury, and the Moon over the paper in the same way. In either case, the banishing symbols should be traced across the altar toward the appropriate direction.

Third, raise your arms to your sides in the Sign of Osiris Slain. Say: "In the name of the Lord of the Universe, who works in silence and whom naught but silence can express, I declare this creature of paper cleansed of all energies." Wrap the paper in the silk or linen, and finish with a Cabalistic Cross. This completes the ritual.

Once cleansed, the paper should be kept wrapped in silk or linen until you're ready to make it into a talisman.

Making the Talisman II: The Symbolism

The symbolism chosen for the talisman needs to be drawn or painted on the prepared paper. This process starts with the rules for choosing the appropriate symbolism explained in Chapter 5, but there are some additional factors involved.

Under most circumstances, as we've seen, purposes that have to do with the physical level are dealt with using elemental symbolism, while the planets are used for purposes in the realm of consciousness. Traditional methods for the making of talismans, though, relied so completely on astrological symbolism that a way of using planetary forces for material ends evolved early on and was quite heavily used.

The key to this system is the difference between the Intelligence of a planet, which is that planet's own indwelling power in the realm of consciousness, and the Spirit of the planet, which is the planet's reflection in the etheric body of the Earth. The Spirit of a planet is a "blind force," in the technical language of magic; it has no consciousness of its own, and for magical purposes must be guided by the ruling Intelligence of its planet.

The twofold application of the planets to talismanic work allows for a greater flexibility of focus; there are purposes, even wholly material ones, that fit the system of the planets better than that of the elements. At the same time, this use of planetary symbolism is especially valuable when, as so often happens, the realms of consciousness and of matter are both involved—for example, in healing work, when even the most concrete of physical damage often has a psychological dimension.

Whichever set of symbolism you choose, you'll need to note the Name of God, Archangel, and Angel governing the energy you intend to summon. For an element, the Ruler will also be necessary; for a planet, the Intelligence will be needed, and if appropriate, the Spirit as well; for a Sphere, the Hebrew name of the corresponding celestial sphere should be used. It's traditional to use Hebrew letters to write these names on a talisman, and you may find it helpful to practice drawing the letters before trying your hand on the talisman itself.

You'll also need to note the flashing colors, numbers, and other symbolism corresponding to the energy you intend to use. In the case of planetary energies, this includes the magical seal of the planet, and the sigils of the Intelligence and Spirit given in Chapter 4.

Finally, there is a set of additional symbols, called the geomantic sigils, derived from the figures used in geomantic divination. These symbols can be a useful addition to the symbolism of a talisman, but it's necessary to have a clear grasp of geomantic symbolism in order to use them effectively. Both the sigils and a basic introduction to geomancy can be found in Volume Four of Regardie's *Golden Dawn*.

By now you're probably wondering what you're going to do with all of this material. Unfortunately, there isn't a simple answer to this most reasonable question. The design of talismans is an art, not a branch of engineering, and each magician needs to develop a personal style in this art that best suits his or her tastes and needs. One common approach is to put names around the rim, and sigils and geometrical figures in the center, but even this should not be taken for a rule.

The one certain rule is that every name and entity you invoke in the consecration ceremony should appear on the talisman as well. Another rule to follow, where possible, is that a talisman using flashing colors should use an equal amount of each color—for example, if the background of the talisman is one color, all the names, sigils, and figures should be in the other.

Two sample talismans, one elemental and one planetary, are shown in Diagram 47 on page 226 to demonstrate one approach. Most older books on magic, and a good many newer ones as well, will provide other examples. With or without these, you may find it useful to begin exploring the demands of the art by drawing a number of practice talismans.

On the practical side, artist-quality colored pencils make one effective way of drawing symbols on a paper talisman, and fine-point colored pens provide another. Other possibilities can be found at any artists' supply store. It's normally a good idea to test your drawing and coloring media on a piece of the paper you intend to use to be sure they won't blur or smudge excessively.

Once the talisman has been drawn, it should be wrapped in silk or linen and left alone until the consecration ritual.

Talisman of Earth

Front   Back

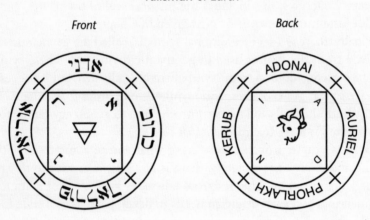

Talisman of Mercury

Front   Back

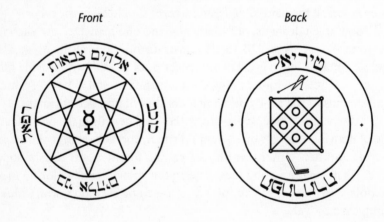

Diagram 47—
Two Sample Talismans

A Basic Ritual of Consecration

There are many different ways of consecrating a talisman, from fairly simple methods that can be done successfully by the beginner, all the way to elaborate two-hour-long ceremonies using the full range of Golden Dawn ritual methods. Three different consecration ceremonies will be given here as examples that can be worked as is or, preferably, used as the basis for ceremonies of your own design.

The first is the simplest ceremony of practical magic given in this book. It can be done by anyone who has learned the Pentagram and Hexagram Rituals and the basic First Degree Opening and Closing. Requirements are those of the Opening and Closing, along with the talisman and its silk or linen wrapper, and a list of the names to be invoked. The ceremony is performed as follows.

First, perform the complete First Degree Opening in the basic form. If you intend to invoke a planet or Sphere in the ritual, perform the Lesser Banishing Ritual of the Hexagram immediately after that of the Pentagram.

Second, unwrap the talisman and set it at the center of the altar. Take the cup of Holy Water in your right hand, dip the fingers of your left hand, and flick Water from your fingertips three times over the talisman, saying, "Creature of talismans, I purify you with Water." Then wave the incense three times over the talisman, saying: "Creature of talismans, I consecrate you with Fire."

Third, perform the Greater Invoking Ritual of the Pentagram or Hexagram corresponding to the energy you intend to invoke.

Fourth, face the direction of the element, planet, or Sphere across the altar and trace the appropriate invoking pentagram or hexagram toward that direction, as though it stood upright on the talisman. Point to the center of the pentagram or hexagram and vibrate the Name of God governing the operation.

Fifth, take the talisman, holding it by means of the silk or linen wrapper so your hand does not touch it directly. Raise it up high, bring it down to face level, and then breathe on it, slowly, three times, concentrating on the idea that energy passes with the breath into the talisman. Return it to the altar and say: "Creature of talismans, I give thee life from my life, as flame is lit from flame, for the fulfillment of this purpose ...." (At this point state slowly and clearly the purpose as you defined it in a single sentence, as described in Chapter 5.) Then return the talisman to its place on the altar.

Sixth, recite the following conjuration to the Ruler of the element, the Intelligence of the planet, or the Spirits of the celestial sphere corresponding to the Sphere of the Tree of Life. (The traditional lore gives no names for the latter; simply use "Spirits of Levanah," in the case of a talisman of Yesod, for the title, and delete references to the name of the spirit.) The appropriate divine, archangelic, and angelic names are inserted at the places noted. The conjuration runs as follows.

"I conjure and command thee, (name of spirit), thou who art Ruler of the element (or) Intelligence of the planet (or) Spirits of the celestial sphere of (name of element, planet, or celestial sphere), in and by the Great Name (Name of God), and in and by the mighty archangel (name), and in and by the angel (or) angelic host (name), that thou wilt direct thy power into this creature of talismans, and give it such strength as it may require to fulfill this purpose ...." Repeat the purpose of the talisman.

For a planetary talisman made for a physical or etheric purpose, add the following section: "And I charge thee likewise to guide and direct (name of planetary spirit), the mighty Spirit of (name of planet), to place the material force of (name of planet) in this creature of talismans for the fulfilment of the same purpose."

In either case, conclude as follows: "And may this creature of talismans fulfill its purpose without evasion or equivocation, ceasing its work only when it is deconsecrated at my hand and its energies return whence they came."

Seventh, wrap the talisman in its wrapper, again being careful not to touch it directly. Then perform the complete basic First Degree Closing; remember to banish with the Hexagram Ritual as well as the Pentagram if you did so in the Opening. This completes the ceremony.

———

Once the consecration is complete, the talisman should be placed in a covering that will not block the flow of etheric energies—small manila envelopes work well—and put in an out-of-the-way location, such as the bottom of a drawer, where it will be safe and undisturbed. Once this is done, leave it alone and, as far as possible, forget about it. The less the physical basis of the talisman is disturbed, the more effectively it can establish the etheric vortex through which it operates, and the less of your energy that goes into worrying about the talisman, the less interference it will have to push through in order to accomplish its purpose.

An Elemental Ritual of Consecration

The second ritual of consecration we'll be examining is based on the same formula as the first, but expands it through a symbolism derived from that of the four elements and used in the Golden Dawn Theoricus Grade. The one additional requirement is a set of elemental working tools or, if you haven't made and consecrated these yet, appropriate elemental symbols of the sort described in Chapter 8. The ritual is performed as follows.

———————

First, perform the complete First Degree Opening in the expanded form.

Second, unwrap the talisman and set it at the center of the altar. Take the cup of Holy Water in your right hand, dip the fingers of your left hand, and flick water from your fingertips three times over the talisman, saying, "Creature of talismans, I purify you with Water." Then wave the incense three times over it, saying: "Creature of talismans, I consecrate you with Fire."

Third, perform the Greater Invoking Ritual of the Pentagram or Hexagram corresponding to the energy you intend to invoke.

Fourth, face the direction of the element, planet, or Sphere across the altar, and trace the appropriate invoking pentagram or hexagram toward that direction, as though it stood upright on the talisman. Point to the center of the pentagram or hexagram and vibrate the Name of God governing the operation.

Fifth, take the talisman, being careful not to touch it directly. Raise it up high, bring it down to face level, and then breathe on it, slowly, three times, concentrating on the idea that energy passes with the breath into the talisman. Say: "Creature of talismans, I give thee life from my life, as flame is lit from flame, for the fulfillment of this purpose ..." and state the purpose as you have defined it.

Sixth, recite the following conjuration to the Ruler of the element, the Intelligence of the planet, or the Spirits of the celestial sphere corresponding to the Sphere of the Tree of Life:

"I conjure and command thee, (name of spirit), thou who art Ruler of the element (or) Intelligence of the planet (or) Spirits of the celestial sphere of (name of element, planet, or celestial sphere), in and by the Great Name (Name of God), and in and by the mighty archangel (name), and in and by the angel (or) angelic host (name), that thou wilt direct thy power into this creature of talismans and give it such strength as it may require to fulfill this purpose ...." Repeat the purpose as you have defined it.

For a planetary talisman made for a physical or etheric purpose, add the following section: "And I charge thee likewise to guide and direct (name of planetary spirit), the mighty Spirit of (name of planet), to place the material force of (name of planet) in this creature of talismans for the fulfilment of the same purpose."

In either case, conclude as follows: "And may this creature of talismans fulfill its purpose without evasion or equivocation, ceasing its work only when it is deconsecrated at my hand and its energies return whence they came."

Seventh, go to the east side of the altar, take up the dagger of Air in your right hand and the talisman in your left. Turn and go to the eastern quarter of the space. Say, facing east: "Creature of talismans, arise and follow me into the realms of Air." Then circumambulate once around the space, saying slowly: "The sphinx of Egypt spake and said: I am the synthesis of the elemental forces. I am also the symbol of humanity. I am life and I am death. I am the child of the night of time." Returning to the east, face east, raise the dagger high, then touch it to the talisman, saying: "In the Great Name YHVH, creature of talismans, I strengthen thee with the energies of Air. Be thou prompt and active as the Sylphs, for the fulfillment of thy purpose."

Eighth, return to the altar, put down the dagger, and take the wand of Fire. Go to the southern quarter. Say: "Creature of talismans, arise and follow me into the realms of Fire." Circumambulate, saying: "I am Osiris, the soul in twin aspect, united to the Higher by purification, perfected by suffering, glorified through trial. I have come where the great gods are, through the power of the mighty Name." Returning to the south, raise the wand and then touch it to the talisman. Say: "Creature of talismans, I strengthen thee with the energies of Fire. Be thou energetic and strong as the Salamanders, for the fulfillment of thy purpose."

Ninth, in the same way, exchange the wand for the cup and go to the west. Say: "Creature of talismans, arise and follow me into the realms of Water." Circumambulate, saying: "I have passed through the gates of the firmament. Give me your hands, for I am made as ye, ye lords of truth! For ye are the formers of the soul." Returning to the west, raise the cup, touch it to the talisman, and say: "Creature of talismans, I strengthen thee with the energies of Water. Be thou flexible and attentive to images as the Undines, for the fulfillment of thy purpose."

Tenth, exchange the cup for the pentacle and go to the north. Say: "Creature of talismans, arise and follow me into the realms of Earth." Circumambulate, saying: "O Lord of the Universe, thou art above all things and thy Name is in all things, and before thee the shadows of night roll back and the darkness hasteth away." Returning to the north, raise the pentacle and then touch it to the talisman, saying: "Creature of talismans, I strengthen thee with the energies of Earth. Be thou laborious and patient as the Gnomes, for the fulfillment of thy purpose."

Eleventh, return to the west of the altar and face east. Set the talisman in the center of the altar. Raise your hands above the altar and say: "Creature of talismans, thou art consecrated and strengthened by the powers of the elements. Let my will in thee be accomplished."

Twelfth, wrap the talisman in its wrapper, being careful not to touch it directly. Then perform the complete basic First Degree Closing; remember to banish with the Hexagram Ritual as well as the Pentagram if you did so in the Opening. This completes the ceremony.

A Telesmatic Ritual of Consecration

The third ceremony for consecrating a talisman makes use of the art of telesmatic imagery described in Chapter 4. In this method, the Rulers, Intelligences, and Spirits used in most consecration rituals in the Golden Dawn tradition are replaced by a telesmatic image of the energy being invoked, which is designed according to the principles of the Cabala and used to focus and direct a balanced array of forces into the talisman. Certain aspects of the Third Degree symbolism, and some of the more advanced Golden Dawn methods of working with the breath, are also put to use. This ceremony is somewhat more demanding to perform than the others given in this chapter, and also more limited—it can't be used, in the form given, to consecrate talismans of the Spheres—but its effects are often a good deal stronger.

Some basic astrological symbolism is involved in the construction of the telesmatic image, as well as aspects of the symbolic structure of the Hebrew alphabet. The twenty-two Hebrew letters are divided into the three Mother letters, which correspond to the elements Air, Water, and Fire; the seven Double letters, which correspond to the seven planets; and the twelve Single letters, which correspond to the signs of the zodiac. (All these can be found in the Appendix.) In astrology, each planet rules either one or two signs, and each element rules three. As a result, it's possible to make a symbolic vibratory name representing the energies of a planet or element by combining the letter of the planet or element with the letters of the signs it rules, and adding the ending ל א, AL.

For the element of Water, for example, the letter מ, Mem, which stands for Water itself, is joined with ח (Cheth), נ (Nun), and ק (Qoph), corresponding to the Water signs Cancer, Scorpio, and Pisces, and with the suffix ל א to form the vibratory name מאקנחם, MChNQAL, Mecheneqal. Similarly, the planet Mars rules the signs Aries and Scorpio; the corresponding letters form the name פהנאל, PHNAL, Pahanel. These names, in turn, can be turned into telesmatic images using the rules given in Chapter 4.

The vibratory name and telesmatic image corresponding to the force you wish to invoke should be worked out before you make the talisman. The vibratory name itself should be written on the talisman in the Hebrew letters, and geomantic sigils that correspond to the signs of the zodiac used in the construction of the name might also have a place there. Both the name and the image should be committed to memory before the consecration.

Other than this—and, of course, the talisman and its wrapper—the consecration ritual has the same requirements as any other First Degree ritual. It is performed as follows.

First, perform the complete First Degree Opening in its expanded form.

Second, unwrap the talisman and set it at the center of the altar. Sprinkle it with Holy Water three times, as in the preceding ceremony, saying, "Creature of talismans, I purify you with Water." Then cense it three times with the incense, saying, "Creature of talismans, I consecrate you with Fire."

Third, perform the Greater Invoking Ritual of the Pentagram or Hexagram corresponding to the energy you wish to invoke.

Fourth, face the direction of the element or planet across the altar and vibrate the Name of God governing the operation, using the Vibratory Formula of the Middle Pillar, as given in Chapter 7.

Fifth, circulate the energies you have invoked by means of the Four Revolutions of the Breath.

Sixth, still facing the direction of the force you have invoked, draw in a deep breath, close your eyes, and silently repeat the letters that make up the vibratory name you've constructed. Take the talisman, being careful not to touch it with your bare skin, and breathe on it slowly, mentally pronouncing the vibratory name as you do so. Repeat this process until you have breathed on the talisman four times.

Seventh, return the talisman to its place on the altar. Take the lotus wand and trace the symbol of the Rose Cross in the air above the talisman, as though the symbol stood upright on it. Make the Signs of Isis, Apophis, and Osiris Risen and say: "May the light descend upon this creature of talismans." Then visualize a shaft of brilliant white light shining down on it from above.

Eighth, with the lotus wand, trace a circle around the talisman. Then, for an elemental talisman, trace the appropriate invoking pentagram five times in the air above the talisman; for a planetary talisman, trace the appropriate invoking hexagram six times over the talisman. In either case, the symbols should be drawn as though standing upright on the talisman, and the vibratory name should be vibrated each time as you trace the symbol. Then say the following invocation, inserting the appropriate names where indicated:

"In and by the Great Name (Name of God), and by the mighty archangel (name) and the powerful angel (name), I summon thee, spirits and powers of (name of element or planet). I conjure and command thine obedience in this work of the magic of light. In and by the mighty Names, I adjure thee to direct the energies of (name of element or planet) into the form of (vibratory name)."

Ninth, visualize the telesmatic image you have designed, placing it in the direction of the invoked force just outside the area enclosed in your banishings at the beginning of the ceremony. Build up the telesmatic image as strongly as possible, seeing it as radiant with light and power. When this has been achieved, say:

"And in and by the Great Name (Name of God), (vibratory name), I call upon thee to direct thy power into this creature of talismans, and to give it such strength as it may require to fulfill this purpose …." Here state the purpose of the talisman. "… and may this creature of talismans fulfill its purpose without evasion or equivocation, ceasing its work only when it is deconsecrated by my hand and its energies return whence they come."

Visualize the telesmatic image making the Sign of Entering toward the talisman. If you watch the talisman at this point, you may see a flickering or flashing of light on or just above it, as the energies lock into place. Hold the visualization until it begins to weaken, and then visualize the telesmatic image making the Sign of Silence and vanishing.

Tenth, wrap the talisman in its wrapper, taking care not to touch it directly. Then perform the complete First Degree Closing in its expanded form. This completes the ceremony.

———

Just as the basic consecration ritual given earlier in this chapter is the easiest practical ritual in this book, so this is in some ways one of the most difficult; it depends on the ability to shape energy directly through the subtle structures of the etheric and astral bodies, rather than indirectly through ceremonial forms. Regular practice of the Middle Pillar exercise is an effective way to develop this ability, and to build toward those levels of magic that lie beyond the realm of ritual.

The formula of the ritual itself is fairly straightforward. The energies awakened in the self through an invocation based on the Vibratory Formula of the Middle Pillar are used to energize the talisman, and are then bound into the talisman's structure through the Third Degree Signs and an appropriate visualization; the vortex of energies thus generated then becomes the anchor for powers drawn from the macrocosm by way of the telesmatic image. The same formula, with appropriate changes, can be applied to many other types of magical work.

Flashing Tablets

One of the most interesting Golden Dawn developments in the field of practical magic is the art of the Flashing Tablet, which combines talismanic ritual with the Order's methods of scrying and Pathworking. This art seems to have been almost entirely abandoned after the collapse of the Order, but it's highly effective and well worth adding to the armory of more advanced magical methods.

A Flashing Tablet is a specialized talisman made using the flashing colors. It should have a relatively simple visual symbolism, centering on a single sigil or image—for example, the seal of a planet or the traditional sign of an element. Because of the way in which a Flashing Tablet is used, it's best to make it square or rectangular rather than circular, and to use very stiff paper. Beyond these points, the same rules given above may be followed for its design and consecration.

The differences in method become important only after a Flashing Tablet is consecrated. Rather than putting the tablet in an out-of-the-way location, it should be kept someplace easily accessible. Each morning, then, the magician places it in a position where he or she can look at it, sits before it in a comfortable position, and uses the Flashing Tablet itself as an astral doorway for scrying.

The detailed Golden Dawn methods for scrying can be found in the Order's papers and in any number of other books on modern magic. Briefly, the scryer takes a symbol of some kind, visualizes it as a door, and then imagines himself or herself walking through that door and into whatever lies beyond it. The imagery that appears in the imagined realm beyond the door will be found, if the procedure is done properly, to reveal something of the inner nature of the symbol. With practice, what start out as little better than daydreams turn into intense and compelling experiences as the scryer's awareness becomes more attuned to the images of the Sphere of Sensation, which correspond to the symbol being used.

In the art of the Flashing Tablet, this same process takes on a more practical form. Having passed through the doorway in the spirit vision and entered into the astral realm beyond, the magician visualizes himself or herself performing an Invoking Ritual of the appropriate Pentagram or Hexagram in that realm. This is done with as much clarity and power as though the same ritual were being done on the physical level. Once the invocation is completed, the magician calls upon the Name of God governing the working and asks for power to accomplish the purpose for which the Flashing Tablet has been made. When this is done, he or she goes back through the doorway, returns to awareness of the physical level, and puts the Flashing Tablet away until the next morning, when the same operation is repeated.

This process, in effect, energizes the Flashing Tablet from within and results in a hypercharged talisman with enormous potential power. By the same token, though, it can be a dangerous method to the practitioner if misused. The link established by the daily charging of the Flashing Tablet will work both ways and lay the worker of destructive or selfish magic open to a backlash of equally heightened power. For this reason, it's a good idea to be very sure of what you are doing before choosing the art of the Flashing Tablet as a way to get it done.

A Ceremony of Deconsecration

Sooner or later, every talisman you make will need to be deconsecrated. This is true of talismans that accomplish their purpose, obviously, but equally true of those that fail; there's a point at which continuing to put energy into a losing cause is a useless act. It's also true, and even more critical, in those cases—which are by no means uncommon, particularly in the early stages of magical training—when a magician decides on a purpose and realizes after the ritual has already been performed that the entire project is a serious mistake.

Fortunately, deconsecrating a talisman isn't a difficult process. The vortex of energies that give it its power can be disrupted by relatively simple methods; an ordinary banishing will often do the job quite efficiently. (This is why you need to wrap the newly consecrated talisman in an insulative substance before closing the ritual.) For a more thorough deconsecration, the following short ceremony can be used to deconsecrate any talisman made by Golden Dawn methods you have in your possession. The one requirement is an an altar. The ceremony is performed as follows.

First, take the talisman out of its covering, without touching it, and place it on the center of the altar. Face the direction corresponding to the energy placed in the talisman and trace the appropriate invoking pentagram or hexagram in the air above the talisman.

Second, using the name of the spirit or the vibratory name you used in the consecration, say: "O (name), thy work is accomplished. Go now in peace, and may the blessing of (Name of God governing the operation) be upon you." Then trace the appropriate banishing pentagram or hexagram in the air above the talisman. If you watch the talisman at this moment, you may notice the change as the energies depart. Say: "Creature of talismans, thy work is accomplished. I deconsecrate thee and return thy energies whence they came."

Third, perform the Lesser Banishing Ritual of the Pentagram, preceded by that of the Hexagram if the talisman was of a planet or Sphere. This completes the ceremony.

A Flashing Tablet should be deconsecrated from within, using the same method used to charge it; simply pass through the tablet in the way described earlier, thank the powers you invoked to accomplish the working, visualize yourself performing the appropriate banishing ritual, and return. Once this is done, the Tablet should be deconsecrated from without, using the method given above.

In the case of a talisman not in your possession, you'll need to perform a more elaborate version of this ceremony. Start with the First Degree Opening, and invoke the energies you originally used to consecrate the talisman by the appropriate invoking ritual. Then visualize the talisman on the altar. (The more precisely you can do this, the better; it's a good idea, for this reason, to make a drawing of any talisman you design and keep it in a safe place.) Then proceed as in the second part of the ritual. When you trace the banishing symbol over the visualized talisman, allow the visualization to disappear. Then banish with the Greater Banishing Ritual of the appropriate Pentagram or Hexagram, and close with the First Degree Closing. Done with focused awareness, this process will disrupt the talisman's energies and allow the etheric vortex to disperse.

CHAPTER 11

EVOCATION

IN THE MAGICAL SYSTEMS OF THE MIDDLE AGES, the practice of evocation was far and away the most important and most thoroughly developed branch of magical work. Rituals of evocation and information about spirits to be evoked account for the great majority of the material given in the old grimoires. It's only a slight exaggeration to say that, for much of Western history, magic could be defined simply as the art of summoning and commanding spirits. This focus on evocation has ancient roots and a tangled web of causes, but it has had a powerful role in shaping attitudes about magic up to the present day.

In the magic of the Golden Dawn tradition, by contrast, evocation plays a much smaller part. Certainly, methods of evocation were taught and practiced by the adepts of the Golden Dawn and its successor groups, and materials on the subject can be found in the published collections of the Order's work. At the same time, these make up a very small part of the total, and certain other branches of practical magic—for example, the making of talismans or the art of telesmatic imagery—receive far more attention. In the curriculum of magical studies used in the original Golden Dawn, in fact, it was possible to advance to the highest grades of adeptship within the Order without ever performing a ritual of evocation.

The reasons behind this relative neglect of evocation are just as complex as those behind its earlier predominance, and had more than a little to do with political factors in the English occult community of the time. Two other reasons, though, are relevant from the standpoint of the modern Golden Dawn magician.

One of these was the Golden Dawn's intensive development of scrying and similar methods of visionary perception. A magician who wishes to communicate with an entity from another realm of being can choose from at least two possible approaches. On the one hand, he or she can attempt to bring the entity through into manifestation in the realm we normally perceive; this is the approach of evocation. On the other hand, he or she can attempt to enter into the realm where the entity normally dwells and communicate with it there; this is the approach of astral clairvoyance. Since the art of voyaging into other realms was much practiced by the Order's adepts—sometimes, as Israel Regardie commented, to the point of becoming little more than a kind of astral tourism—it's not surprising that this latter method became their standard approach, and the substantial body of scrying lore that exists in the Order's papers makes this approach equally available to the modern magician.

The other factor is in some ways more important. Evocation has its dangers; of all the applications of ritual magic used in the Golden Dawn tradition, it involves the most risks, and the most severe ones as well. These risks can be controlled, and there are a number of measures that can be taken to deal with trouble if and when it arises. Still, the risks are there, and the wise magician knows better than to ignore them.

The dangers of the process of evocation arise, for the most part, from the fact that the entities summoned in rituals of evocation are independent beings, with purposes and powers that need not have any relationship to the desires of the magician who summons them. They cannot simply be treated as puppets of the magician's will, and the magician who fails to keep this in mind is likely to end up in trouble.

Imagine for a moment that, instead of summoning spirits, rituals of evocation caused ordinary human beings to suddenly appear outside the circle. One dark and stormy night, using such a ritual, a hypothetical magician evokes a human being to carry out some purpose. The person who appears happens to be friendly and well intentioned toward the magician; they discuss the purpose, and the evoked human agrees to accomplish it. The evocation is a success.

The next night, our imaginary magician uses the same ritual for some other purpose. This time, though, the human who has been evoked is hostile, or simply uninterested, and refuses to help. If our magician has some way of making effective threats, the purpose may still be accomplished—perhaps by pulling a pistol from under the altar and holding the evoked human at gun point until he or she complies— but the help that will be given in this context will be grudging at best, and if the evoked human can find a way to turn the tables on the magician, it's a safe bet that he or she will do so. The evocation may or may not be a success.

The night after that, the magician tries again. This time the ritual summons a human who seems very friendly indeed, who nods and smiles and gets the magician off guard, and then whips out a lead pipe. Our magician regains consciousness late the next morning to find a big lump on his head, his wallet gone, and his house stripped of valuables. The evocation is certainly not a success!

All three of these possibilities have their equivalents in the evocation of spirits. The spirit who appears in answer to an evocation may be well intentioned, but it's far from safe to assume that this must always be the case. An angry or predatory spirit has a number of options at hand if it wishes to make life difficult for a human magician, many of them paralleling the various kinds of magical attack. In the Golden Dawn tradition, most of these activities on the part of hostile spirits are classified under the heading of *obsession*. We'll discuss this more thoroughly later in this chapter.

The Uses of Evocation

It may be worth asking what value the practice of evocation has to the modern magician in the first place. There's little place in magical work for the kind of attitude that treats risk-taking as a sport; magicians in training who are drawn to this kind of behavior would probably be better off taking up bungee jumping or skydiving. If evocation poses more serious risks than other kinds of ritual magic, it needs to offer equivalent advantages—or it needs to be discarded.

A case can certainly be made, in or out of the Golden Dawn tradition, for the second option. On the other hand, there are certain possibilities open to magical evocation that can't easily be achieved by other ritual methods. These arise, for the most part, from exactly that factor which makes evoked spirits potentially dangerous: the fact that they are independent beings, with powers, purposes, and knowledge that differ from those of their summoner.

This factor can be put to work in practical magic in two different ways. On the one hand, it makes spirits of certain kinds extremely valuable as sources of magical information. It's worth noting that a large part of the magical lore used in the Western tradition comes from precisely this kind of source; the Enochian system received by John Dee and Edward Kelley, which makes up an important part of the advanced magical training of the Golden Dawn tradition, is only one of many examples. A magician who seeks a deeper understanding of the secrets of the element of Water, for example, might well choose to perform an evocation of Tharsis, the Ruler of that element; one who seeks a clearer grasp of the mysteries of the planet Venus could do worse than to evoke the Intelligence Hagiel.

On the other hand, spirits can also be evoked to carry out specific magical tasks, and their independence gives evocatory magic many of the same advantages that talismanic magic possesses. Once summoned and set to work at an appropriate task, a spirit will keep working without further action on the part of the magician until the task is accomplished. Importantly, too, spirits associated with a given element or planet have capacities in their own realm that human beings can rarely match; there are very few magicians, for example, who can shape the energies of the element of Water as precisely and forcefully as an undine can. The ability to evoke and direct spirits gives the magician the ability to make use of these powers at second hand. Both these factors make evocation a field of magic that can be worth pursuing if it's handled skillfully and used for appropriate purposes.

The practice of evocation, like the other applications of ritual we've discussed so far, can also be analyzed in terms of the five levels of experience:

On the spiritual level, the spirit to be evoked is linked with a particular planet, element, or other symbolic category, and thus to the corresponding Name of God. This Name therefore plays a central role in the ceremony of evocation, and it is vibrated and contemplated in ritual work before the process of evocation itself begins. In a ritual evocation of a water elemental, for example, the Name ל א , AL, governs both the undine and the whole operation of summoning it.

On the mental level, the spirit to be evoked represents some aspect of the core idea or concept represented by its symbolism, and this mental-level connection determines the spirit's role and place in the universe. The number and geometry that belong to the spirit's symbolism play a part in the ritual, together with certain other geometries—notably, the protective circle itself, and the pentagrams and hexagrams used to invoke and banish. In the case of a ceremony to invoke an undine, the number four and the square (which generally correspond to elemental workings) appear together with the circle and the pentagrams of Water.

On the astral level, the spirit to be evoked has a form by which it appears to the consciousness of the magician. Many of the old books of evocatory magic are full of sometimes lurid descriptions of the shapes taken by spirits, but these should be taken as examples, not as hard and fast rules; the form taken by a spirit in any given evocation will be a function of the interaction between the Spheres of Sensation of the spirit and its summoner. At the same time, this form will also take shape in the context of the whole range of technical methods of astral magic used in the evocation, which may include a range of colors and symbols. In the case of the evocation of an undine, for example, the colors blue and orange, and a range of symbols of water, may appear physically, and will certainly take a role in the inner side of the ceremony.

On the etheric level, much depends on the nature of the spirit being evoked. Of the four types of spirits the rituals in this chapter are specifically designed to summon—the Intelligences and Spirits of the planets, and the Rulers and elemental spirits of the elements—the planetary Spirits and elementals possess complex etheric bodies, able to affect physical matter directly, while the Rulers and Intelligences do not. In the first case, the methods of etheric magic play a subtle, but significant, part in the evocation; in the latter, all that needs to be done etherically is to provide a space of reasonably clear energies that will not impede communication.

On the physical level, a specific choice presents itself to the magician. There are two traditional ways to contact spirits in evocatory ritual. The first is summoning the spirit to appear in a mirror, scrying stone, or similar device. The second, a substantially more difficult feat, is summoning the spirit to appear outside the protective circle in the ritual space itself, usually in a triangle set aside for the purpose.

This latter was the method used in published Golden Dawn evocation rituals, but in most cases, the use of the magical mirror is the better alternative; this was the method used by Dee and Kelley in their Enochian workings, to name only one of many examples. In this method, the mirror or other scrying device provides the physical basis for the working. In the case of evocation to visible appearance, the physical basis is usually made up of large quantities of a strong materializing incense such as dittany of Crete, which can be used by the spirit as the raw material for a body of matter. In either case, the full set of working tools of the magician, plus altar, altar furniture, and circle, provides a physical context.

Dealing with Spirits

The skillful and appropriate use of evocation needs to be rooted in a clear understanding of how the magician and the world of spirits relate to each other. This understanding differs in some important ways from the approaches used by some older traditions of evocation, and it's of some importance to see where the differences lie.

The magicians of the Middle Ages clearly recognized that the practice of evocation had risks as well as benefits, and they set out to deal with the dangers efficiently from the start. The method they used, typical for the time, was sheer brute force. The rituals of evocation from medieval grimoires typically start off with the construction of a protective circle designed, sometimes quite visibly, in the image of the great stone castles of the age. From within this fortified stronghold, the magician readied his arsenal of words of power and consecrated weapons, and then launched his conjurations like assaults, battering the spirit into submission with threats and rhetoric fortified with the Names of God.

A spirit who did not show up quickly enough might have its name and sigil, written on a piece of parchment, scorched over hot coals in the hope that this might torture it into obedience! It's little wonder that spirits, faced with this kind of treatment, were seen as dangerous and treacherous, apt to wriggle out of agreements through any loophole they could find. Most human beings put in the same situation would behave similarly.

This kind of brute-force approach to evocation is an extreme that can be dispensed with in most cases. At the same time, it's important not to go to the opposite extreme, in the fashion of what used to be called trance mediumship and is now usually termed "channeling." This kind of working involves opening up the Sphere of Sensation to whatever entity happens to be present in the astral level, and accepting what comes through—usually at face value.

Golden Dawn teaching materials tended to speak of trance mediumship in very harsh terms, and while some of the rhetoric may have been overdone, there was, and is, a good reason for it. The passive approach of the medium, who hands over control of his or her body and mind to a possessing spirit, is essentially incompatible with the path of the magician as the Golden Dawn tradition understands it.

The magician seeks to strengthen and unify his or her will, to take an active role in the realms of consciousness, and to become free of the domination of external powers and patterns, and none of these things are helped in the least by going through the experience of making oneself a passive mouthpiece for some disembodied presence. Nor, according to magical traditions, are spirits necessarily trustworthy enough to make the extreme vulnerability of possession by spirits a good idea. Whatever the validity of trance mediumship as a path—a question that will not be dealt with here—it's probably true that, as the Golden Dawn papers insist, those who practice one shouldn't practice the other.

Between the overblown forcefulness of the medieval grimoires and the extreme passivity of the modern "channeler," though, lies a saner and more balanced approach to magical evocation—one that recognizes the many characteristics human beings and spirits have in common, and sets out to deal with these entities simply as fellow beings who do not have the blessing and burden of physical bodies. The same qualities of courtesy and caution that make for the graceful handling of human affairs are central to this approach, which can be found in some of the magical writings of the late Renaissance and in the teaching documents of the Golden Dawn.

The "courtesy" side of the equation stands out most clearly when material on evocation from Golden Dawn sources is compared to its equivalents in the grimoires. The Order's writings insist that a magician has no right to injure or torment any spirit, even an "evil" or destructive one, without very good reason. Similarly, spirits are to be commanded only to carry out tasks appropriate to their natures. Even reviling spirits verbally is forbidden; the most one can do is command and banish them by the Names of God—which, admittedly, is all that is necessary.

The "caution" side, on the other hand, stands out most clearly when the Golden Dawn methods of evocation are compared to the approach commonly used by mediums, or any of the other popular methods of evocation (for example, ouija boards) in common use in our culture. The Golden Dawn magician is not dependent on the good will of the spirits he or she summons; a protective circle, appropriate banishing rituals, and the magical sword all play a part in ceremonies of evocation, and natural magic in the form of asafoetida, Holy Water, and the like also offers a means of protection if necessary. The Order's lore also stresses, sensibly enough, that spirits do not always speak the truth in the context of an evocation.

It's possible, and useful, to list some of the principles by which spirits can be successfully evoked and directed: *First, evoke the right spirit for the task*. If the purpose you have in mind corresponds to the element of Fire, don't evoke an elemental of Water, and if the purpose corresponds best to a planet, don't evoke an elemental at all. This is a practical point— undines do a very poor job at Fire-oriented tasks, and elementals an equally poor one at the work of the planets—but a point that also plays an important role in establishing good relations with the world of spirits. It's the nature of undines, for example, to strengthen the influence of Water in the world, to make things colder and wetter. If a magician summons an undine and directs her to do this in some particular situation—for example, to break a fever or a heat wave—there's no need for the threats and imprecations of the grimoires; the undine will happily turn her attention to that situation and then simply do her job.

In the same way, Taphthartharath, the Spirit of Mercury, naturally fosters communication, and a magician who instructs him to do precisely that in some specific case, using the appropriate Names and ritual structure, is unlikely to face much argument.

Another side of this first principle is that in many cases, the spirits who provide information are not the same as the ones who carry out the tasks of practical magic. The Intelligences of the planets and the Rulers of the elements are good sources for knowledge of their respective realms, but to perform magical workings in those realms, the magician will be better off evoking the Spirits of the planets and the elementals of the elements. The difference between these is, in many ways, the same as that between the anima mundi and the spiritus mundi, as described in Chapter 2. One represents the innate intelligence of the element or planet, the other the active power that expresses that intelligence in the realms of concrete form.

Second, always invoke before you evoke. The Name of God corresponding to the appropriate element or planet is an important part of the practice of evocation, and should always be invoked through contemplation and the technical methods of magic before the actual evocation begins. By doing this, you place yourself in contact with the source of the power you are evoking, and help ensure that the effect you seek to produce will be in harmony with the broader patterns of the cosmos. The invocation should also call upon the intermediate powers, those that correspond to the levels between the Unity at the source of being and the specific spirit you intend to evoke. This is done to affirm the descent of the energies of creation down the levels of being.

Third, keep your protections in place. The outward protections that guard you against hostile or treacherous acts on the part of spirits—which are, unfortunately, always a possibility—include the protective circle, the magical sword, the cup of Holy Water, and a bottle of asafoetida next to the censer for emergency use. You should always be certain that these are in place before beginning an evocation. Once you start the initial banishing ritual, you must not cross the circle, or allow anything else to do so, until the ritual is completed. If this means that you have to wet yourself, that's what it means. A puddle of urine on the floor is considerably less trouble to deal with than a case of obsession.

Just as you need to keep these outer protections in place, you need to keep a corresponding set of inner protections ready at hand when attempting evocation. The most important of these are skepticism, common sense, and a distrust of flattery. Keep in mind that spirits can perceive your Sphere of Sensation, and thus your habits of thought and emotion. They can tell you exactly what you most want to hear, and under some circumstances will do so shamelessly and skillfully. Far too many magicians have gone astray into grandiose fantasies of self-importance and, sometimes, into full-blown madness, by taking these deceptions at face value. Any spirit that starts to tell you how special and important you are, however appealing its words may be, should be banished on the spot.

These three principles, followed intelligently, cover most of the critical points in the practice of evocation. The remaining details are best discussed in the context of actual rituals of evocation.

Preparing for Evocation

Like many of the ritual applications discussed in this book, the practice of evocation requires a certain amount of "homework" if it's to be done successfully. Here as elsewhere, you need to be familiar with the ritual before you perform it—memorization is an even better option—and the usual steps of preparing for a ritual, as covered in Chapter 5, need to be followed with great care. In particular, the purpose for the working needs to be formulated with a great deal of precision. This is true above all when you intend to evoke a spirit for the purpose of practical magic, since your exact words will be all the spirit has to go on in performing the task you set it.

The preparation of the space is a somewhat more complex affair than in most other kinds of ritual magic. You'll need, first of all, a protective circle bearing the appropriate Names of God. This can be drawn on the floor using chalk, which is the traditional method, but it's often more useful to make a moveable circle out of a large piece of cloth, such as a king-size unfitted sheet. The design of the circle can be sketched in pencil and then painted using waterproof fabric paints. To draw the circle evenly, tie one end of a piece of string to a chair leg placed at the center of the sheet and tie the other to a pencil; shorten or lengthen the string to produce circles of different sizes. A candlestick may be placed in each of the four pentagrams.

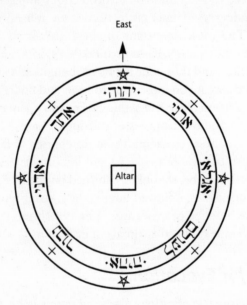

Diagram 48—
A Circle for Evocation

Many different designs of protective circles can be found in books on evocation, and most of them will work well. These circles should be made as large as the sheet or the dimensions of your practice space will permit. At the very least, there must be enough room for you to set up your altar at the center and still move around easily to all sides without stepping over the circle.

The protective circle is the most important requirement. You should also have a censer of the sort that uses blocks of charcoal, if this isn't the kind you ordinarily use in ritual work. The charcoal itself should be the self-starting kind, which can be lit with a match. If you haven't used this kind before, try it several times before relying on it in ritual. Several ounces of asafoetida will also be necessary; most herbal suppliers that cater to magicians carry this herb.

Additionally, you'll need to have made and consecrated the lotus wand, magic sword, lamen, and magical mirror, as described in Chapter 9, and you'll need to have practiced scrying in the mirror until you can reliably see images that correspond to the energy you have invoked.

The Selection of Spirits

Finally, of course, you'll need to choose the specific spirit you intend to evoke. To a great extent, this decision rises from the same process of choosing symbolism, which takes place in the preparation for any ritual working. Once it's clear that the purpose for the ritual corresponds to Venus, for example, it's equally clear that a spirit sharing the same correspondence should be evoked. Either the Intelligence or the Spirit of Venus would be an obvious choice, depending on whether the evocation is being performed for knowledge or for the purposes of practical magic.

On the other hand, the planetary Intelligences and Spirits are far from the only spirits assigned by tradition to the planets, just as the Rulers and elementals are not the only beings corresponding to the elements. Even the briefest glance through books on evocatory magic will turn up a dizzying array of entities that can be summoned by ritual methods. Each of these has its own powers and activities, and some of them can be of substantial value to the practicing magician.

In the Golden Dawn itself, the spirits of the Enochian tablets and those described in the *Key of Solomon* seem to have been the ones most commonly evoked. The methods of the tradition, though, can equally well be used to summon most other kinds of spirits. Issues of sheer space make it impossible to cover these other applications of evocation in detail, but those who wish to make a special study of evocation will have little difficulty finding sources of material.

A word or two should be said about certain classes of beings who are sometimes treated as appropriate subjects for evocation. Archangels and angels make up the first of these. There's a long and very highly developed tradition of angel magic in Western occultism, some of it involving the evocation of angelic beings. Evoking an archangel or angel is a very different matter from summoning a spirit of the kinds we've been discussing.

Angelic beings are active expressions of that primal unity which, in theological language, we may as well call God. Their will is one with the will of unity, and their powers derive from the power of the Absolute. What this means in practical terms is that they cannot be commanded, coerced, bound, or even influenced by magic or anything else. They can be invited to appear, and asked to help; if that request is in harmony with the will of unity, it will be granted; if not, you're out of luck, and that's all there is to it. For this reason, the conjurations and commands given in the rituals in this chapter have no place in angelic evocation and should be replaced by a prayer directed to the Name of God governing the operation, requesting that the archangel or angel appear to you.

Another class of beings that sometimes appears in books on evocation are those spirits of the natural world that are sometimes called elves, faeries, and the like. As mentioned in Chapter 2, these should not be confused with the little flower fairies of Victorian children's literature— or, for that matter, with the equally stereotyped elves of modern fantasy fiction. Folk tradition, usually a sound guide in such matters, portrays them as powerful, amoral, and often dangerous entities who can't be assumed to have good intentions toward human beings. It's possible to contact them using the magical mirror, or by other means, and there's much to be learned by doing so. Still, the encounter will take place on their terms, and there will more than likely be a price to pay for it.

If this kind of work appeals to you, you should plan on learning as much as possible about the folklore of the region in which you live before you attempt practical work. (In North America and Australasia, this includes learning something about the local native peoples and their traditions.) The nature spirits of different areas have different habits, and what draws or repels those of one region can't be counted on to do the same elsewhere. Here, as elsewhere in magical work, the more you know, the more likely you are to get positive results.

Finally, many of the older grimoires, and a few more recent books, discuss the evocation of demons. Here the best advice is a single word: don't. There's nothing of value to be gained by summoning what the Cabala calls the inhabitants of Gehenna, the Kingdom of Shells, and whatever is done with their aid will turn against the doer, sooner or later. They have a place in the universe and a right to exist, but they are as alien and destructive to the fabric of human life as a black hole or the heart of a star. The only time a magician should have any dealings with them is when, as sometimes happens, they intrude on the human world and must be sent back to their own realm through ritual exorcism—a topic we'll explore later in this chapter.

A Ceremony of Evocation for Knowledge

The following ceremony is designed to be used to evoke spirits for the purpose of communication. The ceremony itself is based on a Second Degree formula, as the Second Degree stresses balance and the movement of awareness from lower to higher—two things very useful in a rite of this nature. It also makes use of several elements of Cabalistic symbolism, which can be put to use in a range of other ritual applications as well.

For this ceremony, the magical mirror should be placed at the center of the altar. Some recent books that have covered evocatory magic have suggested the mirror should be placed outside the circle, like the triangle used in summoning spirits to physical manifestation. Still, the more traditional method can be found in the magical manuscripts of John Dee, Dr. Rudd, and Frederick Hockley, all of which were much studied by Golden Dawn adepts and are currently available in print. This method is to place the mirror or shewstone within the circle, on an altar or table. This is much more convenient in practice, and equally safe; the presence of the banished circle and the use of the appropriate Names of God will keep the entity being invoked, or any other, from using the mirror as a gateway.

The mirror should be left wrapped in its protective covering at the opening. The other working tools should be placed around it or, in the case of the lamen, worn. A chair near the altar is often a good idea, and you'll want to have paper and a pen or pencil if you intend to ask the spirit more than a few simple questions. The ceremony is performed as follows.

———————

First, perform the complete Second Degree Opening as given in Chapter 8.

Second, perform the Greater Invoking Ritual of the Pentagram or Hexagram that corresponds to the spirit you have chosen to evoke.

Third, facing the appropriate direction across the altar, trace the proper invoking pentagram or hexagram in the air with the lotus wand, point to the center of the symbol with the lotus, and vibrate the Name of God that governs the element or planet of the spirit. Vibrate the Name four times if you are invoking an element; for a planet, vibrate it as many times as the symbolic number of the planet. (The Vibratory Formula of the Middle Pillar and Revolutions of the Breath, as given in Chapter 7, can be used instead of this step, and can add a great deal of power.)

Fourth, contemplate the invoked force, raise the lotus wand high, and say: "Source of all powers and all beings, vaster than all greatness, stronger than all strength, better than all praise, in the Great Name (Name of God) by which thou rulest over (planet or element), I invoke thee, that my work may go forward in harmony with thy will. Grant thine aid to the higher aspirations of my soul, and guide me in the paths of thy wisdom. May thy presence and thy power be with me, so that the spiritual creatures of (planet or element) may be obedient unto me. May thy mighty archangel (name) keep watch over me, and thy powerful angels of the order of (or) angel (name of order or angel) be my guard and my protection, that I may accomplish this work of the magic of light.

"Therefore, in and by thy Great Name (Name), I propose to summon (name and title of spirit), to appear before me in the mirror of art which I have made and consecrated, that thereby I may learn the secret wisdom of (planet or element). And I affirm that with the help of the Infinite One this work shall be accomplished."

Fifth, unwrap the mirror and set it on its cushion. Trace the invoking hexagram or pentagram before the mirror, five times if a pentagram, six if a hexagram; point with the lotus wand to the mirror and recite the following conjuration: "In the Great Name of God (Name), which ruleth over all the forces of (planet or element), I conjure thee, (name and title of spirit). I call thee to appear to me within this mirror of art, and to truthfully answer the questions which I shall propound to thee, that I may learn the mysteries of thy realm, and lastly to depart from this mirror when I shall command it. Come forth, I conjure thee, in the power of the mighty Name! Show me the mysteries of thy realm. Arise and appear, taking shape in this mirror of art, that I may learn from thee of the works of the Infinite in the realm of (planet or element)."

When this conjuration has been completed, watch the mirror carefully for several minutes. If the spirit is present, you will see a form appear there, although it may be dim and indistinct at first. If nothing appears, repeat the conjuration. It may be repeated up to three times. After each repetition, watch the mirror for a time, waiting for the spirit to appear.

If the spirit has not appeared after the fourth conjuration, lay down the lotus wand and take up the magic sword. Pointing the sword at the mirror, recite the following conjuration:

"O thou mighty Lords of (planet or element) who governeth the spirit (name and title of spirit), I call to thee and I invoke thee in the Great Name (Name). Cause thy servant, the spirit (name), to come forth at once as I have commanded. Let the doors of the Unseen be opened, that (name of spirit) may arise and appear before me without delay.

"O thou spirit (name and title of spirit), I summon thee from thy dwelling in the Unseen. I conjure and command thy immediate presence, in and by the Great Name of God (Name), mighty in the realm of (planet or element); and in and by the name of (name), archangel of (planet or element), and in and by the name of (name), angelic host (or) angel of (planet or element). For I am a child of Adam Cadmon, true microcosm of the macrocosm, made in the image and likeness of the Infinite, and of the ten Stations of the descending light. The crown of glory is above my head. Wisdom and understanding sit upon my brow, mercy and severity are the works of my two hands and beauty the light within my heart. I have girt myself with victory and glory. The strength of foundation is in my loins and the kingdom at my feet. Arise, therefore, and let the secrets of thy realm be opened before me. Come forth and appear unto me in this mirror of art. Come forth without delay. Come forth!"

Again, once this has been done, watch the mirror. The spirit should now appear.

Sixth, once the spirit has appeared in the mirror, say, "In the Great Name (Name), be welcome, (name and title of spirit). I adjure thee to take on clear and visible shape before me, and to answer my questions without deception or evasion." The form of the spirit will then become more stable and definite. You may then begin questioning the spirit. The answers may come in the form of images in the mirror, or of words heard within your mind. Don't forget to take detailed notes of the answers you are given.

If at any point during this process the spirit appears to be coming *through* the mirror into the space within the circle, or the circle is threatened in any other way, take the magic sword and command the spirit to obedience in the divine, archangelic, and angelic names that govern it. More serious threats can be dealt with by sprinkling Holy Water or tracing banishing pentagrams or hexagrams; if this is done over the mirror, you will need to reconsecrate it later, but that's one of the risks of this kind of work.

If at any point the circle is actually penetrated, or you come under any form of direct attack, vibrate the Names YHShVH YHVShH, as in the Rose Cross Ritual, and *burn asafoetida at once*. This will effectively end the evocation, and you should perform a Greater Banishing Ritual of the Pentagram or Hexagram and the Second Degree Closing to finish the working.

Seventh, when you have finished questioning the spirit, take the lotus wand and say, "For thy presence and thy ready answers to my questions, O (name of spirit), I thank thee. Thy work here is now done. Therefore depart now to thy habitations in peace, and peace be between us. May the blessing of the Mighty Name (Name) be upon thee now and in time to come."

Wait for the figure of the spirit to disappear from the mirror. When it has done so, wrap the mirror in its protective cover, then take up the magic sword and trace a banishing hexagram or pentagram of the appropriate type over the altar, facing the direction of the force you invoked in the beginning of the ritual.

Eighth, perform the Greater Banishing Ritual of the appropriate Hexagram or Pentagram to banish the invoked force and ensure the departure of the spirit.

Ninth, perform the complete Second Degree Closing, as given in Chapter 8. This completes the ceremony.

A Ceremony of Evocation for Practical Magic

The ceremony that follows uses the same formula and many of the same words as the one just given, but is intended to summon spirits for the purpose of practical magic. The magical mirror is again the medium for the spirit's appearance, and is handled in the same way as in the last ceremony.

One variation of the formula in this version of the ceremony comes from a point of magical theory. The Spirits of the planets and the elementals are classified as "blind forces"; that is, they are not aware of the wider context of their actions, and in their ordinary work they are guided by higher spirits. The Spirits of the planets are thus directed by the planetary Intelligences.

Elementals have a similar relationship; as centers of force within the *spiritus mundi*, they are governed by the *anima mundi* itself, conceptualized for the purposes of magic in the form of four elemental Kings—Djin the King of Fire, Nichsa the King of Water, Paralda the King of Air, and Ghob the King of Earth—who represent the collective consciousness of the elementals of that element. In evoking these and similar spirits, then, it's necessary to call on the guiding spirit to move and direct the spirit you intend to evoke. The ceremony itself is performed as follows

---

First, perform the complete Second Degree Opening as given in Chapter 8.

Second, perform the Greater Invoking Ritual of the Pentagram or Hexagram that corresponds to the spirit you have chosen to evoke.

Third, facing the appropriate direction across the altar, trace the proper invoking pentagram or hexagram in the air with the lotus wand, point to the center of the symbol with the lotus and vibrate the Name of God that governs the spirit's element or planet. Vibrate the Name four times if you are invoking an element, and for a planet, as many times as the planet's own symbolic number. (Again, the Vibratory Formula of the Middle Pillar and the Revolutions of the Breath can be used instead of this step.)

Fourth, contemplate the invoked force, raise the lotus wand high and say: "Source of all powers and all beings, vaster than all greatness, stronger than all strength, better than all praise, in the Great Name (Name) by which thou rulest over (planet or element), I invoke thee, that my work may go forward in harmony with thy will. Grant thine aid to the higher aspirations of my soul, and guide me in the paths of thy wisdom. May thy presence and thy power be with me, so that the spiritual creatures of (planet or element) may be obedient unto me. May thy mighty archangel (name) keep watch over me, and thy powerful angels of the order of (or) angel (name of order or angel) be my guard and my protection, that I may accomplish this work of the magic of light.

"Therefore, in and by the Great Name (Name), I propose to summon (name and title of spirit, or "one among the spirits of (element)"), to appear before me in the mirror of art which I have made and consecrated, and to accomplish the task which I shall then command. And I affirm that with the help of the Infinite One this work shall be successful and my purpose accomplished."

Fifth, unwrap the mirror and set it on its cushion. With the lotus wand, trace the appropriate pentagram or hexagram before the mirror, five times if a pentagram, six times for a hexagram. Point the lotus at the center of the mirror and recite the following conjuration:

"In the Great Name of God (Name), which ruleth over all the forces of (planet or element), I conjure thee, (name and title of governing spirit—e.g. Intelligence or elemental King). I summon thee to cause (name and title of spirit, or "one among thy servants, the elemental spirits of (element)") to appear to me within the mirror of art, and to accomplish that task which I shall then name, and finally to depart when I shall command it. I so conjure thee, in the power of the mighty Name! Let thy servant arise and appear, taking visible shape within the mirror of art, that I may accomplish my will in the realm of (planet or element). Arise, therefore, (title of governing spirit), and cause thy servant to appear unto me. Let the powers of thy realm be obedient unto the Mighty Name!

"And in and by the same Name, and in and by all the powers of thy realm, I summon thee, (name and title of spirit, or "thou elemental spirit of (element)"), to appear visibly before me in the mirror of art, and to accomplish the task which I shall set thee. Come forth in obedience to the Mighty Name (Name)."

When this conjuration has been completed, watch the mirror carefully for several minutes. If the spirit is present, you will see a form appear; it may be faint and unstable, especially at first. If nothing appears, repeat the conjuration, up to three times. After each repetition, watch the mirror for the appearance of the spirit.

If the spirit has not appeared after the fourth conjuration, lay down the lotus wand, and take up the magic sword. Pointing the sword at the mirror, repeat the following conjuration:

"O thou mighty Lords of (planet or element), and especially thee, (name and title of governing spirit), I call to thee and I invoke thee in the Great Name (Name). Cause thy servant to come forth at once as I have commanded. Let the doors of the Unseen be opened, that (name and title of spirit, or "an elemental spirit of (element)") may arise and appear before me without delay.

"O (name and title of spirit, or "thou elemental spirit of (element)"), I summon thee from thy dwelling in the Unseen. I conjure and command thy immediate presence, in and by the Great Name of God (Name), mighty in the realm of (element or planet); and in and by the name of (name), archangel of (element or planet); and in and by the name of (name), angel (or) angelic host of (element or planet); and in and by the name of (name and title of governing spirit). For I am a child of Adam Cadmon, true microcosm of the macrocosm, made in the image and likeness of the Infinite, and of the ten Stations of the descending light. The crown of glory is above my head. Wisdom and understanding sit upon my brow, mercy and severity are the works of my two hands and beauty the light within my heart. I have girt myself with victory and glory. The strength of foundation is in my loins and the kingdom at my feet. Arise, therefore, and let the powers of thy realm be opened unto me. Come forth and appear unto me in the mirror of art. Come forth without delay. Come forth!"

Again, once this has been done, watch the mirror. The spirit should now appear.

Sixth, once the spirit has appeared in the mirror, say, "In the Great Name (Name), I adjure thee to take on clear and visible shape before me, and to accomplish the task which I shall set thee." Watch the mirror; the form of the spirit should now become clearer and more distinct. At this point, say: "This is the task for which I have summoned thee," and state the purpose for which the spirit has been evoked. The spirit may reply, in words or otherwise, and you may reply in turn as appropriate. Be sure to include in your instructions to the spirit that it must not harm any being in accomplishing the task.

Once again, be ready to use the magic sword, pentagrams or hexagrams, Holy Water, or asafoetida, if any trouble should arise. The Spirits of the planets can also be commanded in the name of their Intelligences, and the elementals in the name of their King; this alone is often enough to put an end to trouble.

Seventh, when the spirit has understood your instructions and agreed to accomplish them, say: "Go, therefore, with the power and the blessing of the Mighty Name, and accomplish the task I have set thee. When it is accomplished, thou art free, and may return to thy dwelling place in the realms of (planet or element)." The figure of the spirit will then disappear. Once this has happened, wrap the mirror in its protective covering. Then, take the magic sword and trace a banishing hexagram or pentagram of the appropriate type above the altar, facing the direction of the force you invoked in the beginning of the ceremony.

Eighth, perform the Greater Banishing Ritual of the appropriate Hexagram or Pentagram to banish the invoked force and ensure the complete departure of the spirit.

Ninth, perform the complete Second Degree Closing, as given in Chapter 8. This completes the ceremony.

The Problem of Obsession

Evocation, as mentioned more than once in this chapter, has its risks, and the most serious of those risks is the possibility of obsession by a spirit. Spirits evoked by ritual means, or any other, enter into contact with the magician's Sphere of Sensation in order to communicate and make their presence known. This is not a problem in the ordinary way of things—the same kind of contact takes place whenever you become aware of anything on the astral level—but a hostile or predatory spirit can make use of this contact to penetrate the Sphere of Sensation and intervene in what the magician thinks of as his or her own thoughts and feelings.

Obsession is not the same thing as possession. An obsessing spirit does not take over the body of its victim, much less start throwing up quarts of split pea soup in the classic Hollywood manner! Instead, obsession typically takes the form that the word itself implies: an irrational idea or compulsion that drives its victim in some more or less self-destructive direction.

There's obviously a lot of common ground between this and certain kinds of mental illness. The adepts of the Golden Dawn clearly recognized this—one of the Order's papers on the subject comments that "obsession is frequently the accompaniment of mania, and still more frequently its cause"—and later students of the tradition such as Dion Fortune have discussed the connection in some detail.

There are probably many more cases of obsession nowadays than anyone suspects. A society that has rejected the notion of magic is poorly equipped to deal with the actions of predatory spirits, and even less equipped to offer help to their victims. Thousands of people, in this age of mental health budget cuts, are left to wander the streets with voices whispering in their ears or personalities that are not their own sharing space in their heads. Attempts to treat such people with scientific methods of psychiatry have had uneven results, and it seems at least possible that what many of these people need is not a pill but an exorcism.

There may someday be a place for magicians in the mental health field, therefore, and recent moves by some psychologists toward studying shamanic cures for mental illness offer some hope in this direction. For the time being, though, major legal and ethical issues stand in the way of magical treatment of this kind, and certainly, magicians who do not have a solid professional background in clinical psychology and medicine have no business taking it up. Dion Fortune, herself both a magician and a psychologist, commented in her highly useful book *Psychic Self-Defense* that there's not much point in carrying out a ritual exorcism against an obsessing spirit when the "obsession" is actually the result of the toxic products of chronic constipation. Similarly, there are many cases of madness that are exactly that, and need to be treated by psychotherapy, not ritual magic.

Still, there are good reasons for the magician in training to understand the process of obsession and the methods by which it can be ended. It's always possible that an evocation can go wrong and leave you facing the attack of a hostile spirit. It's important to realize, additionally, that obsession is not always the result of mishandled magic. There are any number of ways in which human beings and spirits can come into unhealthy kinds of contact. These include extreme emotional states or their chemical equivalents, which touch on the magical realms of human experience—something that happens more often than many people realize. There's also an enormous body of garbled magical or quasi-magical practices at the fringes of modern culture, much of it not even recognized as such, which can have unexpected side effects— including obsession—if mishandled in certain ways.

Finally, places in which any of these things have happened can provide gateways for obsessing spirits unless cleansed with an effective exorcism. This is one of the origins of so-called "hauntings." A house once inhabited by a practitioner of one of the muddier-hued kinds of magic, or by an alcoholic whose binges drew him out into the murky places where magic and madness rub elbows, is likely to have such an effect; most towns more than a few decades old can show at least one dwelling that has had a long history of suicides, tragedies, and mental health problems as a result of exactly this process.

Obsession and the Sphere of Sensation

In any of these cases, clear knowledge and a grasp of the proper procedures can turn a potentially major problem into a situation that can be easily dealt with. The first requirement, then, is to understand how obsession happens, and how it works.

The material on the structure of the human microcosm covered in Chapter 3 is central to this understanding. The parts of the self that exist above the Veil of the Sanctuary, the Higher Self, and Higher Genius, aren't experienced directly by most people at the present stage of human evolution. Still, they are far from inactive. There is a constant stream of guidance that descends from these higher levels into the Lower Self. Much of this guidance remains unconscious, at least from the Lower Self's perspective; some takes the form of intuitions and unexpected insights; some, all too often, is brushed aside when it conflicts with the Lower Self's desires or perceptions. In any case, it plays an important part in leading the whole self through the slow processes of inner evolution.

The basic mechanism of obsession is the cutting off of this connection between the higher and lower aspects of the self. A spirit that seeks to obsess a human being begins with the Sphere of Sensation by introducing some pattern of thought or feeling that is attractive to the Lower Self. Quite often, given human vanity, this involves a fair proportion of flattery. Its next task is to take control of the lower will, dispersing the vital energies and directing the Lower Self's will toward some goal of the spirit's choosing. Finally, it seizes on the awareness itself, focusing on the Daath center in the neck, so that the guidance of the Higher Self can be prevented from reaching the Lower and undermining the spirit's control.

Like most physical illnesses, obsession is at least partly voluntary. If the Lower Self is paying attention during the first part of the process, it's likely to notice that the ideas or feelings that are pressing in on it seem to come from outside, and if it rejects them at this point, the attempted obsession grinds to a halt. Even if the spirit has penetrated the Sphere of Sensation, the Lower Self still has more strength on its own ground than the spirit, as an intruder, can muster. If it fights against the obsessing spirit, and above all if it strives to turn itself and its attention toward the Higher Self, the spirit will be expelled. Only if it responds passively will the obsession become complete.

It's possible, therefore, to come safely through a brush with obsession using nothing but bare will. On the other hand, as with so much in the magical tradition, there are techniques that make the work easier and more effective.

Many of these have already been given. The techniques of natural magic have an important place in dealing with hostile spirits; in particular, problems of this kind in a house or other enclosed place can often be dealt with most efficiently by burning plenty of asafoetida and then airing the place until the stench clears. Among the many benefits of the Middle Pillar exercise is that it banishes outside forces from the Sphere of Sensation and strengthens the link between the Higher and the Lower Self. The Ritual of the Rose Cross is another useful rite to perform whenever obsession might be an issue. Most of the rituals of spiritual development given in the next chapter can also be used to good effect in situations of this kind, and when practiced regularly, make it all but impossible for an obsessing spirit to get a foothold.

On the other hand, there is also a place in the ritual toolkit of the magician for ceremonial work designed specifically to expel obsessing spirits, whether they are attacking a person or simply manifesting in a place. This is the task of rituals of exorcism.

Exorcism

A ceremony of exorcism can be thought of as a ceremony of evocation stood on its head. Where evocation seeks to call spirits into manifestation in the realms of human experience, exorcism seeks to send them back out of manifestation to their own realms. Despite their opposite functions, rituals of evocation and exorcism use similar formulae and require similar skills and precautions.

Preparation for an exorcism is a much simpler process, as the purpose of the working is obvious, and it's not necessary to know the name or nature of the spirit that is to be expelled—although this is useful if it can be found. As with an evocation, a protective circle should be put in place around the altar, and everything necessary should be within the circle before the ceremony begins. The censer and the asafoetida should certainly be present, but the magical mirror won't be needed; the magical sword is the primary working tool, and the same Cabalistic symbolism that appears in the sword's consecration is central to this working as well.

The ceremony is performed as follows.

First, perform the complete Second Degree Opening.

Second, perform the Greater Invoking Ritual of the Pentagram of Spirit.

Third, stand at the west of the altar facing east, with the sword upon the altar, its hilt to the east and its point to the west. Raise your hands, palms down, above the altar. Visualize darkness surrounding you. Say slowly, in a low voice: "The realm of chaos and old night, before ever the Aeons were, when there was neither heaven nor earth, nor was there any sea, when nothing was save the shape unluminous, formless, and void. To and fro in the deeps swayed the coils of the dragon with eight heads and eleven horns. Eleven were the curses of Mount Ebal, eleven the rulers of the Primal Powers, and at their head the two Contending Forces."

Fourth, take the hilt of the sword in both hands and raise the sword above the altar, point down and hilt up. Say: "Then in darkness was spoken the Word!" Then, pausing after each one, vibrate the following Names of God of the ten Spheres in order: AHIH (pronounced "eh-heh-yeh"); YH ("yah"); YHVH ALHIM ("yeh-ho-wah ell-o-heem"); AL ("ell"); ALHIM GBVR ("ell-o-heem gih-boor"); YHVH ALVH VDAaTh ("yeh-ho-wah ell-o-wah vah da-ath"); YHVH TzBAVTh ("yeh-ho-wah tza-ba-oth"); ALHIM TzBAVTh ("ell-o-heem tza-ba-oth"); ShDI AL ChI ("shah-dye ell chye"); ADNI HARTz ("ah-dough-nye ha ah-retz"). Then turn the sword so that the point is up and the hilt down; lower the hilt to the level of your heart and say: "And the Elohim said, 'Let there be light,' and there was light." As you say this, visualize light descending and banishing the darkness; then set the sword upon the altar with its point to the east, and make the Signs of Isis, Apophis, and Osiris Risen.

Fifth, take the sword again, holding it before you, point up, in both hands. Say: "In the ten mighty and terrible Names of the Stations of the Light, before which the darkness rolled back at the dawn of time, I invoke thee, Lord of the Universe, who works in silence and whom naught but silence can express. May the uncreated light of the Infinite Spirit be upon me in this working and strengthen me against the powers of shadow. Help me to perform this ceremony of exorcism, by which that spirit who has here intruded on the world of humankind shall be banished unto its own realm by the power of the Magic of Light. And I proclaim that with the help of the Infinite One, this work shall be accomplished."

Then lower the sword until it points to the east, and slowly turn around with the sun until you are again pointing to the east. Say: "The River Kishon swept them away, that ancient river, the River Kishon. O my soul, thou hast trodden down strength!"

Sixth, go to the east of the altar and face west. Hold the sword in your right hand. Say: "O thou baleful and disobedient spirit who hath trespassed on this world, be thou rebuked by the Mighty Names! Depart at once unto thy proper habitation, and return here no more. By the holy Tetragrammaton, before which the Primal Worlds passed away, I bind thee. By the great Name of strength through sacrifice, YHShVH YHVShH ("yeh-heh-shu-ah yeh-ho-wah-shah"), I compel thine obedience. By the power of the Flaming Sword and the Lightning Flash, I command thee to begone!"

Seventh, turn and go to the eastern quarter of the circle, being careful not to cross it with any part of your body. Say: "In and by the Mighty Names, I banish thee from the realms of active Spirit. Depart unto thy proper place." With the sword, trace a banishing pentagram of active Spirit, then aim the point at the center of the pentagram and vibrate the Name AHIH ("eh-heh-yeh"). Then, still facing east, say: "In and by the Mighty Names, I banish thee from the realms of Air. Depart unto thy proper place." With the sword, trace a banishing pentagram of Air, then aim the point at the center of the pentagram and vibrate the Name YHVH ("yeh-ho-wah").

Go to the south. Say: "In and by the Mighty Names, I banish thee from the realms of Fire. Depart unto thy proper place." With the sword, trace a banishing pentagram of Fire, then aim the point at the center of the pentagram and vibrate the Name ALHIM ("ell-o-heem").

Go to the west. Say: "In and by the Mighty Names, I banish thee from the realms of Water. Depart unto thy proper place." With the sword, trace a banishing pentagram of Water, then aim the point at the center of the pentagram and vibrate the Name AL ("ell").

Go to the north. Say: "In and by the Mighty Names, I banish thee from the realms of Earth. Depart unto thy proper place." With the sword, trace a banishing pentagram of Earth, then aim the point at the center of the pentagram and vibrate the Name ADNI ("ah-dough-nye").

Return to the east, completing the circuit. Say: "In and by the Mighty Names, I banish thee from the realms of passive Spirit. Depart unto thy proper place." With the sword, trace a banishing pentagram of passive Spirit, then aim the point at the center of the pentagram and vibrate the Name AGLA ("ah-geh-la").

Eighth, go to the west of the altar, and face east. Set down the sword. Say: "It is done. Where there was darkness, let there be light. Where there was suffering, let there be joy. Where there was strife, let there be peace."

Take the lotus wand and go to the east. Trace the symbol of the Rose Cross in the east; then go around to the south, west, and north, in turn, tracing the Rose Cross in each quarter. Return to the east, and then to the west of the altar. Set down the lotus wand and perform the analysis of the Keyword INRI (the sixth, seventh, and eighth steps of the Rose Cross Ritual), calling down the Light with all your strength.

Ninth, perform the complete Second Degree Closing. This completes the ceremony.

This ceremony needs little comment, but it's important to note that the eighth step—the invocation of the Light, after the intruding spirit has been banished—is in many ways the most important part of the entire process. It isn't enough simply to chase an obsessing spirit away; there are always others who are ready to take up residence. Only by invoking the Higher, and affirming the link between the human world and the realm of the transcendent, can a case of obsession be definitely and permanently ended.

CHAPTER 12

INVISIBILITY AND TRANSFORMATION

T HE WORKINGS COVERED in the last three chapters all direct magical energies outward from the magician to transform objects in the experienced universe or to interact with other entities on the subtle realms of being. Another kind of magical working turns the flow of energies around to bring about changes within the magician—temporary changes or permanent ones, depending on the needs of the situation. Rituals for permanent change, which most often focus on the magical and spiritual development of the magician, are covered in Chapter 13; ceremonial methods that transform the magician for a period of time are covered here.

The latter include some of the most fascinating of all the ritual methods in the Golden Dawn tradition, and make it possible for the Golden Dawn magician to do things that most people—even most magicians— might consider unlikely or impossible. Who hasn't daydreamed about having the power to become invisible, or to take on the form of another living creature? The Golden Dawn papers include serious, solidly designed rituals for turning these daydreams into realities, and the same formulae can be used for many other kinds of transformation as well.

The key to understanding how these applications of magic work lies in the difference between the magical concept of reality, which we explored back in Chapter 1, and the materialist model that is more common in our culture nowadays. Physical invisibility—in the sense of making one's body completely transparent to light—and transformation of the physical body from one species to another are quite probably impossible, by magical means or any other. The magician isn't limited to a purely physical approach, though; nor is it necessarily true that a thing must be done physically in order to affect the world we experience every day.

The Nature of Invisibility

We'll begin with invisibility. In the legends of the Hermetic tradition, the ability to go about unseen is the stereotypical power of the adept, in much the same way that miraculously healing the sick is the stereotypical power of the Christian saint. Invisibility and Western magic were so deeply connected in the popular imagination during the Renaissance that the French philosopher Rene Descartes, who at one time was suspected of being a Rosicrucian, had to make a point of being seen in public; if people could see him, the logic went, he obviously wasn't involved in occult studies!

There's a certain core of hard fact behind these legends, of course. Being a practicing Hermetic magician in the later Middle Ages and the Renaissance was a dangerous proposition, and those who were too visible and too easily located risked an ugly death. Methods of concealment and evasion, by magic as well as by more ordinary means, were an obvious approach to survival. It's no accident that one of the first Western books on codes and ciphers was written by the same Johannes Trithemius who taught magic to Paracelsus and Cornelius Agrippa. Nor is it an accident that magical techniques for becoming invisible appear in a wide range of magical writings, including the Golden Dawn papers.

There are certain similarities, startling ones, between some of these methods and some of the techniques of invisibility practiced by the ninja, the assassin-mystics of feudal Japan. The art of ninjutsu has deep roots in Asian esoteric traditions, and to this day includes methods of meditation and ritual that, from a Western perspective, can only be called magical. Ninja skills of camouflage, concealment, and silent movement were backed up and strengthened by the invocation of nonphysical powers to shroud the ninja's movements in darkness and blur the vision of those he needed to evade.

The ninja and the Western magician share, as well, an understanding of how it is that these methods work, even though no magical working can keep light from bouncing off the surface of a physical object and carrying its image to a watching eye. The same understanding, in a more philosophical context, is common to most other traditions of mystical thought as well. It rises from the realization that our experience of the universe is at least as much a product of our unnoticed assumptions, our thinking patterns, and our mental habits, as it is a reflection of anything outside ourselves. We see, for the most part, what we expect to see; we confuse our mental models with the realms of experience they are meant to explain. It's because of this that mystics around the world have suggested that for all practical purposes, most people spend their whole lives sound asleep.

To shape thought, then, is to shape perception, to a much greater extent than we tend to realize. The plot of Poe's famous story "The Purloined Letter" depends on exactly this point. A letter is lost, and the most dedicated searching into every dark corner fails to find it—because the whole time it's sitting out in plain sight, where no one thinks of looking for it.

In the same way, a magician who energizes the idea of not being seen or noticed through the trained and focused will, who projects a pattern of forces that whispers "there's no one here" to nearby minds, can walk unnoticed through the middle of a crowd. His or her image will be reflected in the eyes and the nervous systems of the passersby but, like so much else, will not register at all in their awareness. It should always be remembered that it's not the five senses, but the consciousness behind them, that experiences the world. The magician knows this, and when it's appropriate, uses that knowledge.

The Shroud of Concealment

The practical methods of Golden Dawn magic embody this realization in specific forms of imagery, energy, and a specific symbolism. In order to become invisible, the Golden Dawn magician constructs a pattern of astral and etheric forces around his or her Sphere of Sensation. This pattern takes the form of an egg-shaped zone of darkness, the Shroud of Concealment, transparent from within, but opaque to the world outside. Everything within this region is hidden from watching eyes.

The positioning of the Shroud of Concealment at the outer edge of the aura, two or three feet out from the body, is of some importance. In practical terms, of course, being able to include one's clothing and other objects within the zone of invisibility is useful—a method of invisibility that requires complete nudity would risk awkward complications if one's attention falters—but there's a deeper side to it than this. The Sphere of Sensation, as we've seen, is the etheric matrix within which the images of the astral level are seen and reflected. A person's astral presence, his or her energy and personality, are at least as recognizable as the physical form of his or her body. Invisibility depends on not being noticed on any level of awareness, and for this reason, the astral and etheric forces must be veiled as thoroughly as the physical form.

To make the subtle side of this veiling as complete as possible, the energies used to construct the astral and etheric Shroud of Concealment are not drawn from within the self. Instead, they're taken from the macrocosm so that no trace of the magician's own energies can be found in the cloak. This imposes some special requirements on the ritual working, but it also makes the effect of the invisibility working somewhat less dependent on the magician's own condition.

The whole process of magical invisibility can be summed up according to the same system of five levels we've used elsewhere.

On the spiritual level, an invisibility working links with Unity by way of the Name YHVH ALHIM, which corresponds to Binah, the third Sphere of the Tree of Life. This Sphere is the principle of silence, stillness, and limitation, the darkness upon the Great Deep, and it represents the essentially hidden nature of the highest levels of being.

On the mental level, an invisibility working draws on the meaning and abstract symbolism of Binah to formulate the idea of invisibility.

On the astral level, an invisibility working builds up a pattern of astral imagery, the Shroud of Concealment already discussed, which expresses as clearly as possible the idea of invisibility. That pattern is established and energized strongly enough to pass from the magician's Sphere of Sensation and influence the minds of the people he or she encounters.

On the etheric level, an invisibility working establishes a shell of etheric substance around the magician's Sphere of Sensation, veiling it on an etheric level and helping to focus and stabilize the astral pattern of invisibility.

On the physical level, an invisibility working is anchored by, and ultimately conceals, the physical body of the magician.

The Ceremony of Invisibility

There are several different ritual formulae that can be used for an invisibility working; the following ceremony is one example, somewhat simpler to perform than the one included in the Golden Dawn papers. Its requirements are those of any First Degree ceremony. It is performed as follows.

———————

First, perform the complete First Degree Opening in its expanded form.

Second, perform the Greater Invoking Ritual of the Hexagram of Saturn. The ritual should begin and end at the west of the altar, facing east.

Third, move around the altar until you are facing the direction of Saturn. Trace the invoking pentagram of Saturn in that direction with the lotus wand, point to the center of the pentagram and vibrate the Name YHVH ALHIM ("yeh-ho-wah ell-o-heem") three times. Then say: "Supernal Mystery whom none can approach, Lady of silence and of shadow, in whom dwelleth that darkness that was on the face of the Great Deep. In thy mighty Name Aima Elohim, Supernal Mother, I call to thee and I invoke thee. Grant thine aid to the higher aspirations of my soul, and shroud me with thy mystery, that I may walk unseen.

"May thy great archangel Tzaphqiel, the prince of the spiritual strife against evil, be present with me in this work, and thy powerful angels, the Aralim, lend me their aid, so that I may formulate about myself a Shroud of Concealment to veil me from all watching eyes. From the silent places of the sphere of Shabbathai I call the darkness that was before the first day, and weave it into a veil of invisibility, in the Name YHVH ALHIM, that in darkness I may carry forth the works of the Magic of Light."

Fourth, go to the west of the altar and face east. Say: "In the mighty Names YHShVH YHVShH ("yeh-heh-shu-wah yeh-ho-wah-shah"), I conjure and command thee, thou particles of astral darkness. I summon thee from thy abodes. Come, in the Name YHVH ALHIM, to serve me as a shroud of darkness and concealment, so that I may become invisible; so that those who look upon me see me not, nor understand the thing that they behold. Gather about the limits of my Sphere of Sensation, and there be woven into a veil through which no eyes save mine may penetrate. Shroud me in darkness and mystery, that I may pass unseen to accomplish the works of the Magic of Light." As you say this, begin to visualize the Shroud of Concealment, an egg-shaped veil of purple-black light just outside the edges of your aura.

Fifth, take the cup of Holy Water. Dipping the fingers of your left hand in the Water, sprinkle it around you three times, purifying the Shroud of Concealment. Say: "I purify with Water." Set the cup down and take up the incense. Wave it three times, consecrating the Shroud of Concealment. Say: "I consecrate with Fire."

This process has a special importance in the making of the Shroud of Concealment, as the etheric substance present in the Water and incense are said to provide an almost material basis for the barrier you are establishing. This can be helped by visualizing the Water and incense smoke making the cloak denser and more solid.

Sixth, say: "In the Name of the Lord of the Universe, I conjure thee, Shroud of darkness and of mystery. By the Names and powers of the realm of Shabbathai, O particles of astral darkness, I call thee and I command thee. By the Spirit which moved on the face of the Great Deep in the beginning of things, I summon thee to my service. Let the Shroud of darkness and of invisibility be established about me. Let it hide me from all watching eyes until such time as I banish it by the rites of magic. Let it conceal me utterly, so that all who look upon me see me not, nor understand the thing that they behold. Let me pass into the invisible and walk in shadow; let me veil myself from sight and partake in the mysteries of the Unseen! For I am a child of the Supernal Mother, and I hold the balance of darkness and of light."

During this whole conjuration, make the visualization of the Shroud of Concealment clearer and more solid, directing the whole force of your will into giving the form concrete reality. Then turn around three times sunwise.

Seventh, facing east again, make the Sign of Entering, and then follow it with the Sign of Silence. As you take on this second Sign, focus your whole will on actually becoming invisible; see yourself, with as much intensity as possible, actually fading from your own sight, so that you can see right through yourself to the floor. This can be highly disorienting; be careful not to lose your self-control at this point.

Eighth, holding this visualization, say: "In the Great Name YHVH ALHIM, and in the name of Tzaphqiel, and in the name of the Aralim, and in the name of Shabbathai, I conjure and command thee, Shroud of darkness and of mystery. Be thou wholly obedient unto me, and remain under my control and guidance as I go forth invisible into the world, so that all who look upon me see me not, nor comprehend the thing that they behold. Be obedient unto my will, so that I may pass invisibly and go forth to accomplish the works of light."

Ninth, perform the Cabalistic Cross. This completes the first part of the ceremony.

At this point, you have taken on invisibility—or as much of it as your own magical skills will allow. The question that now arises is what you intend to do with it. The usual practical and ethical factors apply, but the subtle nature of magical invisibility brings some additional factors into play as well. For many people, the idea of invisibility wakens childhood fantasies in a way few other kinds of magic can match, and if these fantasies are followed too far, they usually lead the magician in some highly unproductive directions.

There's a story common in magical circles about two people who were having lunch in the Cafe Royal in London early in this century. Halfway through the meal, one of them looked up to see an astonishing spectacle: a portly man in ornate, vaguely Egyptian robes came slowly into the room, a brightly colored wand held before him in one hand and an expression of intense concentration contorting his face. This bizarre figure walked through the cafe, attracting no attention at all, until he had gone out of sight through a door.

"What in heaven's name was that?" the diner asked his friend.

"That? Oh, just that Crowley fellow being invisible," the friend said calmly. "He does it all the time. Don't let him know you've seen him; he gets so upset."

Whether this story is apocryphal or not—certainly it's very much in keeping with Aleister Crowley's known habits—it makes a good cautionary tale for the magician. The key to magical invisibility is nothing exotic; it's ultimately nothing more than not being noticed, and it's rarely a good idea to try to avoid attention by doing exactly those things that are most likely to attract it.

Imagine, by way of comparison, a slightly different story, in which the diner had looked up to see an ordinary-looking gentleman in ordinary

clothes passing through the room without benefit of wand or facial con-
tortions. Odds are that he wouldn't have given the sight a second
thought, and—even without an invisibility working—the whole episode
might never quite have reached the surface of his awareness. Just as the
ninja used dark clothing or clever disguises to supplement their own
inner methods of invisibility, the Golden Dawn magician who seeks to
walk unseen should keep in mind that the decision not to be noticed
needs to be expressed on the physical level as well as on the subtle realms
of astral and etheric force.

It's also worth noting, and remembering, that alarm systems, cameras,
and similar devices aren't usually affected by workings of this kind, since
they have effectively no consciousness to influence. Magical invisibility
isn't absolute, and it's possible to get into a fair amount of trouble if this
point is forgotten.

Returning to Visibility

The state of invisibility can be an unstable one, especially for the beginner; for the first few workings, it's best to hold the image of the Shroud
of Concealment in your awareness the whole time you intend to remain
unseen. With practice, though, the cloak needs less attention, and after
many invisibility workings it can be held in place without any conscious
attention at all.

Remaining invisible all the time isn't especially useful, though—to
mention only one point, it makes crossing busy streets a risky proposition—and it's a good idea, for this and other reasons, to be sure that you
remove the Shroud of Concealment completely and return its energies
to their sources once you've finished using it. The second part of the ceremony is intended to do this. It should be done as soon as you wish to
return to visibility. It follows directly on the end of the part just given,
and is performed as follows.

First, return to the altar, face east, and perform the Cabalistic Cross.
Then say: "In the great Name YHVH ALHIM, I release thee, thou particles of astral darkness which I have fashioned into a Shroud of Concealment. Depart from me, that I may pass from darkness into light."
Visualize the zone of darkness separating from the surface of your

Sphere of Sensation, opening up and moving away from you to the east. At the same time, visualize yourself becoming solidly visible again.

Second, take up the magic sword and point it at the Shroud of Concealment. Say: "By the mighty name YHVH ALHIM, and by the name of Tzaphqiel, and by the name of the Aralim, and by the name of Shabbathai, I dissolve and disperse thee, Shroud of darkness and concealment. I return thy energies to their sources. Yet I conjure thee that thou wilt return to me at my command if I should summon thee, and again conceal me from all watching eyes." With the sword, trace the banishing hexagram of Saturn, and vibrate the Name YHVH ALHIM; as you do this, visualize the Shroud of Concealment dispersing into nothingness. If necessary, repeat this entire step up to three times, until there is no trace of the Shroud of Concealment remaining.

Third, perform the Greater Banishing Ritual of the Hexagram of Saturn. Then perform the complete First Degree Closing in its expanded form. This completes the ceremony.

When this ritual, or another invisibility ritual based on the same principles, is practiced many times, it can become possible for the magician to take on invisibility through a much less complex process—for example, by simply visualizing the Shroud of Concealment, and silently repeating an appropriately designed invocation of Binah. The return to visibility can be accomplished equally easily. This is one of the ways in which the ritual workings of the magician in training begin to shade into the simpler yet more powerful magics of the adept.

The Body of Transformation

The same processes that are used in the rituals of invisibility have another use in Golden Dawn magic, one that opens up some of the most fascinating potentials of the entire system. The cloak of energies created in invisibility workings, formed of astral and etheric forces, is in effect a body—and a structure of this same kind can be used quite precisely as a second body by the magician.

Such a structure is known as a *body of transformation*. The subtle body created and used for astral projection is one kind of body of transformation, and the god-forms that are used in certain classes of lodge ritual are another. A third kind, the one we'll be discussing, is probably the most common type in magical traditions worldwide. This is the animal body of transformation. Like the werewolves and shapeshifters of ancient legend, the magician who learns this technique is able to take on the form of another living creature and experience the world through non-human eyes.

The folklore of shapeshifting, once untangled from the layers of mis-understanding piled on by movies and fantasy fiction, offers a good introduction to the technique. The "wolfman" image created by Holly-wood has more to do with the requirements of filming than with authen-tic werewolf folklore; the shapeshifters of legend were believed to turn completely into animal form, not merely do a somewhat furry variation on Dr. Jekyll and Mr. Hyde. This transformation, though, had some odd features. Old accounts often have it that the werewolf's human body can be found asleep in bed while its owner lopes through the forest and howls at the moon in nonhuman shape.

Nor does the werewolf body seem entirely physical in nature, though it can affect physical matter; in particular, the legends claim that it can be harmed only by silver—a highly conductive metal—or by fire. Finally, of course, there's the one thing about werewolves that almost everyone knows: the fact that they change shape only on the night of the full Moon.

From the standpoint of magical tradition, the truth behind the legends is obvious enough. The animal body of transformation is an etheric struc-ture, not a physical one; the full-scale physical transformations of movies and fantasy fiction are beyond the reach of magic, which is probably just as well. Still, the experience of taking on an animal body of transformation can be intensely real, and not merely to the magician. From within, a body of concentrated etheric substance is hard to tell from one of ordinary physical matter, and the two can function in the physical realm in much the same way, even to the point of leaving physical traces.

Once again, the five levels of experience can be usefully traced in this class of working.

On the spiritual level, the animal body of transformation links to unity through the Names of God governing the particular animal form in question, and through the Name governing the Moon, which rules all such operations.

On the mental level, the animal body of transformation is expressed in an abstract formula specific to the animal form in question, and this is expressed in the ritual of transformation in the usual ways.

On the astral level, the animal body of transformation is a carefully and thoroughly constructed visualization, as complete and detailed as possible, and it is brought into being through the use of the full range of magical symbolism and imagery.

On the etheric level, the animal body of transformation is a lattice of etheric forces built up from the energies of the *spiritus mundi*, the etheric body of the Earth, present in the local environment. The *spiritus mundi*, as mentioned in Chapter 2, has deep connections with biological life and the web of relationships we call "ecology." In it, among many other things, are the etheric templates of life, which function like blueprints for the development of individual living things. This is why shapeshifters normally transform themselves into animals that live (or recently lived) in the surrounding area: the etheric pattern of a wolf, the essential structure of "wolfness," is present in the ether anywhere in North America, in ways that the pattern of a hyena or a panda bear is not.

On the physical level, a transformation body tends to gather small amounts of physical matter in its lattice of forces—your practice area may be unusually dusty after a transformation working—and it also can have effects on the physical body of the magician, as we'll see a little later on.

The Naming of the Animals

Before we go on to the ritual, a certain amount of theory has to be covered in order to clarify the details of this kind of working. Typically enough for Cabalistic magic, the theory in question starts with a legend. A myth from the book of Genesis tells how Adam, the primal human, gave names to all the different animals. As with so many other scriptural myths, the magical traditions of the West took this one in an unexpected way, and saw these original names not merely as convenient labels, but as formulae of power—the expression of the true nature of each on a level that included, and reached beyond, the physical. Considerations of this sort gave rise to a largely forgotten branch of Golden Dawn lore, which worked out a set of special vibratory names for different kinds of animals and plants.

The surviving material on this part of the lore is fragmentary; still, the foundations of the system are given in an essay titled "On the Micro-cosms of Macrocosm," which can be found in Regardie's *Golden Dawn*. Each of the basic types of animal is assigned to one of the four elements: mammals to Fire, fish to Water, birds to Air, and "creeping things," such as reptiles and insects, to Earth. Within these categories, the different kinds of animals are classified by the planets and zodiacal signs. Each animal, then, has an element, a planet, and a sign, and when converted to Hebrew letters, a vibratory name results. The animals of Fire, Water, and Air thus have three-letter vibratory names. The element of Earth has no Hebrew letter assigned to it, and so the creatures assigned to Earth have vibratory names of two letters—a planet and a sign, or (in certain cases) an element and a sign—rather than three.

It's interesting to note that this elemental distinction is mirrored in evolutionary biology. Mammals, birds, and the modern type of fish (teleosts, true bony fish) all emerged at roughly the same time in the Earth's history, late in the Mesozoic era, the age of dinosaurs. All three groups remained small and inconspicuous until the end of the dinosaurs' reign, and then rose to their present dominance. They can be seen as parts of a single wave of evolutionary change, one that also saw the rise of flowering plants; it's the wave to which we ourselves belong. Other kinds of animals—reptiles and amphibians; archaic fish such as sharks, lungfish, and lampreys; and the whole range of invertebrates, from insects and spiders, through mollusks and starfish, to sea sponges and jellyfish—emerged much further back in time.

These more ancient creatures are part of older evolutions than ours, and the differences are reflected, as we've seen, in the way the Golden Dawn tradition symbolizes these animal types. They are also echoed in drastic differences in structure and consciousness, differences extreme enough that the forms of these animals should be taken only by experi-enced magicians. As we'll see, there are certain risks involved in the art of shapeshifting, and some of those risks grow greater as the distance from the human increases.

Among the three more recent animal groups, the twelve signs of the zodiac can be traced in broad patterns of physical form and relationship, while the seven planets can be traced in subtler patterns of behavior and character. The framework underlying the zodiacal classification can be given as follows.

Zodiacal Attributions

Aries animals are strong and often aggressive, and may be noted for jumping or climbing. They are often solitary.

Taurus animals are heavily built, often round in shape and dark in color; like the other Earth signs, Virgo and Capricorn, they tend to live and feed in ways that are literally "down to earth."

Gemini animals are quick and agile, often make a good deal of noise, and rely on social interactions for survival.

Cancer animals are either hard to see or hard to sort out from the group. They are often silver or gray, and are commonly food sources for other animals. Some are associated with the Moon or the tides.

Leo animals, by contrast, are highly visible and often seem proud to human eyes. They may be yellow or golden in color, and tend to be associated with the Sun.

Virgo animals are small, shy, generally brown-colored, and often eat seeds.

Libra animals are graceful in movement, and are often brightly colored or decorated. They may have pairs of ornaments on their bodies.

Scorpio animals are hunters—quick, agile, and merciless—or eaters of carrion. They may have a snakelike body shape.

Sagittarius animals are strong and swift, and often migrate over long distances.

Capricorn animals are long-lived or of ancient types, and may be slow-moving. They tend toward dark and drab colors.

Aquarius animals are eccentrics, adapted to unusual environments. They are often nocturnal.

Pisces animals are associated with water. (Among fish they share many of the characteristics of Cancer, but lack Cancer's lunar symbolism.)

Mammals

The zodiac of the mammals, then, follows a pattern like this:

Aries: climbing or jumping ungulates (sheep, goats, antelope)

Taurus: horned grassland ungulates (cattle, bison)

Gemini: canids (dogs, wolves, foxes); raccoons and their kin

Cancer: the insectivore family (shrews, moles)

Leo: felids (cats, cougars, lions, tigers)

Virgo: rodents (mice, rats, beavers); rabbits and hares

Libra: antlered ungulates (deer, elk, moose)

Scorpio: mustelids (weasels, stoats, badgers, otters)
Sagittarius: odd-toed ungulates (horses and their kin)
Capricorn: large omnivores of several families (bears, pigs and their relatives); armadillos and other mammals of ancient types
Aquarius: bats; primates (monkeys, human beings)
Pisces: marine mammals (whales, dolphins, seals)

Another zodiac, following similar patterns, can be made for the marsupial mammals of Australia, which are governed by the same element of Fire, but which are diverse enough to need a classification of their own. As this demands a knowledge of marsupials I don't have, it has been left as an exercise for readers Down Under.

The zodiacs of birds and fish are less easy to summarize; there are many more types of birds than mammals, and many more types of fish than birds and mammals combined. The following notes may be useful.

Birds

Aries: thrushes, starlings, robins
Taurus: grouse, quail, turkeys
Gemini: swallows, swifts, martens
Cancer: pigeons, doves; snipes, sandpipers
Leo: jays, mockingbirds, catbirds, crows
Virgo: sparrows, finches, juncos
Libra: warblers; hummingbirds
Scorpio: eagles, hawks, vultures; shrikes
Sagittarius: albatrosses, terns, gulls
Capricorn: herons, storks
Aquarius: owls, nighthawks
Pisces: ducks, loons, geese, grebes

Fish

Aries: marlins, mackerel, tuna, jack
Taurus: sole, flounder, halibut
Gemini: croakers, drums, whitings
Cancer: smelt, mullet, silversides
Leo: carp, catfish
Virgo: suckers, cod, hakes

Libra: most brightly colored tropical fish
Scorpio: pikes and pickerels, barracuda, eels
Sagittarius: salmon, trout
Capricorn: sturgeon, gars
Aquarius: flying fish, luminous deep-sea fish
Pisces: herring, anchovy

Planetary Attributions

Planetary attributions within any of these zodiacs can be outlined as follows:

Saturn animals are solitary and long-lived, and may live in isolated habitats such as mountain ranges.

Jupiter animals are usually the largest of their kind; they may be good-tempered, even playful, or have a strong quality of grandeur. They may be associated with water.

Mars animals are fierce and often dangerous. Among predators they are ruthlessly efficient hunters.

Sun animals are intelligent and flexible, and tend to be relatively large. They are often red, orange, or gold in color, and tend to be associated with the Sun.

Venus animals usually have the most beautiful coats, feathers, or skin of their kind, and may be noted for affectionateness.

Mercury animals are swift, elusive, and fond of theft.

Moon animals are generally the smallest of their kind, and may also live near human beings. They may be associated with the Moon.

As an example, the cat family—Leo of the mammal zodiac—can be placed into these attributions:

Saturn in Leo: cougar, snow leopard
Jupiter in Leo: tiger
Mars in Leo: jaguar
Sun in Leo: lion, leopard
Venus in Leo: lynx, panther
Mercury in Leo: cheetah, most small wild cats
Moon in Leo: domestic cat

The vibratory name for the bobcat, the most common North American wildcat, is thus constructed from Fire, Mercury, and Leo; in Hebrew letters, this is ת ב ש, ShBT, and might be pronounced "Shebet." Some other vibratory names that may be of some interest are as follows:

The wolf is Fire, Mars, Gemini, ז פ ש, Shepaz;

The fox is Fire, Sun, Gemini, ז ר ש, Shiraz;

The house mouse is Fire, Moon, Virgo, י ג ש , Shigi;

The otter is Fire, Jupiter, Scorpio, נ כ ש, Shekan;

The brown bear is Fire, Sun, Capricorn, ע ר ש, Sheraa;

The golden eagle is Air, Sun, Scorpio, נ ר א, Aeren;

The blue heron is Air, Saturn, Capricorn, ע ת א, Aethaa.

The rainbow trout is Water, Venus, Sagittarius, ם ר מ, Medes.

Preparing for the Ritual

These names, and others that can be constructed using the system just outlined, provide the foundation for the rituals of transformation we'll be discussing. To build on that foundation requires some careful choices and a fair amount of work.

The first task, of course, is to choose the animal form you intend to take on. This is a significant matter in more ways than one. The animal must be one you find congenial, even attractive. By taking on that animal's form, you will take on some portion of its character as well, and this should be kept in mind. For your first experiments, you'll want to choose an animal that lives (or once lived) in the area where you do; the pattern of that animal's energies will be present in the etheric structure of the Earth in your area, providing a template for the forces you'll use to build the transformation body.

Once the choice has been made, the next task is to learn as much as you possibly can about the animal you've chosen. Books are a good place to start, but it's vital to go beyond bare facts and figures. Pay special attention to the things you learn that bear on the way the animal experiences the world. If you intend to take on the form of a cat, for instance, you'll want to think about the difference between human senses and feline ones: to imagine a world where scent is more important than sight, where sounds come from precise directions and colors don't exist, and where things are seen from six inches off the ground rather than six feet. If you can, make an opportunity to see a living animal of the kind whose form you mean to take; watch it move and rest, and try to get a sense of its inner nature. Don't hesitate to be obsessive. The form you'll be building needs to be as real to you as the body you now inhabit, and any scrap of information that will help you do that is of value.

Older traditions of magic insisted that shapeshifting requires a physical link, some part of the animal that could be used as an etheric template. This works, but it's not necessary to the Golden Dawn method; in a world where animals increasingly have too little place, it's also a bad idea for wider reasons. The one exception is when such a link can be acquired without any harm to the animal. A fallen feather, a piece from a shed antler, a tuft of horsehair from a fence can be a focus for meditation on the animal form, which is a useful preliminary to the act of transformation.

The Ceremony of Transformation

When you feel you've gained a clear sense of the animal whose form you will be taking, the actual ritual is the next step. This should be done on the night of the Full Moon, just as folklore suggests. Shapeshifting should always be done after dark, to avoid the disruptive etheric effects of sunlight, while the full moon provides the maximum possible amount of etheric energy for the working.

The requirements for the ritual will be the same as for any First Degree ceremony, with the addition of a comfortable chair, which is placed halfway between the altar and the east side of the space, facing west. This is where your physical body will be while you're traveling in the transformation body. You'll also need to determine the actual direction of the Moon at the time of the ritual—on a clear night, this can be done simply by looking out the window—and of the planet and sign governing the animal form as well. Time factors are highly variable, so you should arrange to be uninterrupted all night if necessary. The ritual is performed as follows.

First, perform the complete First Degree Opening in its expanded form.

Second, perform the Greater Invoking Ritual of the Hexagram of the Moon. The ritual should begin and end at the west of the altar, facing east.

Third, move around the altar until you are facing the Moon. Raise your hands and vibrate the Name ShDI AL ChI ("shah-dye ell chye") nine times, visualizing the Full Moon before you. Then say: "Mighty God of Life, strong beyond strength, ruler of the animal creation, I invoke thee. May thy wisdom and thy power be with me in this work of the magic of light. May thy powerful archangel Gabriel guide me in the Pathway, and the mighty angels of the Order of Kerubim watch over my footsteps therein; and may the light of the Sphere Levanah, shining now upon the world, assist me in this work of transformation." Pause, and then lower your arms.

Fourth, move around the altar until you face the direction of the element ruling the form you have chosen. With the lotus wand, trace an invoking pentagram of that element over the altar, and draw the letter of that element in the center. Point to the center with the wand and vibrate the Name of God assigned to that element.

Fifth, move around the altar until you face the direction of the planet ruling the form. In the same way, trace an invoking hexagram of that planet over the altar and draw the letter of the planet in the center. Point to the center with the wand and vibrate the Name of God assigned to the planet.

Sixth, move around the altar until you face the direction of the sign ruling the form. Trace an invoking pentagram of the element ruling that sign over the altar and draw the letter of the sign in the center. Point to the center and vibrate the Name of God assigned to the element.

Seventh, go to the east of the altar and face west. Take the lotus wand in your left hand and hold it high above your head; with your right hand, point to an area halfway between the altar and the western edge of the space. This is where the transformation body will take shape. Say: "And the Elohim said, Let us create Adam in our image, after our likeness and let them have dominion over the beasts of the field." (For a bird form, finish this "...over the birds of the air"; for a fish form, "...over the fishes of the sea.") Then vibrate the vibratory name of the animal form, and at the same time begin to visualize the form. Vibrate the name eight more times, and with each vibration make the visualization clearer and more solid, directing the whole force of your will into giving the form concrete reality.

Eighth, holding this visualization, say: "In the name of the Lord of the Universe, arise before me, Form of (vibratory name of animal), into which I have elected to transform myself. So that all who look upon me may see the thing that they see not, and comprehend not the thing that they behold. In the Name of (Name of ruling element), and in the Name of (Name of ruling planet), and in the Name of (Name of ruling sign), be obedient unto my will, Form of (vibratory name of animal), so that I may pass into the shape of a (ordinary name of animal) and go forth to accomplish the works of light."

Ninth, put the lotus wand down, go around the altar, and approach the form, holding the visualization at full intensity. When you reach it, step into it, and at this point strive to inhabit its body and yours at the same time, seeing the space through both sets of eyes, feeling its muscles and movements as well as your own. Once you can do this, move slowly around the altar to the chair in the east. Pace yourself so that both bodies make this movement at the same speed, and maintain a physical over-lap between the bodies. When you reach the east, sit your human body down in the chair and strive to be aware of the animal body alone. (A slight awareness of the human form may remain, but this isn't a serious handicap.) Once your awareness is centered in the animal form, the ceremony is complete.

———

Your first few experiences in a transformation body should be kept fairly brief. That body will be able to pass through walls, unless they are made of metal, but otherwise will function like an ordinary body of its kind. You'll certainly want to venture out into the night, travel through the area close by, and simply explore the experience of inhabiting the animal form. There's a great deal to be learned this way. In later workings, you can cover more territory and begin to use the transformation body for a range of purposes.

If you've chosen to take the form of a fish or a marine mammal such as a dolphin, there are additional complications. Transformations of this sort should be done very close to the body of water where you intend to swim; renting a lakeside or seaside cabin is one good approach. Once you've performed the ritual, visualize the transformation body suddenly leaping through the air toward the water. A half-mile or so seems to be about the limit of such jumps, but this may vary from one magician to another.

Some general cautions are in order. In populated areas, it's best to stay out of sight if you can. Other animals won't bother you—they apparently recognize the difference between transformation bodies and physical ones, and go about their own business—but human beings aren't so clever. The last thing you need is to have the whole neighborhood in an uproar because someone who doesn't know he or she is psychically sensitive saw a wolf trotting down the middle of the street.

There's also the rarer but much more serious risk of repercussion. Anything that affects your body of transformation, according to the traditional lore, will affect your human etheric body in exactly the same way, and take physical shape in the usual manner. A cut on a paw, wing, or fin will turn into a corresponding cut on the hand. If someone drives a conductive object through your transformation form, discharging the etheric energy all at once, it's said that the shock to your system can quite literally kill you. The moral is simple: be careful.

Finally, there's the issue of long-term effects from this kind of magical work. As mentioned above, you'll find yourself absorbing some portion of the character of the animal you've selected, and this can be a problem. If you tend toward vanity already, taking on the form of a cat on a regular basis may make you insufferable! A similar process, if a much slower one, influences the etheric and physical bodies through another kind of repercussion. If work with a single animal form is carried out over a long time, it's said, the magician may begin to take on a noticeable physical resemblance to the animal. This can be awkward, and there are also possible health effects.

One way to help minimize these latter problems is to work with different animal forms, and to choose ones that are fairly close to humankind when possible; this is one of the reasons animal forms from older evolutions aren't a good choice, especially for the beginner. The possibility of problems can also be reduced by banishing the animal form comprehensively at the end of the working, and the following ceremony—which is done when you return to your working space and are ready to take on human form again—is designed with this latter point in mind.

This ceremony follows directly on the end of the one just given, and is performed as follows.

————————

First, return to the chair where your human body is sitting and place your animal form in front of it, physically overlapping it. Then become aware of both bodies at the same time, seeing through both sets of eyes and feeling both sets of movements. Move your human body, slowly, and make sure it will be able to stand and move without fainting before going on.

Second, stand your human body up, and in both bodies move around the altar to the west until you are standing in the place where the animal form took shape. Pace yourself so that both bodies move at the same speed, and remain aware of both the whole time.

Third, shift your awareness entirely to your human body, so that you no longer perceive the animal form from inside. Once this is done, go back around the altar to the east and face west. Take the magic sword in your right hand and hold it high above your head. Say: "And the Elohim created Adam in their own image; in the image of the Elohim created they them." Point the sword at the form and say: "In the name of the Lord of the Universe, be now dispersed, Form of (vibratory name of animal). I return the powers to their sources." Visualize the form fading out. Then, still facing the form, trace the banishing pentagram of the element ruling the sign that governs the form, and trace the letter of the sign inside it; point the sword at the center of the pentagram and vibrate the Name of God assigned to the element.

Fourth, in the same way, use the sword to banish the energies of the planet and the element governing the form. By the end of this process, the form should have vanished completely. If it has not done so, repeat the banishings up to three times. Then go around to the west of the altar and perform the Greater Banishing Ritual of the Hexagram of the Moon.

Fifth, perform the complete First Degree Closing in its expanded form. This completes the ceremony.

———

As a final note, it's usually a good idea to eat as soon as possible after a working of this kind. You'll have used up a great deal of energy in the process and will probably need nourishment. A full stomach is one of the best ways to close down the subtle senses, and doing this is a good idea. It's also wise to wait at least an hour before going to sleep so the energies of the working don't contaminate your dream life too extensively.

Other Transformations

The formulae given here for rituals of invisibility and animal transformation can be used, with appropriate changes, for catalyzing any short-term change you may need or wish to carry out. The usual restrictions are still present; workings based on these formulae are unlikely to change you in ways that violate the natural patterns of the cosmos, or to allow the sort of something-for-nothing nonsense that contaminates too many fantasies about magic. At the same time, it's possible to open up many unexpected possibilities through this kind of working.

One of the most useful applications of these formulae is the temporary expansion of human capacities. Most people have so many unused abilities, so much untouched potential, that rituals designed to focus energy and consciousness through one or another of these can bring about remarkable results. One example is the use of ritual magic to produce, over the short term, eidetic (or as it's often called, "photographic") memory. Another example, one with limited but possibly vital uses, is the use of ritual magic to heighten abilities of physical combat; here, once again, the methods of the Golden Dawn magician and those of the ninja have some relationship to each other, and the warrior-trance techniques of Norse and Celtic traditions are also relevant.

Other possibilities for change will occur to you as you work with the formulae. Some of these may be uncomfortable, even frightening; it's very common to fear changes that affect the self. Still, in the words of the Golden Dawn ritual, "fear is failure and the beginning of failure." One of the central tasks of the magician is to learn to be comfortable with change, so that he or she can shape the currents of change—and approach the still point of the changing world, where change borders on the changeless.

CHAPTER 13

SPIRITUAL DEVELOPMENT

IF THE TEMPORARY CHANGES brought about by the rituals we've just examined can be unsettling, the permanent reshapings of the self that are the result of theurgic magic—the subject of this chapter—are likely to be very much more so. It's one thing to change in some way for a time, knowing that there's a stable base of identity to return to. It's something quite different to leave that stable base behind once and for all and venture out with the whole self into the unknown.

In reality, of course, the "stable base" itself is an illusion. In magical thought, every living being is seen as changing constantly, on every level but one. Scientists have pointed out that the very atoms that make up your physical body at this moment aren't the same as the ones that did so seven years earlier. The physical level is a constant frenzy of change, the etheric level only a little less so; the astral level of thoughts and feelings and perceptions reshapes itself moment by moment; the mental level shows different faces and aspects of itself to the levels below it; only the spiritual level, the hub of the turning wheel, remains unmoved. Certainly the ramshackle structure of memories, images, perceptions, and habits that cluster around the core of awareness, the structure that most of us think of as "I," is anything but changeless. Even the effort to refuse or avoid change in the self—an effort most of us make now and then— produces changes of its own, usually destructive and painful ones.

To the magician, change is a tool to be used, not an enemy to be feared or fought. Since change in the self is inevitable, the magician's goal is to respond to it consciously and constructively, directing the self through the process of change into paths of greater wisdom, compassion, and inner power. Like any other goal, this one can be the foundation for ritual work.

There are any number of ways to conceptualize this goal, and to turn that conceptualization into the framework for a ritual. For the present purpose, though, the tasks of self-initiation discussed in Chapter 3 will provide the needed context. These three tasks—the reorientation of the self from the external world of the senses to the inner world that gives it meaning; the resolution of the whole pattern of unbalanced forces within the self; and the opening up to energies and insights from the higher levels of the self—structure the whole range of spiritual development methods used in the Golden Dawn tradition, and they allow us to make sense of those methods in a practical and useable way.

The first of these tasks includes most of the elementary steps of magical training, and in another sense all of magic is nothing else than a reorientation of exactly this kind. Practices such as concentration, meditation, scrying, and the like, all focus on the inner life of the magician in training, teaching him or her to notice the usually unnoticed workings of awareness, both within and beyond the boundaries of the self. So, in its own way, does ritual, but theurgic ritual work usually plays a fairly small part in the process. Until the first solid steps toward reorienting the awareness have been made, most ritual methods have little effectiveness, and ritual work should focus on fundamental training methods such as the Pentagram Ritual and the Middle Pillar exercise.

The second task draws more deeply on the resources of ritual work. One of the most effective ways of resolving the imbalances of the self uses ceremonial methods to bring energies of the macrocosm into the microcosm, filling gaps in the self's own energy structure. A magician whose emotional and artistic side is undeveloped, for example, might well invoke the energies of the Sphere Netzach or its planetary equivalent, Venus, to strengthen this part of his or her nature. Many of the technical methods we've already covered find an important use in this context.

To continue the example, the magician might make and consecrate a talisman of Venus; she might evoke Hagiel, the Intelligence of Venus, to seek a deeper understanding of Venus and its mysteries; she might choose to take on an animal body of transformation with strong Venus correspondences. All of these methods, and others, can be put to work in the process of inner balancing, and can be strengthened and supplemented with meditations, scryings, and Pathworkings that focus energy in the same direction.

It's with the third task, though, that we pass beyond these applications of practical magic into the realm of most Golden Dawn theurgy. The central feature of the tradition's rituals of spiritual development is that they bring the presence of the Higher into the consciousness of the magician. To some extent, this is an element of all Golden Dawn ritual work—the practice of invocation, after all, can be defined in exactly those words—but the core ceremonial methods of spiritual transformation in the tradition focus on this feature above all else.

At the same time, there are any number of ways in which contact between the awareness of the magician and the presence of the Higher can be brought about using the resources of Golden Dawn ritual magic. These include, among other approaches, relatively straightforward ritual invocations of the Names of God, using formulae identical or similar to ones we've examined in earlier chapters; energy workings that use the tradition's specialized methods of breathing, vibration, and telesmatic imagery; visionary practices that combine ritual methods with the use of Golden Dawn techniques of scrying and Pathworking; and complex ceremonies designed to reshape the relationship between the different parts of the self and bring the Lower Self and the Higher into direct contact. This chapter will give examples of all four of these approaches as an introduction to the work of transformation, which is the heart of the Golden Dawn system.

Despite this diversity of approaches, all of the methods we'll be discussing share common patterns, which can be related to the system of five levels of experience.

On the spiritual level, the work of spiritual development in the Golden Dawn tradition is founded on a recognition that the innermost core of the self remains in constant awareness of the Unity that is before all things. The Names of God used in ritual work are meant to call this primal unity into awareness, and these Names are therefore used in rituals of spiritual development to anchor the entire transformative process in the realities of the Absolute.

On the mental level, the work of spiritual development makes use of the patterns of abstract consciousness in the whole range of ways known to the tradition, using number, geometric form, and other expressions of these patterns to build up structures representing unity, balance, and growth. The goal on this level is to bring the timeless forms of the mental level through as clearly as possible into the realms of space and time.

On the astral level, the work of spiritual development expresses these structures in the form of concrete images and ideas of various kinds, again using any or all of the methods that are part of the Golden Dawn magician's toolkit. These images play a different role in theurgic magic than they do in the different kinds of thaumaturgy we've covered in earlier chapters. In theurgy, images are vessels for the energies of higher levels, not frameworks for manifestation on lower ones, and it's important for them to be as transparent as possible to the Higher. One expression of this point is a tendency for such images to be somewhat less concrete than those used in thaumaturgic work, and to dissolve into light toward the climax of theurgic ritual.

On the etheric level, the work of spiritual development makes use of the basic techniques of breathing and vibration, and in some specific practices, draws on the more intensive methods of energy work as well. The goal of these operations is to call down transcendent energies in as pure a form as possible, and so very often the etheric techniques are used simply to purify and quiet the magician's own etheric aspects so they don't interfere with the work.

On the physical level, the work of spiritual development anchors and grounds itself in the physical body of the magician, and it uses the standard physical methods of posture, gesture, and Signs, as well as physical working tools and ritual equipment, to express itself in ritual form.

The Invocation of the Name

The first example of a spiritual development working we'll examine is a straightforward invocation of one of the Names of God, using the same ritual methods explored in earlier chapters. Invocations of this kind form an excellent method of ritual self-initiation, as well as an effective way to learn and practice the basic elements of ritual technique. The specific ceremony given here invokes the Name ץ ר א ה   י נ ד א, Adonai ha-Aretz, and corresponds to Malkuth, the tenth and lowest Sphere of the Tree of Life. If you've been paying attention, you should have no difficulty constructing ceremonies using the same formula to invoke any of the Names of God.

The requirements of this ceremony are those of the expanded First Degree Opening and Closing. You'll also need the lamp, rose, wine, bread, and salt for the communion of the Elements, as given in Chapter 8; these are placed on the altar in their proper positions before the Opening. The elemental working tools are not needed for this ceremony; the elements of the communion serve as the elemental symbols. The ceremony itself is performed as follows.

First, perform the complete First Degree Opening in its expanded form.

Second, perform the Greater Invoking Ritual of the Hexagram of Malkuth, using the lotus wand. (Remember that this uses the Moon hexagram, but with the Name ADNI HARTz (pronounced "ah-dough-nye ha ah-retz").)

Third, stand at the west of the altar, facing east. Trace an invoking hexagram of the Moon over the altar with the lotus wand, point to the center, and vibrate the Name ADNI HARTz ten times, slowly and strongly. Be aware, as you are doing so, of the presence of the solid Earth beneath your feet, and feel the Name echo through the depths of the planet. Then say the following invocation:

"Adonai ha-Aretz, ruler of Malkuth the Kingdom, master of Earth and of the realms of matter, I invoke thee. May thy presence bless this ceremony of the Magic of Light, and grant thine aid to the highest aspirations of my soul. Lord of Earth, Lord of the Kingdom, a house built upon sand cannot endure, but one founded upon rock will have strength to withstand all the storms and tides of the world. Help me, therefore, to found the house of myself not upon the sands of time and change, but upon that true and unyielding Stone, which is the Stone of the Wise. Teach me strength and firmness of purpose, patience, and self-mastery, that I may better follow the path of thy wisdom; help me to see the presence of the Higher in all material things, and to make my life in the world of matter a solid foundation for the work of the Magic of Light."

Fourth, raise your hands high and say: "Adonai ha-Aretz, Lord and King of Earth! May thy light descend upon these symbols of the elements."

Extend your right hand over the altar, palm down, and direct your awareness toward the four elemental symbols on the altar. Say: "In the Name of Adonai ha-Aretz, I consecrate these symbols of Air (move hand over rose), Fire (over lamp), Earth (over bread and salt), and Water (over wine). May the presence and power of the Lord of Earth overshadow them, and fill them with every virtue, that the kingdom of the elements may be full of the light of the Infinite."

Take the rose and say: "In the Name of Adonai ha-Aretz." Breathe in the scent and return the rose to its place. With the same words, feel the heat of the lamp, eat the bread and salt, and drink the wine. When you finish the wine, set the cup down inverted—it helps to have a saucer in place for it to keep the altar cloth from being stained—and say: "It is finished."

Fifth, remain in silence for a time, being aware of the energies you have invoked and taken into yourself. Then perform the complete First Degree Closing in its expanded form. This completes the ceremony.

———

Perhaps the best way to use this ceremony is as one of a linked series of workings based on the Tree of Life. After invoking Adonai ha-Aretz several times using this ceremony, you can then perform another ceremony the same number of times to invoke Shaddai El Chai, the Name assigned to Yesod; another to invoke Elohim Tzabaoth, the Name corresponding to Hod; and so on up the Tree. The result will be a self-initiation comparable in its effects and intensity to many of the magical lodge initiations currently available.

This same ritual can also be done as a Third Degree working simply by replacing the First Degree Opening and Closing with that of the Third Degree. The difference between the two formulae can be astonishing; the Third Degree tends to produce much higher energy levels, and for this reason it's best to do a full series of First Degree workings first to allow your etheric body to get used to the effects of the process of invocation.

The Vibration of Adonai Ha-Aretz

This ceremony is another method of invoking a Name of God, using somewhat more advanced ritual methods. It makes use of the energy work outlined in Chapter 7, in the context of the Middle Pillar exercise, and applied in another way in the third of the talisman consecration rituals in Chapter 10. It uses telesmatic imagery, etheric focusing through the breath, and vibration to invoke the presence of Spirit through the medium of one of the traditional Names of God. In the Golden Dawn's own curriculum of studies, this specific ceremony was a requirement of the Zelator Adeptus Minor sub-grade, and it had to be practiced and mastered before the advanced levels of ritual magic could be studied.

The requirements of the ceremony are extremely simple—essentially, those of the Middle Pillar exercises—since nearly all the work takes place on nonphysical levels. It is performed as follows.

First, perform the Lesser Banishing Ritual of the Pentagram.

Second, go to the eastern quarter of the space and, facing east, make the Signs of Isis, Apophis, and Osiris Risen. Visualize the descending light. Then trace the symbol of the Rose Cross in the air, as in the Rose Cross ritual; point to the center of the symbol and vibrate the Name IAO. Go to the south, west, and north, in turn, repeating the same actions.

Third, go back around to the east, completing the circle, and then return to the center of the space and face east. Turn your attention to the same point of light far above your head that you've visualized in the Middle Pillar exercises. Breathe in, and with the breath bring a descending current of white light from that point into your heart center. As you breathe out, visualize the light formulating the Name ADNI HARTz in your heart in Hebrew letters, ץ ר א ה י נ ד א, and at the same time vibrate the Name aloud. Repeat this process until you've vibrated the Name eight times. Visualize the letters of the Name blazing more brightly with each vibration. The vibration should be felt to echo outward to the ends of the universe. This forms the Invoking Whirl in the heart.

Fourth, visualize the same Name before you in the air, in letters of brilliant white light, written both vertically and horizontally in the form of an equal-armed cross, as shown in Diagram 49.

Diagram 49—
The Equal-Armed Cross

Be aware, once again, of the point of light far above you, but this time draw a ray of light down from it into this cross. Then, breathing in deeply, vibrate the Name once more, and visualize the cross of letters blazing with intense light, which fills your Sphere of Sensation. This establishes the Expanding Whirl in the aura.

Fifth, after holding the image of the light for a time, allow the following telesmatic image to take shape before you. The image should be of vast size and power, shining with light.

א *Aleph:* a winged crown of brilliant white radiance.

ד *Daleth*: a woman's head and neck, beautiful, but with a sense of great strength and firmness. The hair is long, dark, very full, and waving.

נ *Nun*: arms bare and strong, extended to the sides in the form of a cross. The right hand holds ears of ripe grain, the left hand a golden cup. The figure's wings are dark and slightly spread, and the feathers seem to stir in the wind.

י *Yod:* a deep yellow-green robe covering full breasts and a strongly built torso. The figure's skin is very pale.

ה *Heh:* a square lamen of gold on the chest, bearing a scarlet equal-armed cross in red, and four smaller crosses in the angles. The figure also wears a belt of gold.

א *Aleph:* firm hips and long legs; the hem of the robe reaches to the figure's feet. The golden belt bears a sword in a golden scabbard.

ר *Resh:* dark billowing clouds, shot through with flashes of heat lightning, surround the figure.

צ *Tzaddi:* the robe is rayed with olive toward the hem. The figure's feet are shod in golden sandals.

Build up this image as powerfully as possible in the imagination before you. Once it has been solidly established, imagine it expanding until it fills the universe, and becomes the universe. Be aware of yourself as part of this titanic figure, not as though you have just become part of it, but as though you have always been. Absorb and be absorbed by its radiance and power, until your Sphere of Sensation shines with its light, and then allow the image itself to transform into pure formless light.

Sixth, allow the image of light to fade from your awareness. Pause for a time, and then perform the Cabalistic Cross. This completes the ceremony.

The method given in this ceremony can equally well be used with any of the Names of God, with an appropriate telesmatic image used for each. As with the Invocation of the Name given above, it's a highly effective method of self-initiation to do a series of workings of this kind, using the Names that govern the ten Spheres of the Tree of Life. Each working in the series should be repeated until the imagery is exact and detailed, the sense of presence and energy strong, and the aura filled with light at the end of the ceremony.

Rising on the Planes

Another class of rituals of spiritual development, as mentioned above, makes use of the standard methods of invocation, but combines this with techniques that allow the magician to raise his or her awareness out of the material level. When this is done, the impact of the invoked force is often substantially greater, because the material level no longer stands like a veil between the magician and the power that has been invoked. One effective way of doing this is the process known as Rising on the Planes.

Like the art of the Flashing Tablet discussed in Chapter 10, Rising on the Planes is a fusion of ritual technique with the Golden Dawn's highly developed methods of scrying and Pathworking, which use the focused imagination as a vehicle for experiencing the astral realm of concrete consciousness. The techniques of scrying and Pathworking are covered in detail in the published collections of the Order's papers, and in many other books on magic as well, including *Paths of Wisdom*. Work done with these, or any similar set of techniques, will intensify the effects of Rising on the Planes, and the experienced scryer may find that he or she can obtain the same results with a minimum of ceremony.

The ceremony that follows can be done effectively even by those who don't have this background. It makes use of some of the basic ritual methods we've already explored to provide a context for the visionary journey. The one thing necessary, in addition, is that the magician be willing to use his or her imagination fully, and to accept what it perceives and creates as real on its own level—at least for the duration of the working.

This ceremony makes use of a Second Degree formula, as it involves the movement of awareness from lower to higher levels, and so its requirements are those of the Second Degree Opening and Closing. You'll also need a chair with a straight back, set near the altar, facing east. The ceremony is performed as follows.

First, perform the complete Second Degree Opening.

Second, perform the Greater Invoking Ritual of the Hexagram of the Sun, using all six forms of the hexagram.

Third, standing at the west of the altar, facing east, say: "O thou most glorious light which lighteneth every one who cometh into the world; thou who art in due season shadowed forth by Tiphareth, the Sun of beauty; I invoke thee, that thou mayest direct thy light upon me. Grant unto me that I may rise up from thy Kingdom and pass from the darkness of the world into the light of thy Presence. Help me to enter into the Sphere of Beauty, that I may at length lose and so find myself in that ineffable light which above all other things I seek."

Fourth, sit down in the chair in the standard posture for sitting meditation—feet and knees together, back comfortably straight, the whole body neither tensed nor limp, but in a state of poise, midway between the extremes. Take the lotus wand in both hands, bow your head slightly, and direct the blossom end toward the middle of your forehead.

Fifth, slowly and clearly, say: "In the Name Adonai ha-Aretz, I have set my feet in the Kingdom of Matter." At the same time, visualize the Name in Hebrew letters, ץ ר א ה י נ ד א. Then vibrate the same Name, softly but intensely, four times, and visualize your actual physical surroundings as clearly as possible. Take as much time as you need to make this image solid, detailed, and lifelike. This represents Malkuth, the tenth Sphere, and the material level of experience.

When the image is well established, say, "Let me quit the material and seek the spiritual." Visualize yourself rising to your feet and then rising up into the air, as though floating. See yourself passing through the ceiling and rising up into open air, the landscape spreading out beneath you and beginning to curve away on all sides as you rise high enough to begin to see the curvature of the Earth. The sky around you darkens, and then all at once you pass into a realm of deep indigo light. Say: "In the Name Tetragrammaton Elohim, I enter the Path of Tau."

You continue to rise through the indigo region. This Path is ruled by Saturn, lord of time, age, and limitation, and something of these can be felt in the atmosphere of the Path. Gradually, you become aware of a silvery light descending on you from above. You look up and see the Moon, much larger than it appears from Earth. You approach it, until it fills your field of vision completely.

All at once, you pass into a vast region of violet light. Say: "In the Name Shaddai El Chai, I enter Yesod, the ninth Sphere of the Tree." Visualize the Name before you in Hebrew letters, שד י א ל ח י. Then vibrate the Name nine times, softly but with great intensity. Yesod governs the etheric level of experience, and so swirling currents and tides of energy can be felt (although not seen) around you as you continue to rise.

In time, the violet region gives way to royal blue. Say: "In the Name El, I enter the Path of Samech." This Path is governed by Jupiter, lord of aspiration and mercy, and these qualities influence the atmosphere of the Path around you.

Gradually, you become aware of light shining on you from above, golden sunlight of steadily growing intensity. You look up and see the Sun shining above you, much larger than it appears from the surface of the Earth. It grows steadily larger and brighter as you approach it, reaching blinding intensity as it fills your entire field of vision.

Then you pass into the Sun, and blazing golden light surrounds you on all sides. Say: "In the Name Tetragrammaton Eloah va-Daath, I enter Tiphareth, the sixth Sphere of the Tree." Visualize the Name in Hebrew letters, י ה ו ה א ל ו ה ו ד ע ת, before you, and then vibrate the Name six times, softly but intensely, concentrating on the image of the solar light all around you.

As you reach the center of the Sun, you stop rising. Visualize yourself extending your arms to your sides in the Sign of Osiris Slain, and looking upward into light. Say: "And in the great Name of strength through sacrifice, Yeheshuah Yehoashah, I seek the Light that is beyond."

Turn all of your attention and all of your will toward the distance above you. After a time, you begin to see a change in the light there, as the blazing golden radiance of the Sun gives way to a point of pure white light, unguessably far away: the Star in the East of Tiphareth, the sign of Kether from beyond the Abyss.

Hold this image as long and intently as you can. When your concentration begins to fail, visualize yourself taking on the Signs of Isis, Apophis, and Osiris Risen. Then, remaining in this last Sign, visualize yourself descending the way you came, passing from Tiphareth through the Path of Samech to Yesod, and from there by the Path of Tau to Malkuth. Be aware of the colors and qualities of each Sphere and Path as you pass through them. Finally, return to your practice space and visualize yourself sitting back down in the chair and taking on the posture your physical body has been holding all this while.

Sixth, rise to your feet and slowly, with as much concentration as possible, make the Signs of Isis, Apophis, and Osiris Risen with your physical body, just as you did in the last step with your imagined body. Visualize the Light descending in response. Say aloud: "I.A.O. L.V.X. Such are the Words."

Seventh, perform the complete Second Degree Closing. This completes the ceremony.

———————

The practice of Rising on the Planes needs exactly that—practice—if its full potential is to be awakened by the magician in training. The first few performances of the ceremony are likely to have modest results at best. With time and regular work, though, the journey up the Middle Pillar of the Tree to Tiphareth becomes less "imaginary," in the usual modern sense of that word, and more a perception of realities in the realms of consciousness. This transformation, in turn, makes the ceremony increasingly effective as a means of shaping consciousness and gaining access to the energies of harmony, balance, and unification symbolized, in Cabalistic language, by Tiphareth.

It's possible to construct similar ceremonies in which the magician rises up the Tree along different routes—for example, by way of one of the two side Pillars. Still, this isn't usually necessary; the less ritually based methods of scrying and Pathworking are perfectly suited to the work of exploring the byways of the Tree and opening up their reflections in the microcosm. It's only when the goal is to open up a direct channel for the energies of the Higher that the full ceremonial method of Rising on the Planes given here has its place.

The Holy Guardian Angel

The fourth of the rituals we'll be examining in this chapter aims at goals considerably more advanced than those of the first three. As explained in Chapter 3, the work of spiritual development in the Golden Dawn tradition culminates in the fusion of the Lower Self, the ordinary personality and consciousness, with the Higher Self, the hidden side of the *ruach* or conscious mind beyond the Veil, followed by the opening up of contact between these and the Higher Genius or Spirit, the transcendent aspect of the self that exists beyond the Abyss. The process of calling down energies of the Higher into the consciousness of the Lower Self is but one step, although an important one, in the direction of this goal. It's possible, however, to aim the methods of magical ritual toward these supreme goals of magic in a far more direct way.

The classic method of doing this, one that was much studied by Golden Dawn adepts, is found in a late medieval grimoire called *The Sacred Magic of Abramelin the Mage*. In what has come to be called the "Abramelin operation," the magician dedicates a period of six months to the practice of a set of magical and mystical practices of steadily increasing intensity. The goal of these practices is the experience of contact with "the Holy Guardian Angel," the spiritual power that overshadows each individual person, which can be equated with the Higher Genius of the Golden Dawn system. Once the magician has come into contact with his or her Holy Guardian Angel, the operation culminates with a mass summoning of good and evil spirits, who are commanded and bound by the magician, and may then be used for any of the purposes of practical magic.

The system outlined in *The Sacred Magic of Abramelin the Mage* is an impressive one, and it stands out from the bulk of medieval grimoires as much for its clarity and detail as for the quality of its approach to magic. For all that, though, it's not really suitable for modern magicians. For one thing, its approach to invoking the Holy Guardian Angel comes largely out of medieval religion and involves activities such as the daily confession of all one's sins and the use of self-abasing prayers that, to modern ears, come very close to groveling. For another, it puts the same stress on evocation as most works of medieval magic, neglecting all other types of magical work, and thus lacks a certain amount of flexibility.

Another, and in some ways deeper, problem lies in the basic approach of the Abramelin operation itself. The idea of rising to the summit of magical attainment in a single six-month rush can be an appealing one, but in many cases it simply doesn't work. Most students of magic begin their training with a range of personal imbalances; these need to be cleared up, not merely pushed aside, in order to continue with the process of inner development, and this usually takes time. The alternative—simply pushing ahead and leaving your problems to take care of themselves—is usually a mistake; in magic, just as in electronics, putting too much energy into a system not yet prepared for it is a good way to blow a fuse.

A broader and more gradual approach is often what's needed to make the process of magical training a balanced and constructive one. Such an approach may take many forms, but the kind of basic magical training included in the Golden Dawn system makes up an important part of it in most systems. When these preliminary disciplines and the methods of ritual work have been mastered, though, there's certainly a place for a ceremonial approach to the same goals sought by the Abramelin operation. This ceremony may be called the Invocation of the Higher Self.

The Invocation of the Higher Self

This has been intentionally designed as the most demanding ceremony in this book. Before the Higher Self can be effectively invoked by ritual methods, the whole range of magical skills covered in the previous chapters must be learned and practiced thoroughly, and it also helps if at least one of the series of spiritual development workings given earlier in this chapter has been performed successfully. Most of the ritual techniques given in this book are used here in one form or another, and trying to put them to work all at once, without the necessary preparation, will bring little or nothing in the way of results.

Once the foundations have been laid, though, the Invocation of the Higher Self may be attempted. The requirements of this ceremony are those of the expanded First Degree Opening and Closing. It is performed as follows.

First, perform the complete First Degree Opening in its expanded form.
Second, perform the Greater Invoking Ritual of the Pentagram of Spirit.

Third, standing at the west of the altar facing east, trace the active and passive invoking pentagrams of Spirit over the altar. Using the Vibratory Formula of the Middle Pillar, vibrate the Name AHIH ("eh-heh-yeh") and circulate the energy through the Four Revolutions of the Light. Then do the same with the Name AGLA ("ah-geh-la").

Fourth, recite the following invocation: "Infinite and Eternal One, who dwellest in the bornless beyond, in whom all things have their source, their existence, and their end; lord of the forces of being and of the mysteries of creation, before whom all hidden things are revealed and all secrets made known; creator of all, preserver of all, destroyer of all, redeemer of all, I invoke thee, and I call to thee in this high work of the Magic of Light. Most high and most holy One, I seek to rend the Veil which divides myself from myself, to become one even as thou art One. Grant thine aid, I pray, to the highest aspirations of my soul! May the light of thy presence and the reality of thy power be with me and be shown to me in this hour; may I be made worthy of the transformation which I seek, so that I may accomplish the work of Light in the world.

"I pray that I may be granted the help of thy wise and mighty archangels Metatron and Sandalphon." Visualize the two archangels in the east, Metatron (on the right) a winged male figure in white robes of blinding brilliance, Sandalphon (on the left) a winged female figure in dark robes shining with a gentle light. Say: "Metatron, the Prince of Countenances. Sandalphon, the Reconciler for Earth. Help me and guide me in this high work of the Magic of Light, that I may accomplish the Great Work of uniting the higher and the lower within myself—that I may rend the Veil and enter into Light. For the duration of this ceremony, therefore, let my outer and material senses be bound, so that the inner and spiritual senses may awaken. For the duration of this ceremony, let my thoughts and feelings be bound, so that they stray not from the Great Work. For the duration of this ceremony, let my awareness be bound, so that it may turn only unto the Higher. In the Name of the Infinite One, may thy aid be granted to me."

At this point, imagine yourself plunged into darkness. The archangels disappear, and so does everything else around you. Build up, as strongly as possible, an image of yourself in the midst of absolute nothingness and silence; when this has been established, go on.

Fifth, trace the symbol of the Rose Cross before you in the darkness. Visualize it hanging before you, shining with light. Say: "In the heart of the darkness may be found the seed of the light." Raise your hands high, look up, and say: "Lord of the universe, vast and mighty one, ruler of the light and of the darkness! May light and guidance be granted to me through my Higher Self, whose symbol now shines in the darkness before me. With thy help, let me rend the Veil."

At this point, make the Sign of the Enterer toward the east, and remain in that Sign. While doing so, consider the highest and best idea of the Divine Unity you can conceive, and reach toward it with your whole will.

When your concentration begins to waver, make the Sign of Silence. Allow the Rose Cross symbol to vanish. Then, in the darkness before you, visualize a bright point of light like a faraway star. Hold this image for a time, then say: "I invoke thee, my Higher Self. I invoke thee, my likeness and completion. I invoke thee, in whom I am made perfect and whole."

Sixth, visualize two pillars taking shape before you in the east. The pillar on the right is made of fire, the one on the left of swirling cloud. Both reach from depths far below you to heights far above.

Hold this image for a few moments. Then visualize your own image taking shape between the pillars, facing you. Make that image as complete, exact, and solid as possible. When this has been done, imagine the image walking toward you, until it stands on the other side of the altar, facing you. Kneel, reach out your right hand to the image, and visualize the image clasping your hand with its own.

In the instant of contact, with an effort of imagination, place yourself within the image you have created: looking down through its eyes at your kneeling physical form, clasping your physical hand in its hand, inhabiting the imagined body just as you now inhabit your physical one. Try to make this shift of awareness as complete as possible. (If some awareness of your physical body still remains, it is not necessarily a problem.)

When you have accomplished this, release your physical hand, turn in the imagined body, and return to stand between the pillars of fire and cloud, this time facing east, toward the star of light. There, in the imagined body, make the Sign of the Enterer. Aspire toward the star with your whole will as intensely as you can. When your focus begins to waver, make the Sign of Silence, and be aware of the two pillars beside you. Repeat this process a second time, and then a third time, turning your attention toward the star while making the Sign of the Enterer, and toward the Pillars while making the Sign of Silence.

Seventh, in the imagined body, turn and walk back to the altar, and go around it to the west, so that you are standing above your kneeling physical body. Then, slowly, bring your physical body to its feet, so that both bodies are occupying the same space. At the same time, become aware of the physical body without losing awareness of the imagined one, so that you are inhabiting both bodies at the same time. Make the Sign of the Enterer with both bodies, and say: "Lord of all power and all wisdom, remove the darkness from my spiritual vision!"

Hold the Sign of the Enterer, and strive to see, beyond the pillars, the light of the star growing and taking shape, becoming a human-shaped form of pure light. Make the Sign of Silence, and while still inhabiting both bodies, go around the altar to the east and advance between the pillars in the presence of the Augoeides, the Form of Light.

Eighth, contemplate that Form and gradually imagine its light surrounding and enclosing you. Strive to identify yourself with the light. Visualize yourself taking on the form of a shining Being of immense size, towering above your physical body. Strive to realize that this vast Being is your only true self, and that your body, your personality, and everything you normally think of as yourself is no more than its base and throne. This is the central act of the ceremony, and it should be carried out with as much intensity, clarity, and imaginative power as you can possibly bring to it. Say, finally: "Thus have I been permitted to begin to comprehend the form of my Higher Self."

Ninth, return to an awareness of your ordinary self and physical body, but be aware of the overshadowing presence of the higher dimensions of yourself in the form of a star of light in the Kether center above the crown of your head. Its rays shine down throughout your Sphere of Sensation. Say: "I entreat thee, my Higher Self, that thou wilt guide me and instruct me in those things which are necessary for me to learn, and that thou wilt help me to comprehend both the secrets of the Magic of Light and the events of my life in the world." If there is any specific matter in which you feel you need guidance from the Higher, you may mention this here as well.

Finishing, go to the east of the altar, facing west, and take up the Lotus Wand. Say: "In the name and presence of my Higher Self, and by the Name and Presence of the Infinite One, the creator of worlds, I now proceed to call forth the spirits of the elements." Visualize the darkness around you gradually giving way to colored light. To the east, the light is yellow; to the south, red; to the west, blue; and to the north, green. The space within the limits traced by the banishings in the Opening is illuminated by white light.

Tenth, set the Lotus Wand down and take the dagger of Air. Go to the east and say: "By the power of my Higher Self present in me, I call forth the sylphs of Air." Trace an invoking pentagram of Air to the east with the dagger, draw the symbol of Aquarius, ≈, in the center, and then point to the center and vibrate the Name YHVH ("yeh-ho-wah") four times. Say: "In the Name Tetragrammaton; in the name of Raphael, archangel of Air; in the name of Chassan, angel of Air; and in the name of Ariel, Ruler of Air; spirits and powers of Air in the macrocosm and the microcosm, I call upon you to accomplish the will of the Infinite One. Be prompt and active in the service of the Higher and the works of the Magic of Light."

Visualize the sylphs of Air coming in response to this conjuration. They are slender-winged beings wearing gauzy garments of many colors, and their bodies seem to be slightly transparent. Behind and above them appears a larger figure of the same kind, wearing a winged crown; this is Paralda, Elemental King of Air.

Eleventh, return to the altar, lay the dagger down and take the wand of Fire. Go to the south and say: "By the power of my Higher Self present in me, I call forth the salamanders of Fire." Trace an invoking pentagram of Fire to the south with the wand, draw the symbol of Leo, ♌, in the center, and then point to the center and vibrate the Name ALHIM ("ell-o-heem") four times. Say: "In the Name Elohim; in the name of Michael, archangel of Fire; in the name of Aral, angel of Fire; and in the name of Seraph, Ruler of Fire, spirits and powers of Fire in the macrocosm and the microcosm, I call upon you to accomplish the will of the Infinite One. Be energetic and strong in the service of the Higher and the works of the Magic of Light."

Visualize the salamanders of Fire coming in response to this conjuration. They are dark, humanlike beings with glowing eyes, and their hair and garments seem to be made of living flame. Fire burns around them constantly. Behind and above them is a larger figure of the same kind, wearing a crown of blazing fire; this is Djin, Elemental King of Fire.

Twelfth, return to the altar, lay the wand down and take the cup of Water. Go to the west and say: "By the power of my Higher Self present in me, I call forth the undines of Water." Trace an invoking pentagram of Water to the west with the cup, draw the symbol of the Eagle's head ◁ in the center, and then point to the center and vibrate the Name AL ("ell") four times. Say: "In the Name El; in the name of Gabriel, archangel of Water; in the name of Taliahad, angel of Water; and in the name of Tharsis, Ruler of Water, spirits and powers of Water in the macrocosm and the microcosm, I call upon you to accomplish the will of the Infinite One. Be flexible and attentive to images in the service of the Higher and the works of the Magic of Light."

Visualize the undines of Water coming in response to this conjuration. They are beautiful naked beings with silvery skin and hair the color of the sea. Behind and above them appears a larger being of the same kind, wearing a crown made of shining silver; this is Nichsa, Elemental King of Water.

Thirteenth, return to the altar, lay the cup down and take the pentacle of Earth. Go to the north and say: "By the power of my Higher Self present in me, I call forth the gnomes of Earth." Trace an invoking pentagram of Earth to the north with the pentacle, draw the symbol of Taurus, $\bigcirc\!\!\!\!\!\vee$, in the center, and then point to the center and vibrate the Name ADNI ("ah-dough-nye") four times. Say: "In the Name Adonai; in the name of Auriel, archangel of Earth; in the name of Phorlakh, angel of Earth; and in the name of Kerub, Ruler of Earth, spirits and powers of Earth in the macrocosm and the microcosm, I call upon you to accomplish the will of the Infinite One. Be laborious and patient in the service of the Higher and the works of the Magic of Light."

Visualize the gnomes of Earth coming in response to this conjuration. They are short, heavily built beings, like the dwarfs of legend, with ornaments of metals and gemstones on their earth-colored garments, and tools and weapons in their hands. Behind and above them appears a larger being of the same kind, wearing a crown of gold and bright jewels; this is Ghob, Elemental King of Earth.

Fourteenth, return to the altar, lay the pentacle down and take the Lotus Wand. Standing now at the west of the altar facing east, trace the invoking pentagram of active Spirit with the Lotus Wand, draw the symbol of Spirit, ⊕ at the center, point to the center and vibrate the Name AHIH ("eh-heh-yeh") once. Then trace the invoking pentagram of passive Spirit, draw the same symbol at the center, and vibrate the Name AGLA ("ah-geh-la") once. Raise your hands, look upward toward the light of the Higher Self above you, and say, "And in the great Name of strength through sacrifice, Yeheshuah Yehovashah, I seek harmony and balance in myself and in my actions in the world. Let me be prompt and active as the sylphs, but avoid frivolity and caprice. Let me be energetic and strong as the salamanders, but avoid irritability and ferocity. Let me be flexible and attentive to images as the undines, but avoid idleness and changeability. Let me be laborious and patient as the gnomes, but avoid grossness and avarice. For thus I shall develop the powers of my soul, and rightly command the spirits of the elements. Guide me and teach me, my Higher Self, so that I may accomplish this."

Fifteenth, say: "Spirits and powers of the elements, about me and within me, I therefore summon thee to the service of harmony and balance." Then go to the east, and make the Signs of Isis, Apophis, and Osiris Risen. Trace the Rose Cross symbol there with the Lotus Wand; point to the center, and vibrate the Name IAO. Then say: "In this mighty Name, spirits of Air, I call thee to the Harmony." Go to the south, west, and north, in turn, make the same Signs and symbols, and in the same words summon the salamanders, undines, and gnomes to balance. Return to the west of the altar, facing east, and perform the complete Analysis of INRI from the Rose Cross and Hexagram rituals.

Sixteenth, finishing this, remain in silence in the Light for a time, and then perform the complete First Degree Closing in the expanded form. This completes the ceremony.

————————

The formula for this ritual is built from a combination of several elements of symbolism from the Golden Dawn outer grades and the basic scheme of the Abramelin operation. The first half, steps 1–9, focus on the invocation of the Higher and the establishing of a link between the Lower Self and the Higher Self of the magician; the second half, steps 10–16, brings this link into play as the basis for establishing balance among the elements of macrocosm and microcosm alike.

Like the other ceremonies of spiritual development given in this chapter, this one yields its potentials only to regular practice. A single performance of the Invocation of the Higher Self will bring the magician in training a step closer to the rending of the Veil, but that one step is only the beginning of what is usually a substantial journey. Whatever link with the Higher Self is established in the first few workings—and there may be none, or close to none—will need to be developed and strengthened with further work, and both the symbols and the qualities of character that give the power to control the elements and their spirits must be developed as well. All this takes time and continued effort.

It's often a good idea to begin the journey by doing one performance of the ceremony and then waiting for some time—perhaps as much as a month—before doing the next. In many people, the Invocation of the Higher Self can set off any number of psychological reactions, constructive or otherwise; fear, that fear of change older texts call "The Watcher on the Threshold," is perhaps the most common of these, though troubles with an inflated ego are often seen as well. It's useful to provide room to work through these issues before going on. Gradually decrease the interval between workings and allow the effects to take shape at their own pace. Given steady work, there are quite literally no limits to the power and scope of the results that can be obtained.

CHAPTER 14

THE FORMULA OF
THE EQUINOX

IN THE LAST FIVE CHAPTERS, we've examined some of the ways in which the ritual methods of the Golden Dawn tradition can be applied to both practical and spiritual purposes, and in the process covered a number of different ritual formulae and approaches to ceremonial work. In studying and practicing these applications, it's important to keep in mind that none of them should be treated as fixed, rigid forms. Each is a structure built around the basic framework of the Golden Dawn's Cabalistic magic, using a set of techniques drawn from the traditional lore, and each of them can be reshaped as needed, using different symbolism or seeking different goals. The ability to do this, to use existing ritual forms as the starting point for creative personal work, is one of the things that marks the point of transition between the student of magic and the true magician.

It's precisely this flexible approach to ritual work that gave rise to one of the Golden Dawn's most important magical discoveries. To grasp that discovery and its implications, we'll need to look at some of the background of the rise of the Golden Dawn itself.

All through the eighteenth and nineteenth centuries, as the belief systems of the scientific revolution came to define reality for most people in the West, the magical traditions of earlier times were carried on mostly by small, secretive groups. Most of these groups made use of an organizational structure—the lodge system—borrowed from Freemasonry and similar fraternal orders, which was originally evolved in the craft guilds of the Middle Ages.

From its medieval sources, the lodge system also brought a set of traditions of initiatory ritual. These traditions were expanded and developed fraternal lodges, and as the lodge system became standard among many magical groups, these same ritual methods were borrowed and used there as well. The magical initiations that resulted from this borrowing were in many cases powerful ceremonies. However, they had little or no connection to the practice of ritual magic outside of the lodge setting. In effect, the magicians of these lodges learned two different sets of ritual methods and formulae, one for lodge work and another for personal practice.

One of the supreme achievements of the Golden Dawn was the realization that these two systems could and should be unified. In the Order's work, formulae taken from the grade rituals were put to work in the members' own personal ceremonial practice as well. The same patterns that were used in a Golden Dawn temple to initiate members could be used, and were used, outside of the temple to evoke spirits, consecrate talismans, and accomplish other magical purposes.

This had a twofold effect: first, it enabled the Order's adepts to energize their personal work through a link with the egregor—the collective energy or group soul—of their temple and the Order itself; second, it allowed them to practice and master the formulae of the initiatory grades outside the temple, developing skills and insights that could then be brought back into the temple and used to improve the working of the grade rituals themselves. In addition, it opened up an array of powerful formulae that could be applied to any of the purposes of ritual magic.

The Order's materials on this subject can be found in a collection of papers called Document Z, "The Enterer of the Threshold," which is included in Volume 3 of Israel Regardie's *The Golden Dawn*. In these papers, the Neophyte Grade ceremony is analyzed in detail, and then used as the basis for constructing effective ceremonies of evocation, talisman consecration, invisibility, transformation, and spiritual development, as well as for practical methods of divination and alchemy. These workings represent the summit of the Golden Dawn's ritual magic, and when performed by an experienced magician, they can awaken and direct forces of an intensity few other ceremonies can match.

This same process was applied to other rituals within the Golden Dawn system; for example, the Ring and Disk, divinatory tools used by advanced Golden Dawn adepts, were consecrated using a ceremony based on the Zelator Grade. Little information survives on these more advanced applications, however, and the collapse of the Order itself in 1900 seems to have brought work in this direction to a standstill. Even after the publication of the Golden Dawn documents, little more has been done, and so the Order's most important magical discovery is also in many ways its most neglected one.

The possibilities that are opened up by that discovery can be measured by the fact that it's possible to create effective ritual formulae, using the same approach, starting from *any initiation ceremony whatsoever*. This isn't limited to Golden Dawn ceremonies, or even to the broader tradition of which the Golden Dawn is one part. Wiccan initiations, the degree rituals of fraternal lodges, and the grades of the Ordo Templi Orientis—to name only three of the more obvious examples—could be used by initiates of these traditions as the basis for powerful ritual formulae for personal work. Furthermore, many kinds of group ceremonies besides initiation can be used in the same way.

In order to explore some of the potentials of this approach to ritual work, this chapter will examine a Golden Dawn ritual—the Ceremony of the Equinox—in detail, and will show how it can be transformed into a method of individual magical work. The same methods of transformation, in turn, can be put to use to derive ritual formulae from any other ceremony in or out of the Golden Dawn tradition.

The Marriage of Sun and Earth

The Ceremony of the Equinox is, in many ways, the hidden powerhouse of the Golden Dawn in its work as a magical order. While the grades of initiation serve to energize and transform the Spheres of Sensation of a Golden Dawn temple's members, the Ceremony of the Equinox does much the same thing for the temple and the Order as a whole. Tapping into the energies that flow through two special points in the cycle of the seasons, this ceremony brings those energies into focus within a purified and consecrated space, and uses them to charge and revitalize the group egregor. Importantly, it also renews the effects of the Outer Order initiations in the individual members, strengthening the links that connect the initiate to the energies of the macrocosm and the collective forces of the Order itself.

In order to understand how this is done, it's necessary to know a little about the astronomical basis of the equinoxes themselves. Most people know that the Earth is tilted relative to its orbit around the Sun, as shown in Diagram 50. The angle of the tilt is currently a little over twenty-three degrees. Because of the tilt, the Northern Hemisphere receives more sunlight than the Southern Hemisphere for half the year, and the situation is reversed in the other half, causing the change of seasons.

The same phenomenon causes the "Midnight Sun" of the Arctic and Antarctic regions. For six months at a time, when one of the poles is tilted toward the Sun, the Sun remains above the horizon twenty-four hours a day there, circling around the sky without ever setting; at the same time, the other pole is plunged into six months of unbroken night. Between the poles and the equator, the effects of the tilt are less extreme, but the length of day and night changes throughout the year, and the apparent track of the Sun through the sky moves north and south with the seasons as well. At the equator itself, the Sun passes to the north of an observer for half the year, and to the south for the other half; at only two points during the year does it pass directly overhead.

At these points, the two hemispheres of the Earth receive equal amounts of light, and day and night are of equal length. These points are the equinoxes (from the Latin for "equal night"). The spring equinox happens each year around March 22, the autumn equinox around September 22.

In the Golden Dawn system, these facts of astronomy were combined with the traditional magical idea of the living Earth and a range of

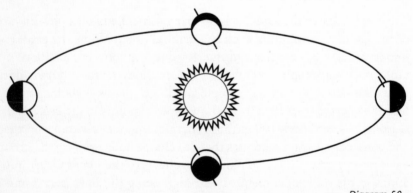

Diagram 50—
The Earth and the Sun

astrological lore to form the foundation on which the Equinox Ceremony was based. The Order's papers include a complex set of teachings
that drew connections between the Tree of Life, the Tarot, the Enochian
tablets, and other magical symbolism, on the one hand, and the stars
and constellations of the night sky on the other. This lore has a number
of practical applications, but the one that is relevant here bases itself on
the idea that these relationships map out the patterns of energy at work
in the Sphere of Sensation of the Earth itself.

In this system, the celestial equator (which is simply the projection of
Earth's equator straight out into space) represents the energies of Earth's
Tiphareth center, its essential life and energy. The Sun has this same role
in the solar system as a whole, and its path through the constellations—
called the *ecliptic*—can represent this broader context of energies. When
the Sun contacts the celestial equator at each equinox, Sun and Earth
come into a relationship that allows their energies to unite. Through this
union, the Earth is revitalized, made fruitful, and brought into harmony
with the wider context of the solar system's energies. In the language of
an older symbolism, each equinox is the marriage of Sun and Earth, and
from this mating, all life on Earth is born.

Another aspect of the lore of the heavens plays a role here as well. Like
many of the magical traditions of its time, the Golden Dawn system
includes some strange speculations on the role of the Earth's axial tilt as a
factor in human evolution. (Many traditional teachings on this theme
have been collected by Joscelyn Godwin in his excellent book *Arktos*.)
The Order's lore held that the Earth's North Pole presently points toward
the part of the heavens assigned to Binah, the third Sphere, source of the
principle of limitation. This in turn can be seen as having more than a little
to do with the realities of life on Earth at the present time.

According to these teachings, the North Pole once pointed toward
the part of the heavens assigned to Kether, in the constellation Draco.
This point is also the pole of the ecliptic that is the axis of the Earth's
revolution around the Sun—and an Earth oriented to that point would
have no axial tilt at all, and no seasons or extremes of temperature. In
magical terms, the equator and the ecliptic would be the same, and the
energies of Earth and Sun thus would be in constant union. This situation
corresponds at least symbolically to the primal age of peace that the
Golden Dawn's Cabalistic lore, borrowing a term from Judeo-Christian
mythology, describes as Eden.

It's anyone's guess whether these speculations are anything more than mythology themselves. The Earth's axis does point to different parts of the heavens, turning in a 25,920-year cycle that also drives the precession of the equinoxes and the change of astrological ages, but the evidence for major shifts in the angle of the tilt—rather than simply the direction toward which the tilted axis points—is a good deal less certain. To the modern Golden Dawn magician, on the other hand, such questions are of little practical importance. The critical point is that the intersection of equator and ecliptic, the marriage of Sun and Earth, takes place twice a year. For a short period each spring and fall, Eden is renewed in the world, and the magician can participate in the union of energies that results. This is the purpose of the Ceremony of the Equinox.

The Ceremony of the Equinox

In the Golden Dawn and in many of its successor orders, the coming of each equinox played a central part in the activities of each temple or lodge. It was at the equinox that new officers took their positions and were empowered to carry out their functions in the grade rituals, and at the equinox that the password for the next six-month term was issued. The Ceremony of the Equinox carried out these and other organizational functions, as well as accomplishing its magical work, and the combination of these different purposes was handled with a great deal of skill.

The text of the ceremony can be found in Volume 2 of Regardie's *The Golden Dawn*. It begins with the opening of the Neophyte Grade, the basis for the First Degree Opening used elsewhere in this book. The password of the previous term is abrogated, and then the temple officers in the four quarters and the center establish a pattern of polarities: first between east and west, then between north and south, and finally among all four quarters. All are brought into focus and reconciled by the Hegemon at the center.

Next, the officers at the quarters exchange the working tools of their offices for symbols of the elements, and all present invoke the Divine Unity in its elemental expressions, facing each of the four quarters in turn, and then facing the center. During this process, the symbolism of the Middle Pillar is used to open a channel for the descent of the solar light. Air, as the firmament, is equated with Kether; Fire with the solar

Sphere Tiphareth; Water with the lunar Sphere Yesod; and Earth with Malkuth. These invocations thus function on two levels at once, the level of the elements and that of the Spheres, and prepare a way for the shift between levels that follows.

The temple officers then give way to the three chief officers; the new password is proclaimed, the officers for the next term are announced, and the officers of the past term surrender their regalia.

At this point, the energies of the ceremony, in effect, change gears. All members who have not yet attained the Portal Grade are ushered out, and the symbolism of the rite shifts completely from the elemental realm to the spiritual in a process whereby the Outer Order temple is assumed into the Inner. In the presence of the Inner Order members, the adept who has been chosen to lead the temple as Hierophant is formally installed, and when this is finished, the ceremony shifts back to the First Degree, the temple is remitted to the Outer, and the Outer Order members return to their places.

The new Hierophant is next presented to the members and makes his "confession" or statement of purpose. He or she then installs the other temple officers and presents them with their regalia, and they take up their working tools from the altar. The Kerux returns the symbols of the elements to the altar, and there is an interval for official announcements and for the new Hierophant to address the temple. The ceremony finishes with the Neophyte Grade closing, which includes the communion of the elements described in Chapter 8.

To make sense of this sequence of ritual actions, two points must be kept in mind. The first is that the Ceremony of the Equinox, like the Neophyte Grade, belongs to the First Degree. Like any other First Degree ceremony, its purpose is the creation of a link between higher and lower levels. The second point is that the Neophyte and Equinox ceremonies make this link in sharply different ways. In the Neophyte Grade, the energy that forms the link has to be built up through a gradual process in which circular movement plays a central role. The Equinox Ceremony, by contrast, draws on energies that are already present at high intensity in the macrocosm, and attracts and seals these energies into a balanced, stable matrix of forces.

The difference between these approaches is not unlike that between the two ways to start a car that has a dead battery. The car can be pushed into motion down a slope so that the alternator can begin generating current and fire the spark plugs, or another car can be used to provide the current through jumper cables. The first of these methods, in essence, is that of the Neophyte Grade; the second is that of the Ceremony of the Equinox. Depending on the circumstances, and the particular "dead battery" that has to be brought to magical life, either of these approaches will serve.

In the Equinox formula, this magical "jump-starting" involves three major phases. First, the ground has to be prepared for the incoming energies. In the ceremony, this is done first of all by abrogating the password of the previous term, which represents the energies brought through at the last equinox; next, by creating a balanced pattern of polarities between the elements, reconciled by Spirit; and finally, by bringing this pattern into relationship with the higher energies of the Spheres of the Middle Pillar. This phase ends with the proclamation of the new password, which serves as a seed around which the macrocosmic energies can coalesce.

The second phase establishes the link with the energies. This is done by a sudden change of level from the material to the spiritual, in which the symbolism of the elements centered on Spirit gives way to that of the Tree of Life centered on Tiphareth. At this higher level, the core work of the ceremony is accomplished. Once this has been done and the energies have been brought through, a second change of level returns the temple to the realm of the elements and the Outer Order.

In the third phase, the link that has been made is anchored in the temple by the installation and investiture of the temple officers, and in the members, by the elemental communion that is part of the ceremony of Closing.

This three-step process may seem oddly familiar, and it should. The same sequence, in a much simpler form, makes up the framework for the basic rituals of invoking and banishing covered in Chapter 6. A rite such as the Lesser Ritual of the Pentagram, in a real sense, can be seen as a Ceremony of the Equinox in miniature: it establishes a stable matrix of forces, and then shifts up a level in order to bring energy through from higher levels, in the same way the Equinox Ceremony does.

An Equinox Ceremony for Solitary Use

The formula outlined above can have any number of practical uses in ritual magic. Probably the most obvious is a version of the Ceremony of the Equinox for use by individual magicians who don't belong to a working lodge or temple in the Golden Dawn tradition. The benefits of invoking the solar energies at the equinox can be a source of power and healing for the solitary magician, just as they are for the member of a lodge, and the ceremony itself can easily be adapted so that it can be performed by a single magician.

The following ritual is designed to serve this purpose. It should be performed within forty-eight hours of the actual time of the spring or autumn equinox, which can be found in an astrological calendar or almanac. This is the window of time in which the energies of the Sun and the Earth are in direct contact with one another, and performing the ceremony earlier or later than this will result in a greatly weakened effect.

The requirements of the ritual are those of the First Degree Opening and Closing, and you'll also need the rose, lamp, wine, bread, and salt for the elemental communion. In addition, you'll need to choose a watch-word, which is the personal equivalent of the password used in a lodge setting. The watchword should express an idea, a theme, or a direction you intend to develop during the six months to come; if at all possible, it should be a single word, and may be in English or any other language.

Examples of watchwords might be "compassion," for a magician who seeks to develop this quality; "Netzach," for one who wants to deepen his or her experience of the side of life represented by this Sphere of the Tree; or "awake," for one who has chosen to work on mental clarity. A watchword should be chosen with the same care you would use in selecting the purpose for a ritual working. Whatever it represents is likely to come up again and again in your life over the six months to come. The ceremony is performed as follows.

First, perform the complete First Degree Opening, in either the basic or expanded form.

Second, go to the east of the altar and face west. Holding the Lotus Wand high, say: "In the Name of the Lord of the Universe, who works in silence and whom nothing but silence is expressed, I proclaim that the (spring or autumn) equinox is here." If you have previously performed this ceremony and took a watchword at that time, say: "...and that the watchword (word) is abrogated."

Third, say: "I consecrate according to ancient custom the return of the equinox.

"Light: Darkness. East: West. Air: Water." While saying these words, build up the following imagery for the directions: behind you, in the east, a morning sky with high billowing clouds and rays of sunlight; in front of you, in the west, a dark sea at sunset. When this has been established, knock once with the lower end of the Lotus Wand on the top of the altar and say: "I am the reconciler between them.

"Heat: Cold. South: North. Fire: Earth." Here the images are: to your left, in the south, a desert scene beneath a burning noontide Sun; to your right, in the north, a winter scene at midnight, with leafless trees dark against a sky ablaze with the northern constellations. Knock once with the Lotus Wand and say: "I am the reconciler between them."

"One Creator. One Preserver. One Destroyer. One Redeemer." Here visualize all four of the images around you and strive to feel the presence of a unity of creative power working in and through all of them. Knock once with the Lotus Wand and say: "One Reconciler between them."

Fourth, set the Lotus Wand down. Take the rose from the altar and go to the east. Say: "I invoke the Lord of the Universe. Holy art thou, Lord of the Air, who hast created the firmament." Make an equal-armed cross in the air with the rose, and then make the Sign of the Enterer to the east, followed by the Sign of Silence. During this process, visualize the presence of a vast sphere of pure white brilliance immeasurably far above you.

Return to the altar, set the rose down, and take up the lamp. Go to the south and say: "I invoke the Lord of the Universe. Holy art thou, Lord of the Fire, wherein thou hast shown forth the throne of thy glory." Make a cross of the same kind in the air with the lamp, and then make the Signs to the south. During this process, visualize a stream of light descending from the sphere of brilliance to another vast sphere, still far above but much closer, which shines like a golden Sun.

Return to the altar, set the lamp down, and take the cup of wine. Go to the west and say: "I invoke the Lord of the Universe. Holy art thou, Lord of the Waters, whereon thy spirit moved in the beginning." Make a cross in the air with the cup, followed by the Signs; be careful not to make the Sign of the Enterer too forcefully or the wine will spill. During this process, visualize the light descending from the golden sphere to another, high above you but again much closer, which is a deep violet color and has a sense of immense power about it.

Return to the altar, set the cup down, and take the dish with bread and salt. Go to the north and say: "I invoke the Lord of the Universe. Holy art thou, Lord of the Earth, which thou hast made for thy footstool." Make a cross in the air with the bread and salt, followed by the Signs. During this process, visualize the light descending straight down onto the place where you are performing the ritual and passing through it into the Earth.

Fifth, return to the altar, and set the bread and salt down. Stand at the east of the altar facing west, take the Lotus Wand, and say: "I invoke the Lord of the Universe. Holy art thou, who art in all things—in whom are all things. If I climb up to heaven, thou art there, and if I go down to Hell, thou art there also. If I take the wings of the morning and flee unto the uttermost parts of the sea, even there shall thy hand lead me and thy right hand hold me. If I say, peradventure the darkness shall cover me, even the night shall be turned light unto thee.

"Thine is the Air with its movement.

"Thine is the Fire with its flashing flame.

"Thine is the Water with its ebb and flow.

"Thine is the Earth with its enduring stability."

Make an equal-armed cross over the altar with the Lotus Wand, and follow it with the Signs. During this whole process, be aware of the pillar of light descending from immeasurable heights to the Earth beneath your feet.

Finally, say: "In thy Name, I confer the new watchword. It is (word)."

Sixth, lay the Lotus Wand down, go around to the west of the altar and face east. Make the Signs of Isis, Apophis, and Osiris Risen, and say: "Now, in the presence of the Lord of the Universe, may this external and visible sanctuary of the Magic of Light be assumed into the House not made with hands, builded of living stones—the Company of the Adepts."

Go to the east. Make the three Signs again, trace the symbol of the Rose Cross in the air, point to its center, and vibrate the Name IAO. Do the same in the south, west, and north; return to the east, and then to the west of the altar. Perform the complete Analysis of the Word INRI, as in the Rose Cross Ritual, and call down the Light. Say: "And it is so assumed accordingly."

At this point, visualize yourself rising and expanding, as in the opening of the Cabalistic Cross. Your surroundings fade out, replaced by pure golden light, and the altar before you is of gold.

Seventh, trace the Rose Cross symbol over the altar and say: "In the great Name YHShVH YHVShH ("yeh-heh-shu-ah yeh-ho-wah-shah"), I invoke the forces of the Solar Light. Eternal and spiritual Sun, whose visible image is the light and the life of Earth, grant that I may be given whatever of thy blessing and thy power I may be fit to receive during the next six months. Strengthen me that I may bear the trials of the path; guide me that I may walk thereon in harmony with the will of the Infinite; teach me that I may learn the mysteries of the Magic of Light."

Bow your head. Say: "And unto thee, sole wise, sole mighty, and sole Eternal One, be praise and glory forever, who hath permitted me, who now standeth humbly before thee, to enter thus far into the sanctuary of thy mysteries. Not unto me but unto thy Name be the glory. Let the influence of thy divine ones descend upon my head and teach me the value of self-sacrifice so that I shrink not in the hour of trial, but that thus my name may be written on high and my genius stand in the presence of the Holy Ones, in that hour when the Son of Man is invoked before the Lord of Spirits and his name in the presence of the Ancient of Days."

Eighth, pause for a time, and then say, "The work of the Light for which this sanctuary has been assumed is accomplished. In the presence of the Lord of the Universe, may it be remitted into its due place in the outer world, taking with it the gifts which have been bestowed therein." Make the Signs of Isis, Apophis, and Osiris Risen. "And it is so remitted accordingly."

At this point, visualize yourself descending and contracting to your ordinary size, and become aware again of your surroundings.

Pause, and then say: "In virtue of the power to me committed, I consecrate these symbols of the elements." Then perform the ceremony of the communion of the elements, as given in Chapter 8, blessing and then consuming the elemental symbols.

Ninth, perform the complete First Degree Closing, in whichever form—basic or expanded—you did the Opening. This completes the ceremony.

Applications of the Equinox Formula

The Equinox Ceremony for solitary working given above is only one of the many ritual uses of the formula we're examining. Any of the other classes of magical operation covered in this book can be done using a ritual structure built up on the same lines. The one requirement is that the ceremony be used to attract and seal an energy already present in strength in the macrocosm. Nearly any kind of magical working can be done in this way, given a little imagination and an attentiveness to the cycles of macrocosmic energies.

The patterns traced by these cycles are discussed in Chapter 2, but some practical notes might be useful at this point. The energies of the Spheres are for all practical purposes a constant presence in the magical universe, and any working that is done with Sphere energies in their pure form can take place any time at all. Such workings, as mentioned earlier, are best limited to the purposes of spiritual development, but this certainly has a place in the life of any magician worth the name.

The energies of the planets are best tracked by astrological methods. It's possible to take this to a high degree of complexity, using the techniques of electional astrology to combine planetary forces with a great deal of precision, but this isn't strictly necessary for the use of the formula. The essential rule is that the planet you intend to invoke should be in a harmonious aspect (conjunction, trine, or sextile) with the Moon, while at the same time neither conjunct the Sun nor in a hostile aspect (opposition or square) with Mars or Saturn. A little time spent with an astrological calendar will make this easy enough to work out.

For the elements, in turn, the placement of the Moon is the dominant factor. The cycles of the elements are less clearly defined than those of the planets, and the scheme for tracking them used in the Golden Dawn itself—the tattwa system, borrowed from Hindu occultism—doesn't fit well with the rest of the tradition and has been abandoned by most groups.

The role of the Moon as the great determinant of elemental forces, on the other hand, is a major theme of Renaissance magical philosophy, and it offers an effective way to track elemental energies for workings with this formula. Here the phase and sign of the Moon are the important points. Ceremonies of the Equinox formula invoking one of the elements should be done when the Moon is in a sign of the zodiac assigned to that element; thus, a ceremony invoking Fire should be done when the Moon is in Aries, Leo, or Sagittarius. As always, works of increase should be done in the waxing Moon, works of decrease in the waning.

There are any number of ways to use the Equinox formula for spiritual and practical magic, and some fairly simple rules for doing so. In most cases, the establishment of the matrix of balanced forces is done in the same way, and with much the same words, as in the Ceremony of the Equinox itself. The upward shift is directed toward the Sphere that corresponds to the operation, or simply to the realm of Spirit, and the major invocation of forces is done from this level. The downward shift that follows brings the invoked force into manifestation, and the magician then directs that force toward its intended target, just as the new Hierophant directs the energies he or she has received to install the temple officers.

Two rituals based on this formula have been included in this chapter as examples of the ways in which this can be done. One, an Equinox formula consecration ceremony for a scrying mirror, can be used as a model for practical workings; the second, a spiritual development ceremony, serves as a model for theurgic workings. Either or both can also be performed by the student as written.

Consecration Ritual for a Scrying Mirror

This ritual is presented to show how the Equinox formula can be used to call upon highly specific energies for the purposes of practical magic. Requisites are the same as those of the First Degree expanded Opening and Closing, plus a scrying mirror to consecrate and a silk bag in which the mirror may be placed. The mirror design described in Chapter 9 will be suitable, but symbolism appropriate to the Moon (or its correspondence on the Tree of Life, Yesod) should be worked into the design and construction; for example, the cushion may be partly stuffed with herbs attributed to the Moon, or it may be made of purple velvet.

The ritual should be performed nine times in succession, each time on the night of the full moon. It will be most effective if done in a place where the light of the moon can shine onto the altar at the center of the ritual space during the time of the ritual. Glass blocks some of the denser etheric forces, so an open window or skylight is preferable, and—where this is possible, and safe—an outdoor ritual space for the working is best of all.

At the beginning of the first performance of the ritual, the scrying mirror should be resting on top of the silk bag on the altar. In all subsequent performances, the mirror should be in the bag, so that the banishing rituals do not disrupt the forces already present. The ritual is performed as follows.

First, perform the complete First Degree Opening in its expanded form.

Second, if the mirror is in its bag, take it out at this point; do not touch it with your bare skin. Then perform the Greater Invoking Hexagram Ritual of the Moon, using the Lotus Wand.

Third, stand at the altar facing the direction of the Moon across the altar. Raise the Lotus Wand high in your right hand and say, "Light: Darkness. East: West. Air: Water." Point at the mirror. "Thou shalt be the reconciler between them. Heat: Cold. South: North. Fire: Earth." Point at the mirror again. "Thou shalt be the reconciler between them. One Creator: One Preserver: One Destroyer: One Redeemer." Raise both hands skyward, looking up. "One Reconciler between them." As before, while naming the polarities, visualize the opposed elements in their quarters; while invoking their reconciliation, though, visualize a sphere of intense violet light above the altar, large enough so that the scrying mirror is within it.

Fourth, take the mirror in your left hand, being careful not to touch it with bare skin; with mirror and Lotus Wand, go to the east. Trace the Fire form of the invoking hexagram of the Moon with the Lotus Wand. Vibrate the Name ARARITA and say: "In the Great Name ALHIM ("ell-o-heem"), I call the visions of Fire into this mirror of art. Spirits of Fire present in this place, consecrate this mirror with thy power to the service of the Magic of Light." Go around to the south and trace the Earth form of the invoking hexagram of the Moon; repeat the invocation, but replace the Name ALHIM with ADNI ("ah-dough-nye") and the word "Fire" with "Earth." Do the same in the west with the Air form of the hexagram, the name YHVH ("yeh-ho-wah"), and Air, and in the north with the Water form of the hexagram, the Name AL ("ell"), and Water.

Fifth, return to the altar and set the mirror down. If possible, place the mirror so the moonlight shines directly on it, and position yourself so you can see the Moon mirrored in the glass. (If circumstances don't allow this, face the direction of the Moon and visualize the full Moon in the mirror.) Trace the Earth form of the invoking hexagram of the Moon over the image, and then repeat the word "Levanah"—the Cabalistic name of the sphere of the Moon—nine times, slowly and intently, focusing all your attention on the image of the Moon in the mirror. Then say: "Mistress of the night, lady of visions! Behold this scrying mirror, consecrated in the four directions by the power of the four elements. As thy image is reflected in it, so may power in thy realms of vision pass into it, that it may show me true images of hidden things in the service of the Magic of Light."

Sixth, go to the west of the altar and face east. Raise both your hands and vibrate the Name ShDI AL ChI ("shah-dye ell chye") nine times. Be aware of a new presence in the consecrated space, an energy lunar in nature but greater and more spiritual than that of the Moon itself. Visualize your working space surrounded by violet light. Build the perception and the visualization as strongly as possible, and then say:

"In thy mighty and holy Name Shaddai El Chai, I invoke thee, Infinite and Eternal One, in whom is all power and from whom comes all life. Be with me, and grant thine aid to the highest aspirations of my soul. Be thou my firm foundation, that I may accomplish this work of the magic of Light, and make of this scrying mirror a true instrument whereby to see into the Unseen. May thy mighty archangel Gabriel be present with me in this work, and thy powerful angels, the Kerubim, lend me their aid, that I may truly consecrate this scrying mirror with the forces of the Sphere of Yesod, the Foundation."

Seventh, bow your head and allow the awareness of Yesod to fade. Go to the east of the altar and face west. Raise the Lotus Wand high in your right hand and say: "In the Great Name ShDI AL ChI, and by all the names and powers of Levanah, the sphere of the Moon, I therefore ordain you, mirror of art, to the service of the Magic of Light; and I charge you to show me true images of hidden things at my command." Lower the Lotus Wand, go to the west of the altar and face east. Carefully, without touching the glass with your skin, wrap the mirror in its bag so that the energies invoked into it are not discharged by the closing and banishing.

Eighth, perform the First Degree Closing in its expanded form. This completes the ceremony.

———————————

After the ninth performance of this ritual, the mirror can be used for scrying. The visions that come through a lunar scrying mirror of this kind will be more concrete and detailed than those seen in a mirror of the sort covered in Chapter 9; some of the more advanced types of mirror work, such as projecting consciousness through the mirror, are also helped by the much more extensive etheric patterning of the Moon mirror. On the other side of the balance, it's very hard to bring abstract information through a mirror of this kind, and no attempt at scrying through it should be made in the last three days before the New Moon.

In working, an invocation of the Moon or of Yesod, the ninth Sphere of the Tree of Life, should be used in place of the invocation of the Angel Hru given in Chapter 9. The mirror itself, like any other scrying mirror, should never be exposed to sunlight or touched directly with bare skin.

The Ceremony of the Descending Light

The following ceremony for spiritual development uses the Equinox Formula to call on the powers of Spirit to balance and harmonize the four elements in the cosmos and the self. The references to "the Harmony" in the ritual are inspired by passages in old Hermetic writings, and are based on a vision of the universe as music in which every existing thing is a harmonious tone.

Requirements for the ceremony are the same as those of any First Degree ceremony. As a Sphere working, it isn't dependent on energy cycles in the macrocosm, and so can be done at any time. The ceremony is performed as follows.

———

First, perform the complete First Degree Opening in its expanded form.

Second, perform the Greater Invoking Pentagram Ritual of Spirit, using the Lotus Wand.

Third, stand at the east of the altar, facing west. Raise the Lotus Wand and say: "In the Name of the Lord of the Universe, who works in silence and whom nothing but silence can express, I proclaim the Harmony, the presence of the infinite and eternal within the universe of space and time."

Fourth, pause and say, "Light: Darkness. East: West. Air: Water." Knock once on the altar with the Lotus Wand. "I am the reconciler between them." While naming the polarities, visualize the presence of the elements of Air and Water in their symbolic quarters, using the visualizations from the solitary Equinox Ceremony; when you knock, be aware of yourself as the point of balance between these two, balancing the opposed forces.

Say: "Heat: Cold. South: North. Fire: Earth." Knock again. "I am the reconciler between them." Again, visualize the elements as you name the polarities, and then yourself as the one resolving them.

Fifth, say: "One Creator: One Preserver: One Destroyer: One Redeemer." Knock again. "One Reconciler between them." Once again, visualize the elements—all four, in this case—but this time, strive to perceive the presence of the Divine in each of the elements. The image of Spirit unifying and balancing them is not yourself, but a vast figure of light that seems to stand where you are standing, but to tower far above you.

Sixth, take the Lotus Wand and go to the east. Trace the invoking pentagram of Air toward the eastern quarter with the wand. Say: "In the Great Name YHVH ("yeh-ho-wah"), and in the name of the Archangel Raphael, and in the Name of the Angel Chassan, and in the name of the Ruler Ariel, spirits and powers of Air, I call you to the Harmony." Trace the symbol of the Rose Cross, as given in the Rose Cross Ritual in Chapter 6, over the pentagram with the Lotus Wand. As you trace the pentagram, visualize the spirits of Air coming in response to the summoning; the imagery described in the Invocation of the Higher Self in Chapter 13 may be used here.

Seventh, go to the south and trace the invoking pentagram of Fire toward the southern quarter. Say: "In the Great Name ALHIM ("ell-oh-heem"), and in the name of the Archangel Michael, and in the name of the Angel Aral, and in the name of the Ruler Seraph, spirits and powers of Fire, I call you to the Harmony." Then trace the symbol of the Rose Cross over the pentagram. Again, visualize the spirits of Fire responding to the summoning. In the same way, using the same words with the appropriate names, invoking pentagram, and the Rose Cross, call the spirits and powers of Water to the Harmony in the west, and those of Earth in the north in the Name ADNI.

Eighth, return to the east of the altar and face west. With the Lotus Wand, trace invoking pentagrams of active and passive Spirit over the altar and say, "In the Great Names AHIH and AGLA ("eh-heh-yeh" and "ah-geh-la"), and in the names of the Archangels Metatron and Sandalphon, spirits and powers of Spirit, I call you to the Harmony." Once again, trace the Rose Cross over the pentagrams. As you trace the pentagrams, visualize a circle of tall, luminous winged beings gathering outside the circle of elemental spirits.

Ninth, make the Sign of Osiris Slain and contemplate the four elements and their spirits balanced in and by Spirit. Imagine your vision opening outward, so that you perceive not only the elemental beings present around you, but the angelic and archangelic powers behind and above them, and at the outermost edge of the universe an ocean of infinite light in all directions, in which all these have their source. Hold this image for a time, and then say: "I stand in the place of balanced forces at the center of all things. Let Harmony within me mirror Harmony without me: as above, so below." Make the Signs of Isis, Apophis, and Osiris Risen, and say: "In the Great Name of strength through sacrifice, YHShVH YHVShH ("yeh-heh-shu-ah yeh-ho-wa-shah"), I invoke the descent of the Light." Visualize a shaft of light descending from far above your head and shining upon you, through you, and on into the depths of the Earth. Hold this visualization as long and forcefully as possible. When your attention begins to falter, perform the Cabalistic Cross to equilibrate the Light.

Tenth, facing east, say, "By the power of Spirit and the Descending Light, and by my Higher Self present within me, spirits and powers of Air, I ordain you to the service of the Magic of Light. Be ye obedient and faithful in the Harmony." Go to the south, and repeat the charge, replacing the word "Air" with "Fire." Do the same to the west for the spirits and powers of Water, and to the north for those of Earth.

Eleventh, perform the complete expanded form of the First Degree Closing. This completes the ceremony.

Further Applications of the Equinox Formula

In the Golden Dawn instructional papers on the Neophyte ceremony, the applications of the Neophyte formula to personal ritual work were given in outline form and it was left to individual members to fill them out into complete ceremonies. There's something to be said for this approach. The outlines made it easier to grasp the essential structure of the formula being used, while at the same time forcing the magician to take a more personal approach to the invocations and other ritual practices. Using the outline form requires a certain amount of experience in Golden Dawn magic, but readers who have worked their way through this book should have no trouble using outlines of this kind to create complete and effective ceremonies.

For these reasons, and also to make it easier to compare Equinox formula workings to those of the Neophyte formula, the following section gives outlines of ceremonies for each of the categories of magical ritual found in the Golden Dawn's Document Z. These include ceremonies for the evocation of spirits, the consecration of talismans, the production of natural phenomena such as specific kinds of weather, and for invisibility, transformation, and spiritual development. Students of the Golden Dawn tradition who are familiar with the papers in question may find the outlines a useful guide to the uses of the Equinox formulas.

The ceremony for spiritual development, which is included in the outline below, differs in a number of ways from the Ceremony of the Descending Light described above. This should be a reminder that a given formula can be used for a given purpose in any number of different ways!

Document Z also gives outlines for applying the Neophyte formula to two other classes of operations: divination and alchemy. I have not given equivalent uses for the Equinox formula, although both of these can certainly be done. In the case of divination, the Golden Dawn's tendency to make divination a hugely cumbersome and time-consuming process—a tendency that shows up clearly in the idea of using a major ceremonial formula for divinatory purposes—is one of the main reasons the Order's methods of divination have been so little used in this century.

My own experience with divinations performed according to the Neophyte formula system is that they can be done, but that there's no particular benefit in doing so. Those who feel otherwise should have no trouble constructing an Equinox formula divinatory process from the materials in this chapter.

In the case of alchemy, by contrast, the Golden Dawn's methods are clear, effective, and well worth using, and the Equinox formula as an alchemical process holds some intriguing possibilities. The alchemists of old put a great deal of effort into drawing the creative energies of nature into their processes, and a method based on the Equinox Ceremony seems likely to be highly useful in this context. My only reason for not providing one is that my own studies in alchemy have not yet reached the point where I could devise such a process with any confidence.

The following index provides a general reference for the Equinox Ceremony and the phases of its applications.

Index for the Equinox Ritual

A. The ceremony itself; the place of the temple.

B. The Hierophant.

C. The officers.

D. The solar light and influence.

E. The recipient of the solar light: in the broadest sense, the Earth; in a more specific sense, the members, the temple, and the Order.

F. The ceremony of Opening.

G. The equinox is proclaimed and the previous password abrogated.

H. The polarities between the quarters are established and reconciled by the Hegemon.

I. The officers surrender their working tools at the altar and take the symbols of the elements out to the quarters.

J. The Kerux goes to the four quarters in turn. Invocation of the Divine in its elemental aspects, all members participating. Formation of the Middle Pillar in the macrocosm.

K. The Hegemon reconciles the energies of the quarters and seals the influx of solar light down the macrocosmic Middle Pillar.

L. Assumption of power by chief officers. The new password and officers of the new term are proclaimed. The officers of the previous term surrender their regalia at the Hierophant's throne in the east.

M. Outer Order members depart. The temple is assumed from Outer to Inner by the Chief Adept.

N. Ceremony of installation and investiture of the new Hierophant.

O. The temple is remitted from Inner to Outer. Outer Order members readmitted. Presentation and Confession of new Hierophant.

P. The New Hierophant installs and invests the new temple officers.

Q. The Kerux returns symbols of the elements to the altar. Chief Officers make announcements and new Hierophant addresses the members.

R. The ceremony of Closing.

I. ᾿

Evocation

A. The magic circle.

B. The magician.

C. The names and formulae to be employed.

D. The planetary, elemental, or other force in the macrocosm to which the spirit to be evoked corresponds.

E. The evocation itself.

F. The construction of the circle, its purification and consecration, and the performance of the banishings and the ritual of opening.

G. The invocation of the Higher. Announcement of the object of the working, naming the spirit or spirits to be evoked. This is pronounced standing at the center of the circle, holding the Lotus Wand and facing the direction that corresponds to the spirit.

H. The magician recites the words from the Equinox Ceremony that establish and reconcile the polarities in the East and West, in the South and North, and around the circle of the directions.

I. The magician lays the Lotus Wand down, and takes the Magic Sword. He or she then calls aloud the name of the spirit, summoning it to appear in either the mirror or the triangle, stating the purpose of the evocation, and finally affirming solemnly that the spirit will be evoked and the purpose accomplished.

J. The magician goes to the four quarters in turn, beginning in the east, and repeats at each a conjuration by the Name governing that direction and element, commanding the spirit to appear and binding it by the forces of the element.

K. The magician returns to the center, faces the quarter corresponding to the circle, and recites a long and powerful conjuration by the Name that governs the spirit, commanding the spirit to visible appearance in the mirror or triangle, and making use of all appropriate names, symbols, and the like.

L. The magician raises his or her arms on high, holding the Magic Sword upright in the right hand, and stamps thrice on the ground with the right foot, then proclaims that the time for the spirit's appearance has arrived and commands "Come forth!" thrice.

M. The magician performs an invocation of the Sphere of the Tree of Life that has governance over the spirit, using the Vibratory Formula of the Middle Pillar or any other convenient method of invocation; he or she contemplates the invoked force, making every effort to enter into the energies of the Sphere; from this vantage, addressing the Divine by the appropriate Name, asks that he or she may receive the power necessary to accomplish the evocation.

N. He or she then recites a conjuration addressed to the spirits and powers governing the spirit that is to be evoked, calling upon them to command the spirit to appear at once, and to render it faithful and obedient to the commands that will be given it.

O. The magician turns to the mirror or triangle and reads a powerful conjuration of some length, calling upon the spirit to appear at once. This conjuration may be made up to four times if necessary. In most cases, the spirit will already have appeared by the time the first conjuration is spoken, if it has not appeared earlier, but the ceremony is to be performed up to this point whether this happens or not.

P. The magician commands the spirit to take on clear and visible form, and then communicates with the spirit, stating the purpose for which it has been summoned, binding it to harm none and to faithfully carry out the task it has been given.

Q. The spirit is blessed and licensed to depart, and the magician banishes with the appropriate Greater Banishing Ritual.

R. The ritual of closing is performed.

II. ה

Consecration of Talismans or Generation of Natural Phenomena

A. The place where the operation is done.

B. The magician.

C. The names and formulae to be employed.

D. The forces of the macrocosm employed and attracted.

E. The talisman or material basis.

F. For talismans, the selection of the matter to form the talisman, the preparation and arrangement of the place, the making of the talisman, and the ceremony of opening. For natural phenomena, the preparation of the operation, the selection of the material basis, such as a piece of Earth, a cup of Water, a flame of Fire, a Pentacle, or the like, the preparation of the circle, and the ceremony of opening.

G. The invocation of the Higher. The announcement of the nature of the working.

H. The polarities are established by means of the words from the Equinox Ceremony, slightly altered; in each of the first two speeches, the talisman is addressed, "Thou shalt be the reconciler between them." The third speech is unaltered.

I. The magician takes the talisman or material basis from the altar and states aloud the purpose of the working, solemnly affirming that it will be achieved.

J. The magician takes the talisman or material basis to the four quarters and in each invokes the element of that quarter, calling on the spirits and powers of that element to give the talisman or material basis power for the attainment of its purpose.

K. The magician returns to the altar, faces the direction of the force to be invoked, and recites a strong invocation of that force, calling it forth by the appropriate names and symbolism.

L. The magician smites the talisman or material basis thrice with the flat of the Magic Sword, and raises the sword and the talisman or material basis high in the air, sword in the right hand, stamping thrice on the ground with the right foot. He or she then proclaims that the time for the consecration of the talisman (or the induction of the natural phenomenon) has arrived.

M. The magician performs an invocation of the Sphere of the Tree of Life that has governance over the working, using the Vibratory Formula of the Middle Pillar or any other convenient method of invocation, contemplates the invoked force, making every effort to enter into the energies of the Sphere, and from this vantage, addressing the Divine by the appropriate Name, asks that he or she may receive the power necessary to accomplish the working.

N. The magician recites a conjuration addressed to the spirits and powers governing the working, calling upon them to empower the talisman or set the natural phenomenon in motion.

O. The magician, standing in the east, reads a powerful conjuration of some length addressed to the talisman or the natural phenomenon, reiterating the names and symbols that govern the working, and commanding that the talisman be consecrated or that the natural phenomenon commence. At the end of this conjuration, he or she makes the Sign of the Enterer toward the talisman or material basis, focusing on it the whole force of his or her will.

When the current of will begins to falter, the magician makes the Sign of Silence, drops his or her hands, and then looks toward the altar. At this point, a faint light should be seen to flicker over the talisman or material basis, and in the case of natural phenomena, a first appearance of the phenomenon should be observed. This conjuration may be made up to a total of four times if necessary, concluding each with a new projection of will in the Sign of the Enterer.

P. The magician then commands the energies of the talisman or natural phenomenon, stating clearly the scope, duration, and nature of the effect to be produced, and binding them to harm none and to faithfully carry out the task they have been given. At this point, the talisman should flash visibly, or the natural phenomenon should definitely begin.

Q. The talisman or material basis is then wrapped in silk to preserve it from the effect of the banishings. A talisman consecrated by this formula may be treated in the same way as any other. In the case of natural phenomena, the material basis should be kept wrapped in silk until the phenomenon has finished its work, and then banished thoroughly and discarded.

R. The ceremony of closing is performed.

III. ש

א —Invisibility

A. The Shroud of Concealment.

B. The magician.

C. The guards of concealment.

D. The energies of the planet or element invoked to create the Shroud. The planet Saturn or the element of Air may be invoked for this purpose, but the Moon in her eld, the last three days before the New Moon, is best.

E. The etheric body of the magician.

F. The ceremony of opening, and the awakening of the symbols in the Sphere of Sensation.

G. The invocation of the Higher. The announcement of the nature and purpose of the working.

H. The polarities are established, using the words from the Equinox Ceremony.

I. The magician clearly formulates the idea of becoming invisible, defining the distance at which the shroud encloses the body, and solemnly affirms that the working will be accomplished. The cloak is purified with Water and consecrated with Fire to begin establishing its etheric basis.

J. The magician goes to the four quarters in turn, and at each conjures the powers of the elements to help construct the shroud, using appropriate names and symbols.

K. Returning to the center, the magician recites a conjuration to the Shroud of Concealment, calling upon it to render him or her invisible. The magician then turns around three times with the Sun and says, "In the Name of the Lord of the Universe, who works in silence and whom naught but silence can express, I conjure thee, O Shroud of darkness and of mystery, that thou encircle me so that I may become invisible, so that all who look upon me see me not, nor comprehend the thing that they behold."

L. The magician formulates the Shroud of Concealment as intensely as possible, visualizing his or her physical body fading from sight within it.

M. The magician then performs an invocation of the Sphere of the Tree of Life that has governance over the working, using the Vibratory Formula of the Middle Pillar or any other convenient method of invocation, contemplates the invoked force, making every effort to enter into the energies of the Sphere, and from this vantage, addressing the Divine by the appropriate Name, asks that he or she may receive the power necessary to accomplish the working.

N. He or she then recites a conjuration addressed to the celestial or elemental power governing the working, calling upon it to formulate the Shroud of Concealment and empower it to grant the magician invisibility.

O. The magician, standing in the west—the quarter of symbolic darkness—reads a powerful conjuration of some length addressed to the Shroud of Concealment, reiterating the names and symbols that govern the working. At the end of this conjuration, he or she makes the Sign of the Enterer to the east and focuses the whole force of his or her will on becoming invisible, visualizing his or her body fading from sight until it cannot be seen at all.

P. The magician addresses a conjuration to the shroud, commanding it to remain under his or her control until it is dispersed and banished, and stating exactly what is intended to be accomplished.

Q. The magician then goes forth invisible and accomplishes his or her purpose.

R. Having done so, the magician invokes the powers of the Light, opens and steps out of the Shroud of Concealment, and disperses and banishes the energies of the shroud, commanding them to return again if summoned. He or she then performs the ceremony of closing.

ב—*Transformations*

A. The astral form.

B. The magician.

C. The names and formulae used to create the form.

D. The energies of the element, planet, and sign governing the form. If at all possible, the planet should be in the sign, or in trine or sextile aspect to the sign, at the time the ritual is done.

E. The form to be taken.

F. The ceremony of opening and the awakening of the symbols of the Sphere of Sensation.

G. The invocation of the Higher. The announcement of the nature and purpose of the working.

H. The polarities are established, using the words from the Equinox Ceremony.

I. The magician clearly formulates the form intended to be taken. This is defined exactly as a clear form and is purified and consecrated by Water and Fire. The magician then solemnly affirms that the working will be accomplished.

J. The magician goes to the four quarters in turn, and at each conjures the powers of the elements to help construct the form, using appropriate names and symbols.

K. Returning to the center, the magician recites a conjuration to the form, calling upon it by the names and symbols governing it, and by its vibratory name. The magician extends the blossom end of the Lotus Wand over the place where the form is to take shape and says, "In the Name of the Lord of the Universe, who works in silence and whom naught but silence can express, arise before me, O form of (name of form), into which I have elected to transform myself. So that all who look upon me see the thing that they see not, nor comprehend the thing that they behold."

L. The magician then formulates the form as intensely as possible, visualizing it in as much detail as possible.

M. The magician performs an invocation of the Sphere of the Tree of Life that has governance over the working, using the Vibratory Formula of the Middle Pillar or any other convenient method of invocation, contemplates the invoked force, making every effort to enter into the energies of the Sphere, and from this vantage, addressing the Divine by the appropriate Name, asks that he or she may receive the power necessary to accomplish the working.

N. He or she then recites a conjuration addressed to the element, planet, and sign governing the working, calling upon them to formulate the astral form and enable the magician to enter into it.

O. The magician, standing in the east, reads a powerful conjuration of some length addressed to the form, reiterating the names and symbols that govern the working, and takes on the form, functioning for a time in both human and transformation bodies.

P. The magician addresses the form, commanding it to remain under his or her control until it is dispersed and banished, and stating exactly what is intended to be accomplished. He or she then leaves his or her human body in a convenient place.

Q. The magician goes forth in the astral form and accomplishes his or her purpose.

R. Having done so, the magician resumes his or her human form and, in both bodies, invokes the powers governing the form. He or she steps out of the form, and disperses and banishes the energies of the form, commanding them to return again if summoned. He or she then performs the ceremony of closing.

ש—Spiritual Development

A. The Sphere of Sensation.

B. The Augoeides or Higher Genius.

C. The symbols and formulae of the working.

D. The Spheres of the Tree of Life.

E. The Lower Self of the magician.

F. The ceremony of opening; the awakening of the symbols in the Sphere of Sensation.

G. The invocation of the Higher. The limiting and controlling of the Lower, and the closing of the material senses, to allow the spiritual to awaken.

H. Attempting to make the Lower Self aware of the Higher by orienting it to the place of balance between the elemental polarities. In doing this, the words and visualizations from the Equinox Ceremony are to be used.

I. The aspiration of the whole Lower Self toward the Higher Self, and a prayer for light and guidance through the Higher Self, addressed to the Lord of the Universe.

J. The magician goes to the four quarters in turn, invoking the Divine Light in its elemental forms and calling upon that light to purify and balance the corresponding elemental aspect of the magician's own body, soul, and spirit. At the same time, the descent of light down the Middle Pillar is visualized, as in the Equinox Ceremony.

K. Returning to the center, the magician visualizes the descending light reaching and illuminating his or her physical body, and recites an invocation of the Light, calling on the Infinite to remove the darkness from his or her spiritual vision.

L. The magician stands for a few moments in silence, with arms raised, the Magic Sword in his or her right hand, head thrown back and eyes lifted up, and aspires with his or her whole will to the best and highest ideal of the Divine he or she can conceive.

M. The magician endeavors to perceive a vast image of light present in and above the place of the working, an image of his or her own physical form made luminous and perfect. This image surrounds and rises above the magician's body and Lower Self, as though these latter are its base and throne. The image is built up as clearly as possible; then, the magician strives to identify himself or herself with the image, realizing that this is the only true self, and that the Lower Self is merely its vehicle and expression on the levels of manifest existence.

N. The magician, as the Higher Self, becomes aware of his or her place in a great gathering of beings of equal beauty and power, which are recognized as the seen and unseen inhabitants of the Earth in their inner and spiritual forms. The magician then becomes aware of the vaster universe of which the Earth is a part of its powers and inhabitants, and finally he or she reaches out in awareness to a light and presence that surrounds and contains the universe, and that extends out to infinity in every direction.

O. The magician remains in this contemplation for a time and then returns to awareness of his or her Lower Self and physical surroundings, while still perceiving the image of the Higher Self as an overshadowing presence. He or she then proclaims aloud: "Thus at length I have been permitted to begin to comprehend the form of my Higher Self."

P. The magician prays that a link may be formed between the glory of the Higher Self and his or her own selfhood, and asks also that he or she may be kept from the pitfalls of fanaticism and arrogance.

Q. He or she addresses the Higher Self, seeking guidance in the work of the Magic of Light, and in any other matter that may be of concern.

R. The magician then allows his or her consciousness of the Higher Self to fade, and performs the ceremony of closing.

APPENDIX

CABALISTIC SYMBOLISM

THE TABLES THAT FOLLOW give the basic Cabalistic correspondences of the elements, planets, Spheres, and letters of the Hebrew alphabet, as used in the ceremonies in this book. Most follow standard Golden Dawn practice. The founders of the Golden Dawn, however, drew their symbolism from a wide array of sources, and too often failed to sort out the gold from the garbage; as a result, the Order's tables of correspondences are garbled, contradictory, or inaccurate in a few places. I have, therefore, inserted a few corrections where it was appropriate. Those who wish to use the Order's system in its original form will find the neccesary information in Regardie's *Golden Dawn*.

I have also included a discussion of the symbolic meanings of the regular polygons and polygrams, which can be used in the design of talismans and in alternative invoking and banishing rituals.

The Elements

Element of Earth

Symbol: ▽

Letter of Tetragrammaton: ה , final Heh

Name of God: א ד נ י , ADNI, Adonai (Lord)

Archangel: א ד ו י ר א ל , AVRIAL, Auriel (Light of God)

Angel: פ ו ר ל א כ , PVRLAK, Phorlakh

Ruler: ‎כ ר ו ב‎, KRVB, Kerub
Elemental King: Ghob
Elementals: Gnomes
Hebrew Name of Element: ‎א ר ץ‎, ARTz, Aretz
Direction: ‎צ פ ו ן‎, TzPVN, Tzaphon, the North
Season: Winter
Time of Day: Midnight
Qualities: Cold and dry
Nature: Stability

Element of Water
Symbol: ▽
Letter of Tetragrammaton: ‎ה‎, Heh
Name of God: ‎א ל‎, AL, El (God)
Archangel: ‎ג ב ר י א ל‎, GBRIAL, Gabriel (Strength of God)
Angel: ‎ת ל י ה ד‎, TLIHD, Taliahad
Ruler: ‎ת ר ש י ס‎, ThRShIS, Tharsis
Elemental King: Nichsa
Elementals: Undines
Hebrew Name of Element: ‎מ י ם‎, MIM, Mayim
Direction: ‎מ ע ר ב‎, MAaRB, Mearab, the West
Season: Autumn
Time of Day: Sunset
Qualities: Cold and wet
Nature: Union

Element of Fire
Symbol: △
Letter of Tetragrammaton: ‎י‎, Yod
Name of God: ‎א ל ה י ם‎, ALHIM, Elohim (Gods and Goddesses)

Archangel: ל א כ י מ, MIKAL, Michael (He who is as God)

Angel: ל א ר א, ARAL, Aral

Ruler: ף ר ש, ShRP, Seraph

Elemental King: Djin

Elementals: Salamanders

Hebrew Name of Element: שא, ASh, Aesh

Direction: ם ו ר ד, DRVM, Darom, the South

Season: Summer

Time of Day: Noon

Qualities: Hot and dry

Nature: Energy

Element of Air

Symbol: △

Letter of Tetragrammaton: ו, Vau

Name of God: ה ו ה י, YHVH, Tetragrammaton

Archangel: ל א פ ר, RPAL, Raphael

Angel: ן ש ח, ChShN, Chassan

Ruler: ל א ר י א, ARIAL, Ariel

Elemental King: Paralda

Elementals: Sylphs

Hebrew Name of Element: ה ו ר, RVCh, Ruach

Direction: ה ר ז מ, MZRCh, Mizrach, the East

Season: Spring

Time of Day: Dawn

Qualities: Hot and wet

Nature: Separation

Element of Spirit

Symbol: ✸

Names of God: ה י ה א, AHIH, Eheieh (active)

א ג ל א, AGLA, Agla (passive)

Archangels: מ ת ת ר ו ן, MTTRVN, Metatron (active)

ס נ ד ל פ ו ן, SNDLPVN, Sandalphon (passive)

Direction: Center

Qualities: Union of all qualities

Nature: Balance

The Planets

Saturn

Symbol: ♄

Letter of Ararita: א, Aleph

Name of God: י ה ו ה א ל ה י ם, YHVH ALHIM,
      Tetragrammaton Elohim

Archangel: צ פ ק י א ל, TzPQIAL, Tzaphqiel

Angelic Host: א ר ל א י ם, ARALIM, Aralim

Intelligence: א ג י א ל, AGIAL, Agiel

Spirit: ז א ז ל, ZAZL, Zazel

Hebrew Name of Planet: ש ב ת א י, ShBThAI, Shabbathai

Element: Air

Direction: West

Jupiter

Symbol: ♃

Letter of Ararita: ר, Resh

Name of God: א ל, AL, El

Archangel: צ ד ק י א ל, TzDQIAL, Tzadqiel

Angelic Host: ח שמ ל י ם, ChShMLIM, Chashmalim

Intelligence: י ה פ י א ל, IHPIAL, Iophiel

Spirit: ח ס מ א ל, HSMAL, Hismael

Hebrew Name of Planet: צ ד ק, TzDQ, Tzedek
Element: Fire
Direction: East

Mars

Symbol: ♂
Letter of Ararita: א, Aleph
Name of God: א ל ה י ם   ג ב ו ר, ALHIM GBVR, Elohim Gibor
Archangel: כ מ א ל, KMAL, Kamael
Angelic Host: ש ר פ י ם, ShRPIM, Seraphim
Intelligence: ג ר א פ י א ל, GRAPIAL, Graphiel
Spirit: ב ר צ ב א ל, BRTzBAL, Bartzabel
Hebrew Name of Planet: מ ד י ם, MDIM, Madim
Element: Water
Direction: North

Sun

Symbol: ☉
Letter of Ararita: ר, Resh
Name of God: י ה ו ה   א ל ו ה   ו ד ע ת, YHVH ALVH VDAaTh, Tetragrammaton Eloah va-Daath
Archangel: מ י כ א ל, MIKAL, Michael
Angelic Host: מ ל כ י ם, MLKIM, Malakim
Intelligence: נ כ י א ל, NKIAL, Nakhiel
Spirit: ס ו ר ת, SVRTh, Sorath
Hebrew Name of Planet: ש מ ש, ShMSh, Shemesh
Element: Fire
Direction: East

Venus

Symbol: ♀

Letter of Ararita: י , Yod

Name of God: ת ו א ב צ ה ו ה י , YHVH TzBAVTh,
        Tetragrammaton Tzabaoth

Archangel: ל א י נ א ה , HANIAL, Haniel

Angelic Host: ם י ש י ש ר ת , ThRShIShIM, Tarshishim

Intelligence: ל א י ג ה , HGIAL, Hagiel

Spirit: ל א מ ד ר כ , KDMAL, Kedemel

Hebrew Name of Planet: ה ג ו נ , NVGH, Nogah

Element: Earth

Direction: South

Mercury

Symbol: ☿

Letter of Ararita: ת , Tau

Name of God: ת ו א ב צ ם י ה ל א , ALHIM TzBAVTh,
        Elohim Tzabaoth

Archangel: ל א פ ר , RPAL, Raphael

Angelic Host: ם י ה ל א י נ ב , BNI ALHIM, Beni Elohim

Intelligence: ל א י ר י ת , TIRIAL, Tiriel

Spirit: ת ר ת ר ת פ ת , ThPThRThRTh, Taphthartharath

Hebrew Name of Planet: ב כ ו כ , KVKB, Kokab

Element: Air

Direction: West

Moon

Symbol: ☽

Letter of Ararita: א , Aleph

Name of God: י ח ל א י ד ש , ShDI AL ChI, Shaddai El Chai

Archangel: ל א י ר ב ג , GBRIAL, Gabriel

Angelic Host: ם י ב ו ר כ , KRVBIM, Kerubim

Intelligence of Intelligences: ד ע ו ם י ס י ש ר ת ב א כ ל מ
ם י ל ח ש ת ט ח ט ר

MLKA BThRShISIM VAaD RVChVTh ShChLIM, Malkah Be-Tarshishim Ve-ad Ruachoth Shechalim

Spirit of Spirits: ן ת ת ר ש ה ת ע מ ש ר ב ש ד , ShD BRShMAaTh HShRThThN, Shad Barshemoth ha-Shartathan

Spirit: י א ד ו מ ש ח , ChShMVDAI, Chashmodai

Hebrew Name of Planet: ה נ ב ל , LBNH, Levanah

Element: Earth

Direction: South

The Spheres

Kether, the First Sphere

Hebrew Spelling of Name: ר ת כ , KThR

Meaning of Name: Crown

Name of God: ה י ה א , AHIH, Eheieh

Archangel: ן ו ר ת ת מ , MTTRVN, Metatron

Angelic Host: ש ד ק ת ו י ת ח , ChIVTh HQDSh, Chaioth ha-Qodesh

Astrological Correspondence: ם י ל ג ל ג ה ת י ש א ר , RAShITh HGLGLIM, Rashith ha-Gilgalim, the Primum Mobile (the Galaxy)

Element: Air

Chokmah, the Second Sphere

Hebrew Spelling of Name: ה מ כ ח , ChKMH

Meaning of Name: Wisdom

Name of God: ה י, YH, Yah
Archangel: ר ז י א ל, RZIAL, Raziel
Angelic Host: ם י נ פ ו א, AVPNIM, Auphanim
Astrological Correspondence: ת ו ל ז מ, MZLVTh, Mazloth, the
Zodiac
Element: Fire

Binah, the Third Sphere

Hebrew Spelling of Name: ב י נ ה, BINH
Meaning of Name: Understanding
Name of God: י ה ו ה א ל ה י ם, YHVH ALHIM,
Tetragrammaton Elohim
Archangel: צ פ ק י א ל, TzPQIAL, Tzaphqiel
Angelic Host: א ר א ל י ם, ARALIM, Aralim
Astrological Correspondence: ש ב ת א י, ShBThAI, Shabbatai, Saturn
Element: Water

Chesed, the Fourth Sphere

Hebrew Spelling of Name: ח ס ד, ChSD
Meaning of Name: Mercy
Name of God: א ל, AL, El
Archangel: צ ד ק י א ל, TzDQIAL, Tzadqiel
Angelic Host: חשמ ל י ם, ChShMLIM, Chashmalim
Astrological Correspondence: צ ד ק, TzDQ, Tzedek, Jupiter
Element: Water

Geburah, the Fifth Sphere

Hebrew Spelling of Name: ג ב ו ר ה, GBVRH
Meaning of Name: Severity

Name of God: ר ו ב ג ם י ה ל א, ALHIM GBVR, Elohim Gibor
Archangel: ל א מ כ, KMAL, Kamael
Angelic Host: ם י פ ר ש, ShRPIM, Seraphim
Astrological Correspondence: ם י ד מ, MDIM, Madim, Mars
Element: Fire

Tiphareth, the Sixth Sphere

Hebrew Spelling of Name: ת ר א פ ת, ThPARTh
Meaning of Name: Beauty
Name of God: ת ע ד ו ה ו ל א ה ו ה י, YHVH ALVH
                VDAaTh, Tetragrammaton Eloah va-Daath
Archangel: ל א כ י מ, MIKAL, Michael
Angelic Host: ם י כ ל מ, MLKIM, Malakim
Astrological Correspondence: ש מ ש, ShMSh, Shemesh, the Sun
Element: Air

Netzach, the Seventh Sphere

Hebrew Spelling of Name: ח צ נ, NTzCh
Meaning of Name: Victory
Name of God: ת ו א ב צ ה ו ה י, YHVH TzBAVTh,
                Tetragrammaton Tzabaoth
Archangel: ל א י נ א ה, HANIAL, Haniel
Angelic Host: ם י ש י ש ר ת, ThRShYShYM, Tarshishim
Astrological Correspondence: ה ג ו נ, NVGH, Nogah, Venus
Element: Fire

Hod, the Eighth Sphere

Hebrew Spelling of Name: ד ו ה, HVD
Meaning of Name: Glory

Name of God: ת ו א ב צ ם י ה ל א, ALHIM TzBAVTh, Elohim
Tzabaoth

Archangel: ל א פ ר, RPAL, Raphael

Angelic Host: ם י ה ל א י נ ב, BNI ALHIM, Beni Elohim

Astrological Correspondence: ב כ ו כ, KVKB, Kokab, Mercury

Element: Water

Yesod, the Ninth Sphere

Hebrew Spelling of Name: ד ו ס י, YSVD

Meaning of Name: Foundation

Name of God: י ח ל א י ד ש, ShDI AL ChI, Shaddai El Chai

Archangel: ל א י ר ב ג, GBRIAL, Gabriel

Angelic Host: ם י ב ו ר כ, KRVBIM, Kerubim

Astrological Correspondence: ה נ ב ל, LBNH, Levanah, the Moon

Element: Air

Malkuth, the Tenth Sphere

Hebrew Spelling of Name: ת ו כ ל מ, MLKVTh

Meaning of Name: Kingdom

Name of God: ץ ר א ה י נ ד א, ADNI HARTz, Adonai ha-Aretz

Archangel: ן ו פ ל ד נ ס, SNDLPVN, Sandalphon

Angelic Host: ם י ש א, AShIM, Ishim

Astrological Correspondence: ת ו ד ס י ם ל ו ע, AaVLM YSVD-
VTh, Olam Yesodoth, the World of the
Elements, Earth

Element: Earth

The Hebrew Alphabet

Letter	Path	Title	Number	Astrological Correspondence	Color (King Scale)
א , A	11	Aleph, Ox	1	Air	Pale yellow
ב , B	12	Beth, House	2	Mercury	Yellow
ג , G	13	Gimel, Camel	3	Moon	Blue
ד , D	14	Daleth, Door	4	Venus	Emerald green
ה , H	15	Heh, Window	5	Aries	Scarlet
ו , U, V	16	Vau, Nail	6	Taurus	Red orange
ז , Z	17	Zayin, Sword	7	Gemini	Orange
ח , Ch	18	Cheth, Fence	8	Cancer	Amber
ט , T	19	Teth, Serpent	9	Leo	Greenish yellow
י , I, Y	20	Yod, Fist	10	Virgo	Yellowish green
כ , K	21	Kaph, Hand	20	Jupiter	Violet
ל , L	22	Lamed, Goad	30	Libra	Emerald green
מ , M	23	Mem, Water	40	Water	Deep blue
נ , N	24	Nun, Fish	50	Scorpio	Green-blue
ס , S	25	Samech, Prop	60	Sagittarius	Blue
ע , Aa	26	Ayin, Eye	70	Capricorn	Indigo
פ , P	27	Peh, Mouth	80	Mars	Scarlet
צ , Tz	28	Tzaddi, Hook	90	Aquarius	Violet
ק , Q	29	Qoph, Back of head	100	Pisces	Magenta
ר , R	30	Resh, Head	200	Sun	Orange
ש , Sh	31	Shin, Tooth	300	Fire	Scarlet-orange
ת , Th	32	Tau, Cross	400	Saturn	Indigo

The following letters have different shapes and number values when written at the end of a word:

Letter	Final Form	Number
Kaph	ך	500
Mem	ם	600
Nun	ן	700
Peh	ף	800
Tzaddi	ץ	900

Note that Hebrew is written right to left, not left to right as English.

Polygons and Polygrams

In the Golden Dawn system, elements of traditional sacred geometry were taken over and used as part of the symbolism of ritual magic, particularly in the making of talismans and similar devices. One of these elements is the lore of regular polygons and polygrams.

In geometry, *a regular figure* is one made of equal lines meeting at equal angles. *Polygons* are made of lines that meet only at their endpoints; *polygrams* are starlike shapes with a more complex structure. There is only one regular polygon with any given number of sides, while there may be zero, one, two, or more polygrams.

In Golden Dawn symbolism, polygons represent the outward dispersion of a force, while polygrams represent the inward concentration of a force. Polygons are therefore used magically to initiate a vortex of energy and to spread that energy outward, while polygrams are used to concentrate and to seal.

The Triangle

The triangle, or trigon, is the simplest lineal figure. It corresponds to the Supernal Triad among the Spheres, to Saturn among the planets, and to the element of Fire. Its three angles can also be used to represent the three principles of alchemy—Mercury, Sulfur, and Salt.

Diagram 51— The Triangle

The Square

The square, or tetragon, represents stability and equality, the four letters of the Tetragrammaton, and the four elements. It corresponds to Chesed among the Spheres, Jupiter among the planets, and Earth among the elements. Its angles can represent any of the many fourfold patterns in magical symbolism.

Diagram 52— The Square

The Pentagon and Pentagram

With the number five, a new factor enters the picture. There's only one regular figure with three sides, and only one with four. With five sides, there are two: the pentagon and the pentagram. Both correspond to Geburah among the Spheres. The pentagon represents the dispersal of the five elements through Nature.

The pentagram as shown, with one point up, symbolizes the dominion of Spirit over the four material elements, and the power of the Name YHShVH. It is the special symbol of the human microcosm, and of the power of consciousness over matter. It also has a special relationship

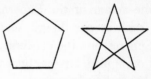

Diagram 53—
The Pentagon and Pentagram

with the planet Mars, and with the letter Heh of Tetragrammaton, since Heh's number is five.

The pentagram with two points up, over which so much fuss has been made, represents consciousness submerged beneath the blind energies of matter.

The Hexagon and Hexagram

There are two regular six-sided figures, the hexagon and the hexagram, and one irregular one, the hexangle or pseudohexagram, which also plays a role in symbolism. The first two correspond to Tiphareth, the sixth Sphere of the Tree of Life. The hexagon represents the dispersal of the rays of the

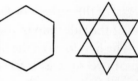

Diagram 54—
The Hexagon and Hexagram

planets and of the signs of the Zodiac. The hexagram is the special symbol of the macrocosm and represents the concentrated force of the planets centered on the Sun.

The hexangle or pseudohexagram, because of the different size of its angles, can be used to represent the rulership of the Sun and Moon over the five elements.

The Heptagon and Heptagrams

With the number seven, it becomes possible to trace a polygram in more than one way, and each of the resulting heptagrams has its own meaning. All seven-sided figures correspond to Netzach, the seventh Sphere. The heptagon represents the dispersal of planetary energies through the cycles of the week and the year.

Diagram 55—
The Hexangle or
Pseudohexagram

The first form of the heptagram, connecting every other point around a circle, is formed of seven triangles touching at their basal angles. It therefore represents the power of the number three within the number seven, the action of the Supernal Triad in the lower seven Spheres, and the concentration of planetary energies in the week and the year.

Diagram 56—
The Heptagon and Heptagrams

The second form of the heptagram, connecting every third point, is the special symbol of the planet Venus, and represents the powers of Nature harmonized through love.

The Octagon and Octagrams

As with the heptagram, there are two ways of forming an eight-sided regular polygram, each with its own meaning. All eight-sided figures correspond to the eighth Sphere, Hod. The octagon represents the dispersal of the powers of the elements in their positive and negative forms under the rulership of the two Names YHVH and ADNI.

The first form of the octagram, connecting every other point, is made up of two squares interlaced, and represents the concentration of elemental force in both positive and negative aspects. It is also formed of eight triangles joined at their basal angles, and can symbolize the power of the Supernal Triad, and of other threefold symbolisms, within the elemental world. It has a special application to alchemy.

The second form of the octagram is the special symbol of the planet Mercury, and represents the union of positive and negative forces through the medium of intelligence.

Diagram 57—
The Octagon and Octagrams

The Enneagon and Enneagram

There are three ways to make a regular enneagram, and each of these has its own meaning. All nine-sided figures correspond to Yesod, the ninth Sphere. The enneagon represents the dispersal of the rays of the seven planets and the lunar nodes—the "Dragon's Head" and "Dragon's Tail" of ancient astrology—throughout Nature.

The first form of the enneagram, connecting every other point around the circle, is made of nine triangles jouned at their basal angles, and represents the power of the Supernal Triad or of any other threefold symbolism within the energies of the heavens. The second form, connecting every third point, is made of three interlaced triangles, and represents the three alchemical principles combined and interacting.

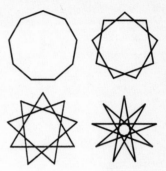

The third form of the enneagram, connecting every fourth point, is the special symbol of the Moon, and symbolizes her role as the channel for energies descending from the planets.

Diagram 58—
The Enneagon and Enneagrams

It may be worth noting, finally, that the so-called "enneagram" devised by G. I. Gurdjieff, and more recently introduced to a wider audience by a number of popularizers, belongs to a different class of symbol and partakes of a wholly different symbolism.

The Decagon and Decagrams

All figures with ten sides have a special relationship to the Tree of Life as a whole, and also correspond to the tenth Sphere, Malkuth. The decagon represents the dispersal of the powers of the ten Spheres through Nature.

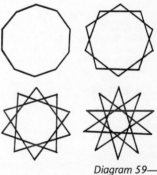

The first form of the decagram, connecting every other point, is the special symbol of Malkuth. Formed of two interlaced pentagons, it represents the stable combination and concentration of the five elements in positive and negative forms under the governance of the Spheres.

Diagram 59—
The Decagon and Decagrams

The second form, connecting every third point, represents the concentrated and continuous operations of the ten Spheres in Nature. The third form, connecting every fourth point, is formed of two interlaced pentagrams, and represents the dynamic revolution and interaction of the five elements in positive and negative forms under the governance of the two forms of the Pentagrammaton.

BIBLIOGRAPHY

Agrippa, Henry Cornelius. *Three Books of Occult Philosophy.* Translated by James Freake. Edited by Donald Tyson. St. Paul: Llewellyn, 1993.

Bardon, Franz. *Initiation Into Hermetics.* Kettig uber Koblenz: Osiris-Verlag, 1962.

_____. *The Practice of Magical Evocation.* Graz-Puntigam: Rudolf Pravica, 1967.

_____. *The Key to the True Quabbalah.* Wuppertal: Dieter Ruggeberg, 1971.

Butler, W. E. *Apprenticed to Magic.* Wellingborough: Aquarian, 1962.

_____. *Lords of Light.* Rochester: Destiny, 1990.

_____. *Magic: Its Ritual, Power and Purpose.* Wellingborough: Aquarian, 1975.

_____. *The Magician: His Training and Work.* North Hollywood: Wilshire, 1959.

Cicero, Chic, and Sandra Tabatha Cicero. *Self-Initiation into the Golden Dawn Tradition.* St. Paul: Llewellyn, 1995.

_____. *Secrets of a Golden Dawn Temple.* St. Paul: Llewellyn, 1992.

Crowley, Aleister. *Book Four.* York Beach: Weiser, 1980.

_____. *The Book of Thoth.* York Beach: Samuel Weiser, 1969.

_____. *Magic in Theory and Practice.* New York: Dover, 1976.

_____. *Magick Without Tears.* Phoenix: Falcon, 1986.

_____. *777.* York Beach: Weiser, 1973.

Davidson, Gustav. *A Dictionary of Angels.* New York: MacMillan, 1967.

Fortune, Dion. *Applied Magic.* Wellingborough: Aquarian, 1978.

_____. *The Cosmic Doctrine.* Wellingborough: Aquarian, 1988.

_____. *The Mystical Qabalah.* York Beach: Weiser, 1984.

_____. *Psychic Self-Defence.* Wellingborough: Aquarian, 1988.

_____. *Sane Occultism.* Wellingborough: Aquarian, 1987.

Gilbert, R. A., editor. *The Magical Mason*. Wellingborough: Aquarian, 1983.

_____. *The Sorcerer and His Apprentice*. Wellingborough: Aquarian, 1983.

Godwin, David. *Godwin's Cabalistic Encyclopedia*. St. Paul: Llewellyn, 1989.

Godwin, Joscelyn. *The Mystery of the Seven Vowels*. Grand Rapids: Phanes, 1991.

_____. *The Theosophical Enlightenment*. Albany: SUNY Press, 1994.

Guthrie, Kenneth Sylvan, editor. *The Pythagorean Sourcebook and Library*. Grand Rapids: Phanes, 1987.

Hamill, John, editor. *The Rosicrucian Seer: Magical Writings of Frederick Hockley*. Wellingborough: Aquarian, 1986.

Iamblichus. *On the Mysteries*. Translated by Thomas Taylor. San Diego: Wizards Bookshelf, 1984.

Kaplan, Aryeh. *The Bahir*. York Beach: Weiser, 1979.

_____. *Meditation and Kabbalah*. York Beach: Weiser, 1982.

_____. *Sefer Yetzirah*. York Beach: Weiser, 1990.

King, Francis, editor. *Astral Projection, Ritual Magic and Alchemy*. Rochester: Destiny, 1987.

King, Francis, and Stephen Skinner. *Techniques of High Magic*. New York: Warner, 1976.

Knight, Gareth. *Experience of the Inner Worlds*. Cheltenham: Helios, 1975.

_____. *Occult Exercises and Practices*. Wellingborough: Aquarian, 1982.

_____. *The Practice of Ritual Magic*. Wellingborough: Aquarian, 1976.

_____. *The Rose Cross and the Goddess*. New York: Destiny, 1985.

Lawlor, Robert. *Sacred Geometry*. New York: Thames & Hudson, 1982.

Mathers, S. L. MacGregor, editor. *The Key of Solomon the King*. New York: Weiser, 1972.

McLean, Adam, editor. *The Magical Calendar*. Edinburgh: Magnum Opus, 1979.

_____. *A Treatise on Angel Magic*. Grand Rapids: Phanes, 1990.

Mead, G. R. S. *Thrice Greatest Hermes*. York Beach: Weiser, 1992.

Plato. *Collected Dialogues*. Edited by Edith Hamilton and Huntington Cairns. Princeton: Princeton University Press, 1961.

Plotinus. *The Enneads*. Translated by Stephen MacKenna. Burdett: Larson, 1992.

Regardie, Israel. *Ceremonial Magic*. Wellingborough: Aquarian, 1980.

_____. *Foundations of Practical Magic*. Wellingborough: Aquarian, 1979.

Regardie, Israel. *The Golden Dawn*. St. Paul: Llewellyn, 1971.

_____. *The Middle Pillar*. St. Paul: Llewellyn, 1970.

_____. *The Tree of Life*. York Beach: Weiser, 1972.

Sadhu, Mouni. *Concentration*. North Hollywood: Wilshire, 1959.

_____. *Meditation*. North Hollywood: Wilshire, 1967.

_____. *The Tarot*. North Hollywood: Wilshire, 1962.

_____. *Theurgy: The Art of Effective Worship*. London: George Allen & Unwin, 1965.

Underhill, Evelyn. *Mysticism*. New York: Dutton, 1961.

Wang, Robert. *The Secret Temple*. New York: Weiser, 1980.

Waterfield, Robin, translator. *The Theology of Arithmetic*. Grand Rapids: Phanes, 1988.

Westcott, William Wynn, editor. *The Chaldean Oracles of Zoroaster*. Wellingborough: Aquarian, 1983.

_____. *Sepher Yetzirah*. San Diego: Wizards Bookshelf, 1990.

Yates, Frances. *The Art of Memory*. Chicago: University of Chicago Press, 1966.

_____. *Giordano Bruno and the Hermetic Tradition*. Chicago: University of Chicago Press, 1964.

Yeats, William Butler. *A Vision*. New York: MacMillan, 1966.

Zalewski, C. L. *Herbs in Magic and Alchemy*. Bridport: Prism, 1990.

Zalewski, Patrick. *Secret Inner Order Rituals of the Golden Dawn*. Phoenix: Falcon, 1988.

INDEX

A

Abramelin operation, 299-300, 306

Abyss, 53-55, 62, 113, 165, 189, 297

Adam Cadmon, 140, 253, 257

Adeptus Minor, 57-58, 187, 196, 293

Agrippa, Cornelius, 35, 266

Air, Sign of, 71-72, 144-145, 177-178, 204

alchemy, 28, 38, 53, 91, 121, 152, 165, 170, 202, 310, 328

altar, 125-126, 128-130, 132, 172-178, 180, 182-185, 188-191, 198-200, 203, 207, 211-212, 214-216, 223, 227-231, 233, 236-237, 241, 244, 248-255, 258, 262, 269, 272, 281-283, 285, 291-292, 296, 301-306, 315, 317-326, 329, 332-333

angel, 31-32, 53, 87, 190, 199, 214-216, 224, 228, 230, 233, 250, 252-253, 256-257, 299, 304-305, 325-326

anima mundi, 38, 246, 255

animal, 89-90, 114, 221, 274-276, 280-286, 289

Apophis, Sign of, 74, 76, 148, 156, 191

arch-fays, 34

archangel, 177, 190, 199, 203, 211-212, 224, 228, 230, 233, 250, 252-253, 256-257, 269, 282, 304-305, 324, 326

Ars Notoria, 113

asafoetida, 41, 246-247, 249, 254, 257, 261-262

astral static, 156

astrology, 22, 26, 35, 38, 50, 79, 121, 126-128, 232, 321

aura, 42, 44, 48, 50, 68-69, 91, 156, 167, 169-170, 267, 270, 294-295

B

banishing, 41, 95-96, 98-100, 102, 137-139, 141, 143-147, 149, 151-153, 155, 162, 164, 168, 171-174, 176, 178-181, 184-188, 191, 205, 207-208, 214-216, 223, 227, 236-237, 245, 247, 254, 263-264, 273, 284-285, 293, 316, 322, 324, 331

Bardon, Franz, 222

body of transformation, 273, 284, 289

C

Cabala, 9, 15, 44, 54, 79-80, 87, 103, 140, 176, 186, 231, 251

celestial system, 125

chakras, 157-159

Chaldean Oracles, 174

channeling, 17, 244

Christianity, 82, 146

closed position, 67, 73

Closing of the Veil, Sign of the, 73-74, 185, 191

contemplation, 64, 109, 194, 212, 246, 338

Crowley, Aleister, 6, 53, 271

Cup, 7, 128-130, 172-173, 182-183, 188, 194-195, 197-198, 208, 213, 223, 227, 229, 231, 247, 270, 292, 294, 305, 318-319, 332

D
Dagger, 197-198, 213, 230, 304
Dee, John, 242-243, 251
demons, 31, 34, 251
Descartes, Rene, 266
dittany of Crete, 40, 244
divination, 32, 115, 216, 225, 310, 328
Dukes of Edom, 184, 186

E
Earth, Sign of, 71, 144, 177, 180, 204
ecliptic, 313-314
Eden, 203, 313-314
egregor, 59-60, 310-311
elementals, 33-34, 38, 200, 243, 246, 249, 255, 258
Emerald Tablet, 186, 202
Enterer, Sign of the, 69-70, 78, 167, 169, 173, 175, 177, 184-185, 302-303, 310, 318, 333, 335
equinox, 37-38, 124, 182, 309, 311-323, 325, 327-335, 337
ether, 10, 12-13, 15, 23, 36, 39-40, 42-43, 166, 220, 275
etheric condenser, 39
etheric double, 44, 48, 50, 64-65
ethics, 117-118
evocation, 40, 205, 209, 239-251, 253-255, 257-259, 261-263, 299, 310, 328, 330-331
exorcism, 209, 251, 259-263

F
faery, 34
Fire, Sign of, 71-72, 144, 177-178, 204
First Degree, 57-58, 61, 69, 132, 172, 175-176, 181-185, 187, 190, 193, 198-200, 202, 204, 207-208, 211-212, 214-215, 227-229, 231-234, 237, 269, 273, 281, 285, 291-292, 300, 306, 314-315, 317, 320, 322-325, 327
five elements, 9, 28, 44, 46, 93, 186
flashing colors, 86, 222, 225, 235
flashing tablet, 86, 235-237, 295

fluid condenser, 222-223
formulae, 21, 58, 69, 123-124, 172, 187, 262, 265, 269, 275, 286, 289, 292, 309-311, 330-331, 335, 337
Fortune, Dion, 259
Fourfold Breath, 69, 77, 163, 167, 169-170
frankincense, 40-41, 153

G
geomancy, 115, 225
godforms, 91
heart center, 73, 160, 164-166, 168-170, 293
Hermetic Brotherhood of Luxor, 213
Hermetic Order of the Golden Dawn, 69

H
hesychasm, 164
Higher Genius, 53, 55, 62, 260, 299, 337
Higher Self, 51, 53, 111, 260-261, 299-300, 302-307, 326-327, 337
Holy Guardian Angel, 53, 299
Holy Water, 40, 128-130, 172, 227, 229, 233, 246-247, 254, 257, 270

I
incense, 40-41, 128-130, 132, 153-154, 172-173, 183, 188, 190, 208, 222, 227, 229, 233, 244, 270
initiation, 45, 55-60, 62, 69, 122, 172, 187, 222, 311
intelligences, 32, 108, 231, 243, 246, 249, 255, 258
invisibility, 124, 265-273, 286, 310, 328, 333-334
invocation, 40, 53, 109, 126-127, 138, 140-141, 146, 149, 153, 156, 167, 175, 181, 184, 186, 190, 199-200, 203, 208, 211, 215, 233-234, 236, 247, 264, 266, 273, 289-292, 295, 300-301, 306-307, 322-323, 325-326, 329-332, 334-337

iron, 41-42, 198, 205-206, 209
Isis, Sign of, 74, 148, 156, 191

J
Jesus, 81-82, 92, 149, 164
Jung, Carl, 5

K
kamea, 103-105
Kingsford, Anna, 114-115, 118-119
kundalini, 158

L
lamen, 96, 200-204, 213, 217, 249, 252, 294
larvae, 34, 42
Levi, Eliphas, 195
Lotus Wand, 209-213, 217, 233, 249, 252-257, 264, 269, 282-283, 291, 296, 304, 306, 317, 323, 330, 336
Lovelock, James, 38
Lower Genius, 53
Lower Self, 53, 260-261, 289, 299, 306, 337-338

M
macrocosm, 13-15, 19-21, 23, 25, 27, 29, 31, 33, 35, 37, 39, 41, 43-45, 48, 55, 58, 64, 66, 85, 92, 96, 110, 157, 166, 170, 174, 193, 220, 234, 253, 257, 268, 276, 288, 304-305, 307, 311, 315, 321, 325, 329-331
magical mirror, 48, 213-214, 243, 249-251, 255, 262
Magical Sword, 204-208, 212, 246-247, 262
microcosm, 13-15, 43, 45, 47-49, 51, 53-55, 57, 59, 61, 63-64, 93, 96, 103, 110, 157, 170, 174-175, 193, 253, 257, 260, 288, 298, 304-305, 307
Middle Pillar, 48-49, 77, 132, 157-163, 165-171, 233-234, 252, 255, 261, 288, 292-293, 298, 301, 314, 316, 329, 331-332, 334, 336-337

Moon, 4, 23, 28, 36, 41, 46, 83, 85, 97-103, 105, 108, 122, 127-128, 150-153, 217, 223, 274, 277, 279-282, 285, 291, 297, 321-325, 333

N
Names of God, 21, 77, 79-80, 82, 150, 159, 181, 194, 199-200, 203, 207-208, 220, 244-245, 248, 251, 262, 274, 289-291, 293, 295
natural magic, 28, 39-42, 121, 205, 246, 261
ninjutsu, 266

O
open position, 67, 73, 142, 166, 168-169
Osiris, 73-76, 144-145, 147-149, 155, 182-183, 190, 207, 211, 223, 230, 233, 263, 293, 297-298, 306, 319-320, 326-327
Osiris Risen, Sign of, 75-76, 148, 156, 191
Osiris Slain, Sign of, 74, 76, 148, 156, 190-191, 223, 297, 326

P
Pentacle, 197-199, 213, 231, 305-306, 332
Pentagrammaton, 81-82
phases of the Moon, 23, 36
Picatrix, 87
planetary spirit, 228, 230
pranayama, 75
protective circle, 243, 245, 247, 249

Q
Qlippoth, 34, 186

R
Regardie, Israel, 69, 162, 196, 225, 240, 276, 310, 314
Rending of the Veil, Sign of the, 73, 184, 190
Ring and Disk, 216, 310
Rosicrucian, 81, 93, 165, 201, 266

S

sacred geometry, 91, 93, 100, 103, 202

scrying, 40, 125, 213, 235, 240, 243, 249, 288-289, 295, 298, 322-325

Second Degree, 57-58, 62, 73, 183, 186-188, 191-192, 251-252, 254-255, 258, 262, 264, 295-296, 298

self-initiation, 58-62, 176, 288, 290, 292, 295

shewstone, 213, 251

Shroud of Concealment, 267-270, 272-273, 333-335

sigil, 105-108, 235, 244

Silence, Sign of, 68-70, 167, 169, 173-175, 177-178, 184-185, 234, 270, 302-303, 318, 333

sitting posture, 66

Sphere of Sensation, 44, 48, 50-51, 56, 59, 162, 167, 169-170, 235, 244, 247, 258, 260-261, 267-269, 273, 294, 303, 313, 334-335, 337

spirits, 6, 22-24, 29, 31-34, 40-41, 87, 100, 108, 138, 177-181, 184-186, 189, 191, 198, 200, 204-205, 209, 213, 216, 228, 230-231, 233, 239-247, 249-251, 255-261, 299, 304-307, 310, 320, 323, 326-328, 330-332

spiritus mundi, 38, 246, 255, 275

standing posture, 66-67, 69-70, 73, 77

Sun, 22, 28, 36-38, 40-41, 46, 74, 83, 85, 89-90, 99-104, 107, 122, 127, 149-150, 152-153, 163, 165, 170, 175, 183, 203, 217, 222, 263, 277, 279-280, 296-297, 311-314, 317-318, 320-321, 334

sword hand, 68, 141, 143

T

talisman, 46, 48, 78, 87, 89, 100, 105, 188, 219-237, 288, 293, 310, 331-333

telesmatic image, 89, 231-232, 234-235, 294-295

terrestrial system, 125

Tetragrammaton, 80-82, 145, 166, 178, 186, 192, 211, 263, 296-297, 304

thaumaturgy, 17, 290

theurgy, 17, 54-55, 289-290

Third Degree, 58, 62, 73, 82, 93, 187-188, 191-192, 232, 292

tide, 37

Tiphareth, 26, 47, 57, 84-85, 93, 146, 149-151, 153, 156, 158, 160, 162-164, 166, 169, 183, 201, 203, 296-298, 313, 315-316

transformation body, 111, 275, 280-283

Tree of Life, 9, 26, 47, 50, 56, 85, 93, 96, 121, 123, 127, 130, 140, 146, 149, 158-159, 201, 205, 208, 212, 228, 230, 268, 291-292, 295, 313, 316, 322, 325, 331-332, 334, 336-337

Trithemius, 266

U–V

Veil of the Sanctuary, 51-53, 57, 184, 190-191, 260

vibratory name, 232-234, 237, 276, 279, 282-283, 285, 336

W–X–Y–Z

Water, Sign of, 71-72, 144, 177, 179, 204

werewolf, 274

working tool, 68, 129, 188, 193-195, 197-200, 205, 209, 211, 213, 217, 219, 262

Stay in Touch . . .

Llewellyn publishes hundreds of books on your favorite subjects.

On the following pages you will find listed some books now available on related subjects. Your local bookstore stocks most of these and will stock new Llewellyn titles as they become available. We appreciate your patronage!

Order by Phone

Call toll-free within the U.S. and Canada, **1–800–THE MOON.**
In Minnesota call **(612) 291-1970.**
We accept Visa, MasterCard, and American Express.

Order by Mail

Send the full price of your order (MN residents add 7% sales tax) in U.S.funds to:

> **Llewellyn Worldwide**
> **P.O. Box 64383, Dept. K313-1**
> **St. Paul, MN 55164–0383, U.S.A.**

Postage and Handling

- $4.00 for orders $15.00 and under
- $5.00 for orders over $15.00
- No charge for orders over $100.00 to U.S.,Canada, and Mexico

We ship UPS in the continental United States. Orders shipped to P.O. boxes and to Alaska, Hawaii, and Puerto Rico will be sent first-class mail. Orders to Canada and Mexico will ship via surface mail.

International orders: Airmail—add freight equal to price of each book to the total price of order, plus $5.00 for each non-book item (audiotapes, etc.); surface mail—add $1.00 per item.

Allow 4–6 weeks delivery. Postage and handling rates subject to change.

Group Discounts

We offer a 20% quantity discount to group leaders or agents. You must order a minimum of five copies of the same book to get our special quantity price.

Free Catalog

Get a free copy of our color catalog, *New Worlds of Mind and Spirit*. Subscribe for just $10.00 in the United States and Canada ($30.00 overseas, first-class mail). Many bookstores carry *New Worlds*—ask for it!

Prices subject to change without notice.

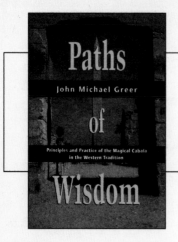

Paths of Wisdom
Principles and Practice of
the Magical Cabala in
the Western Tradition
John Michael Greer

Unlock the hidden potentials of your self and the universe—of macro-cosm and microcosm—with the key of the Cabala. *Paths of Wisdom* gives you a complete set of instructions to perform Cabalistic magick. This general introduction to the magical Cabala in the Golden Dawn tradition can be used by the complete beginner. *Paths of Wisdom* also contains practical material on the advanced levels of Cabalistic work, based on a perspective inherent in most of the Golden Dawn-derived approaches to magic.

Originating as a secret mystical school within Judaism, Cabala was transmitted to the great magicians of the Renaissance and became the engine behind the body of Western magical methods. From Cornelius Agrippa to the adepts of the Golden Dawn, the magicians of the West have used the Cabala as the foundation of their work. Central to this tradition is an understanding of magic that sees esoteric practice as a spiritual Path, and an approach to practical work stressing visualization and the use of symbolic correspondences. Through meditation, path-working, magical rituals, and mystical contemplation, you'll incorporate the insight of the Cabala into your daily life.

ISBN: 1-56718-315-8, 6 x 9, 416 pp., illus.   **$20.00**

The Golden Dawn
Israel Regardie

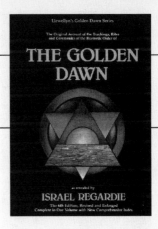

Originally published in four bulky volumes of some 1,200 pages, this revised and enlarged edition has been entirely reset in half the pages (while retaining the original pagination in marginal notation for reference) for greater ease of use. Corrections of typographical errors in the original and subsequent editions have been made, along with revisions, additional text, and notes by noted scholars and actual practitioners of the Golden Dawn system of Magick.

Also included are initiation ceremonies, rituals for consecration and invocation, methods of meditation and magical working based on the Enochian Tablets, studies in the Tarot, and the system of cabalistic correspondences that unite the world's religions and magical traditions into a comprehensive and practical whole.

This volume is designed as a study and practice curriculum suited to both group and private practice. Meditation upon, and following with the Active Imagination, the Initiation Ceremonies are fully experiential without need of participation in group or lodge. A very complete reference encyclopedia of Western Magick.

0–87542–663–8, 840 pp., 6 x 9, illus., softcover   **$29.95**

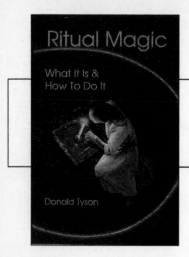